Japanese Pride, American Prejudice

ASIAN AMERICA
A series edited by Gordon H. Chang.

The increasing size and diversity of the Asian American population, its grow-ing significance in American society and culture, and the expanded appreci-ation, both popular and scholarly, of the importance of Asian Americans in the country's present and past—all these developments have converged to stimulate wide interest in scholarly work on topics related to the Asian American experience. The general recognition of the pivotal role that race and ethnicity have played in American life, and in relations between the United States and other countries, has also fostered this heightened attention.

Although Asian Americans were a subject of serious inquiry in the late nineteenth and early twentieth centuries, they were subsequently ignored by the mainstream scholarly community for several decades. In recent years, however, this neglect has ended, with an increasing number of writers examining a good many aspects of Asian American life and culture. Moreover, many students of American society are recognizing that the study of issues related to Asian America speak to, and may be essential for, many current discussions on the part of the informed public and various scholarly communities.

The Stanford series on Asian America seeks to address these interests. The series will include work from the humanities and social sciences, including history, anthropology, political science, American studies, law, literary criti-cism, sociology, and interdisciplinary and policy studies.

Japanese Pride, American Prejudice

MODIFYING THE EXCLUSION CLAUSE
OF THE 1924 IMMIGRATION ACT

Izumi Hirobe

STANFORD UNIVERSITY PRESS

STANFORD, CALIFORNIA 2001

Stanford University Press
Stanford, California

© 2001 by the Board of Trustees of the
Leland Stanford Junior University

Printed in the United States of America
On acid-free, archival-quality paper

Library of Congress Cataloging-in-Publication Data

Hirobe, Izumi.
    Japanese pride, American prejudice: modifying the exclusion clause
of the 1924 Immigration Act / Izumi Hirobe.
        p.   cm. — (Asian America)
    Includes bibliographical references (p.) and index.
    ISBN 0-8047-3813-0 (acid-free paper)
        1. United States—Relations—Japan.   2. Japan—Relations—
United States.   3. United States—Foreign relations—20th century.
4. Japan—Foreign relations—1912–1945.   5. United States—Emigration and immigration—History—20th century.   6. Japan—
Emigration and immigration—History—20th century.   7. Emigration and immigration law—United States—History—20th century.
8. Clergy—United States—Political activity—History—20th century.
10. Non-governmental organizations—United States—History—20th
century.   I. Title.   II. Series.

E183.8.J3 H597   2001
325'.252'0973—dc21   2001020016

Typeset by BookMatters in Garamond 11/14

Original Printing 2001

Last figure below indicates year of this printing:
10   09   08   07   06   05   04   03   02   01

Acknowledgments

First and foremost, my greatest debt is to Professor Akira Iriye, who served as my dissertation adviser and provided invaluable comments on the entire manuscript over the years. I am also grateful to various members of the faculty at Harvard University, especially members of the Department of History, and at the University of Tokyo, especially members of the Graduate School of Arts and Sciences, for supporting this work. The comments and suggestions of the anonymous readers at Stanford University Press improved this work greatly.

Many friends have helped me in this project. Tadashi Anno, Pat Katayama, David Nickles, Fumiko Nishizaki, and Futoshi Shibayama, among others, kindly read and commented on the manuscript in part or in its entirety. Professors Sadao Asada, Gordon Chang, Albert Craig, Yuji Ichioka, Ken'ichirō Hirano, Nagayo Homma, Ernest May, Kensaburo Shinkawa, and Daizaburō Yui also gave me valuable advice. Special thanks go to Guy Genin and Mari Yoshihara, who have helped me since the first stages of this work.

I received valuable assistance from staff members at the Archives du Ministère des Affaires Étrangères in Paris; the Center for American Studies at the University of Tokyo; the Diplomatic Record Office in Tokyo; the Herbert Hoover Presidential Library; the Hoover Institution on War, Revolution, and Peace; the Library of Congress; the National Archives; the Public Record Office at Kew; and the Presbyterian Department of History in Philadelphia. I would further like to thank the staff of the Bancroft Library of the University of California at Berkeley and also those in Special Collections at the University of California at Los Angeles, Harvard University, Columbia University, Clark University, Swarthmore College, and Knox College. Financial assistance from the Charles Warren Center at Harvard University, the Harvard University History Department, and the Reischauer Institute of Japanese Studies helped fund my research.

Finally, my deepest gratitude is to my father, Eiichi, who cultivated my interest in writing; and to my mother, Kyōko, who opened my eyes to international affairs.

Contents

Abbreviations

ABCFM   American Board of Commissioners for Foreign Missions

AFSC   American Friends Service Committee

AMAE   Archives du Ministère des Affaires Étrangères, Paris

BHNG   Beikoku ni okeru hainichi mondai ikken: 1924 nen iminhō seiritsu ni taisuru naigai no hantai undō [Documents Relating to Anti-Japanese Movements in the United States: Protests against the 1924 Immigration Law at Home and Abroad], Diplomatic Record Office, Tokyo

BHZIS   Beikoku ni okeru hainichi mondai zakken: Iminhō shūsei kankei [Miscellaneous Documents Relating to Anti-Japanese Problems in the United States: Documents Relating to the Amendment of the Immigration Law], Diplomatic Record Office, Tokyo

BIHJ   Beikoku ni okeru hainichi mondai zakken, Beikoku iminhō ni taisuru haibei jōhō [Miscellaneous Documents Relating to Anti-Japanese Problems in the United States, Anti-American Information Relating to the United States Immigration Law], Diplomatic Record Office, Tokyo

CCOR   California Council on Oriental Relations

CCRCE   Citizens Committee to Repeal Chinese Exclusion

CIJG   Commission on International Justice and Goodwill

CJIC   California Joint Immigration Committee

CO   Colonial Office, Public Record Office, London

CRIA   Papers of the Council on Religion and International Affairs, Butler Library, Columbia University, New York

DWH   Department of War History, National Institute for Defense Studies, Tokyo

FCCCA   Federal Council of the Churches of Christ in America (later called National Council of the Churches of Christ in the United States of America)

FCN   *Foreign Commerce and Navigation of the United States*

FO   Foreign Office, Public Record Office, London

FRUS   *Foreign Relations of the United States*

IPR   Institute of Pacific Relations

JACL   Japanese American Citizens League

JDRO   Diplomatic Record Office, Tokyo

KHZB   Kakkoku ni okeru hainichi kankei zakken: Beikoku no bu [Miscellaneous Documents Relating to Anti-Japanese Movements in Foreign Countries: United States], Diplomatic Record Office, Tokyo

KTGS   *Kizokuin tsūjōkai giji sokkiroku* [Proceedings in the Imperial Diet of Japan, House of Peers]

NCAJR   National Committee on American-Japanese Relations

NCCCA   Papers of the National Council of the Churches of Christ in the United States of America, Presbyterian Department of History, Philadelphia

NCCWP   National Committee on the Churches and World Peace

NGB   *Nihon gaikō bunsho* [Documents on Japanese Foreign Policy], Ministry of Foreign Affairs, Tokyo

NGBNK   *Nihon gaikō bunsho: Nichibei kōshō, 1941 nen* [Documents on Japanese Foreign Policy: Japan–U.S. Talks in 1941], Ministry of Foreign Affairs, Tokyo

NGBSK   *Nihon gaikō bunsho, Shōwa-ki* [Documents on Japanese Foreign Policy: Shōwa Era], Ministry of Foreign Affairs, Tokyo

NGBTIM   *Nihon gaikō bunsho: Taibei imin mondai keika gaiyō* [Documents on Japanese Foreign Policy: Summary of the Course of Negotiations between Japan and the United States concerning the Problems of

Japanese Immigration in the United States], Ministry of Foreign Affairs, Tokyo

NSGW   Native Sons of the Golden West

OCOR   Oregon Council on Oriental Relations

PCCOR   Pacific Coast Council on Oriental Relations

SD   U.S. Department of State Files, Record Group 59, National Archives, Washington, D.C.

STGS   *Shūgiin tsūjōkai giji sokkiroku* [Proceedings in the Imperial Diet of Japan, House of Representatives]

WAIFTC   World Alliance for International Friendship Through Churches

WCOR   Washington Council on Oriental Relations

WO   War Office, Public Record Office, London

A Note on Japanese Names

In this volume, Japanese names are given in Western form—that is, the given name precedes the family name. Not a few Japanese appearing in this work were active both in Japan and the United States. They often wrote their names with the given name first in the United States and in the opposite order in Japan. Moreover, sometimes their identities were not clear or changed from time to time. Therefore, in order to avoid confusion, I have standardized the order.

Japanese Pride, American Prejudice

Introduction

July 1, 1924, was a day of anger against the United States in Japan. At rallies across the country, speakers denounced America as a treacherous nation and were met with enthusiastic applause. Theaters boycotted American movies: interpreters who were supposed to help audiences understand silent films refused to go on the job. This day of national action was the culmination of a period of protest during which a man had even committed hara-kiri outside the former embassy of the United States in Tokyo, and the nation's leading intellectual—Inazō Nitobe, who was at the time undersecretary general of the League of Nations and whose portrait today graces Japan's 5,000-yen note—had vowed never to set foot in the United States again.

The source of all this outrage was a new law that completely barred Japanese immigration to the United States. Today, this law—and Japan's aggrieved response to it—is recognized as one of the principal causes of the deadly clash between the United States and Japan that began in 1941. Indeed, Emperor Hirohito allegedly referred to the rejection of Japanese immigrants in California as one of the original causes of the Pacific war.[1] In 1941, Kikuichi Fujita, commander of the Eighth Squadron heading to Pearl Harbor, wrote in his diary that whereas the Japanese had previously just endured the treacherous behavior of the Americans, such as the exclusion of Japanese immigrants, it was now time to teach them a lesson.[2]

Although U.S.-Japanese relations were cordial in theory for much of the period during the 1920s (especially after Japan accepted the framework of international cooperation in the Far East embodied by the Washington Conference in 1921–22), the American immigration law nevertheless had serious psychological consequences and thus stands out as one of the few disputes to disturb relations during those years.

To fully understand the impact of the enactment of the exclusion law on the Japanese mind, one needs to contextualize the significance of the immigration issue in the history of U.S.-Japanese relations.

From the time when the United States fleet first "opened" Japan in the 1850s until the end of the nineteenth century, U.S.-Japanese relations had been relatively smooth and without much conflict, mostly because neither country displayed much interest in expanding its power in the Pacific. During the latter half of the nineteenth century, the United States was busy developing its territory within the North American continent. The fact that it was concentrating its energy on the establishment of a stable internal political system also made it difficult for the country to pay attention to affairs overseas. The Civil War, which lasted from 1861 to 1865, in particular drained the country's energy away from Asian entanglements. Although the United States was rapidly growing into a world power, it was not yet ready to become a major player in world politics in the manner of the European powers. The United States even showed some distaste for imperial politics. For those reasons, until the late nineteenth century, the United States made few aggressive overtures outside the American continent.[3]

Neither was Japan ready to embark on imperial activities in the Pacific. The nation had just opened its doors to the world and was still economically and militarily vulnerable. Relations between Japan and the Western powers were characterized by unequal treaties: Japan had no tariff autonomy and the Western powers enjoyed extraterritoriality in Japan. Japan focused its energy on removing these inequalities and, therefore, was not in a position to compete with the United States.

This mutual indifference ended in the 1890s, when the dynamics of international relations in the Pacific were transformed, on the one hand, by Japan's victory over China and the annexation of Taiwan in 1895, and on the other, by the annexation of Hawaii and the Philippines by the United States in 1898. For the first time, the United States and Japan encountered one another as growing imperial powers facing each other across the Pacific. It is significant that in 1897 Japan sent a battleship to Hawaii for the purpose of checking on the activities of the United States. The Japanese Minister in the United States even advised his government to annex Hawaii.[4] The two countries had come to regard each other as rivals across the Pacific.[5] The Japanese victory over Russia convinced the United States that Japan was no longer a small, weak country in Asia. Japan, too, detected the rise of American interest in Asia, especially in China. While the U.S. navy drafted a war plan against Japan, called "War Plan Orange," in 1907, in the same year the Japanese navy added the United States to the list of its potential enemies.[6]

This strategic confrontation between the United States and Japan at the turn of the century coincided with the rise of anti-Japanese movements on the Pacific Coast of the United States. The flow of Japanese immigrants into the United States had begun late in the nineteenth century, at a time when U.S.-Japanese relations had been characterized by mutual indifference. In those days the presence of Japanese immigrants in the United States did not give rise to any massive anti-Japanese movement, partly because the number of Japanese was not large and partly because the Japanese were composed mostly of *Shosei imin* (student immigrants), who were eager to study American culture and society. However, around the turn of the century the number of Japanese immigrants to the U.S. mainland began to greatly increase, and these new immigrants were more interested in earning money than in studying American culture. It was then that conspicuous anti-Japanese movements began to appear in communities along the Pacific Coast, where the Japanese population was clustered. The majority of these new immigrants became farmers and peasants who, despite their initial intention to return to Japan after having earned enough money, turned from being sojourners to settlers as they realized the difficulties of economic success in the face of exclusionist laws and limited occupational niches. As these immigrants gradually came to play an important role in local agriculture and began to compete with American farmers, they came to be seen as a threat to American agricultural enterprise.[7]

Since the sudden increase of Japanese immigrants coincided with Japan's emergence as an imperial power, their arrival and their gradual establishment was viewed by many as part of a Japanese scheme to conquer the United States, or at least the Pacific Coast. This image of Japanese immigrants as a threat to America linked the domestic concern of immigration to foreign relations, and the Japanese immigration issue came to occupy an increasingly central place in debates over U.S.-Japanese relations.[8]

As the number of Japanese on the West Coast increased, the anti-Japanese movement strengthened, especially in San Francisco. Most symbolic was the formation of the Japanese and Korean Exclusion League in May 1905. The League was basically an extension of the labor movement in San Francisco, and its leaders mainly came from labor unions such as the Building Trade Council and the Sailors' Union.[9] Although the League was active in anti-Japanese propaganda, it temporarily ceased its anti-Japanese campaign when its leader, Patrick Henry McCarthy, became mayor of San Francisco and found it necessary to suppress the anti-Japanese campaign in order for the city to be selected as host for the Panama-Pacific Exposition in 1915.[10]

The United States and Japan tried to settle the problems concerning Japanese immigrants in the United States at the government level. The Japanese immigration question, which had previously been a local issue, reached the federal level when the San Francisco Board of Education segregated Asian children into a separate public elementary school in 1906. Although this incident was settled through the good offices of the federal government, it became clear that it would no longer be possible to dismiss the Japanese immigration issue as simply a local issue. The incident was reported in Japan as an example of American discrimination against the Japanese. *Kokumin Shimbun* declared that the segregation of Japanese children was a terrible offense to Japanese pride that should not be accepted meekly. For the Japanese, who had made every effort to obtain Great Power status since the advent of the Meiji Restoration, the incident became a matter of national dignity that threatened to undermine everything Japan had achieved (*Kokumin Shimbun*, 11 December 1906 and 4 January 1907). The Gentlemen's Agreement of 1907–1908 was the result of the efforts of both governments to solve the Japanese immigration issue through diplomatic channels. The Japanese government agreed that it would greatly decrease the number of immigrants by restricting the issuance of passports. Although, according to this agreement, restrictions on immigrations were to be implemented bilaterally, given that there were very few immigrants from the United States to Japan, the agreement was in fact a face-saving measure for

Japan. In fact, it was imperative that Japan, eager to assert its equality with the Western powers, be able to preserve its honor.

However, the Gentlemen's Agreement did not succeed in resolving the anti-Japanese problems on the Pacific Coast, in part because the number of Japanese who were resident in the United States did not decrease, and in part because the wives of earlier Japanese immigrants, who were still permitted to enter the United States under the agreement, continued to arrive. As the Japanese moved out from the cities into rural areas, anti-Japanese sentiment that had at first been mainly concentrated in San Francisco spread throughout California. In 1913 the California state legislature passed a bill to ban land ownership by aliens, the unstated target of which was the Japanese immigrants. This anti-Japanese land law aroused anti-American sentiments in Japan. However, these anti-American sentiments were limited around this time, because many Japanese viewed the law as a local incident and considered that most Americans not actually living on the Pacific Coast would not agree with the law.

Anti-Japanese sentiments in the U.S. eased temporarily during World War I, partly because Japan participated in the war on the same side as the United States, and partly because American attention became diverted from the Japanese immigration question. In fact, even as anti-Japanese sentiments on the Pacific Coast eased during this period, organizational movements directed against the anti-Japanese movement began to emerge. The first of these was organized by the Protestant clergy, especially those who had formerly been missionaries in Japan. The central figure was Sidney Lewis Gulick, who had taught at Dōshisha University in Kyoto between 1906 and 1913. He worked through the organizations he established, including the National Committee for Constructive Immigration Legislation and the Commission on Relations with Japan. The second pro-Japanese movement developed from those members of the business community who already had trade relations with East Asia. Members of the San Francisco Chamber of Commerce were enthusiastic about the anti-exclusion movement, for example. The central figure was Wallace Alexander, who organized the Japanese Relations Committee in the chamber of commerce in 1915. Finally, some intellectuals who were devoted to the peace cause were also engaged in the pro-Japanese movement.[11]

While the failure of the Versailles Conference to insert a racial-equality clause into the League of Nations Covenant shocked the Japanese,[12] they nevertheless gained confidence in their position as one of the great world powers by securing status as a permanent member of the Council of the League. Although some Japanese navy officers were deeply dissatisfied over the disarmament agreement, the success of the Washington Conference further contributed to the improvement of U.S.-Japanese relations. The Conference created a postwar world order controlled by the Anglo-American powers, with which Japan chose to cooperate. Although the rejection of the racial-equality clause left a deep scar on the Japanese mind, at the beginning of the 1920s, U.S.-Japanese relations entered a relatively stable phase.

Anti-Japanese sentiment along the Pacific Coast soon became prevalent again, however, since West Coast residents were little affected by expectations at the governmental level. In 1920 a California referendum was proposed to tighten up the 1913 alien land law. California politicians, including State Senator J. M. Inman, State Controller John S. Chambers, and U.S. Senator James Phelan, took advantage of the issue to augment their influence and popularity.[13] As a result of an energetic campaign promoted by some exclusionist state officials, including the governor, two-thirds of the California voters approved the referendum. Exclusionists in California, who were not fully satisfied with the anti-Japanese land laws at the state level, now turned their focus to the prohibition of Japanese immigrants at the federal level. In September 1920 a new exclusionist organization, the Japanese Exclusion League of California, was organized, headed by State Senator Inman, and backed by the Native Sons of the Golden West (NSGW), the American Legion, the California State Federation of Labor, the California Federation of Women's Clubs, the State Grange, the Farm Bureau, and the Loyal Order of Moose.[14] The new Japanese Exclusion League soon suffered from financial difficulties, however. Fundraising efforts did not work well and, finally, in 1922, the organization ceased to function as a membership organization, although its executive members continued to meet regularly. After 1922, the financial support of two of its most dedicated members, retired newspaperman Valentine Stuart McClatchy and former U.S. Senator James Phelan, became particularly significant.[15]

Also in 1922, a decision of the U.S. Supreme Court concerning Japanese immigrants' eligibility for U.S. citizenship aided the anti-Japanese cause. Federal law had restricted the right of naturalization to aliens who were either "free white" or of "African nativity and persons of African descent." Since the former category was not precisely defined, the status of the Japanese remained ambiguous. Some felt that the "free white" category should be interpreted inclusively, so as to allow Japanese immigrants to become naturalized citizens. As a matter of fact, some lower federal courts had issued naturalization documents to some Japanese immigrants at the turn of the century.[16] Although this practice was ended by order of the U.S. Attorney General in 1906, after unfavorable decisions by the lower federal courts, the Supreme Court did not take up the matter of Japanese naturalization until *Takao Ozawa v. United States* in 1922. Takao Ozawa was a perfect candidate to test the Supreme Court's views because he satisfied all requirements for naturalization other than the racial one. Ozawa was born in Japan in 1875 and immigrated to San Francisco in 1894. Since this time, he had lived continuously in the United States. He had studied at the University of California. He was fluent in English and worked for an American company. However, the court declared Ozawa "ineligible to citizenship" because the naturalization right was reserved for "free whites" and "persons of African descent." The court's ruling in November of 1922, that Japanese, as "Mongolians," were "aliens ineligible to citizenship," gave exclusionists the justification for their cause.

In the meantime, anti-Japanese measures were also being prepared at the congressional level. Only a couple of months after the court decision, a bill to ban Japanese immigration was submitted by the House Committee on Immigration and Naturalization. Since there was not enough time to pass the bill in the 67th Congress, a clause barring all Japanese immigrants from entry into the United States was inserted into an immigration bill proposed in the 68th Congress, which convened in December 1923. Although the main targets of the immigration bill were immigrants from southern and eastern Europe, whose influx into the United States had increased dramatically around the turn of the century, anti-Japanese Californians did not miss their opportunity to insert a clause to ban the entrance of "aliens ineligible to citizenship." Although the term "Japanese" was not used, it was clear that they were the object of the bill's new language, since most other "aliens ineligible to citizenship," such as Chinese and Asian Indians, were already banned. Worried that the bill, if passed, would disturb American-Japanese relations, the State Department and the Japanese Foreign Ministry worked diligently to abort the clause. The Japanese Foreign Ministry sent frequent letters of protest to the State Department, and the State Department promised the Foreign Ministry its full support in opposition to the bill. The State Department considered that it would be possible to prevent the inclusion of the anti-Japanese clause simply by requests to individual legislators.

Such anti-Japanese measures were not supported unanimously by politicians. Although the House of Representatives did not oppose the insertion of the Japanese exclusion clause, which was supported by Albert Johnson, chairman of the Committee of Immigration and Naturalization, the Senate was reluctant to accept the clause. Some senators favored quotas on Japanese immigration instead. Whether the Japanese exclusion clause passed would depend on the Senate. Since immigration policy was made by the legislative branch, the State Department had no direct means to influence Congress. Urged on by Secretary of State Charles Evans Hughes, Masanao Hanihara, the Japanese ambassador, sent him a letter explaining Japan's position on this issue and asking the Senate not to include the clause, which would totally prohibit immigration from Japan.

> The manifest object of the [exclusion clause] is to single out Japanese as a nation, stigmatizing them as unworthy and undesirable in the eyes of the American people. . . .
>
> It is needless to add that it is not the intention of the Japanese Government to question the sovereign right of any country to regulate immigration to its own territories. Nor is it their desire to send their nationals to the countries where they are not wanted. On the contrary, the Japanese Government showed from the very beginning of this problem their perfect willingness to cooperate with the United States Government to effectively prevent by all honorable means the entrance into the United States of such Japanese nationals as are not desired by the United States, and have given ample evidence thereof, the facts of which are well known to your Government. . . .
>
> Relying upon the confidence you have been good enough to show me at all times, I have stated or rather repeated all this to you very candidly and in a most friendly spirit, for I realize, as I believe you do, the *grave consequences* which the enactment of the measure retaining that particular provision would inevitably bring upon the otherwise happy and mutually advantageous relations between our two countries. (emphasis added)[17]

Use of the phrase "grave consequences" had unexpected results, however. Senator Henry Cabot Lodge interpreted the phrase as "a veiled threat," and scholars have generally agreed that the Hanihara letter, rather than convincing legislators to strike the exclusion clause, actually prompted passage of the bill.[18] A provision added to the bill that would have endorsed the Gentlemen's Agreement of 1907–1908 was defeated in the Senate by a vote of 76 to 2.[19]

Historians have attributed Southern senators' approval of the exclusion clause to their racism, but Southerners were in fact mostly indifferent on the race issue. Rather, their reluctance to support exclusion reflected the ill-feeling they harbored toward Senator Samuel M. Shortridge from California, who was attempting to push an anti-lynching bill through the Senate. The Southerners decided to support Japanese exclusion only after the senior senator from California, Hiram Johnson, intervened. Craving the insertion of the exclusion clause and feeling an antipathy against Hughes, Johnson made a deal, promising to dissuade Shortridge from pushing the anti-lynching bill in return for the Southerners' support. Passage of the exclusion clause was therefore assured. It was only necessary to find a plausible reason to explain the sudden change in the views of the Southern senators. The Hanihara letter provided them with a convenient excuse.[20] In the end, the House passed the Johnson bill, which included the exclusion clause, on April 12, and the Senate passed a similar bill on April 15, 1924.[21]

It was not practical national interest that caused the resulting Japanese indignation. Even if the exclusion clause had not been included in the bill, the number of immigrants permitted into the United States would have amounted to less than two hundred per year. Japanese reacted vehemently to the bill because, in their eyes, the ban was a betrayal of trust. After all, many Japanese felt that the immigration question had been settled with the implementation of the Gentlemen's Agreement of 1907–1908. The racial implications of the law also aggravated Japanese sentiment. Japan, which had chosen to cooperate with the Western powers at the Washington Conference, was not given the immigration quota allowed all European countries. In Japan, the total ban of Japanese immigrants to the United States in 1924 was interpreted as a rejection of Japan, made exclusively on the grounds of race, by the existing world order, controlled by the Western nations. The Japanese interpreted this to mean that no matter how hard Japan tried to cooperate with the United States, they would never be treated as America's equal. Thus, the clause became a thorn in the flesh of the Japanese people and continued to be a disturbing factor in U.S.-Japanese relations in the interwar years, a period during which economic, political, and cultural issues were becoming increasingly interconnected. In this period, whenever the interests of the two countries collided, the exclusion clause sprang to the Japanese mind as evidence of American racism against the Japanese.

This history is all relatively well known today. Less well recognized are the efforts that were made during the 1924–1941 period to rectify the situation. One might get the impression, especially from studying the policies of the two governments during that period, that no one took much interest in repairing U.S.-Japanese relations once they had been damaged by the exclusion provision. But that was not the case, and therein lies the purpose of this study, which is to investigate how internationalists in America tried to build cordial U.S.-Japanese relations by opening America's doors at least a crack to Japanese immigrants.[22] Recent scholarship has emphasized that not only governments but also civic groups such as business associations and private foundations play a critical role in the shaping of America's foreign relations. That is especially true of the period before World War II, and yet the number of studies focusing on the private sector during that period is surprisingly small. The weight of scholarship continues to lie on the side of works studying intergovernmental relations. Since the main players in the battle over the Japanese exclusion clause came from the private sector, a study of their activities will shed new light on how non-governmental groups can influence American foreign relations.

The necessity of emphasizing the private sector is much more apparent when we turn to American–East Asian relations. Since American foreign policy traditionally places much less importance on relations with non-European countries, the influence of non-governmental groups rises correspondingly outside of Europe. Private Americans, especially businessmen and missionaries, were always in the forefront of American expansion into the Far East. Taking advantage of close connections with the government and of public ignorance of the region, and exercising extensive influence upon public opinion, businessmen and clergymen had a significant influence on American relations with East Asia. Moreover, American foreign relations in the Far East were also greatly influenced by the non-governmental sector because the Department of State could not afford sufficient staff and budget for its activities in the region.

This study focuses in particular on clergymen, particularly missionaries, and businessmen, two of the most prominent private-sector groups that advocated cordial U.S.-Japanese relations. Missionaries have played a significant role in American relations with non-European countries since the early nineteenth century. They were in the field many years before the first professional diplomats were assigned, and their devotion and commitment went far beyond those of other groups. Their role in East Asia has not been totally ignored; scholars have noted their influence in American foreign relations. However, those studies concentrate mostly on the role of the China mission. A good example of such work is Jane Hunter's *Gospel of Gentility*, which reveals the important role American missionaries played in the shaping of U.S. foreign relations in China.[23] Very little, however, has been written about Japan missionaries' influence upon American attitudes toward Japan. Although their activities in Japan were much less extensive than those of missionaries in China, it is also true that clergymen who spent years in Japan continued to be active in advocating amicable U.S.-Japanese relations in America. Sandra Taylor's *Advocate of Understanding* is one of the few works dealing with relations between American missionaries to Japan and American attitudes toward Japan; she clearly demonstrates the significant role those missionaries played, through the examination of a former missionary in Japan who spent his life promoting cordial U.S.-Japanese relations.[24] Nevertheless, despite its significance for its detailed biography of one of the most outspoken former American missionaries to Japan, Taylor's study devotes only five pages to Gulick's post-1924 activities on the Japanese immigration issue. By building on Taylor's biographical study, this work will focus on missionaries' visions of peaceful U.S.-Japanese relations.

Businessmen, especially traders, have also influenced American relations with East Asia. They have always been among the first Americans to arrive in "new" areas around the globe, even preceding the missionaries. A few works demonstrating business influence upon American foreign relations have appeared. Emily Rosenberg's *Spreading the American Dream* is a good example of a work in the scholarly tradition of focusing on non-governmental factors, and, as she demonstrates, business interests have played a vital role in

American international relations.[25] Joan Hoff's *American Business and Foreign Policy, 1920–1933* remains an important work, examining the business community's influence upon American foreign policy.[26] But although American business groups were among the few interested in U.S.-Japanese relations in pre–World War II America, not much has been written about their attitude toward Japan throughout the 1920s and 1930s, with the exception of some studies on particular investment plans to Japan (and regions under its influence) or on specific trade conflicts.[27] Nevertheless, they played a significant role during this period, and their reluctance to join the anti-Japan cause affected American attitudes toward Japan during these decades.

The Japanese immigration issue provides an excellent perspective from which to examine the role of private Americans, because non-governmental interests were the main actors in U.S.-Japanese relations concerning this issue. Neither the Japanese nor the U.S. government made any significant move with regard to the question after 1924. Although the issue was discussed at every major U.S.-Japanese diplomatic meeting, both governments had their own reasons for not moving to resolve the question. The Foreign Ministry in Tokyo wanted to avoid being regarded as interfering in U.S. domestic affairs. The Department of State, on the other hand, did not want to appear to be infringing on the domain of Congress. It was thus left to private groups to take action regarding the exclusion clause.

Americans advocating the modification of the immigration law, most of whom were in the private sector, can be broadly classified into two groups. The first group, made up of clergymen and peace advocates in the eastern part of the United States, was primarily active from the immediate aftermath of the enactment of the law until the late 1920s. The main figure in this group was Sidney L. Gulick, a former missionary in Japan. Born in 1860, the son of a missionary attached to the American Board of Commissioners for Foreign Missions (ABCFM) in Hawaii, Gulick followed in his father's footsteps and went to Japan in 1887 as a missionary. He taught at Dōshisha University from 1906 to 1913, when he returned to the United States and began to work to counter the anti-Japanese movement on the Pacific Coast. He took advantage of his position in the Federal Council of the Churches of Christ in America (FCCCA) in his work for the anti-exclusion cause. After he failed to bar the adoption of the exclusion clause in the immigration law of 1924, he immediately started the movement to give Japan an immigration quota by modifying the immigration law, thereby hoping to restore amicable U.S.-Japanese relations.

The second group of Americans who wanted to modify the immigration law were businessmen, chiefly traders on the Pacific Coast who were engaged in trade with Japan. This group was active between the end of the 1920s and the late 1930s. The San Francisco Chamber of Commerce was the central organizing resource of the movement and its main figure was Wallace M. Alexander. Alexander was born in Hawaii in 1869 and inherited from his father large holdings of sugar proprieties on Maui. He was president of Alexander & Baldwin Ltd. and a director of many Pacific-oriented companies such as the Matson Navigation Company and the Honolulu Consolidated Oil Company of California. He had been advocating amicable U.S.-Japanese relations since the 1900s, establishing the Japan Relations Committee in the San Francisco Chamber of Commerce and serving as a trustee of the Carnegie Endowment for International Peace. Since San Francisco was the largest port on the Pacific Coast and a large portion of its trade was with Japan, the chamber of commerce there was greatly interested in U.S.-Japanese relations. In addition to the San Franciscans, lumber traders in Washington and Oregon were also active in the movement to modify the exclusion clause. Since their lumber export business was heavily dependent on Japan, they also placed great importance on amicable U.S.-Japanese relations.

In addition to these two major groups, several other groups or individuals also advocated the modification cause. Some intellectuals, like Professor George Blakeslee of Clark University, who participated in organizations dealing with international relations such as the Institute of Pacific Relations and the Institute of Politics, belong to this category. Such intellectuals argued that jeopardizing U.S.-Japanese relations by excluding a mere two hundred or so immigrants a year was irrational.

The Japanese themselves also advocated the modification of the immigration law. Foreign ministers continued to mention the issue at successive openings of Diet sessions. The *Gaikō Jihō*, the semi-official publication of the Japanese Foreign Ministry, published articles concerning the immigration question every July on the anniversary of the implementation of the law. While the Japanese army, whose interests were focused on Asia, tended to link the United States with its Asian policy, the navy, which faced the United States across the Pacific, was much more directly interested in affairs with the

United States. Naval officers could not overlook American racial prejudice against Japanese, and as a result some of them bore a grudge. However, these opinions were relatively subdued in the public sector. More outspoken were the rightist organizations, many of which attacked the exclusion clause. These included such famous groups as Kokuryū Kai (the Amur River Society, known as the Black Dragon Society in the West) and Taikōsha (the Great Forward Society), as well as small, local, and often single-issue groups such as Kyokutō Renmei Kyōkai (the Far East Allies Association) and Ajia Renmei Kyōkai (the Asia Allies Association).[28] All of them cited the exclusion clause as the foremost example of American racial prejudice against Asians and continued to advocate its modification from time to time, once the outrage of the bill's passage had abated. While the exclusion clause was merely one more example of American racism for rightist groups in Japan, it represented a deadly blow to such pro-American Japanese as Eiichi Shibusawa, a prominent businessman; Inazō Nitobe, the great educator and undersecretary general of the League of Nations; and Kentarō Kaneko, a politician and a classmate of Theodore Roosevelt at Harvard College. Now these men shouldered the burden of proof: when they argued that Japan should be on friendly terms with the United States, they had to prove that the exclusion clause was not based on a consensus of American citizens.[29]

There was also opposition to modification from within the private sector in the United States. After the enactment of the immigration law of 1924, the anti-Japanese movement became much less profitable politically, since most of the anti-Japanese agenda had been realized by the law. Therefore, anti-Japanese agitators such as California state senator Inman and California state controller Chambers, who had been active before 1924, now appeared to be uninterested in the anti-modification movement. The main force of the anti-modification movement was the California Joint Immigration Committee (CJIC), based in San Francisco. While this organization was backed by four California organizations, it was mostly operated by one man, Valentine Stuart McClatchy, who devoted much of his personal fortune and most of his time to the activities of the organization.

V. S. McClatchy was born in Sacramento, the son of a newspaperman, James McClatchy, who had migrated to the United States from Ireland in 1840. The young McClatchy inherited a half-ownership of the *Sacramento*

Bee and established the *Fresno Bee* with his brother C. K. McClatchy. While V. S. McClatchy ran the newspaper business, he was also engaged in the anti-Asian immigrant movement as a sideline, working for the Japanese Exclusion League of California and conducting anti-Japanese campaigns in his own papers until 1923, when he sold his interest in both papers to his brother. He then began to devote most of his energy to the exclusion movement, setting up his own organization, the CJIC. This committee represented the four organizations that had earlier supported the Asiatic Exclusion League (predecessor of the CJIC). By organizing the CJIC, McClatchy became the leader of the exclusion movement in California both in name and reality.

The largest of the four supporting organizations was the California State Federation of Labor, whose membership was around nine thousand in the mid-1920s.[30] Although California labor had traditionally opposed Asian immigration, beginning with the influx of Chinese in the nineteenth century, the growth in the ranks of the State Federation of Labor at the turn of the century strengthened the tendency. At that time, the organization started to include many members from unskilled trades such as "butchers, cooks, waiters, stablemen, street-railway employees, retail clerks, laundry workers, teamsters, barbers, hodcarriers, tanners, and laborers."[31] Most in those unskilled trades were directly threatened by the influx of Japanese immigrants. Paul Scharrenberg, secretary-treasurer for the organization, spoke for these members. He was born in Hamburg, Germany, in 1877 and had come to the United States in his teens and worked as a seaman. After a ship he was on was wrecked off the coast of California, he settled in the state and joined the American Seamen's Union, working as an editor of its *Coast Seamen's Journal.* He enlisted himself in the California State Federation of Labor around 1904 and served as the group's secretary from 1910 to 1936. Throughout his incumbency, he was an enthusiastic supporter of the exclusion cause. Even after the enactment of the 1924 immigration law, he continued to be active in the CJIC, representing the labor federation. His presence had a very negative effect on the anti-exclusion movement, especially after 1924, because he deceived many Japanese elites into believing he was sympathetic to them, which later caused disappointment and confusion.

The second supporting organization for the CJIC was a group of small farmers who competed with Japanese farmers. There were two major farm organizations in California in the 1920s: the California State Grange, made up of small and part-time farmers, and the California Farm Bureau Federation, which represented relatively large farmers. Neither had expressed opposition to Japanese immigrants as cheap labor in the early years of Japanese immigration and settlement. However, once the Japanese ceased being low-paid workers and gradually became landowning farmers, they found themselves under attack by both groups. After 1924, however, the two groups diverged on the issue of Japanese farmers. The large farmers of the Farm Bureau Federation were no longer directly threatened by newly established Japanese farmers, and therefore unenthusiastic about continuing the anti-Japanese movement. Moreover, the Farm Bureau's original aims had been educational, and its membership was more than twice as large as that of the Grange, two more factors that mitigated against continuing the anti-Japanese cause. On the other hand, the small farmers in the Grange, who had to compete directly with Japanese farmers, did not easily drop the anti-Japanese cause from their agenda. The Grange thus became another of the four supporting organizations of the CJIC at the time of its founding. However, their support for the CJIC was short-lived. After 1924, they soon realized that they were far more threatened by Mexican and Filipino immigrants, whose entrance was neither banned nor controlled by the 1924 immigration law. In addition, the financial burden of CJIC membership weighed heavily on the small farm organization, whose membership never surpassed 10,000 in the 1920s. The Grange, therefore, gradually lost its interest in participating in the activities of the CJIC.[32]

The third supporting organization for the CJIC was the NSGW, a fraternal society, incorporated in 1876, which strictly restricted its membership to men born in California "under the American flag."[33] It expanded greatly around the turn of the century, from 113 members at the time of its founding to 160 "parlors" and 30,000 members by 1924. Unlike the California State Federation of Labor and the California State Grange, the primary concern shared by its members was not economic but nativistic. Its monthly publication, the *Grizzly Bear*, started in May of 1907, published racist articles, and almost every issue carried anti-Asiatic pieces. The NSGW was disproportionately influential in California, because its membership included many prominent Californians, such as Frank M. Angellotti, a California Supreme Court Justice between 1915 and 1921; James Rolph, Jr., mayor of

San Francisco between 1912 and 1931; and Angelo J. Rossi, mayor of San Francisco between 1931 and 1943. Hiram Johnson, who served as governor of California between 1911 and 1917 and became a powerful U.S. senator between 1917 and 1945, and James D. Phelan, who was mayor of San Francisco between 1897 and 1902 and U.S. senator between 1915 and 1921, were also members.[34]

The fourth supporting organization of the CJIC, the California Department of the American Legion, which chose "aggression of Orientals" as one of the first matters to be considered at its first convention in San Francisco, had been anti-Japanese from its foundation. It did not change its attitude after the passage of the 1924 immigration law.[35] Although its actual membership never exceeded 4,000 in the 1920s, politicians could not ignore the united voice of the veterans.[36]

This study focuses on those groups in the American private sector, in cooperation with some Japanese, that tried to promote positive U.S.-Japanese relations, primarily through their efforts to modify the Japanese exclusion clause, during the years between the enactment of the law in 1924 and the attack on Pearl Harbor in 1941. While foreign policy in these years is often characterized as nativist and isolationist, it is important to note that there were strong voices in the private sector trying to promote cordial U.S.-Japanese relations within the generally hostile atmosphere. American society in the 1920s was characterized by its nativistic and exclusionistic mood, and the immigration law of 1924 was a part of that environment. But, at the same time, we cannot ignore the forceful parallel trend of internationalism, which advocated peaceful international relations. This intellectual trend was manifested in a movement within the private sector to modify the exclusion clause. Except for short periods of time during the Manchurian and Shanghai incidents, and for the years of the Sino-Japanese War, the 1930s were characterized by an isolationist mood and, since most other groups in the United States did not pay much attention to U.S.-Japanese relations during these years, voices from the private sector increasingly influenced American attitudes toward Japan. It is important to note that even after the Manchurian crisis of 1931, when internationalism became increasingly unpopular, these businessmen's internationalist voices grew stronger and continued to advocate cordial U.S.-Japanese relations. An examination of their activities reveals that the non-official sector played a significant role in defusing U.S.-Japanese tensions during the critical period following 1924 by suggesting an alternative peaceful vision of U.S.-Japanese relations. This study also looks at the exclusion debate in Japan. Examination of the debate in Japan shows how widely and seriously the immigration issue was discussed in Japan, and demonstrates the interplay between the exclusion debate and other disputes regarding U.S.-Japanese relations. Further, by focusing on issues such as the regional variations in opinion on exclusion legislation, this study situates the debate over the exclusion question in the broader context of American racism and anti-racism. The examination of those issues will reveal the complex ways class and economic interests cut across racist predispositions. As a whole, this approach to the topic enables us to reexamine our prevalent views of American society in the 1920s and 1930s.

PART I

The Missionary Initiative

ONE

The Immediate Aftermath

The Japanese Response

The immigration bill which included the exclusion clause was passed on April 12, 1924 in the House of Representatives, and, in the Senate, a similar bill with the exclusion clause was passed on April 15. Without waiting to see whether the president would sign or veto the bill, Japan reacted to the passage of the law almost at once.

Initial Japanese reaction was universally hostile. From the government on down, everyone maintained that the law was based on racial discrimination and stained the prestige of Japan. According to a report made by Ambassador Cyrus Woods in Tokyo to the Department of State, protests came from "groups and organizations of varied character[:] educational, religious, social, political, commercial, industrial, financial, et cetera."[1]

The Japanese media led the charge. Many editorial writers viewed the issue from the perspective of race and argued that the law was not only a national challenge to Japan, but also an insult to the yellow race in general. The *Tokyo Nichinichi Shimbun* proclaimed that a great race war was imminent.[2] The *Teikoku Daigaku Shimbun*, the newspaper of the Imperial University of Tokyo, published an article by Hikomatsu Kamikawa, an associate professor, in which he argued that the immigration law symbolized white ethnocentrism and marked the onset of a race war.[3] To emphasize this aspect of racial affront, some newspapers published the anti-exclusion views of non-Japanese Asian intellectuals, who advocated the solidarity of all Asians on this issue.[4]

While some newspapers regarded the law's passage as an insult to Asians as a whole, others revealed a different kind of prejudice. The law, they argued, was an insult especially to Japan because Japanese were superior to other Asian nationals, whose immigration was already banned. The *Osaka Asahi Shimbun*, for example, not only declared the immigration law to be a product of incorrigible racial prejudice, but further argued that it could not accept the law because the Japanese were not inferior but superior to other peoples.[5] Even the *Chūgai Shōgyō Shimpō*, a newspaper that specialized in commerce, declared that the law would not only cause great losses to countries in the East but would also lead to racial tensions.[6] On April 21, 1924, fifteen major newspapers in Tokyo published a joint declaration about the exclusion issue. Since they still hoped that the law would be vetoed, the declaration was not radical. It read: "It is very clear that the anti-Japanese bill which was passed in both houses is unfair and immoral. . . . If the bill becomes a law, there will be no recourse other than to regard it as the defined will of the American people, and, as a result, it will injure deeply the traditional friendship between the nations."[7]

American diplomats in Japan experienced the Japanese indignation firsthand. Immediately after Congress passed the bill, a staff member of the American embassy in Tokyo found a leaflet on his car from the Taibei Mondai Yūkoku Seinendan (Patriotic Young Men's League Regarding the Japan-American Question), which was an offshoot of Nihon Rikkōkai (the Japanese Strenuous Efforts Society), a Christian organization founded by Hyōdayū Shimanuki to assist Japanese students who wished to study abroad. The leaflet urged Japanese patriots to "punish the hypocritical and cruel America."[8] The leaders of Suihei-sha, an anti-discrimination league, handed Ambassador Woods a note of protest, which said that it was unreasonable for the United States, which had been an advocate of liberty, an emancipator of slaves, and a promoter of peace, to take an anti-Japanese attitude.[9]

Mass rallies against the exclusion clause took place throughout Japan. As early as April 20, a national convention was held in Tokyo under the leadership of Ryōhei Uchida, head of Kokuryū Kai, a major patriotic organization interested in foreign affairs.[10] Kokuryū Kai had been organized by Uchida in

1901, at a time when there was a strong sense of the impending danger of Russia's seizing Manchuria. Mitsuru Tōyama, an influential rightist activist, became its adviser. The organization preached pan-Asianism and Japanese expansion onto the Asian mainland. After World War I, Kokuryū Kai expanded its interests, expressing alarm at the uncomplaining acceptance of the Washington Treaty and the exclusion of Japanese immigrants by the United States and Australia. It also worried about social turmoil in Japan, especially the development of Taishō democracy. Kokuryū Kai's agenda included promoting harmony between the East and West and making Japan the leader of East Asia.[11] On April 22, the *Kokumin Shimbun* sponsored an evening of speeches on U.S.-Japanese relations. According to a report by the Metropolitan Police, the event attracted as many as three thousand people. The speakers ranged from moderates to radicals, but radical views were the more numerous. Among the invited speakers was Kiroku Hayashi, president of Keiō University, who emphasized that the immigration law was against the spirit of peaceful cooperation. Other speakers endeavored to stir up nationalistic feelings among the Japanese; Jirō Hayasaka, a reporter for the *Kokumin Shimbun*, proclaimed that if the United States did not heed the protests from Japan, the Japanese must prepare to respond to this racial affront, and Kōki Hori, a professor at Tokyo Commercial College, argued that the American law was unwise because propagation of the Japanese was for the good of mankind.[12]

A compilation of these speeches was published within a month of the meeting. The preface examined the history of U.S.-Japanese relations and highlighted the inconsistency in U.S. policy toward Japan. The United States had opened Japan seventy years earlier by force, yet now persecuted the Yamato race by barring immigrants from entering the spacious territory of America. The book insisted that Japan's voice was being ignored because its military was not strong enough, and thus maintained that a military buildup was necessary.[13]

The view that Japan should build its military strength was common, as is apparent from a series of twelve articles on the immigration issue that appeared in *Kaizō*, a progressive monthly magazine. In one of them, Tatsukichi Minobe, a well-known scholar of constitutional law, maintained that it had become clear that the anti-Japanese movement in the United States was forged out of contempt for the Japanese and argued that since the strength of the United States was far beyond that of Japan, cooperation with Asian nations should be promoted.[14] The general tone of these articles was not violent, but the possibility of war against the United States appeared in many essays. An editor's note, in particular, declared that if the U.S. president failed to veto the law, Japan would have to either accept the insult or go to war.[15] Launching a war with the United States was not considered realistic by most Japanese, however, even in the first heat of outrage. Educated Japanese, moreover, also realized that without the backing of considerable military strength their voices would not be heard by the United States; their silence on the issue did not necessarily mean that they were satisfied with the situation.

Nihon oyobi nihonjin was a rightist publication, put out by Seikyōsha, an organization founded in 1888 that strongly criticized the unquestioning imitation of all things Western in Japan. The magazine responded to the passage of the immigration bill quickly, basically regarding the immigration question as the beginning of a race war between whites and non-whites. After expressing its deep regret over the exclusion clause in the May 1 issue, this bimonthly magazine gave extra space to special articles on the immigration question in the May 15 issue, calling it the "issue of indignation against the U.S." The author of the editorial for the issue said that he could only laugh at those who saw a ray of hope in the possible veto of the bill by the U.S. president because he knew that the president would not do so. He argued that what the United States really wanted was to build a white America, and so the rejection of the Japanese revealed their true intentions. He concluded that Japanese exclusion was neither a simple immigration question nor an economic question, but was rather part of a racial struggle.[16]

Outside the Tokyo area, demonstrations against exclusion were no less prevalent. On April 21, a women's group organized a public protest in Nagoya.[17] In Osaka, four major newspapers and a local business organization convened a mass meeting that drew a lot of attention. The participants passed a declaration demanding reconsideration of the law by the U.S. Congress and sent telegrams requesting a veto to President Calvin Coolidge.[18] In Manchuria, anti-exclusion protests were also heard among the Japanese community there. Since Manchuria was not a part of Japan territory, the Japanese community there emphasized the importance of cooperation among all nonwhite peoples, and especially between Japanese and

Chinese. *Manshū Nichinichi Shimbun*, a newspaper published in Dairen, argued that the Christians in the West who professed an inclusive love for humankind nonetheless harbored deep racial prejudice against non-white races.[19] At a civic convention that was organized in Dairen, speakers advocated cooperation between the Japanese and Chinese to counter Western domination of the world. An editor of the *Manshū Nichinichi* argued that since the world was controlled by the white race and non-whites were looked down upon as slaves, Japanese and Chinese should end their "marital quarrel" and cooperate to cope with Western racial discrimination. The convention concluded with the passage of a resolution which requested that the United Stated agree to an amicable settlement of the immigration question.[20]

The Japanese cabinet took the issue seriously. Before the bill was passed, the cabinet had been very optimistic about the development of the U.S. immigration bill. In early April, Foreign Minister Keishirō Matsui simply gave it as his opinion that "Mr. Hughes's view would prevail in the end, and that nothing would be enacted prejudicial to the international status and dignity of Japan."[21] This optimistic attitude had to be changed. On April 14, British Ambassador Charles Eliot thought Masui "grave and despondent." Immediately after passage of the bill, Premier Keigo Kiyoura indicated to Viscount Nobuatsu Makino that, as prime minister, he felt obliged to take responsibility for the incident. Makino felt that, depending on the course of events, Kiyoura was actually prepared to resign. Matsui expressed his pessimistic expectation that President Coolidge would not veto the bill.[22]

The Japanese Foreign Ministry remained basically calm on the issue of the exclusion clause, doing little except submitting official protests through diplomatic channels. However, this did not mean that officials harbored no ill-feelings about the clause. Although they rarely criticized the U.S. government in their official capacity, the negative views of Foreign Ministry bureaucrats appeared in the *Gaikō Jihō*, a semi-official bimonthly magazine on foreign affairs. The journal criticized the 1924 immigration law harshly. The May 15 issue declared that the Japanese should work ceaselessly for the abrogation of the exclusion clause, and should do so by instilling righteous indignation into the public conscience of the United States.[23] The succeeding issue called the American anti-Japanese legislation not only a diplomatic problem but also a sin, from the perspectives of morality, pure reason, and humanity.[24] While the Foreign Ministry, as the official agency of the Japanese government, remained calm, the *Gaikō Jihō*, its civilian offshoot, attacked the law vehemently. This sort of split attitude, which was observed in many sectors in Japan, would continue until the end of the 1930s.

The split psychology, which was observed in diplomatic circles, was also evident in the military sector in Japan. The Imperial Headquarters' calm attitude toward the immigration issue did not mean that there was no individual indignation against the anti-Asiatic attitudes of the Americans. Officers of the navy, whose number-one potential enemy after the Russo-Japanese War was the United States, were particularly indignant about American racism. When the first imperial defense principles were formulated in 1907, one of them concerned the issue of race and accepted the possibility that Japan and the United States might collide on the issue in the future.[25] That possibility became more likely with the newly revised defense principles of 1923:

> Japanese exclusion in California gradually extends to neighboring states
> and the situation concerning the Japanese question in Hawaii is not
> promising. It is extremely difficult to solve long-time complications
> based on economic problems and racial prejudice, and conflicting interests
> and emotional alienation will greatly grow in the future. If the Asia policy
> of the United States, which secures footholds in the Pacific and Far East
> and possesses great military power, follows this trend, it is inevitable for
> the United States to collide with the Japanese Empire sooner or later. The
> U.S. is, therefore, most central to our defense policy.[26]

Some individual officers spoke out more explicitly on this point. In a rally held in Toyama prefecture, a major-general of the Imperial Army argued that the United States had intentionally timed the passage of the immigration law to take advantage of the disorder in Japan caused by the earthquake that had destroyed Tokyo in 1923.[27] Some Japanese naval officers held extremely radical opinions on this issue. According to a security police report on the opinions of the top officers at the Yokosuka naval base, some officers complained of the inconsistencies in American policy, pointing out that the United States had proposed disarmament at the Washington Conference of 1921–1922 in an atmosphere of mutual conciliation, but that it had nonetheless expanded its air force and passed an anti-Japanese immigration law in 1924. These officers argued that since the capabilities of the Japanese fleet exceeded those of the American fleet, and since there were no soldiers ready to protect U.S. warships passing through the Suez Canal, there would never be a better opportunity to declare war against the United States.[28] After a meeting at Yokosuka, the Kaigun Rōdō Kumiai Renmei (Naval Federation of Labor) sent a declaration condemning the immigration bill to Samuel Gompers and President Coolidge.[29] The Maizuru Division of the Naval Federation of Labor also telegraphed Foreign Minister Matsui, asking him to make every effort to abrogate the exclusion bill.[30] And so, in military circles, too, although anti-exclusion feelings ran high, official outward appearances remained calm. But this pent-up indignation would later emerge, when the two countries' material interests came into direct conflict.

To the surprise of foreign observers, exclusion did not become an issue during the general election campaign, which culminated with the vote on May 10, because all parties had agreed not to take advantage of the issue during the campaign. The insult felt by the nation was so great that it was not difficult to reach such an agreement. This agreement was a wise one from the perspective of cordial U.S.-Japanese relations because any discussion would only have increased Japanese resentment toward the United States. The fact that it was not difficult to reach such an agreement among the different political parties also reveals how seriously they took exclusion as a national crisis which demanded a unified national response. Since the ruling party failed to win a majority vote, it became inevitable that the cabinet would change, and so the question of whether the Kiyoura cabinet should resign on account of the exclusion issue simply faded away.[31]

Meanwhile, behind the scenes, some Japanese were putting pressure on American friends to use their influence to persuade President Coolidge to exercise his veto. For example, Japanese women activists wrote to their American counterparts asking for their support on this issue. Tomi Wada of Kyūshū Imperial University sent a letter to Jane Addams describing the Japanese as "very much troubled about the new immigration law which had passed in the U.S. Congress."[32] The Ladies Association of Nagoya City also wrote to Addams, informing her that they trusted her "Christian spirit of love and justice to aid [them] in the solution of the present difficulty."[33] Even before she received those letters, Addams had asked Coolidge to veto the immigration bill. Addams's telegram to the president read: "Organized as we are for the promotion of international peace and good will, we are deeply

Fig. 1. "Look at this fatal crack!"
Cartoon published in the *Tokyo Asahi
Shimbun* after President Coolidge signed
the Immigration Act of 1924.

concerned over a situation which may so easily lead to grave misunder-standings and discord."[34]

These efforts, however, were in vain. President Coolidge signed the bill on May 26—ironically, on the very day that the Foreign Ministry in Tokyo was expressing its expectation of a veto in a telegram to Ambassador Masanao Hanihara. Coolidge's decision disappointed those Japanese who had hoped he would veto the bill, and boosted anti-American sentiments in Japan. The *Osaka Mainichi Shimbun* regarded Coolidge's action as an affront to Japan and claimed that Japanese nationals would never cease to fight against the immigration law.[35] On May 28, a cartoon in the *Tokyo Asahi Shimbun* (see Figure 1) depicted a huge jar labeled "Nichibei yūgi," or "Japanese American friendship." A big crack ran down the center of the jar. The caption read: "Look at this fatal crack!"[36] The *Chūgai Shōgyō Shimpō* maintained that the Japanese government should submit a formal protest.[37] The *Tokyo Asahi* proclaimed July 1, the day the law went into effect, a day of humiliation, and published a picture of a big signboard in the United States which read: "JAPS. . . . KEEP MOVING."[38] To allay the feelings of the Japanese, Coolidge expressed his regret over "the impossibility of severing from [the immigration bill] the exclusion provision." Coolidge also wrote that he hoped the enactment of the law would not "imply any change in our sentiment of admiration and cordial friendship for the Japanese people."[39]

The shock felt by liberal intellectuals in Japan, who were generally pro-America, was intense. The enactment of the immigration law seriously diminished the influence of Japanese internationalists who advocated cordial U.S.-Japanese relations. Inazō Nitobe, who had become a Quaker in the United States and who identified himself as a "bridge" between Japan and the United States, was terribly shocked by the enactment of the immigration law, especially since he had been an optimist who believed that the war scare had been created by yellow journalists and arms manufacturers in the United States, and that anti-Japanese problems in California could be solved through goodwill and mutual accommodation. The impact of the immigration law on Nitobe was so great that he swore he would never set foot on U.S. soil again unless the exclusion law were abrogated.[40]

Kanzō Uchimura, a devout Christian and a graduate of Amherst College, was also tremendously shocked by the law. Since he had regarded the United States as a country of true Christian love, he felt betrayed: "No words can express my pain and sorrow (and indignation, too,) at the grave and disastrous consequences of what I cannot but characterize as the mad and thoughtless act of the American Government in its dealing with the Japanese question."[41] He even wrote, "[at] the Golden Gate of heaven, many shall be excluded who excluded others on earth."[42] These Christians had such a strong faith in America that their disappointment was enormous.

Viscount Kentarō Kaneko, a classmate of Theodore Roosevelt at Harvard, who had sent a telegram to Coolidge to request his veto on April 25, "more or less cut himself off from his American friends" after Coolidge signed the bill. He finally resigned as president of the Japan-America Society, a position he had occupied since the organization's founding.[43] In his letter of resignation, he wrote:

> When Americans in foreign countries experience racial discrimination, the American Government make[s] a protest and assert[s] their rights; but when a Japanese in America is treated with the same discrimination, they say it is a domestic question for America, and the Japanese Government [has] no right to interfere. . . . When I learned the Immigration Bill

was passed in so drastic a manner and with such an overwhelming majority, I felt as if the hope of my life were destroyed. . . . When my hope to serve my country and my second home—America—is frustrated, I cannot conscientiously occupy the post of . . . President of the Society any longer.[44]

The total prohibition of immigration from Japan seriously debilitated pro-America liberals. Sohō Tokutomi, a patriot and the prolific publisher of the *Kokumin Shimbun*, criticized such liberals, claiming that they regarded the United States, not Japan, as their "spiritual mother country."[45]

Compared with the liberal idealism of the Japanese intellectuals, Japanese businessmen, who viewed U.S.-Japanese relations mainly from a commercial perspective, responded more calmly. Eiichi Shibusawa, a Japanese business tycoon, sent telegrams to influential Americans to request them to use what influence they had to pressure Coolidge to veto the bill.[46] Even after Coolidge signed the bill, Shibusawa suspected that the exclusion law was not supported by the majority of Americans, and believed that the Japanese should stay calm.[47] At the end of 1924, he wrote to his American friends to express his appreciation for their "very sympathetic attitude throughout the painful crisis," and to indicate his belief that any initiative on this matter should originate from among the Americans.[48] Takuma Dan of Mitsui, who believed the enactment of the immigration law was "far from reflect[ive of] the feelings of a great majority of the American people," offered a reassuring interpretation of the angry Japanese response, saying that the great magnitude of the disappointment was "due principally to the fact that the feeling of confidence in the American friendship has been steadily growing in the hearts of the Japanese people in general, as amply shown at the Washington Conference, and thereafter especially strengthened by the generous action . . . at the time of the great earthquake disaster." He explained that anti-American movements were "sporadic" and did not embody "the national feelings at large."[49]

There existed yet another view, different from both the passionate anti-American views and the unperturbed business views. Tanzan Ishibashi, a publicist and politician, criticized the Japanese public for its lack of a pan-Asian perspective and its Japan-centered views. He attacked the attitude that accepted discrimination against other Asians so long as the Japanese themselves were treated as equals by whites. This attitude was exemplified by the foreign minister's strong protest against exclusion on the grounds that it "lump[ed the Japanese] together with Chinese or Hindus as undesirable aliens." Ishibashi argued that the Japanese should not focus on a token immigration quota but should speak on behalf of all Asians excluded by the United States.[50]

The passage of the immigration act, while not immediately explosive, had enduring practical effects on the young elite at the Foreign Ministry. Jefferson Caffery, chargé d'affaires at the American Embassy, reported: "Prior to the passage of the Act the younger officials [at the Japanese Foreign Ministry] were more than ready to grant favors or to supply information, whereas requests now are often acceded to with evident reluctance." He also explained that an atmosphere in the Foreign Ministry had been created in which friendly relations with Americans could work against the young Japanese diplomats' careers. Discriminatory measures against Japan by the United States would continue to affect young Foreign Ministry recruits. Yōji Hirota, an official who belonged to the "Progressive" School within the Japanese Foreign Ministry, regarded the Anglo-Saxon diplomacy toward Japan as nothing but oppression against Japan, based on his observations of the peace conference at Paris, the Washington Conference, and the immigration law.[51] Although it is difficult to demonstrate whether these younger officials had an influence on Japan's foreign policy, it can at least be said that many younger officials who dealt with anti-Japanese issues by the United States tended to lean toward the Axis powers in the late 1930s. Chūichi Ōhashi who served as consul at Seattle in 1924 is a good example. The topic remains to be examined.

The reaction of Japanese Christian clergymen was divided. A small group of Japanese Christians held radical views on the future of U.S.-Japanese relations. The Reverend Naomi Tamura, for example, argued that unless the United States changed its discriminatory policy toward non-white peoples, a clash between Japan and the U.S. would be inevitable, and that "one hundred years from now the American Territory [w]est of the Rocky Mountains will be Japanese territory."[52] At a synod, it was proposed that all American missionaries should be expelled from Japan, though it was eventually agreed that such a vengeful act would simply show that the Japanese had as little Christianity as the Americans.[53] However, the majority view was much less extreme. In an open letter to Japanese Christians, Bishop Kogorō Usaki, the presiding officer of the Japan Methodist Church, pointed out that "almost all the Christian organizations of America took a positive stand against [the immigration law]," arguing that both the Japanese and Americans must be patient and love each other as brethren.[54] The Federal Council of Churches of Christ in America (FCCCA), which represented more than twenty million American Protestants, reinforced this point of view by writing to the Churches of Christ in Japan that they "deplore[d] the action of Congress and consider[ed] that it did violence both to Christian and to American ideals," adding that "American goodwill toward the Japanese people has not changed."[55] The FCCCA also said that it would work for modification of the immigration law, although it did not spell out how in its letter.

Although the Japanese government took the immigration issue seriously, it had no intention of initiating any effort to rectify the situation. The central members of the government only tried to find out who was to blame, whereas the Foreign Ministry merely tried to keep U.S.-Japanese relations on an even keel, while at the same time soothing the Japanese public by showing that the Ministry was making every effort to solve the problem. When the U.S. Senate passed the immigration bill, Prime Minister Keigo Kiyoura expressed his disappointment to foreign correspondents.[56] However, top Japanese politicians were much more interested in understanding why the law had not been stopped than in fighting its discriminatory nature. When the Privy Council took up the issue on April 23, the foreign minister, Keishirō Matsui, expressed the view that both the Republican and Democratic parties had supported the anti-Japanese clause in order to attract the California vote in the forthcoming presidential election. Matsui deplored the passage of the immigration law, and the Privy Council spent a great deal of time trying to determine who on the Japanese side was responsible.[57]

While promising that it would use "every effort to allay public feeling and to prevent popular outbreaks,"[58] the Japanese government officially protested that "international discriminations in any form and on any subject . . . are opposed to the principles of justice and fairness." It asked the American Government to "take all possible and suitable measures for the removal of such discrimination."[59] But the Japanese foreign minister did not seriously believe that his memorandum would force the U.S. government to immediately adopt measures to rectify the situation. Matsui admitted to British Ambassador Eliot that his memorandum was for "home consumption" only, to show "the Japanese people that the Government was not submitting tamely to the insolence of America."[60]

The protests of the Foreign Ministry were not enough to calm public indignation in Japan. On May 31, a Japanese man committed hara-kiri, the traditional Japanese form of suicide, in front of the former American embassy in Tokyo. In addition to a note requesting the disposal of his remains, two letters were found near his body. The first was addressed to the ambassador and people of the United States and said, "I request by my death the withdrawal of the Japanese exclusion clause." The second letter urged "the nation to rise up to avenge the insult embodied in the action of America." The *Tokyo Asahi* reported that the police officers who had been called to the scene were impressed by the suicide, calling it "tragic but magnificent."[61]

This act of hara-kiri boosted anti-American feeling in Japan. Shinkichi Uesugi, a professor at Tokyo Imperial University and a leader of the "national spirit movement," stated that "hara-kiri shows that a solution of the exclusion question cannot be reached by speeches and notes, but by the heroic resolution thus typified."[62] Many people who sympathized with Uesugi, including Ryōhei Uchida, visited the temple where the body of the suicide was being held to offer sticks of incense.[63] Several more Japanese followed the example of this unknown man and committed suicide in protest against the exclusion clause.[64] Responding to this surge of public sentiment, nineteen major newspapers in Tokyo and Osaka issued a joint declaration which stated that although the Japanese people would wait patiently and prudently for the right time to act, they would never be content to accept such discriminatory treatment.[65]

On June 5, the Kokuryū Kai held a national convention at Ryōgoku, which, according to a report by the Metropolitan Police, was attended by thirty thousand people. According to its invitation letter, the purpose of the convention was to enhance national dignity by emphasizing Japanese national unity and by refusing to overlook American anti-Japanese behavior. The convention declared that since the American anti-Japanese action was extremely high-handed and infringed upon Japanese national honor, it was impossible for the Japanese to forgive it. Shinkichi Uesugi delivered a radical address maintaining that since war with the United States was unavoidable, Japan should lead the other non-white peoples by initiating this war. The convention resolved to hold a funeral for the anonymous man who had committed suicide, and Tōyama was appointed as chairman of the funeral. It was unanimously decided to create a small organization within Kokuryū

Kai, to be called Kokumin Taibeikai. This smaller group, to be established within the publication division of Kokuryū Kai, would concentrate on relations with the United States and would continue its activities until the U.S.-Japanese problem was solved.[66]

On the following day, bands of young Japanese men who belonged to Taikōsha, or the Great Forward Society, a rightist organization whose original object was the "purification" of social and political institutions in Japan, intruded into the elegant, Western-style Imperial Hotel, which at that time housed the American embassy chancery. Although the organization had recently been established, it was not merely a "single issue" group. The Taikōsha was a collateral organization, an offshoot of Yūzonsha, a larger organization led by Kametarō Mitsukawa and Shūmei Ōkawa, which was dedicated to the reform of the Japanese empire and the liberation of Asian races.[67] Upon entering the hotel, one demonstrator raised his voice and urged the upper-class guests of the hotel to take the lead in eliminating the imitation of Western customs such as dancing. While some of the intruders performed a traditional Japanese-style sword dance in front of the guests, others distributed copies of a pamphlet that demanded the removal of American missionaries in Japan, the prohibition of American movies, the boycotting of American goods, the abrogation of Japanese-American treaties, and a ban on the entry of Americans to Japan. The intruders did not harm any of the guests and no injuries were reported.[68] Ryūtaro Satō, a novelist and editor, characterized the incident as "joyful."[69]

The surge of anti-American sentiment also affected the film industry in Japan. Some film interpreters, whose job it was to help audiences understand American silent films, simply refused to explain the American movies.[70] On June 8, several leaders of Japan's biggest movie companies, fearing tumult in the movie theaters, decided to refrain from showing American movies.[71] Although most movie theaters stopped showing American movies for a while, some theaters continued to do so, and as a result received threatening notes from rightist organizations.[72] Kōa Kinema Kaisha, a film company, decided to stir up anti-American sentiment by making a "white peril" movie, in which Chinese who had been tricked by American and British villains would be saved in the end by a Japanese hero.[73]

The Japanese antagonism toward the United States kept growing. On June 9, department stores in Tokyo were visited by some of the same anti-

American activists who had invaded the Imperial Hotel. They requested cooperation in the boycott of American goods; the stores were generally cooperative and agreed to refrain from selling American goods, at least for a while.[74] A Japanese man visited the American Consulate at Yokohama carrying a dagger. He denounced the U.S. immigration law as unjust before being arrested.[75] A nationalist organization called Dokuritsu Haibei Dan (Independent Anti-American Society) sent a threatening note to the American embassy. Having learned that the embassy had warned the Japanese government regarding the boycott of American films, Dokuritsu Haibei Dan responded that the embassy should give such warnings not to the Japanese government, but to its own government in Washington, and concluded: "We [don't] like violence but if you continue in this way we may be driven to exasperation and take direct action in dealing with members of your Embassy staff."[76] Eugene H. Dooman, a junior diplomat at the American embassy in Tokyo, concluded that "the Japanese were hurt right down to the bone."[77] Kyokutō Renmei Kyōkai (the Far East Allies Association), a nationalist group that had come into being in the upsurge of anti-America sentiments in Osaka, organized a convention at the Nakanoshima Convention Hall on June 9. According to a report by the Osaka governor's office, the hall was packed full with an eager audience of five thousand, who heard the United States accused of hypocritically advocating world peace under the mask of justice, but that with the passage of the immigration law, U.S. wickedness had at last been revealed.[78] On June 17, the organization convened a second anti-American convention, which attracted two thousand people, where the United States was accused of humiliating the Republic of China and the Japanese Empire. Yet a third anti-American convention was planned for July 1, the date when the immigration law would go into effect. Alarmed, the Japanese Ministry of Interior warned Kyokutō Renmei Kyōkai against behaving rashly, in the light of the effects such actions might have on U.S.-Japanese relations. According to the report of the Ministry of Interior, as many as five hundred thousand fliers urging veterans, labor unionists, Koreans, and Chinese to attend the July 1 convention had been distributed.[79]

The Japanese government, which hoped to keep U.S.-Japanese relations undisturbed, made considerable efforts to protect American citizens living in Japan. In Kanagawa Prefecture, which included the city of Yokohama with its large American population, the prefectural government dispatched policemen to the districts with American residents and increased the frequency of patrols.[80] Apparently, American residents and the American embassy were satisfied with the efforts of the Japanese government to protect Americans. A group of prominent Americans living in Yokohama, surprised by newspaper reports claiming that Japanese in America were being harassed by locals retaliating for what they mistakenly believed was the mistreatment of Americans in Japan, passed a resolution which stated that even the most radical groups in Japan had declared they would not harm Americans. Expressing their earnest desire to have this resolution publicized in the United States, especially on the Pacific Coast, they sent it to the National Chamber of Commerce in Washington, D.C., and to newspapers in Japan and the United States.[81] The U.S. chargé d'affaires at Tokyo told British Ambassador Eliot that the Japanese government's attitude had been "beyond reproach;"[82] the American embassy in Tokyo reported to Washington that "Japanese authorities [were] endeavoring to take every reasonable precaution for the protection of American lives and property here."[83] The chargé d'affaires also made a considerable effort to keep American correspondents in Tokyo from exaggerating the anti-American incidents in Japan. And the Japan Tourist Bureau, worried about reports in the American media of anti-American activity in Japan, paid for advertisements that said rumors of danger to travelers in Japan were "groundless."[84]

On June 16, the State Department responded to the Japanese government's May 31 memorandum requesting the repeal of the immigration law. Secretary of State Hughes said he regarded the law as a closed matter, reiterating that the "legislative action [was] mandatory upon the executive branch." Hughes's response consisted primarily of historical references to immigration control and some legal arguments. Despite a perfunctory reference to the "mutual goodwill and cordial friendship" between the United States and Japan, he made it plain that the U.S. government had no intention of trying to modify the law.[85]

Not surprisingly, Japanese public sentiment was not eased by this response. The secretary's failure to mention the issue of race, which the Japanese believed was at the heart of the matter, disappointed the Japanese badly. The *Kokumin Shimbun* claimed that while the Japanese government opposed discrimination based on race, the U.S. government skirted the issue by continually insisting that restriction of immigration was a domestic right.[86] The *Osaka Asahi Shimbun* agreed that Japanese indignation was based not on the secretary's argument about the sovereignty of U.S. immigration policy, but on his failure to mention racial discrimination.[87] Sohō Tokutomi, president of the *Kokumin Shimbun*, wrote that no Japanese were satisfied with the American response because it ignored the essence of the issue.[88]

The Japanese government, however, generally looked upon the secretary's statement favorably. After the Kiyoura cabinet resigned en masse following the general election defeat of June 7, Taka'aki Katō formed a new cabinet and chose Kijūrō Shidehara as foreign minister. So as not to aggravate U.S.-Japanese relations by clinging to the immigration issue, Shidehara made no changes to existing foreign policy, although the government continued to protest the American immigration law. An episode that Shidehara recounted indicates his own attitude toward the issue: when he asked the late Lord James Bryce, then British ambassador in Washington, how he would respond to the fact that the U.S. Senate had passed the bill including a clause violating the Hay–Pauncefote Treaty, Lord Bryce had replied that he would do nothing because he believed that protest would only make things worse and that the American sense of justice would rectify the situation in the long run. Shidehara's recounting of this episode indicated that he took a similar course on the immigration issue.[89] The foreign minister told American correspondents that he was satisfied with its good-willed intentions, and that "he could state that the Japanese Government . . . were prepared to study it in the same spirit." Shidehara also said that Japanese authorities were "endeavoring to take adequate measures to prevent the growth of anti-American agitation as well as to break up the anti-American boycott," and that "the big business interests including Mitsui, Mitsu[b]ishi and the Tokyo Chamber of Commerce are all backing up the government in this."[90]

Despite protests from the Japanese, the law went into effect on July 1. On that day, designated "National Humiliation Day" in Japan, protests took place all over the country. At eight in the morning, ceremonies were held at Shintō shrines throughout Japan. At the Meiji Shrine in Tokyo, the chief priest characterized the enforcement of the American immigration law as a deed that defiled the imperial spirit. He prayed for Americans to be guided to the right path. Prominent figures such as the minister of justice and the governor of Tokyo paid their respects at the Shrine. The *Tokyo Asahi* described July 1 as a day of "American peril" to commemorate national dishonor, whereas the *Kokumin Shimbun* described it as a day of unforgettable humiliation for both Americans and Asians, and warned that the United States would have to reap what it sowed.[91]

Organized mainly by the Kokuryū Kai, the ceremony at the Zōjōji temple in Shiba attracted ten thousand people. Ryōhei Uchida delivered the opening address, in which he urged the Japanese to respond decisively now that the Americans had ignored Japanese protests against the immigration bill and had put it into effect. Many prominent figures, including several politicians, also delivered speeches. Daisuke Sakai, a representative of Japan's Lower House, asserted that the Japanese, as the leader of all oppressed Asians, should resolve firmly to struggle against whites and give a crushing blow to the United States.[92] Distributing anti-American fliers which said, "Alas, tyrant America ignoring humanity and disturbing peace," members of Taikōsha rushed to Akasaka Sannōdai, where another large-scale assembly took place. Having observed the anti-America gathering in Tokyo, Professor Uesugi rushed to his house and wrote a book on the matter, in one sitting, entitled *Nichibei shōtotsu no hisshi to kokumin no kakugo* (*The Necessity of the Japan-U.S. Clash and National Determination*). Uesugi explained that in Westerners' thinking only whites were considered human beings and non-whites were considered to be something closer to monkeys. Accordingly, the rise of the Japanese made Westerners determined to suppress the Japanese, sooner or later. He concluded that the United States and Japan would not be able to avoid the fatal clash, which he regarded as a divine destiny.[93]

Many similar events concerning the immigration issue were held throughout Japan. Rightist organizations participated in great numbers in these activities. Members of Taikōsha distributed tens of thousands of fliers in major cities. Although the fliers accused the United States of disturbing the peace and appealed to Japanese nationals to build up national power, they also urged the Japanese to be calm and show perserverance.[94] In Osaka, four anti-American rallies took place.[95] One of these was organized by the Kyokutō Renmei Kyōkai (the Far East Allies Association) and attracted an audience of several thousand.[96] The convention passed a resolution saying that by barring immigration from Japan, China, and India, the United States was disturbing world peace.[97] At its previous convention, the Kyokutō

Renmei Kyōkai had not mentioned India in the resolution, so it is clear that by this time it was consciously taking up the cause of Asianism.

Such anti-American gatherings were generally orderly. British Ambassador Eliot, who traveled to the Kansai area and observed these events, described them as "perfectly orderly and even picturesque." He noted that although "all classes of Japanese [were] profoundly hurt by the decision of the United States to discriminate between [the Japanese] and the white races," the present tendency [was] not to seek revenge or to attack the United States but rather to keep the question open."[98] French Ambassador Paul Claudel's opinion was a bit more ominous. Although he noted that the impact of the boycott of American products was decreasing, he nonetheless predicted that July 1 might become a great turning point in history, marking the moment when Japan departed from the circle of Western powers and joined the Asian powers. He concluded that public sentiment about the exclusion issue was beyond the control of the authorities and that it was possible that public sentiment might erupt unexpectedly at any moment.[99]

Zaigō Gunjin Kai, the national veterans' association, also organized anti-America rallies all over Japan. The Fifteenth Division of the Zaigō Gunjin Kai in Tokyo held a rally at the Yasukuni Shrine on May 25 which attracted eight thousand participants, the largest-ever turnout for the organization. The leadership swore an oath that it would be ready to punish whatever would threaten the imperial country and distributed the declaration to the group's divisions nationwide.[100] Officers on active service often lectured on those occasions.[101] A lieutenant general delivered an address to seven thousand people at a lecture meeting of the greater Osaka area on June 19.[102] Some divisions sent declarations not only to other divisions of Zaigō Gunjin Kai but also to the regional headquarters of the army. For example, the division of Zaigō Gunjin Kai in Tokyo sent to regional army and navy headquarters and its local divisions declarations regarding the exclusion clause as extremely humiliating and demanding a build up of national power to dissipate the humiliation. According to research by the security police, reactions to the declarations were generally positive and some commanders forwarded them to subdivisions in their districts.[103]

A high-ranking army general privately revealed his own radical ideas. Kunishige Tanaka, an army general in the 1920s who had participated in the Washington Conference, and president, in the 1930s, of the Meirinkai, an organization of retired military officers, set out his thoughts in a letter to Yūsaku Uehara, general of the army. He thought that if the immigration law damaged Japanese admirers of America, one should thank the anti-Japanese activists in the United States. Moreover, he argued that the final solution to the issue of U.S.-Japanese relations was not protest to the U.S. nor appeal to public sympathy nor diplomatic negotiation, concluding that even a three-year-old child knew that the final solution to the Japanese American question could only be achieved through military force.[104]

However, the army headquarters in Tokyo tried to suppress these anti-American activities. The undersecretary of war sent divisional headquarters an official notice to guide veterans' associations to be prudent in their behavior.[105] Here again, a split attitude was evident. While some officers vehemently attacked the United States and veterans organized rallies nationwide, the mainstream of the Imperial Army and Navy Headquarters did not show any opposition to the immigration law in public, and even made efforts to prevent military-related organizations from organizing anti-American rallies.

Army officers tended to see the immigration issue as connected with Japanese prestige in the world. Yasakichi Hayashi, an army attaché to the Japanese legation in China between 1922 and 1925, submitted a report regarding the effects of the exclusion clause on Sino-Japanese relations. He argued that the enactment of the immigration law exerted a bad influence on Sino-Japanese relations because one result of the poor U.S. treatment of Japan was that Chinese intellectuals had come to regard Japan with contempt. While he did not attack the United States, he instead attributed the cause of exclusion to the Japanese and urged the Japanese to make efforts to sort things out for the best.[106] In his letter to Uehara, Tanaka had warned that the immigration question would make Japanese Asian policy more difficult because, due to the humiliation of Japan by the United States, China and Russia would take Japan less seriously.[107] A report by the General Staff Office concluded that since it would be impossible to expunge the racism represented by the German Kaiser's "yellow peril" and Australia's "white" policy, officers should expect that racial war would take place sooner or later, and that, therefore, they should build up their power and cease to fight their brother-Asians, and instead start to prepare with them to fight for an Asia for Asians.[108] Another secret report written by the General Staff Office in April 1924 also recognized that the immigration law dealt a blow to Japan's national power. It said that it was unquestionable that the immigration law would have a prolonged influence on Japan's future. This humiliation, it concluded, would prevail all over the world, and Japan's diplomats would encounter many difficulties. The report predicted that the law had sown the seeds of the future consolidation of non-white peoples.[109] It is remarkable that the General Staff Office placed so much importance on the immigration law. Although the issue ceased to be a main topic of discussion by top army officials after 1924, it had made a great impression on Japan's military elite and these racial issues would reemerge in the future, whenever the United States appeared to thwart Japan's national interest. In his book, *Nichibei sensō: Nihon wa makenai* (*U.S.-Japan War: Japan Won't Be Beaten*), navy Lieutenant Commander Tōta Ishimaru argued that Japan should abandon its pro-Anglo policy and instead emphasize its ties with Russia and China. According to Ishimaru, faced with the American enactment of anti-Japanese legislation, Japan should stop being a pawn of the Anglo powers and turn toward Asia.[110]

Officers who did not openly criticize the United States were not necessarily unconcerned about this problem. They did not criticize the United States because they thought it would be of no use, and they tended to conclude quietly that they would simply have to build up Japanese military power. Although most officers were rational enough not to urge an immediate attack on the United States, it is probable that the exclusion clause had a deep effect on their state of mind.

Also active were Buddhist temples, which regarded the controversy as an opportunity to minimize the influence of the Christian churches. At Chionin, the headquarters of the Jōdo sect, lectures were organized concerning Japanese American relations and pamphlets containing the monks' views on the immigration issue were distributed. These pamphlets advised against taking direct action under the influence of radical nationalists. However, it concluded that if a rightful solution were not realized and if the United States continued its hostility toward justice and humanity, then the Japanese should "unsheathe a sword," even against their will.[111] At Honganji, the headquarters of the Jōdoshinshū sect, another pamphlet entitled *Hainichi mondai to kokumin no kakugo* (The Japanese Exclusion Question and National Determination) was published, which argued that since the true character of Americans was that they valued material interests rather than justice and humanity, the Japanese needed to build up material power rather than make purely verbal demands.[112]

Rallies protesting the immigration law were held even outside of Japan. In Manchuria, for example, a festival to enhance the national dignity of Japan took place at the Dairen Shrine in China. The principal of Shinmei Girls' High School in Dairen criticized the immigration law in front of the whole school, students and teachers.[113] And in Harbin, a rally presented a resolution unanimously criticizing the United States.[114]

These anti-American rallies in Japan and Manchuria never disintegrated into uncontrollable riots, partly because of the meticulous care taken by the authorities. The Japanese government, which had chosen to cooperate with the United States at the Washington Conference, did not want to see U.S.-Japanese relations deteriorate over the immigration issue. The American embassy reported that although the Japanese expressed "violent resentment" against the immigration law, "their conduct has been quite orderly."[115]

The immigration issue became a major topic at the Imperial Diet. In his address on foreign policy to the Lower House, Foreign Minister Shidehara took up three important issues: (1) the American immigration law, (2) negotiations with the Soviets, and (3) the general situation in China. The immigration law, he said, was mainly targeted at immigrants from eastern and southern Europe and was unlikely to be changed in the near future. Nonetheless, Shidehara told the Diet that he was dissatisfied with the law and won applause when he declared that the issue could not be regarded as closed and that he would continue efforts to resolve the problem until the Japanese were satisfied with the results.

After Shidehara's address, forty-eight representatives submitted a resolution stating:

> The Lower House of the Imperial Diet expresses strong opposition toward the American insertion of a clause discriminatory toward the Japanese into the new immigration law because it is not only against the principles of justice and equality of international relations but also disturbs the Japanese American seventy-year friendship.

One after another, representatives expressed views supporting this proposal. A statement by Shigeho Kawahara that attributed American anti-Japanese attitudes to racial prejudice was received with applause. Another representative criticized the Foreign Ministry, asserting that its overly euphemistic approach and softly worded complaints had facilitated the passage of the law. The representative further maintained that the Japanese should instruct the Americans on the principles of liberty, equality, humanity, and fraternity. This resolution was passed unanimously.[116]

The situation was almost the same in the House of Peers. Six peers, with the support of forty others, proposed a resolution which expressed their deep regret over the immigration law. Eikichi Kamata, one of the proposers, asserted that the immigration law was unlawful, unreasonable, and unjust, and insisted it be abolished. Baron Shōzō Yabuki explained that though he considered America a friendly nation, he supported this resolution in the hope that it would awaken America. This resolution was also passed unanimously.[117] Baron Yoshirō Sakatani maintained that the government's underestimation of the resentment among the Japanese people had resulted in a failure to adequately protest against anti-Japanese movements in the United States, which in turn had brought about the enactment of this immigration law. Sakatani asked Shidehara if there was any way to solve this issue. The criticism backed the foreign minister into a corner, since he could hardly admit to being weak-kneed but nonetheless wanted to avoid provoking tensions with Washington. He denied that the Japanese government had underestimated the issue and stated that he was determined to take every possible measure to solve it, but he also noted that he had yet to see a "national awakening" of the American consciousness.[118]

Disturbances related to the immigration law continued in Japan for some time. On July 1, a Japanese man sneaked into the American embassy in Tokyo, pulled down the American flag, and ran away with it. Acting ambassador Jefferson Caffery quickly expressed deep dismay over this incident and visited Shidehara at the Foreign Ministry to ask for a full investigation. Shidehara dealt with this matter with scrupulous tact. He paid a personal visit to Caffery that night, believing that although this was an incident caused by an individual acting independently of the government, it would be wise to express his regrets.[119] A suspect was captured in Osaka on July 2, and the flag was returned to the American embassy.[120] The State Department also wanted to keep the effect of this incident to a minimum. On July 9, Secretary of State Hughes sent a statement to Shidehara that the United

States regarded the flag incident as "the act of an irresponsible individual." Hughes also said that he had "the fullest confidence in the desire and the ability of the Japanese authorities to handle the matter appropriately to the situation."[121]

As time passed, the number of articles in the media expressing emotional outrage at the immigration law decreased. Ryūtarō Saitō, in an article in *Bungei shunjū*, hinted at his inclination to attack every American he saw; yet in the same issue Sane'atsu Mushanokōji, a noted writer, cautioned readers against jingoistic talk. Observing the surge of nationalism, Mushanokōji feared that Japan was about to go astray.[122] In *Chūō kōron*, Yasaka Takagi, a professor of American politics at the Imperial University of Tokyo, argued that it would be wrong to consider the passage of the immigration law as an insult from all Americans, and that the criticism of Congress by Coolidge and many American newspapers deserved notice.[123] The August issue of *Chūō kōron* criticized the anti-foreign sentiment in Japan caused by the American anti-Japanese law. Some articles in this issue argued that since Japan was not strong enough to defeat the United States, it should make efforts to become stronger rather than attempt to fight the United States. Others argued that anger about the anti-Japanese exclusion act was not the response of a great nation. What these articles had in common was the assertion that it was not the time to fight the United States over the immigration issue.[124]

Partly because of stringent controls by the authorities, as exemplified by their swift response to the flag incident, and partly because of subsiding media attention, the anti-American protests did not expand into a mass movement.[125] The interest of ordinary people shifted to other issues. Although rightists continued to criticize Japanese for watching American movies, claiming that watching movies based on American racism meant humiliating themselves,[126] American movies remained so popular in Japan that the boycott was lifted on July 10, and movie offerings were brought back to normal by July 18.[127]

The enforcement of the immigration law had minimal material impact on Japanese immigrants living in the United States. The most serious practical difficulty was that the immigrants could no longer bring family members to the United States or return to Japan. Transpacific liners overflowed with Japanese passengers who were eager to enter the United States before July 1. Because of the immigration law, some Japanese living in the United

States permanently lost the opportunity to marry. However, since most immigrants who wanted to marry brought their spouses into the country before the enforcement of the law, this effect of the ban was limited.

Nonetheless, the psychological blow to Japanese immigrants caused by the immigration law was far from negligible. Japanese-language newspapers published in the United States understood the exclusion clause in racial terms. The *Taihoku Nippō*, a Seattle Japanese newspaper, described the enactment of the law as the planting of "the seeds of a racial war." The *Shinsekai*, a major Japanese newspaper in San Francisco, also argued that the racial affront to the Japanese would cause "a racial struggle."[128] Responding to a request from the Japanese Foreign Ministry for information about the impact of the enforcement of the law on Japanese immigrants, the Japanese consuls, in San Francisco and Portland, in particular, emphasized the crushing mental anguish felt by Japanese immigrants in America.[129]

Overall, however, the response of Japanese immigrants in the United States seemed to be less emotional than that of residents in Japan. The Japanese consulate in Portland reported that although the mental anguish was great, Japanese immigrants believed that they had no other recourse than to put up with the present situation, because they believed life in Japan would be economically more severe. The report observed that the enforcement of the immigration law was generally not taken as a direct personal insult by immigrants already in the United States.[130] No mass protest rallies took place. While many Japanese-language newspapers in the United States interpreted the issue in a racial context, they protested the law in a more restrained manner than did their counterparts in Japan.[131] There were far fewer expressions of fiery nationalism in Japanese-language newspapers in the United States, for example. Immediately after the passage of the bill in Congress, the *Rafu Shimpō*, the largest Japanese newspaper in Los Angeles, advised Japanese immigrants not to bear hatred against the United States or protest, since nothing could be done now that the immigration bill had passed. It cautioned against pessimism and encouraged immigrants to push forward in high spirits.[132] The newspaper even argued that it would be better to have the exclusion law come into effect all at once, since even if some face-saving measures were to be taken, there would be little improvement from the perspective of national honor.[133] Akira Togawa, a Japanese immigrant who would be active in literary circles during World War II, wrote in his diary on July 1: "It seems that fellow countrymen in the United States were not so shocked [as the Japanese in Japan]. It is also the case with me. I wonder why I think the United States is a good place even after I was excluded and insulted."[134] The *Rafu Shimpō* continued to report developments on the immigration issue in a subdued manner. The May 29 issue argued that the United States should take responsibility for any racial conflict that might occur in the future. However, this same article expressed the hope that once the total ban on Japanese immigration came into effect, problems relating to the treatment of Japanese immigrants in the United States would be discussed and solved in a fair way by Americans.[135]

The *Nichi Bei*, a major Japanese newspaper in San Francisco, was equally restrained in its attitude toward the United States concerning this issue. It did not accuse Americans of racial prejudice, as newspapers did in Japan. Rather, it admonished the Japanese for their contempt of Koreans and Chinese, and encouraged them to regard their Asian neighbors as equals. If equal relations with other Asian nations could be established, the newspaper argued, the Japanese footing in the world would be solidified and the Japanese would not have to take account of tiny things such as the immigration exclusion problem.[136]

These newspapers also feared that anti-American activities in Japan might provoke anti-Japanese activities in the United States. The *Rafu Shimpō* argued that no matter how forcefully the Japanese as a nation attacked the United States, nothing would be gained and only the feelings of Americans would be hurt.[137] The *Nichi Bei* explained that although the immigration law was a national insult for the Japanese, it would not necessarily be considered an insult from the American point of view, since the United States regarded the immigration question strictly as a domestic issue. According to the *Nichi Bei*, the injury the law inflicted on Japanese national pride was an unintended consequence, and American respect and friendship toward Japan and the Japanese people remained unchanged after the law's passage.[138] The *Nichi Bei* criticized anti-American activists in Japan, complaining that their boycotts and protests achieved little, apart from threatening the peaceful lives of Japanese immigrants in the United States. While activists on both sides of the Pacific were kicking up a fuss, the newspaper said, neither side was suffering the consequences of the bad feelings.[139] Jūji Kasai, secretary of the

Los Angeles Japanese Association, explained, "As long as we keep quiet and make no move the public forgets us."[140]

There were at least three reasons why the reaction of Japanese immigrants in the United States was much more moderate than that of Japanese nationals in Japan. First, racial discrimination, which was a shock to Japanese nationals, was nothing new to Japanese immigrants. Second, although the immigration law insulted their national honor and prevented family members from joining them in the United States, Japanese immigrants in the U.S. could continue with their lives as before, safe in the knowledge that their American-born children were already U.S. citizens. There were worse fates—for instance, the Nisei (second-generation Japanese immigrants) could be denied the right to citizenship—and the exclusion clause might actually have a positive impact if it led to the cessation of anti-Japanese movements. *Rafu Shimpō*, however, cautioned that first-generation immigrants must remain vigilant since it could happen that their American-born children might also lose their rights of citizenship later.[141] The *Nichi Bei* argued that since efforts to promote cordial U.S.-Japanese relations were nullified by the immigration law, Japanese immigrants in the United States should make a fresh start by cooperating with the Americans.[142] Third, since many Japanese immigrants intended to continue living in the United States at least for a while, they were not in a position to attack the immigration law for fear of antagonizing Americans.

The enactment of the immigration law had two different effects on the Japanese immigrants. First, they began to think that the future of the Japanese in the United States depended upon the Nisei. Although no new Japanese immigrants could enter the United States and existing immigrants had no hope of becoming naturalized, American-born Nisei were already American citizens. Accordingly, Japanese newspapers in the United States now emphasized the importance of the Nisei. Kyūtarō Abiko, publisher of the *Nichi Bei*, in particular, saw the Nisei as a bridge across the Pacific.[143] The second effect of the law was that many Issei (first-generation Japanese immigrants) lost their interest in Americanization and reoriented themselves toward Japan. Even Japanese Protestants, who had been most eager to Americanize, began to take a pro-Japan stance.[144] Compared with the response of the Japanese in Japan, the responses of the Japanese immigrants in the United States were much more complicated. These ambivalent attitudes, coupled with the Ozawa case, which completely closed the door to the possibility of naturalization for Japanese immigrants, contributed to a passive attitude toward the possibility of modifying the exclusion clause among Japanese immigrants in the 1920s and 1930s.

In this period, the Chinese neighbors of Japanese immigrants in California also paid great attention to the Japanese exclusion bill, not primarily because they sympathized with the Japanese but rather because they thought that the bill would have a bad influence on the Chinese exclusion issue. *Chung Sai Yat Po*, a major Chinese-language daily published in San Francisco, attacked the Japanese exclusion clause, pointing out that the issue was closely aligned with the Chinese immigration problem. In an editorial, it warned that Chinese in the United States should not make light of the Japanese exclusion issue, because the enactment of the new immigration law would make modification of the Chinese exclusion law much more difficult. It also argued that the addition of the Japanese to the exclusion list would exacerbate the neglect of Asia as a whole, and if the bill became law, there would be repeated demands for its modification. Although the Chinese in California attacked the exclusion bill from their own perspective, they at least considered the Japanese as fellow Asians who were being rejected by the United States.[145]

News of the exclusion clause also had repercussions outside of the United States and Japan. Europeans tended to focus on the effects of the law on world politics. For example, the *Stockholm Dagblad* argued that the exclusion clause carried implications for continued peaceful international relations in the Pacific, and warned that "the question of whether the slant-eyed coolie shall be allowed to eat his rice in Los Angeles and send home to Nippon his dollar savings seems to be a question very closely related to big politics."[146] The countries that had colonies in Asia worried about possible repercussions in those areas. In the Netherlands, the *Handelsblad* of April 17 predicted that "the attitude of the American Senate with respect to Japanese immigration, in the end, may have very serious consequences." A report from the Netherlands to Washington revealed that "apprehension of Japanese aggression is very general in the Netherlands."[147]

Paul Claudel, the French ambassador to Tokyo, observed the issue with interest, and predicted that latent anger among the Japanese could become manifest in relations between the United States and Japan at any moment and in any area. He reported to the Foreign Ministry in Paris that French merchants would be able to take advantage of the Japanese boycott of American merchandise. He also believed that the Japanese would turn toward Asia and that solidarity between the Japanese and Chinese would therefore be strengthened. He speculated that the actions of the Anglo-Saxons would bring consequences in China, Manchuria, and Siberia.[148]

The United Kingdom, which faced a similar immigration problem in its Asian colonies, paid close attention to the United States in its relations with Japan. The British ambassador in Tokyo, Charles Eliot, who had witnessed Japanese indignation against the American immigration law at first hand, cautioned his government regarding colonial attitudes toward Japanese immigrants. He explained that while the Japanese understood the necessity of the restriction of Japanese immigrants, they felt offended by the American method of limiting immigration: the Americans had excluded the Japanese immigrants by unilaterally abrogating the Gentlemen's Agreement. Eliot argued that the Japanese "put manner before the matter, their national dignity before the material advantage," and he explained that the Japanese did not want to be singled out as inferior to white peoples. He suggested that the "British colonies follow procedure which [would be] considered courteous," and warned that "if any British colony acts in the way . . . offensive to Japan it [would] be [a] severe blow to Anglo–Japanese friendship."[149] His suggestion was taken seriously and circulated to British officers in colonies such as Canada, Australia, New Zealand, South Africa, and Southern Rhodesia.[150] The issue of Japanese exclusion was not only a matter of interest within the government in the United Kingdom; it was also taken up in the House of Commons.[151] A member of the British general staff also attached importance to the immigration issue. In a report examining Japan's population expansion, the major concluded, "There is bound to be a clash sometime in the future when the vested interests of European powers in the Pacific are challenged by the pressure of Japanese expansion."[152]

The Soviet paper *Russki Golos* published in Harbin, China, regarded the controversy over Japanese exclusion as a positive development. The Russians apparently thought that the conflict between the United States and Japan would eventually cause a great war. It seemed to them that whichever side won, "bright perspectives would be opened for Soviet Government and the Committee of the Internationale, who from now on have selected Asia to be the field for experiments in sovietization" of the globe.[153]

On the other hand, newspapers in East Asia, and particularly China, tended to interpret the exclusion clause within the context of East-West relations. For example, the *Harbin Dawning* said, "No matter how the Immigration Problem has been eased, the yellow peoples should not feel happy," and proclaimed that Asians "should worry about the latent danger" of American racism toward Asians and cooperate against it. G. C. Hanson, the American consul in Harbin, warned that "the immigration problem has drawn the Japanese and Chinese closer together."[154] The *Shanghai Times*, a British newspaper with pro-Japanese views, observed that "none but the narrow-minded can class [the exclusion clause] as other than unfair: it offensively assumes the existence of superior and inferior races, thus violating the spirit of equality which is avowedly so strong an element of Americanism."[155] The *Chen pao*, an important Chinese newspaper in Beijing, argued that the immigration bill would "create bad blood between the white and colored races and sow the seed of a race war in the future." The paper urged all colored peoples to join together to make a combined effort to fight against racial discrimination.[156] However, different views were not necessarily nonexistent. John Powell, editor and publisher of the *China Weekly Review*, a magazine published in Shanghai, disagreed that the exclusion issue would draw the Japanese and Chinese closer together. He thought it was "scarcely to be considered" that Asia would "be able to cooperate with Japan to the extent of a trial at arms with the West," for "several generations at least," and "certainly not over such a question as the exclusion of low-priced Japanese labor from the United States."[157]

The view that it might not be easy for Japan and the other Asians to cooperate against the Western powers was especially prevalent among those Koreans under Japanese rule. Censored articles of nationalist newspapers reveal their opinion on this issue. An article in *Tonga ilbo*, which was censored from the May 2 edition, argued that it was extremely mean and inferior of Japan to praise pan-Asianism without any penitence regarding its past actions, and concluded that the difficulty Japan faced regarding the immigration issue might be regarded as "generous punishment." *Chŏson ilbo*, another nationalist paper, pointed out that while Japan behaved aggressively toward neighboring weak and small nations, it behaved conservatively and self-demeaningly toward powerful nations in the far-off distance. Regarding the Japanese attitude toward pan-Asianism, another article in this paper, which was also repressed, argued that Japan should stop following the shallow policy of throwing out what was bitter and swallowing what was sweet. It proclaimed that Japan's first priority should be repentance, and that only after reflecting on and repenting its actions could it talk about pan-Asianism.[158]

According to the American consul general in Melbourne, Australia, there was "a reticent undercurrent of anxiety" among Australians regarding the American exclusion of the Japanese that was "finding manifestation in different forms," and "public opinion, accordingly, [was becoming] more and more attracted by the particular gravity of the issues involved, in relation especially to their possible consequences and results as affecting the future situation of Australia." Australians evidently felt that the exclusion clause posed a serious threat. The British had failed to construct an impregnable naval base at Singapore, and as a result Australians tended to feel vulnerable to Japanese military attack. An article in the *Melbourne Herald* argued that since the exclusion clause meant "the hastening of the inevitable conflict between East and West," and that those "who dwell in the Pacific and especially those who declare that trespassing Asiatics [should] be prosecuted must look to their defense." When the American consul general had occasion to sit beside the Australian prime minister at a luncheon meeting in mid-May, the prime minister expressed his concern over the issue. The consul general reassured the prime minister that although it was obvious "how deeply Japanese pride seemed to have been hurt," the prime minister's concern was nonetheless an overreaction. A commander of a British battleship wrote a letter to the American consul general in Melbourne, in which he directly accused the United States of causing a problem for Australia, arguing that Americans had shifted their "Asiatic immigration problems to the shoulders of the Australian people." The consul general worried about the possible negative effects of his ideas.[159]

American diplomats, worried that the immigration law would unite Asians, especially Chinese and Japanese, against the United States, tried to justify the new law. Jacob Gould Schurman, the American minister to China, defended the law at a Rotary Club dinner at Tientsin, China, arguing that "the protection of the personal identity of a people . . . is self-preservation in its highest potency" and "a right which every free nation in the world either actually exercises or keeps in reserve against the possibility of danger."[160]

The American Response

U.S. response to the enactment of the 1924 immigration law differed considerably according to region. On the West Coast, where most of the interested groups were concentrated, a few newspapers such as the *San Francisco Chronicle*, the *Daily Commercial News*, and even some Republican newspapers such as the *Sacramento Republican*, spoke out against exclusion. The *Daily Commercial News* was a San Francisco paper catering to the finance, shipping, oil, mining, and insurance industries. Arguing that the Japanese exclusion clause was an unnecessary affront to Japan, it called for the approval of a quota for Japanese immigrants, believing that such an alternative solution would "cement the pleasant relationship that at all times existed" between the two countries.[161] Such voices were virtually lost in the roar of anti-Japanese vitriol, however. In Los Angeles, all the major newspapers favored the anti-Japanese clause. The *Los Angeles Times* believed that "the menace of a peaceful penetration by oriental labor has been conjured away," although the paper acknowledged that the exclusion of Japanese "might have been done more diplomatically." The Hearst newspapers, such as the *San Francisco Examiner* and the *Seattle Post-Intelligencer*, all carried the same editorial, entitled "Japanese Exclusion Policy Is Vital to American People," on April 21. Moreover, the *Post-Intelligencer* of June 14 asserted that the Japanese were willing to criticize the American exclusion only because State Department officials had shown their sympathy with the Japanese.[162]

Since the Hearst newspapers were quite influential in the West, their pro-exclusion stance must have had a considerable effect. Research conducted by the Japanese Foreign Ministry showed that among nineteen California newspapers, ten were in favor of the Japanese exclusion clause, five were against exclusion, and the rest were neutral. Newspapers in the state of Washington were generally pro-exclusion: thirteen out of sixteen papers expressed support for the exclusion clause.[163]

Labor on the Pacific Coast strongly supported Japanese exclusion. The May 17 issue of *Organized Labor*, the official publication of the State and Local Building Trades Councils of California, argued that Japanese were not being discriminated against on the grounds that the United States "excludes all Orientals, Chinese, Koreans, Japanese, Hindus, and other Far Eastern peoples because they are ineligible to citizenship."[164] The *Labor Clarion*, the official journal of the San Francisco Labor Council, fell in line behind Representative Albert Johnson, chairman of the House Committee on Immigration and Naturalization. Johnson explained that Congress had terminated the Gentlemen's Agreement because, after careful consideration, it had concluded that it would be reasonable to do so and not because it resented the Hanihara statement.[165] At the annual convention of the California State Federation of Labor, the Committee on Officers' Reports commended the group's secretary-treasurer Paul Scharrenberg "for his active participation in the Japanese Exclusion by law activities," saying "much of the responsibility of obtaining the [desired] results . . . [could] be traced directly to the activities of Brother Scharrenberg."[166]

In other areas of the United States, opinion was generally divided between those who were against exclusion and those who were indifferent on the issue. The East Coast was mostly sympathetic to the Japanese. According to the same Japanese Foreign Ministry research, only one out of eleven newspapers in New York supported the exclusion clause.[167] The *New York Times* argued that the immigration act was a "rude means of obtaining an object [suspension of Japanese immigration] which Japan was more ready to agree to diplomatically" and emphasized the importance of friendly relations between the two nations.[168] In Boston, the *Christian Science Monitor* opposed the exclusion clause for two reasons: first, because Congress had chosen a "method . . . highly offensive to a Nation with whom the United States should take especial pains to remain on terms of peace and amity," and second, because "it is more than doubtful whether the exclusion law will effect that complete stoppage of Japanese immigration which its promoters desire."[169]

Pennsylvania newspapers also generally opposed the exclusion clause. The *Philadelphia Evening Bulletin* lamented the jingoism that surrounded passage of the law and argued that it would make "harder the task of the President and the Secretary of State in maintaining, not merely the peace of the Pacific, but the international friendship which underlies and underwrites that peace."[170]

In the Washington, D.C. area, opinions differed. Whereas the *Baltimore Sun* opposed the exclusion clause, the *Washington Post* applauded it, noting that the policy would "not be modified, no matter how serious . . . the interruption of good relations between the two countries" might be.[171]

In Chicago, the majority of the newspapers stood against the exclusion clause. The key newspaper in the region, however, the *Chicago Daily Tribune*, praised the law, and asked why Japan criticized only the U.S. exclusion clause, while it did not protest those of other countries, such as Australia and New Zealand. The paper also noted that Japan itself excluded "fellow yellows" from other Asian countries such as China and Mongolia.[172]

In the South, newspapers were either indifferent to or critical of the exclusion clause. Southern congressmen had supported the clause, not because they linked the Japanese immigration problem with their own racial problem, but because they had been persuaded to the cause by their California colleagues, especially Hiram Johnson. Southerners, in general, were mainly indifferent to the question of whether fewer than two hundred Japanese should be permitted to enter the United States. And other southerners were generally anti-exclusion, especially those in the cotton-growing areas whose export economy was linked to Japan. During the early 1920s, Japan was mostly the third largest importer of raw cotton, after Germany and the United Kingdom, and purchased about 10 percent of U.S. exports of unmanufactured cotton.[173] The *Atlanta Constitution*, in its anti-exclusion editorial, celebrated the U.S. government's "friendly commercial and diplomatic relations with Japan," pointing out that "the latter nation is rapidly becoming one of the great civilized powers of the world."[174]

Several magazines published in the East also criticized the immigration act. The *Atlantic Monthly* argued that the law "wantonly sacrificed" the achievements of Theodore Roosevelt and insisted that "exclusion is not a purely domestic problem nor does it rest upon an obvious natural right."[175] The editors of *Life* magazine named Congress as the winner of "LIFE's War Contest," "in recognition of its inestimable services in furthering the cause of war by passing . . . the Immigration Bill containing the Japanese Exclusion clause." Certificates were sent to all members of Congress "with best wishes for a Happy War."[176] *Asia*, a magazine dedicated to "commercial and financial intercourse" between the United States and the Far East, published an article by lawyer-journalist K. K. Kawakami, who characterized the exclusion law as an American challenge to Japan.[177] Kawakami also wrote an article for *Outlook*, in which he described how the clause "would provoke the most unpleasant feeling in the hearts of seventy million people of the Empire."[178]

African American media in the United States kept a close eye on Japanese

Fig. 2. "Perhaps It Wasn't Intended for Us, But—" Cartoon published in the *Chicago Defender*, 19 April 1924. Apparently drawn at the time of the 1913 or 1920 alien land disputes, the cartoon clearly shows an African-American perspective on the issue.

reactions to the exclusion clause. Black newspapers may have differed from each other in nuance, but they generally criticized the exclusion clause. Some directly attacked the clause, regarding it as foolish and arrogant, and suggesting that it might cause a war between the United States and Japan. Leading bishops of the African Methodist Episcopal Church noted that exclusion was against the basic principles of the American government.[179] The *Kansas City Call* also regarded the American government's behavior as arrogant.[180] The *Negro World* observed that "the whole question of Japanese exclusion [is] based upon [a] false assumption of racial superiority," and compared the situation of African Americans in the United States with that of the Japanese, saying "The American Congress and a large section of the American press, affect not to understand the Japanese sensitiveness in this business any more than they . . . understand the sensitiveness of the Negro." The paper ominously predicted that "the race worm trod upon has begun to turn upon its tormentors."[181]

The *Chicago Defender*, however, one of the most influential black papers at the time, admitted the necessity of a reduction of immigration and argued that the Japanese were "less assimilable than any other nationality," justifying its argument with the formulaic, "once a Japanese always a Japanese." In the end, however, the paper opposed exclusion, arguing that "there is no just reason for singling out the Japanese as the goat in framing immigration laws." The paper warned that although the discriminatory measure was not intended for African Americans, this sort of discrimination could be targeted against them at any time (see Figure 2).[182] The *Defender* had also criticized Takao Ozawa's legal struggle to be declared white for the purposes of naturalization, and now suggested that the Japanese should stop currying favor with whites and instead join forces with non-whites: "[the] lesson to the proud Japanese [is] to watch his white brother a little more closely and show more sympathy to his other dark skinned relatives."[183]

Newspapers all over the United States commented on the official protest memorandum handed by Ambassador Hanihara to the U.S. Secretary of State on May 31. As with the initial announcement of the passage of the immigration act, newspapers in the East tended to be sympathetic to the Japanese, while those in the West extolled the virtues of the exclusion clause. On June 1, the *New York Times* reported Hanihara's protest on the front page, but waited until the following day to express an editorial opinion. The June 2 editorial criticized Congress for "its rough and needless riding over the sensibilities of the Japanese people." After the suicide of a Japanese man, the *Times* once again focused on how badly Japanese sentiments were hurt. It warned its readers against slighting these suicides, arguing that although such incidents seemed to Americans "absurd or pathetic," to the Japanese they reflected the fact that the Japanese people had taken "the very gravest offense at the discrimination."[184]

The *Seattle Post-Intelligencer*, on the other hand, interpreted Hanihara's May 31 note as a "threat." The *San Francisco Examiner*, without mentioning Hanihara's formal protest, devoted its entire editorial page that day to the Japanese immigration issue. The paper assailed the Republicans for attempting to permit the entrance of the "Japanese Mouse," and argued that "this foolish Republican elephant doesn't represent the feeling of the American people," because "the United States does not intend to permit Asiatic immigration."[185]

Intellectuals and peace movement activists opposed the exclusion clause. Immediately after passage of the bill, Jane Addams implored President Coolidge to veto it. James W. Garner, a professor of political science at the University of Illinois, Urbana, wrote a similar letter to Coolidge, and also wrote to members of the cabinet asking them to use their influence to "induce [Coolidge] to veto the proposed immigration act." In his letter to Herbert Hoover, the Secretary of Commerce, Garner argued: "The effect of this legislation will be to affront the Japanese people, to brand them with the stigma of racial inferiority, to wound their national sensibilities and to humiliate them in the eyes of the rest of the world."[186] These actions were reported in Japan and boosted expectations of a veto.[187]

Thirty college presidents, including Charles W. Elliot, president emeritus of Harvard, John G. Hibben of Princeton, and W. H. P. Faunce of Brown, signed a message which "Condemns [the] 'Inconsiderate Action' of Congress." This message, drafted by Elliot, stated that the action of Congress "does not represent the sentiments of the American people toward Japan." The signatories also included two Californians, David Starr Jordan, president emeritus of Stanford University, and W. W. Campbell, president of the University of California.[188]

Americans reacted in various ways when pressed by friends or business contacts in Japan to oppose the bill. The directors of the Nippon Electric Company wrote to its associated company in America, the International Western Electric Company in New York, expressing their fear that if the bill became law, "it will have an unfortunate effect upon American business." Reacting to this letter, P. K. Condict, a vice-president of the American company, wrote to Coolidge and Hoover to request exclusion of Japanese immigrants "in such a form as not to offend the Japanese people."[189]

Eiichi Shibusawa sent a telegram to Thomas Lamont of the financial giant J. P. Morgan after the Senate passed the bill: "All past efforts for promotion of good feelings between two nations [will] be nullified."[190] But Lamont was careful not to encourage pro-American Japanese to expect too much. While he sent a telegram to Coolidge requesting a veto, Lamont did not convey optimistic views; the content of his quick response to Shibusawa's telegram was limited to "a bare acknowledgment and an assurance that he was for good relations."[191]

Roland S. Morris, a former ambassador to Japan, wrote to Count Kabayama, expressing his hope that "the Japanese people will realize that the Congressional action does not . . . represent the real feeling or the considered judgment of [American] citizens." He suggested that it was better for "Japanese publicists and thinkers" to come to the United States and "express a real grievance than to nurse it in silence."[192]

American businessmen who had connections with the Far East joined the veto effort. The president of the St. Paul & Tacoma Lumber Company, which exported lumber to Japan, asked Hoover to influence Coolidge in this regard.[193] The president of the American Exporters' and Importers' Association, which comprised trade companies in New York, also sent a letter to his congressmen explaining how the immigration law could cause "unnecessary damage to American trade with Japan" and urging them "to take such action as will avoid needless affront to Japan."[194]

The Chamber of Commerce of the United States was against the exclusion clause. The Foreign Commerce Section of the annual convention approved a declaration against the exclusion clause unanimously. Edward A. Filene of Boston proposed a resolution which read: "We heartily support the Secretary of State in his efforts to deal with exclusion of those ineligible to citizenship by friendly negotiation instead of by act of Congress." Those who seconded this resolution included C. M. Clark of the Portland Chamber of Commerce, and E. G. Griggs, who had written to Hoover in April. Robert N. Lynch of the San Francisco Chamber of Commerce also delivered an address which, according to a report, "revealed a marked unanimity of cordial regard for the Japanese position."[195] The resolution, with minor modification, was adopted the following day.[196]

Even in California, the home of anti-Japanese activism, many organizations opposed the exclusion clause. A group of influential businessmen and college presidents expressed their unanimous view against the exclusion clause at a conference attended by the "best minds" of California, including

W. W. Campbell, president of the University of California; Harry Chandler of the *Los Angeles Times*; Wigginton E. Creed, president of Pacific Gas and Electric Company; Ray Lyman Wilbur of Stanford University; and Wallace M. Alexander of the sugar conglomerate Alexander & Baldwin Ltd., who had established the American Japanese Relations Committee in the San Francisco Chamber of Commerce in 1915. The conference attendees unanimously agreed that Coolidge should veto the immigration bill and stated that his doing so "would not lose him [the] California electoral vote" in the coming presidential election.[197] The California State Federation of Women's Clubs, led by J. C. Urquart, also criticized Coolidge for his failure to veto the immigration bill.[198]

The Commonwealth Club of California, comprised primarily of businessmen and professionals whose objective was "to investigate and discuss problems affecting the welfare of the Commonwealth and to aid in their solutions" and "to maintain . . . an impartial position as an open forum for the discussion of disputed questions," put the Japanese immigration issue before its immigration section, and the section concluded that the "so called Japanese exclusion clause should be omitted, and the Japanese put under the quota." Although the immigration section was against "general Oriental immigration," it regarded the exclusion clause as not only unnecessary but even an "international blunder."[199]

Many American anti-exclusionist businessmen's efforts to urge Coolidge to veto the immigration bill were doomed. Although he understood the undesirability of the exclusion clause, Coolidge, who did not want to alienate congressmen from California who supported the clause, had no other choice but to sign the bill. Hoover, through whom the businessmen tried to pressure the president, was not useful on this matter. Actually, Hoover favored the exclusion of the Japanese because he thought that "a definite exclusion law would make in the long run for better [U.S.-Japanese] relations," and told a friend, "The biological fact makes mixture of bloods disadvantageous."[200]

Clergymen generally opposed the exclusion clause. The Methodist Board of Foreign Missions sent Coolidge a resolution urging him to veto the immigration bill. A part of this resolution read:

We deplore the present form of the pending legislation on [the exclusion clause] and express the hope that a way may be found by the Congress and the Executive of the United States to maintain that international good-will which is so important to both lands in which the churches of America have so vital an interest.[201]

On May 22 the Congregational Conference in New York also urged the president to veto the immigration bill.[202] On June 5, the Congregational Committee on Friendly Relations with Japanese and Other Citizens, established in Los Angeles, resolved that racial discrimination in the naturalization laws should be abolished.[203]

The FCCCA "deplored" the exclusion clause and took several steps in response. The organization sent a letter to "all mission boards suggesting action on their part," and to "all the local councils and federations of churches urging that . . . they secure as wide a protest as possible." The FCCCA also sent a special letter to the California State Federation of Churches, urging the group to "secure as vigorous a reaction as possible from California."[204] Responding to the appeal from the FCCCA, the California State Federation of Churches sent Coolidge a telegram asking him to veto the immigration bill.[205]

The FCCCA, through its subsidiary body, the Commission on International Justice and Goodwill (CIJG), requested every senator and representative to regulate Japanese immigration in the "right way."[206] For example, John H. Finley, chairman of the CIJG, wrote to Senator William E. Borah, suggesting that exclusion might be "secured in a friendly and conciliatory way."[207] The CIJG regarded the adoption of the exclusion clause as a "hasty and ill-considered action" and said that it was "a severe blow to all lovers of just dealing and to all who [feel] that friendly relations between America and Japan [are] of vital importance for world peace."[208] The CIJG released a statement urging "the Senate and the House to reconsider their action and . . . to find a more satisfactory method of dealing with the problem."[209]

The National Committee on American-Japanese Relations (NCAJR), an organization that was established over the winter of 1920 and spring of 1921 in order to "replace animosity with feelings of amity and goodwill between the two countries," strongly opposed the exclusion law.[210] Sidney Gulick, as executive secretary, asked its members to urge senators and representatives to "give the Appeal serious consideration."[211] Even before the president signed the bill, George W. Wickersham, chairman of NCAJR and a former U.S.

attorney general, stressed the necessity of meeting the "pressing need of educating the responsible citizenry of the United States" in regard to the issue.[212]

On June 27, twenty-four prominent East Coast clergymen, lawyers, and businessmen, including Lamont and Wickersham, entrusted to Hiroshi Saitō, the Japanese consul general in New York, a letter of vindication addressed to the American Japanese Society. Admitting that some expressions used in the debate over the immigration bill in Congress were unjustifiable, the letter said that the statements "do not represent the real feeling of the American people" and that "the real America realizes that it has a part to play in the sympathetic and generous treatment of its fellow nations and in the reasonable consideration shown to their traditions and susceptibilities."[213]

State Department senior officials were displeased with the immigration act. William R. Castle, chief of the Division of Western European Affairs, feared that it would leave to future generations "a heritage of hatred across the water which in future years might burst into flame."[214] He said Congress could not understand how important "gentlemanly" conduct was in international affairs.[215] Castle was also concerned that the immigration law might push Japan into a Sino-Japanese-Russian alliance. He concluded that the Senate was unable to see into the future and that this act would become a blot on Secretary of State Charles E. Hughes's record.[216] Joseph Clark Grew, undersecretary of state and future ambassador to Japan, felt that "a separate treaty [could] be negotiated with Japan along the lines of the Gentlemen's Agreement which would supersede the Immigration Act" before the enactment of the law.[217] John Van Antwerp MacMurray, chief of the Far Eastern Division, considered it "incontrovertible" that the exclusion clause was "most unfair, as it put Japan definitely on a lower plane than the rest of the world."[218]

Although officials at the State Department complied with the policy of Japanese exclusion, most of them would have preferred a less extreme approach. However, some officials who specialized in Chinese affairs, such as Stanley K. Hornbeck of the Economic Adviser's Office, held a more restrictionist view. At a meeting for the chiefs of divisions, Hornbeck maintained that "the press should emphasize [the American] right to keep out the Japanese rather than find a solution satisfactory to Japan."[219] Nelson T. Johnson, consul general at large, also saw no change in U.S.-Japanese relations necessarily following from the immigration law. He believed that "the action of . . . congress was an inevitable thing, the inevitableness was well known to every one, not least of which were the Japanese unless the Japanese were fools."[220] Though they differed in their preferred methods of excluding Japanese, the officials agreed that Japanese immigrants should be excluded.

Many Americans believed that the immigration law placed Americans living in Japan in a seriously compromised position. In spreading their religious doctrines, American missionaries in Japan had benefited from the reputation of their homeland as the nation of freedom and equality. However, this idealized image of the United States was seriously tainted by the enactment of Japanese exclusion, and missionaries found themselves confronted with severe opposition from the Japanese people. A missionary from Japan warned that the exclusion clause would "affect [their] missionary work adversely because—in the popular mind—the missionary, Christianity, and the United States are very closely related."[221] A letter from a Japanese urged the teachers of the leading Methodist Episcopal school in Tokyo to leave Japan on the grounds that "Japan is better off without the Americans' 'un-Christian ideas.'"[222] The missionaries complained of difficulties as a result of the immigration act. A report from missionaries in Japan said: "It is no exaggeration to say that the method and spirit of the immigration legislation has made it much more difficult for the missionary to be thought of as a minister of religion. The color of his skin and the accident of his birth as a Britisher, a German, or an American put his message at a handicap."[223] Dr. A. K. Reischauer, executive secretary of the Women's Christian College in Tokyo, said that "the situation of native Christians as well as of missionaries and other Americans residing in Japan has been made very serious."[224]

The fifty-second annual meeting of the Japan Mission of the American Board of Commissioners for Foreign Missions (ABCFM), held in Arima, Japan, expressed "its sincere regret at the recent action of the United States Government in legislation" and "pledged itself to work actively . . . for the removal of all unjust discrimination."[225] To realize this end, two experienced missionaries, the Reverend Frank A. Lombard and the Reverend Dwight W. Learned, were appointed to form a committee to attract due publicity to this issue.[226]

On July 2 the secretary of the Presbyterian Board of Foreign Missions expressed the resolve that "no American Protestant missionaries would be withdrawn from Japan." Although he admitted that the missionaries were "very much concerned about the situation created by the American Exclusion

Act," he proclaimed, "This is the time of all times when missionaries ought to be at their posts, for they are the chief aids by which the Japanese people can learn the real sentiment of intelligent Christian people in America."[227]

Though both clergymen and businessmen opposed the exclusion clause, their perspectives on the immigration issue differed. While the businessmen emphasized the harmful influence on trade in their criticism, clergymen emphasized justice. The annual presidential address by Corwin S. Shank of Seattle at the Northern Baptist Convention held in Milwaukee clearly revealed this difference:

> I have said nothing here with reference to the effect of this exclusion act upon the commerce between two great countries. . . . We are, however, concerned in everything which bears upon the religious aspects of this question and we must get within our vision the fact that there will be a reaction throughout all the East against the great teachings for which the Christian church has stood through the centuries.[228]

The attitude of the clergymen toward this issue, which was revealed in this address, would later shape their approach to the immigration issue.

As time passed, concern over the immigration law diminished, not only in the East but also along the West Coast. Although the Hearst newspapers, such as the *Seattle Post-Intelligencer*, occasionally published anti-Japanese articles, most of the press regarded the Japanese immigration question as settled and dropped the issue. Although Coolidge, in his address accepting the Republican nomination for the presidency, mentioned the Japanese immigration issue and expressed his preference for methods other than the exclusion clause to control immigration from Japan, he added, "the law has been passed and approved, and the incident is closed." Newspapers in the East also stopped paying attention to the issue; even a letter by former ambassador Cyrus E. Woods, which recommended modification of the law, went unreported in the major newspapers in the East.[229]

As a last resort, Foreign Minister Shidehara prepared a draft of a treaty under which both governments would mutually prohibit immigration. Since the number of American immigrants to Japan was negligible, the mutual prohibition was thought to be the best measure to preserve Japan's national honor. This treaty would also have guaranteed the rights of Japanese immigrants already in the United States. For example, Article III read, in part: "Japanese subjects lawfully resident within any State or Territory of the United States shall enjoy . . . the same rights as are accorded by such laws to the subjects or citizens of other countries, without distinction of nationality." However, it was apparent that the State Department would not accept this treaty because it stood no chance of being passed by the Senate. Frederick Moore, an American adviser to the Japanese embassy in Washington, told Shidehara that Hughes would reject the treaty because of the traditional attitudes of the Senate. In Hughes's opinion, Moore informed Shidehara, "the undoing of the exclusion legislation is impossible."[230]

Sadao Saburi, acting chief of the Bureau of Commerce at the Foreign Ministry and former counselor of the Japanese embassy at Washington, attempted to solve this problem by modifying the exclusion clause. He consulted John K. Caldwell of the American embassy at Tokyo about the necessity of rectifying the exclusion clause, and suggested that if the United States were to give an immigration quota to Japan, the Japanese government would promise to send far fewer immigrants to the United States than the quota would allow.[231] Nevertheless, the Japanese government decided not to raise this issue, and apparently never officially submitted a draft of the treaty to Washington.

Eventually, the Japanese government stopped exchanging notes with the State Department concerning the immigration law, on the grounds that such exchanges "would only tend to arouse popular agitation in both countries and to complicate further the situation without serving any useful purpose." On September 16, Acting Ambassador Isaburō Yoshida conveyed this decision to Secretary Hughes. However, this did not necessarily mean that the Japanese government had abandoned the immigration issue; the Japanese government made clear that it could not regard the issue as "closed" and hoped that "some satisfactory solution . . . [will] be reached as soon and as far as possible." This communication meant only that the immigration question ceased to be an immediate diplomatic issue.[232]

In the autumn of 1924, public interest about Japan in the United States focused on its role in the League of Nations conference at Geneva. When Japan opposed Article V of the discussed Protocol for Pacific Settlement of International Disputes, which stated that the League could not take action on any matter lying within a nation's domestic jurisdiction, some newspapers in the United States attributed Japan's motive to its intention to bring

Fig. 3. "A Persistent Fellow." Cartoon published in the *San Francisco Examiner*, 9 October 1924.

the immigration issue to the League of Nations.[233] Newspapers in the South were generally critical of Japan because of this assumption,[234] whereas newspapers in the East, such as the *New York Times*, reported the developments in Geneva more dispassionately.[235] Even newspapers that did not support the exclusion clause, such as the *San Francisco Chronicle*, assumed that the exclusion question lay behind Japan's proposed amendment. Several newspapers published articles similar to one published in the *Chronicle* entitled "Japan Thought Ready To Quit if Turned Down."[236] Hearst newspapers on the Pacific Coast were much more suspicious in their coverage of the Japanese amendment. Although Foreign Minister Shidehara informed Acting Ambassador Caffery that the Japanese amendment was not directed against the United States, and although claims by the Foreign Ministry in Tokyo to the effect that Japan had no intention of introducing the immigration issue to the League of Nations were reported in the United States, Hearst newspapers on the Pacific Coast ignored such statements.[237] On October 9, the

San Francisco Examiner published a cartoon in which a man named "Japan" tried to climb up a wall on a ladder labeled "League of Nations" because the "immigration gateway to U.S." was closed to him (see Figure 3).[238] Two days later, the paper editorialized: "If we . . . protest that Japanese immigration is, under international law, a purely domestic question, and that we deny the Court's or the League's jurisdiction, we shall be told that unless we obey the League's mandate we shall be denounced as an aggressor—all the nations in the League will unite against us."[239]

Surprised at this sort of reaction in the United States, the Japanese government repeatedly denied having any intention to bring the immigration issue to the League of Nations. A statement from the Japanese embassy in Paris on October 13 maintained that the motive to modify the protocol was "'purely a question of a juridical nature, a question of principle, with the loyal intention of keeping the Covenant free from patent inconsistency and illogicalness.'"[240] Japanese newspapers, which earlier had vehemently criticized the immigration law, largely ignored the protocol issue in connection with the law.[241] An editorial in the *Tokyo Asahi* argued that there was no intention to fight other countries over the immigration issue and explained that since the rapid development of international traffic had caused numerous international disputes on topics such as immigration, it would be wiser to create a system for solving such disputes internationally.[242] The denials by the Japanese government and the calmness of Japanese newspapers did not halt the Hearst papers' flow of anti-Japanese propaganda. The *Seattle Post-Intelligencer* published a cartoon in which a big hand representing the "League of Nations" was supporting a Japanese soldier who presented to Uncle Sam a sheet of paper which said "JAPAN DEMANDS THE RIGHT TO REGULATE U.S. IMMIGRATION."[243]

Public interest in the immigration issue, however, did not last long. Secretary Hughes emphatically denied the "groundless agitation over relations between [the United States] and Japan," then departed "from diplomatic precedent . . . to issue a formal statement of cordial greetings to Tsuneo Matsudaira as the next Japanese Ambassador."[244] And Matsudaira "expressed his appreciation of the statement" and said that his government shared "the view of the American Government 'that there are no issues whatsoever between the two countries endangering the existing cordial relations.'"[245] The intense public concern had eased.

The Origins of Pro- and Anti-Quota Movements

As public attention turned toward other issues of international relations, such as the possibility of war between the United States and Japan, public concern about the Japanese exclusion issue declined, along with newspaper coverage. However, the beginnings of movements to modify the exclusion clause, as well as countermovements, were evident immediately after the enactment of the immigration law.

The State Department continued to monitor the effect of the immigration law on the Japanese. Although Secretary of State Hughes understood that Japan had not recovered from the shock of the exclusion, he also believed that there was "no reasonable prospect of a reversal of the action taken by Congress," and so did not support efforts to amend the law. Hughes believed that the best way to heal the psychological injury caused by the exclusion clause would be to maintain a moderate diplomatic stance toward Japan. He instructed Edgar A. Bancroft, the new ambassador to Japan, to take every precaution so that "our intercourse with Japan be kept upon a consistently friendly, dignified and candid basis." Hughes further instructed Bancroft to approach the issue with "exceptional delicacy" since it involved "racial and national pride." "The mere lapse of time will . . . abate the intensity of local feeling on these questions in our western states,"[1] he wrote, but until then, the U.S. government would have to "maintain the attitude that that [the immigration issue] is a closed question."[2]

Whereas the State Department regarded the immigration issue as "closed," private organizations in the United States did not, and movements to reignite interest in the immigration question and pursue further efforts to amend the law developed along the East Coast. Clergymen and professionals in the eastern part of the United States made up the core group of those who opposed exclusion. Immediately after the law went into effect on July 1, some of them told Dr. Tsunejirō Miyaoka, a leading Japanese lawyer and former counselor of the Japanese embassy in Washington, that they would "never cease their agitation until Congress [had] repealed its recent act." The views of George W. Wickersham, a former U.S. attorney general, were typical: "I am perfectly confident that Congress did not represent the views of the great body of American citizens who do not approve of offending a friendly nation."[3]

Soon after the law's passage, the Commission on International Justice and Goodwill (CIJG) and the National Committee on American-Japanese Relations (NCAJR) began a campaign to modify the exclusion clause. The CIJG was a subsidiary organ of the Federal Council of the Churches of Christ in America (FCCCA), a Protestant federation that had been organized in New York City in 1908 to represent the group's one hundred fifty thousand churches and twenty-two million members. The CIJG itself was established within the FCCCA in 1911, and its aim was to establish world justice and peace. Since its founding, the CIJG had played a significant role in Protestant peace movements. Sidney L. Gulick, a former Japanese missionary, whose lifework was to promote cordial U.S.-Japanese relations and who opposed any anti-Japanese measures in the United States, played a leading role in the CIJG. The CIJG released a public statement urging "the Senate and the House to reconsider their action."[4]

The NCAJR had been organized in New York City on Gulick's initiative in 1920 to prevent the further deterioration of U.S.-Japanese relations. So as to avoid giving the impression that the committee placed more importance on Japan's welfare than on American interests, the NCAJR membership was composed solely of American citizens. Its stated purpose was to cultivate "an informed and rational public opinion in the United States in regard to Japan, inspired by a friendly spirit and sympathetic understanding of her needs and problems." In 1924, the NCAJR's chair was Wickersham and its secretary was Gulick. The list of honorary members included prominent peace activists such as Jane Addams and John R. Mott. The mainstay of this committee were professionals who had a keen interest in peace movements.[5] They believed that the exclusion clause ran counter to international justice and was detrimental to international peace. Both of these anti-exclusion movements, then, were situated within the peace movement, generally, and especially the internationalist peace movement, as represented by Wickersham, and the social progressive peace movement, as represented by Gulick.[6] Both groups acted together for the same objective: to rectify the U.S. exclusion law.

Early on, the two groups could not agree on how to tackle the problem. An NCAJR pamphlet entitled *National Committee on American-Japanese Relations*, published before the exclusion law was enacted, had advocated a "new treaty . . . to take the place of the present Gentlemen's Agreement." However, a later version urged that the "Japanese be included in the quota provisions of the new immigration law,"[7] probably because the granting of a quota seemed a more convenient way to soothe Japan's psychological wounds.[8] The two leaflets reveal that the friendship between the United States and Japan was much more important to anti-exclusionists than the welfare and equal treatment of Japanese immigrants in the United States.

For its part, the CIJG issued *Japan Wonders Why?* Published in June 1924 and written by the missionary William Axling, the pamphlet called attention to the serious effect of the immigration law on Japanese public sentiment toward the United States. Axling wrote that Japan was "the key to the situation in the Orient" and called on the U.S. government to "grant equal treatment to Japan by giving her a quota" in 1927 when new quotas were scheduled to be fixed.[9] This pamphlet was also used to invite influential people to join the anti-exclusion organizations.[10]

Gulick himself was also very active in writing similar pamphlets, and both the NCAJR and the CIJG used them in their publicity campaigns. Gulick's goal was to "present the facts with a view to re-establishing right relations with Japan." The NCAJR distributed Gulick's pamphlets to all its new members, and through these pamphlets also succeeded in gaining the support of other pro-Japanese organizations. They included *America and Japan*, a pamphlet that contained many facts about Japan and the Japanese presented in question-and-answer form, and written on the premise that "Americans have been misled by many mistaken assertions regarding Japanese in America and Americans in Japan." Though the main purpose of this short pamphlet was to educate Americans about Japan, it also proposed a quota system for Japan.[11]

Another pamphlet written by Gulick and entitled *Reestablishment of Right Relations between America and Japan* explained how Japan had been hurt and humiliated by the immigration law. Gulick argued that the action of Congress appeared to be a betrayal to the Japanese for two reasons: first, the Japanese had thought it would be possible to meet the U.S. demand for a reduction in the number of immigrants through the Gentlemen's Agreement; and second, the Japanese had believed that America was a nation of freedom and equality, and so the ban on Japanese immigration conflicted with their respect for the American nation. Gulick cautioned against the simplistic view that "the question was 'settled,' 'a closed incident,'" and then proposed some ways to recover the previously cordial relationship between the United States and Japan. He wrote that the only solution was "another act of Congress placing Japan under the operations of the quota provisions of the law," and suggested that such an adjustment should be made when new quotas went into effect on July 1, 1927.[12]

In the immediate aftermath of the law's passage, businessmen in general were relatively inactive in the campaign for a quota system. So long as the Japanese appeared to have forgotten the dispute and it was not having a major impact on trade, businessmen felt it best not to interfere in such a delicate issue. The annual convention of the Foreign Trade Council criticized the exclusion clause only in the vaguest terms, saying, "The regulation of the admission of Aliens. . . . should be handled without needless impairment of our friendly relations with other countries." Even Pacific Coast traders were unenthusiastic about the pro-quota movement. J. J. Donovan, vice-president of a lumber mill that exported its products to Japan, made a speech in support of the immigration law, arguing that Asian countries would still be able to send students, traders, and diplomats to the United States under the new law.[13] An influential businessman in Seattle also noted that Eastern businessmen would be the ones to push for abolition of the exclusion law, because although trade with Asia was carried out through Pacific ports such as Seattle and San Francisco, most of this trade originated in the East. He argued that those who were most damaged by the Japanese exclusion were businessmen in the East.[14]

The anti-exclusion movements were closely monitored by Californians who had organized themselves under the Japanese Exclusion League. The League had been a driving force in the exclusion movement which had culminated in the enactment of the 1924 immigration law.[15] After the law's passage, the Japanese Exclusion League of California went through a structural reorganization, and Valentine Stuart McClatchy, former part-owner of the *Sacramento Bee* and the *Fresno Bee*, took over its leadership. He was highly praised for his untiring efforts to exclude the Japanese, and the *Grizzly Bear* declared, "No person has done more for California and the Pacific than McClatchy in the Japs controversy."[16] While McClatchy had, up to that point, directed most of the League's propaganda activities by being "in the office and furnishing information," he now decided to act "in [his] own name, personally, and without using the League's name." Also, partly "because of the prejudice which the name of the organization created," a change of name was considered.[17] McClatchy now focused his attack not on Japanese residents in America, but on efforts to modify the exclusion language of the law.[18] Even the enactment of the immigration bill had not completely satisfied McClatchy, because there still existed strong opposition to the exclusion clause, such as that of the U.S. Chamber of Commerce. He found it necessary, then, to continue with his education campaign, at least for a while, at least "until the opening of Congress, and thereafter if it appears necessary," so that before the reconvening of Congress that December, "our position and that of Japan will be thoroughly appreciated, and the action taken by Congress [will] receive general approval."[19]

McClatchy named his new organization the California Joint Immigration Committee (CJIC), and its structure was radically different from that of its predecessor, the Japanese Exclusion League of California. McClatchy became executive secretary of the new organization, and James K. Fisk of the American Legion was named chairman. Other principal members included Paul Scharrenberg of the State Federation of Labor, John T. Regan of the Native Sons of the Golden West, and U. S. Webb, the California State Attorney General. Scharrenberg, born in Germany, had lobbied for the exclusion clause since having arrived in California, first as an editor of the *Coast Seamen's Journal*, and then as the secretary of the California State

Federation of Labor. He had worked with McClatchy for the passage of the 1924 immigration law.[20] At the CJIC's first meeting, former U.S. Senator James Phelan was elected treasurer. Phelan was the son of an Irish immigrant and a strong supporter of the exclusion movements. While the composition of the principal group of members changed, most of the Committee's supporting organizations remained unchanged. These included the California Federation of Labor, the California Department of the American Legion, the State Grange, and the NSGW, all of which had also been supporters of the Japanese Exclusion League of California.[21] Labor unions opposed Asian immigration because they worried that their members would be replaced by cheap immigrant laborers. The California Department of the American Legion attacked the "aggression of Orientals" and what it viewed as the intrusion of alien elements into American society.[22] The *Grizzly Bear*, official organ of the Native Sons, had written about the "threat" from Asian immigrants throughout its publication history.[23] Since the California State Grange consisted mainly of small farmers who were threatened by the advance of Japanese immigrants into farming, this group, too, strongly opposed Japanese immigration.

With the establishment of the CJIC, the Japanese Exclusion League of California was disbanded and its executive committee transferred the group's funds over to the CJIC. The CJIC vowed to use the funds to "continue in the work of protecting the State and the Nation from oriental immigration so long as action in that direction is necessary."[24] However, these monies were not sufficient to support the CJIC, so the main financial burden of the organization was initially assumed by McClatchy.[25]

Since the CJIC was quick to attack anything it deemed detrimental to the exclusion movement, the FCCCA immediately became its target. The CJIC distributed a pamphlet in which McClatchy accused the FCCCA of rehashing the "closed" Japanese immigration issue. Since the FCCCA's focus was on the effect of the exclusion clause on international relations, McClatchy was able to avoid allegations of racial discrimination. Without mentioning the motivation behind the naturalization law, he declared it was not discriminatory against Japan. He asserted that the effort to modify the exclusion clause "would be fruitless in the result" and merely "increase friction and ill will between the two nations," and that "the movement was started in ignorance of important facts."[26]

When the FCCCA backed Japan's demand for amendments of the protocol at the League of Nations by arguing that the enactment of the exclusion clause did not have "the approval of the President, or the Secretary of State, or the American public," the CJIC issued a pamphlet denouncing the FCCCA's action and asserting that "the action of Congress . . . should not be condemned by these organizations until they have made the most searching and unprejudiced investigation." This pamphlet concluded by declaring, "Neither insistent plea nor covert threat should induce loyal Americans, or their Congress, to take action in this matter in violation of long established policy and in manifest detriment to the ultimate interest of nation and race."[27]

The CJIC concentrated on disseminating propaganda to organizations within California, especially groups which opposed the exclusion clause, such as the California State Federation of Churches, whose headquarters was located in Los Angeles; the Missionary Education Movement of Dr. Harvey H. Guy; and the Congregational Committee on Friendly Relations with Japanese and Other Citizens. Women's clubs also became targets of CJIC's propaganda campaigns when the Executive Board of the State Federation of Women's Clubs revealed its support for the movement to amend the exclusion clause. The CJIC tried to win over individual women's groups by sending them literature and dispatching speakers.[28] In their letters, the CJIC argued that the sovereign right to executive control of immigration was a purely domestic question and requested reconsideration of their anti-exclusion stand.[29] At least five local clubs approved the pro-exclusion stand of the CJIC and "deprecated the action taken by their State Board."[30]

McClatchy traveled to Southern California to spread his group's propaganda, delivering speeches at prominent private clubs such as the City Club of Los Angeles and the X Club. He also met with leaders of the International Goodwill movement, who tended to be anti-exclusionists, including K. S. Bean, secretary of the State Church Federation; C. H. Matson of the Los Angeles Chamber of Commerce; Professor George Day of Occidental College; George Gleason, executive Secretary of the YMCA. of Los Angeles; and Mrs. J. C. Urquhart, president of the Federation of Women's Clubs. Although McClatchy did not convert these prominent leaders into supporters of his cause, his speeches attracted lots of public interest.[31]

McClatchy also met with Japanese immigrant leaders, including Paul M.

Hiratsuka of the Central Japanese Association of Central California, and Jūji Kasai of the Japanese Association of Los Angeles. What these Japanese immigrant leaders sought was not a modification of the immigration law, but the resolution of what the CJIC considered to be "other less important matters," such as "land cropping contracts, naturalization of resident Japanese and admission of brides for Japanese bachelors." Indeed, the national honor of their homeland was not necessarily foremost in the minds of at least some Japanese immigrants.[32]

The CJIC was pleased to see this kind of attitude among Japanese immigrants. A report presented at the Findings Conference at Stanford University said, "The Joint Immigration Committee . . . has expressed itself as ready to see that the Japanese actually in the United States should receive fair and friendly treatment insofar as this involves no modification of existing laws." This report also concluded that "since the enactment of the land laws and the federal exclusion law, the Pacific Coast has had a kindlier feeling toward its Japanese population."[33] This evaluation of the treatment of Japanese on the Pacific Coast was validated by Japanese immigrants themselves. The *Nichi Bei* published an article revealing that it had a high opinion of the improvement in American attitudes toward the Japanese after the enactment of the immigration law.[34] The CJIC was happy to promote fair treatment toward Japanese immigrants as long as Japanese immigrants did not advocate modification of the immigration law, as few Japanese immigrants apparently did.

In early November, McClatchy was still optimistic about obtaining quick results. Although he realized that some forces were "making a determined effort to have the Immigration Act amended as to admit Japan to the quota" and argued that it was "all the more necessary . . . to solidify sentiment in California," he felt that the fight would end within a year with his victory: "If we win the fight before this Congress it is probable that no future effort will be made to reopen the question; and we can close up our office and be at no further expense in that event."[35]

In the hope that the anti-exclusion movement would fold if the exclusionist movement became strong enough before the forthcoming Congress, McClatchy stepped up his activities. The CJIC circulated propaganda which emphasized the threats posed by Japan and Japanese. For example, one pamphlet, released on November 12, warned of the possibility that Hawaii's electorate would soon be controlled by Japanese,[36] while another, released on November 17, pointed out the danger posed by Japanese who were born in the United States and who chose to retain Japanese citizenship.[37] McClatchy also argued that the Japanese had already evaded the immigration law of 1924, claiming that Japanese women who were prohibited from entering the United States came anyway as tourists and played "the part of wives while here for the six months stay permitted as such tourists, then return to Japan, to come again next year or the year after as tourists."[38]

When the newly appointed ambassador to Japan, Edgar Bancroft, passed through San Francisco on his way to Tokyo, both exclusionists and anti-exclusionists seized the opportunity to try to influence him. McClatchy and Phelan visited Bancroft to promote the exclusionist side and David Starr Jordan, former president of Stanford University, as well as many other prominent Californians, visited him to argue for the anti-exclusionists. Bancroft himself remarked that he hoped that "California will some day realize . . . the wisdom and advantage of moderation and restraint in all matters affected by race prejudice."[39]

The CJIC's supporting organizations backed McClatchy's efforts. The annual convention of the American Federation of Labor (AFL), which began on November 17 in El Paso, Texas, passed a resolution submitted by delegates of the California Federation of Labor, including Paul Scharrenberg, expressing the AFL's "determined opposition to any modification of the clause in the general immigration law . . . which reaffirms the long-established policy of this nation to exclude all immigrants ineligible to citizenship." Another resolution opposed "exclusion by treaty," which evidently alluded to the Gentlemen's Agreement.[40] The National Conference of Department Adjutants of the American Legion, held in Indianapolis from November 17 to 19, endorsed the pro-exclusion activities of the four organizations supporting the CJIC in California. The National Director of the Americanism Department of the American Legion also expressed his willingness to back the activities of the CJIC.[41] The Convention of the National Grange in Atlantic City also resolved to oppose changing the exclusion clause.[42]

Some anti-exclusion people on the Pacific Coast felt apprehensive about McClatchy's renewed anti-Japanese propaganda campaign and thought that anything capable of further stimulating the anti-Japanese factions, such as movements to modify the exclusion clause, should be avoided. They feared that the pro-quota movement would simply antagonize the anti-Japanese forces which, apparently satisfied by the passage of the immigration law, had become dormant. This fear of a resurgence of anti-Japanese sentiment can be seen through the actions of business and religious leaders in San Francisco, who urged William Axling, on a nationwide lecture tour, not to "make frontal attacks on the immigration Bill on the Coast at the present time."[43]

Despite the fear of stimulating the McClatchy factions, some local organizations continued to criticize McClatchy's stand and supported Japanese demands. The State Executive Board of the Federation of Women's Clubs still strongly opposed the CJIC and called its efforts "unusual and unethical."[44] The Southern California Council of Religious Education, comprised of Protestant Sunday-school workers, resolved to oppose Japanese exclusion. Some clergymen argued that "in the interests of the Christian spirit and the brotherhood of man, Japanese and all aliens should be placed on the same plane as to admission and naturalization as is conceded to the white race."[45] In addition to this criticism from local forces in California, national organizations whose headquarters were located on the East Coast also offered resistance to McClatchy by maintaining that Japan should be given an immigration quota. At the ninth annual meeting held at Buffalo, the World Alliance for International Friendship Through Churches (WAIFTC), a Protestant international organization established in 1914 whose purpose was "to enlist the churches in a joint endeavor to achieve the promotion of international friendship,"[46] passed a resolution expressing the hope that "the recent legislation on this subject [the Japanese immigration] may be revised, even to the extent of admitting ultimately the Japanese to the quota provisions of the new Immigration Law."[47]

Since these pro-quota voices were not diminishing as he had anticipated, McClatchy had to reevaluate his estimation of the persistence of the anti-exclusion forces. In a letter to a congressman from California, he admitted that "there is still apparent determination on the part of certain interests to assist Japan in securing a place under the quota," and concluded that "in view of the general situation this committee has deemed it necessary to maintain an office and an active campaign in defense of the victory that was won in May."[48]

The anti-exclusion movements of national organizations consisting of clergymen and peace activists began to catch the attention of newspapers on the East Coast. The NCAJR received some negative press in the *Washington Evening Star*, which reported the group's activities in an article entitled "Move To Placate Japan Launched."[49] The *Philadelphia Inquirer* gave more favorable coverage to the Presbyterian Board of Foreign Missions, which made public a document, signed by 330 American missionaries of various denominations in Japan, protesting the exclusion clause.[50]

The FCCCA, one of the largest organizations which publicly opposed the exclusion clause, had by this time fully adopted the strategy of working to place Japan on the quota basis. In its quadrennial meeting, held at Atlanta from December 3 to 9, President Robert E. Speer read former Ambassador Woods's letter, which argued that the exclusion clause was "a disaster to American business, a disaster to religion and the effective work of our American Churches in Japan," insisted that this question was one "Christian leaders must face," and advocated that "Japan be placed on the quota basis." At this meeting, the Reverend A. K. Reischauer, representing the National Christian Council of Japan, also suggested that Japan be put "on the quota basis."[51] On December 8, a series of resolutions entitled "The 1925 Program of the Federated Churches for a Warless World" were adopted. One of them said: "Let American Christians urge such change in the law as would put Japan upon the quota basis."[52]

Those active in the modification movement were not necessarily optimistic about the results of their labors. However, as Gulick said to Moore, while he was pessimistic about the outcome of his movement, he firmly believed that the modification movement itself would contribute to improving U.S.-Japanese relations.[53] Moore analyzed the movement and reported to Yoshida, "Many of Dr. Gulick's supporters believe the campaign should be conducted because of its righteousness, although they doubt the probability of its success."[54] These movements contributed to the promotion of cordial U.S.-Japanese relations in that they gave some hope to pro-American forces in Japan; however, they also stimulated anti-Japanese forces in California.

The CJIC observed carefully the anti-exclusion movements and articles about the immigration issue, and sometimes responded to them. When an editorial in *Collier's* criticized the enactment of the exclusion clause by stating that "Congress . . . quickly undid much of the good of the Washington Conference by the needless insult of the Immigration Act," McClatchy wrote to the editor, arguing that the misunderstanding and friction were caused by Japan and its friends in the United States who had "imperfect knowledge."[55]

The minutes of its meetings show that the CJIC was interested in the "continued activity of . . . church organizations in approaching Congressmen." However, the CJIC did not aggressively counteract these activities at this point.[56] To those who criticized the exclusion clause, McClatchy just repeated his argument that the "exclusion law against all aliens ineligible to citizenship was not intended and cannot be fairly construed as either discrimination or insult against Japan."[57] He also tried to refute the argument that the Gentlemen's Agreement had been successful and that the exclusion clause was "an unnecessary affront to Japan" by citing data showing that immigration from Japan decreased after the enforcement of the immigration law.[58] McClatchy never dreamed that he would have to continue his exclusion campaign against Japanese immigration for at least another ten years. In 1924 he only thought that he would have to "continue aggressive operation at least for a year."[59]

While the CJIC focused on the Japanese immigration issue, its supporting organizations adopted individual campaigns that did not necessarily concentrate on the Japanese issue. The Native Sons of the Golden West was the most aggressive in attacking the pro-quota movements. The group worried about "an intensive campaign in behalf of the yellow pests" by anti-exclusionists in the United States.[60] The organization drew attention to the beginnings of the modification movements, proclaiming that "Japs in Japan and the white- and yellow-Japs in the United States are preparing to use every means at their command to open the immigration question."[61] The January 1925 issue of the *Grizzly Bear* bitterly criticized the clergymen's pro-quota movement, arguing that it contributed to the deterioration of U.S.-Japanese relations. "If the American missionaries were kicked out of all foreign countries there would be fewer international tangles, and if the Protestant Church Federation . . . would get out of politics and cease their efforts to Japanize the Western states, they could accomplish much more real good in this country," the *Grizzly Bear* said.[62]

Since their major objective was to stop cheap foreign labor from entering the United States, labor organizations in California were less interested in the pro-quota movement and came to place more importance on the issue of Mexican laborers. Labor unions said that they were "glad that after twenty years of ceaseless and continuous agitation by organized labor, Congress has at last heeded our warning and has saved us from that great menace [of Japanese immigration]," declaring that they were "now compelled to raise [their] voice in protest against the influx of Mexican labor."[63] The *Labor Clarion* also dropped the Japanese immigration issue and instead focused on Mexican laborers.[64] Since labor organizations were among the strongest supporters of the CJIC, McClatchy might have ceased fire at this point save for the aggressive pro-quota campaigns.

In summary, most groups who had expressed anti- or pro-exclusion views before and immediately after the passage of the immigration law of 1924 soon lost interest in the issue, but a few groups continued to lobby for the Japanese cause. The most active of these groups were composed of clergymen in the Eastern part of the United States, who had been pro-Japan for more than a decade. Believing that the exclusion clause was a mistake, they continued to promote the anti-exclusion movement, some of them arguing for immigration quotas for Japan to be based on the system in effect for non-Asian countries.

The CJIC, the successor of the Japanese Exclusion League, also continued its interest in the Japanese immigration issue. But the CJIC's agitation on behalf of the anti-Japanese cause would have been extremely difficult to maintain had there been no concrete target to attack. As 1924 drew to a close, it seemed likely that anti-Japanese agitation would die out for lack of interest. However, the Gulick faction, whose judgment was obscured by its firm belief in justice, failed to see this, and their activities soon inadvertently aroused countermovements.

THREE

The Clergymen's Political Campaign

Since many Japanese continued to harbor ill-feelings about the immigration law, even after the issue no longer demanded media attention, some clergymen in the United States endeavored to remedy the situation by urging Congress to modify the law. However, it soon became apparent that to modify the law within a year of its passage by a substantial majority in Congress would not be an easy task. Furthermore, the movement for modification rekindled the fervor of exclusionists in California, who might otherwise have shifted their attention to other groups to be excluded, such as Mexican and Filipino immigrants who were exempted from immigration restriction.

The protests of Japanese nationals also aggravated the situation in California. Although reports about anti-American demonstrations faded from Japan's mass media, and although the Japanese government also ended its criticism of the U.S. government's stance, well-educated Japanese continued to be antagonistic toward Americans because of the exclusion issue. Jefferson Caffery, the American chargé d'affaires in Tokyo, reported that although conspicuous agitation subsided after the flag incident, "a strong steady undercurrent of bitter resentment and wounded pride" remained. Caffery enumerated many examples, among them: younger officials at the Foreign Ministry, who had been "more than ready to grant favors or to supply information," now were reluctant to deal with requests by American diplomats; and a family with whom the American embassy was negotiating for the rental of a house for an ambassadorial residence became unwilling and instead rented the house to the French-Japanese Society. Caffery predicted that these ill-feelings would "probably take years to burn out."[1]

On October 1, 1924, the *Japan Times and Mail* published a special edition entitled "Message from Japan to America," which contained statements by influential Japanese who expressed dissatisfaction with the exclusion clause. Baron Yoshirō Sakatani stated: "Nothing is settled when justice is found lacking." Some suggested that not only America but also Japan should be blamed, and some tried to appeal to the conscience of the American people. A poll taken by the *Japan Times* indicated that the vast majority of Japanese citizens believed that the underlying motive for the law was racism, and that most people considered it impossible to regard this issue as closed.[2] The CJIC responded to the special issue of the *Japan Times* with a pamphlet entitled *California's Answer to Japan*, in which McClatchy restated his argument that passage of the exclusion law was due neither to racial prejudice nor to the manipulation of political schemers, and that the Gentlemen's Agreement had been inefficient. He argued that "Japan's Honor [Was] Not Hurt by the Immigration Act."[3]

The Japanese government wanted to avoid becoming further entangled in this matter. Foreign Minister Shidehara felt there was little he could do, and he tried to argue that the resolution of the issue depended entirely on the American public. He told a reporter from the *Tokyo Asahi* that if the Japanese would simply remain calm, that would bring about the best results, and he reiterated that he was not trying to influence the U.S. State Department concerning the problem.[4]

When Shidehara discussed the immigration issue at the opening of the Fiftieth Imperial Diet, he sounded moderate. Although he expressed regrets at the enactment of the immigration law, he explained that since the administrative and legislative branches of government were totally separate in the United States, talks between the two governments would not lead to a satisfactory solution. Rather, he said, Japan must wait for the transformation of American public opinion, and he cautioned that impatient speeches and actions would never improve international understanding.[5]

Neither Japanese immigrants nor Japanese in Japan were pleased with Shidehara's position. Even the *Nichi Bei*, which had attacked the anti-American attitude of the Japanese immediately after the enactment of the law, expressed dissatisfaction. While admitting the necessity of waiting for a shift in American public opinion, the *Nichi Bei* also believed that the Japanese government should take every possible measure to change American opinion and to impress upon Americans the strength of their resolution to modify the law. Otherwise, the newspaper argued, Japan would never be given a quota.[6]

Some politicians within Japan also were dissatisfied with Shidehara's weak response. In the Lower House of the Diet, Representative Keijirō Nakamura criticized Shidehara for avoiding the immigration issue, which forced the foreign minister to affirm that he would never cease to work toward building a wholesome understanding about the Japanese among Americans.[7] In the House of Peers, Baron Sakatani took issue with Shidehara's rationale about the separation of powers between the administrative and legislative branches of government in the United States, maintaining that Japan must nevertheless continue its fight against exclusion. Shidehara, in order to satisfy Sakatani and others, once again expressed the great importance he attached to the removal of discriminatory treatment of Japanese immigrants and reiterated that he did not regard the immigration issue as closed.[8]

Internal politics, then, forced the Japanese government to openly express dissatisfaction with the unfair treatment of Japanese immigrants by the United States. This, despite the fact that it would have preferred to see the issue fade from public view. And across the Pacific, Gulick and Wickersham struggled to maintain interest among the American public by promoting an even more aggressive campaign to give a quota to Japan. Wickersham declared, "The time has come to begin the educational drive in support of the whole program of this Committee and especially of Article 5: 'To urge that after July 1, 1927, Japanese be included in the quota provisions of the new immigration law.'"[9] The NCAJR continued to distribute a pamphlet entitled *Reestablishment of Right Relations with Japan*, which asserted that Japan should be given a quota.[10] The CIJG printed pro-quota information in its biweekly newsletter, *International Goodwill*, and included in the March 12 issue a resolution in which the World's Sunday School Association expressed its dissatisfaction with "that part of the recent immigration law that affects the Japanese people." The association recommended that Congress either "appoint a High Commission to study the situation" or "enact a law that will allow Japanese to be eligible to citizenship."[11]

The Gulick–Wickersham faction made two policy adjustments around this time. First, they added China to their statement of policy and began to advocate an immigration quota for China. The shift was mainly due to tactical considerations. Gulick continued to regard a quota for Japan as the primary objective, but he thought that the change would "free the Article from the appearance of discrimination."[12] Second, the Gulick–Wickersham faction, which had carried out its campaigns mainly in the East, finally began to extend its activities to California, the stronghold of the anti-Japanese agitators. Realizing that without transforming the opinions of Californians it would be impossible to modify the law, the NCAJR wrote to influential Californians on April 8, 1925, inviting them to join the group's national committee.[13]

Some California activists harbored misgivings about the possible unintended consequences of renewed pro-quota movement there. Pro-Japanese forces on the Pacific Coast, who were relieved that the anti-Japanese faction had calmed down, regarded Gulick's intervention as harmful. Robert N. Lynch of the San Francisco Chamber of Commerce and Corwin S. Shank of the Seattle Baptist Church told Ambassador Tsuneo Matsudaira that Gulick and Wickersham might provoke the McClatchy faction anew.[14] Moreover, unlike anti-exclusionists in the East, business interests on the Pacific Coast had little interest in reigniting Japanese protests. They were content to leave things as they were just as long as U.S.-Japanese trade continued to be prosperous.

Gulick himself was apprehensive about the possible effects of his movement and sought the opinion of Japanese diplomats, including a visit to the new Japanese ambassador Tsuneo Matsudaira almost immediately after his appointment. Matsudaira could not provide any useful advice, however, and sent Gulick away with the explanation that the Japanese government could neither encourage nor discourage the movement because it would be dangerous if it was thought that Gulick's movement had any relation with the Japanese government.[15] Matsudaira's comment represented the typical stance of Japanese diplomats, that while they could not interfere with American domestic problems, they would not discourage anti-exclusion efforts as long as Americans made such efforts at their own risk.

Some American diplomats had a clear understanding of the danger of the quota movement. When Gulick met Secretary of State Frank B. Kellogg to ask for advice, Kellogg said that he had no objection to Gulick's education campaign, but that he could not agree it was wise to place Japan on a quota at this time. J. V. A. MacMurray, assistant secretary of state and former chief of the Division of Far Eastern Affairs, said that Gulick and Wickersham's movement was as dangerous as setting fire to explosives.[16]

The NCAJR's activities did indeed refire the rage of anti-Japanese factions. In a letter to George Gleason of the YMCA, McClatchy declared his intention to "inaugurate an aggressive campaign against [pro-quota movements] in the East."[17] McClatchy responded to the NCAJR's efforts to recruit members in California by arguing that the advocates for the modification of the immigration law had personal interests in Japan; he pointed out, for example, that Wickersham had previously worked as a lawyer for Mitsui. McClatchy argued that the members of the NCAJR did not report the truth, and that they attached less importance to the welfare of the United States than to that of Japan.[18]

By the spring of 1925 the renewed pro-Japanese movements which originated in the eastern part of the United States had attracted the attention of Pacific Coast newspapers. The *San Francisco Bulletin*, for example, reported the beginnings of a "definite movement to establish better relations between the United States and Japan" by modifying the exclusion clause.[19]

Other newspapers joined in McClatchy's attack in May. On May 1, the *Illustrated Daily Herald* of San Francisco denounced the work of NCAJR members as unpatriotic. The Hearst papers could not ignore the resumption of the pro-Japanese movements either. The *San Francisco Examiner* published an article with the headline "Fight Begun to End Jap Exclusion," which reported the beginning of "renewed efforts to revive the Japanese exclusion issue and effect a revision of the present immigration act."[20] The *Seattle Post-Intelligencer* wrote, "All attempts to revive [the anti-exclusion movement] will be in vain."[21] Through the Hearst newspapers, McClatchy issued a statement warning that Wickersham and Gulick's efforts were "a mistake and will not accomplish the end sought." McClatchy denounced Gulick as "the instigator of this movement" and said that "his counsel in this matter is as unwise as that which he has generally given Japan and the friends of Japan in the United States since he came to this country."[22]

At the same time, a Japanese diplomat perceived the dangerous nature of the modification movement. Surprised by the *Post-Intelligencer*'s articles,

Seattle consul Chūichi Ōhashi worried that the publication of articles detailing efforts to modify the immigration law might arouse anti-Japanese feelings which had finally begun to subside. He concluded that the time for launching a modification movement was not ripe, and that renewed efforts to modify the immigration law would only give new ammunition to anti-Japanese agitators.[23]

Despite Ōhashi's warning, the Foreign Ministry in Tokyo could do little to impede the movement. McClatchy focused his efforts on discrediting the Gulick–Wickersham faction. In a May 11 speech, he argued that the renewed anti-exclusion movement was being promoted "in Japan's interest by Sidney Gulick, who came here from Japan ten years ago," and that through the "influence of Gulick and Wickersham, the Federal Council and allied organizations are being used in an un-American attempt to discredit Congress."[24] McClatchy also wrote to members of the Advisory Council of the NCAJR, trying to convince them that "loyal Americans, fully advised as to the facts, will not countenance the campaign now being conducted" by Gulick and Wickersham. He argued that church, good will, and women's organizations in California "have ceased to promote the Wickersham–Gulick campaign," and that organizations which cooperated in this campaign would "lose influence with loyal Americans."[25]

McClatchy considered it necessary to conduct "an aggressive campaign in opposition . . . [throughout] the eastern territory, reaching newspapers, Congressmen and prominent church organizations and church members." He placed considerable importance on the influence of church organizations along the East Coast and focused on destroying Gulick's influence among these organizations. McClatchy even wrote to Gulick to explain that the CJIC had had to "undertake an aggressive [exclusion] campaign" only because of Gulick's pro-quota movement, and that his "attempt to reopen the question . . . [would] greatly increase the present friction with Japan" and "markedly decrease church influence among loyal Americans within and without the church fold."[26] The CJIC distributed copies of McClatchy's letter to influential people and asked them to "pass these [copies] after reading, to some prominent churchmen, preferably in the Eastern States, whose church organization is concerned in the movement."[27] McClatchy also wrote to the members of the NCAJR to urge them to reconsider their support for the organization, emphasizing that "loyal Americans . . . will find little reasonable ground for criticizing the practically unanimous action of Congress."[28]

Among the four organizations that were represented by the CJIC, the California Federation of Labor and the Native Sons of the Golden West (NSGW) were especially active in assisting McClatchy's activities against the Gulick–Wickersham movement. The Grand Parlor of the NSGW resolved to "deplore and condemn the activities of those individuals and organizations who either for pay or through misguided motives are endeavoring to inject . . . Japanese influence into a matter which is purely within the sovereign jurisdiction of the American people." It also criticized Gulick by resolving that its members "regret that any organization . . . should permit the use of its name and prestige by executive officers who are willing to subordinate the nation's honor and welfare to their own selfish interests."[29]

Although the California State Federation of Labor had shifted its main focus to Mexican immigrants, it too lent its voice against the Gulick faction. Paul Scharrenberg, secretary of the California State Federation of Labor, wrote:

> It is clear to a student of the matter that the missionary and church are acting in this case, not as American citizens, bent upon safeguarding the interest of nation and its citizenship above all other considerations, but as internationalists, thinking first of the welfare, physical or spiritual, of the alien individual, and concerned only in a minor manner, if at all, with the safety and dignity of this nation.[30]

Scharrenberg's assertion that the clergy were not acting as American citizens was not accurate. They were very much acting as Americans who attached the utmost importance to cordial U.S.-Japanese relations and to whom the avoidance of international conflict was seen to be in the American people's best interest. Indeed, as the passage shows, it was Scharrenberg who attached little importance to the issue of international conflict, choosing to focus instead on the fear of average Americans living on the Pacific Coast that Japanese immigrants posed a threat to the American public.

Anti-quota reverberations caused by the renewed quota movement did not forestall pro-quota clergymen such as Gulick. When the executive committee of the FCCCA met to discuss future policies on the Japanese immigration problem, all members agreed that the immigration law was unjust to

Japan. Opinion was split, however, over how to deal with this issue. A majority felt that the quota movement would arouse counterproductive countermovements and therefore recommended the discontinuation of FCCCA efforts to modify the law. Instead, they recommended concentrating on a public education campaign to promote better U.S.-Japanese relations. A minority took the position that the organization had an obligation as clergymen to recognize the law as unjust, and they insisted that the Council continue its efforts to modify the law, regardless of the consequences. This faction placed more importance on racial equality than on issues of world peace. Because of this minority opposition, the executive committee decided to put off a decision in favor of more research on the immigration question; a special committee was formed for the purpose, and at least for the time being, the issue remained alive.[31]

The *Christian Century* continued to emphasize the harmful effects of the exclusion clause and to press for its modification, arguing in the January 15 1925 issue that it was necessary to modify the law in order to "maintain friendship with . . . the orient as a whole." The publication claimed in its April 16 issue that the Japanese did not trust Americans because of "exclusion based on racial discrimination," and the April 23 issue noted that the immigration law had contributed to a resurgence of militarists in Japan.[32]

The policy of both governments toward the Japanese quota question was basically to do nothing, but whereas the U.S. State Department could adopt such a position openly, the Japanese government had to protest whenever anyone called the issue closed. For example, when Russell Kennedy, the Tokyo correspondent of the *Chicago Daily News*, reported that "well informed Japanese were reconciled to the American immigration policy and were not inclined to believe the movement headed by George W. Wickersham had the slightest chance of success," the Japanese Foreign Ministry quickly proclaimed that "Japan does not regard the immigration problem as settled."[33] Kennedy's remarks once again reanimated public discussion on the immigration issue in Japan, to the extent that the American embassy reported to the State Department that "the Japanese . . . are not reconciled to [the exclusion clause]."[34] Foreign Minister Shidehara told Assistant Secretary of State MacMurray that the only purpose of public meetings on the anti-immigration law scheduled for July 1 was "to overcome the effect of Mr. Kennedy's erroneous reports."[35] The *Osaka Mainichi* criticized Kennedy directly, calling his article "fabricated news" and stating bluntly that "we cannot believe in the mental sanity of a certain American correspondent in Tokyo."[36]

State Department officials believed they should refrain from discussing the Japanese immigration problem so as to prevent further damage to the already bruised image of the United States. Frank Lockhart, former chief of the Division of Far Eastern Affairs, advised Secretary of State Kellogg that "the less that is said the better off we will be."[37] Kellogg accepted Lockhart's advice and immediately sent off a telegram to Ambassador Bancroft: "The Department considers it inadvisable to issue any statement, as anything which could properly be said would seem likely to have an adverse rather than a beneficial effect upon the situation in Japan."[38]

Although Ambassador Bancroft, a Chicago lawyer unexpectedly appointed ambassador to Japan, was not much interested in the Japanese exclusion issue, he gradually came to realize, in the process of communicating with the Japanese people, how important it was in the context of U.S.-Japanese relations, and began to send telegrams explaining how seriously the Japanese had been hurt and humiliated by the immigration law. On January 5, 1925, Bancroft wrote to Secretary of State Hughes about his personal impression of Japan:

> My conclusions are that the Japanese people, with substantial unanimity, keenly felt that a humiliating slight was put upon their race by the form of the Immigration Act; that this feeling of insult was intensified by the friendship of the Japanese toward America, and their confidence that America was their friend. That feeling still continues. With the more intelligent and sober-minded, it has softened into disappointment and sadness, with a brave effort to cherish the hope that the wrong will be fully righted. With others, there is still a bitter resentment that time seems to fix rather than to lessen; and still others who calmly regard it as an injury that had best be forgotten. . . . It is this attitude of suppressed sadness and deep disappointment coupled with gracious courtesy, that is very appealing to me.[39]

Japanese-language newspapers in California also reported on the renewed anti-exclusion movement. While the *Rafu Shimpō* favored it,[40] the *Nichi Bei* was critical of the Gulick–Wickersham campaign, primarily because it was based on the East Coast. Such a movement should be concentrated in

California, the paper argued, since sentiments in California were the key issue on the question.[41] Although there were small differences of opinion regarding the movement, Japanese newspapers, in general, were pro-quota.

As July 1, 1925 approached, there were plans for a demonstration on the anniversary of "National Humiliation Day" in Japan, which drew the attention of the United States. Gulick, fearing repercussions, backed off and denied the existence of any such political movement. After sending a telegram to the prominent Japanese businessman Eiichi Shibusawa with a request not to publicize his movement in Japan, Gulick set about collecting relevant information on the immigration problem to reevaluate whether he should carry through with his plans to modify the law.[42] In Japan, only a few public speeches concerning the immigration law took place on July 1,[43] and these did not attract much attention in the media. Two meetings planned for that day by the Kokuryū Kai were canceled out of "sympathy with the victims of the Santa Barbara earthquake."[44]

On July 1, newspapers in the United States were generally indifferent to the Japanese immigration issue. No major newspaper in San Francisco published articles about it, with the exception of the *San Francisco Examiner*, whose editorial argued that "the restriction against Japanese immigration is today overwhelmingly accepted by the American people as a wise, sensible and well-working provision which is effectively protecting America."[45] In the East, the *New York Times* simply reported that the anniversary of "Humiliation Day" had been generally subdued in Japan and that only small radical groups had used the day to denounce the immigration law.[46]

The relative indifference of the Japanese toward the immigration issue did not necessarily mean that the year-old psychological wound had healed, and indeed a few national newspapers still debated the issue. *Seiyū*, the organ of a Japanese major political party, published an article about the immigration issue which criticized the Japanese Foreign Ministry's way of dealing with the problem, claiming that the ministry acted as if nothing racial was involved in this issue. The article dismissed American and Japanese Foreign Ministry arguments that the main reason of exclusion was economic, and declared the main cause to be racial.[47] The *Tokyo Asahi* reviewed the previous year's events and expressed its dissatisfaction with the status of the exclusion problem.[48] The *Chūgai Shōgyō Shimpō* reported on National Humiliation Day activities and attacked the views of McClatchy.[49] Arguing that the United States had compelled Japan to declare a "spiritual war" against America, the *Kokumin Shimbun* urged the Japanese government to make yet another protest in order to maintain the honor of the Japanese Empire.[50]

Moreover, newspapers in Tokyo tended to focus not on the general indifference of American newspapers toward the immigration issue, but rather on those anti-Japanese articles that appeared in a few newspapers, which must have given Japanese readers the wrong impression of American public opinion. The *Tokyo Asahi*, for example, reported that the *San Francisco Examiner* called the exclusion law "wise."[51] The *Chūgai Shōgyō Shimpō* warned that it would be shortsighted to assume that the low-key public reaction on July 1 was an indication of subsiding anti-American sentiment. Clearly, Japan had not resigned itself to accepting the immigration law, as was further shown by a *Chūgai Shōgyō Shimpō* article which attacked McClatchy for demanding that the Japanese remain quiet over the immigration ban, which the paper said was akin to asking one not to protest after being slapped.[52] These reports, mainly covering the exclusionist tendencies of Californians, must have had a negative influence on Japanese feelings toward the United States. Anti-American sentiments were still observed among Japanese military officers. At the breakup dinner of the Imperial Military Academy, for example, a plaque could be found carrying the inscription, "First Division of the Expedition against America." On another occasion, at an event held at the Osaka garrison, the walls were full of anti-American posters. The British ambassador observed that "the idea that America is a hostile Power with whom there will be a struggle some day is becoming more and more familiar."[53]

Japanese protests against the exclusion clause were also heard at the first convention of the Institute of Pacific Relations (IPR), a new international organization which first met in conference from June 30 to July 14, 1925. It was one of many groups founded through private initiative in this period, when the idea that international communication and exchange would promote peace continued to be influential. Organized by prominent figures in the private sector, including businessmen, educators, scholars, and professionals from the Pacific countries, the idea for the organization was originally conceived within the YMCA. Founding members included Ray Lyman Wilbur, president of Stanford University; John R. Mott of the YMCA; and the former ambassador to Japan, Roland S. Morris.[54] The 1925 conference focused on the advancement of mutual understanding among Pacific nations, and Japanese delegates used the opportunity to publicize Japan's view that the immigration question was not closed. Japanese delegate Masatarō Sawayanagi explained that "Japan does not intend to claim for her people the right of free entry into the territory of another country," but that the Japanese objected to "discrimination on account of race," and he implicitly demanded a change of the immigration law, saying: "The more thoughtful among us still have sufficient confidence in the traditional sense of justice and fair play on the part of the American people to cherish the hope that in due course of time this wrong will be righted with honor to both nations."[55] Professor Kenzō Takayanagi of the Imperial University of Tokyo echoed Sawayanagi's views, admitting the right of a country to control immigration, but arguing that this right "should be exercised in such a manner that (a) it should not discriminate between states, and (b) it should be based on personal grounds . . . rather than upon race or nationality."[56]

Although most American participants were sympathetic to the Japanese position, a few from California supported the exclusion clause. California journalist and civic leader Chester Rowell, for example, criticized the "lack of courtesy" in excluding the Japanese immigrants, but he supported the immigration law on the grounds that "now [that] we have it we must live up to it."[57] Paul Scharrenberg, representing the voice of labor, said that as long as movements like Gulick's to modify the immigration law continued, labor would persistently oppose them. Still, he also stated that if the immigration law were to be recognized as a closed case, he thought that the Japanese would then be given the same treatment as other nations in the future.[58]

While anti-exclusionist groups praised the advent of the IPR, traditionally exclusionist bodies did not. Labor in California did not have a high opinion of the IPR, and *Organized Labor*, the magazine of the state's building trade councils, deemed the Institute as "part and parcel of the Japanese propaganda campaign, fostered by the Federal Council of the Churches of Christ in America and other friends of the Japanese in this country."[59] According to the *Honolulu Star-Bulletin*, Congressman John F. Miller of the state of Washington deplored the attacks on the immigration law as "unwise and futile," and proclaimed that "exclusion represents the voice of the American people."[60]

Japanese newspapers in the U.S. regarded the IPR as a useful instrument for solving the immigration issue. The *Nichi Bei* wrote that the Institute would be useful in helping ordinary Americans to recognize the historical background of the Japanese opposition to the immigration law,[61] and the *Rafu Shimpō* emphasized the possibility that the IPR would contribute to the fusion between Eastern and Western civilizations if the participants would wholeheartedly accept racial equality.[62]

Coinciding with the first conference of the IPR, the *Nippu Jiji*, a Japanese-American newspaper in Hawaii, published a poem written by an American friend of Inazō Nitobe named Alexander Irvine, which expressed his sorrow over the exclusion clause. A portion of this poem, entitled "Be Patient, Neighbor Japan," read:

> BE PATIENT, NEIGHBOR JAPAN,
> One day, we shall
> Feel ashamed
> Of the wall we've built
> And when we do, we'll raze it.
> Nothing built on lies
> Can permanently endure,
> And this spite-fence
> Of the Pacific
> Is built on the lies
> That might makes right
> And man is not
> His brother's keeper!

Irvine wrote the poem after being surprised by Nitobe's refusal to set foot in the United States because of the immigration law.[63] By showing American sympathy with Japanese feelings, this newspaper tried to promote understanding between the two peoples.

The CJIC, however, continued to denounce the Gulick–Wickersham movement, and issued a new pamphlet, written by McClatchy, entitled *America and Japan*, the chief purpose of which was to vitiate the movement by attracting the attention of "prominent church leaders, particularly in the East" and making "loyal Americans . . . realize how their church organizations are being used in a cause detrimental to American interests."[64]

McClatchy argued that the movement reopened the discussion of the Japanese immigration issue "with little probability of securing any change in the law, but with the certainty of reviving racial friction and misunderstanding," and that the campaign by the Gulick faction would only "increase misinformation and misunderstanding."[65] This new pamphlet was sent out accompanied by a letter requesting cooperation with the CJIC in opposing the Gulick–Wickersham movement. McClatchy wrote to the members of women's clubs, the State Federation of Farm Bureaus, and the American Legion, warning that "the better feeling developed [by the enactment of the immigration act of 1924] is now threatened by the campaign" of Gulick and Wickersham.[66] Copies of the pamphlet were also distributed to "all members of Congress, all newspapers, . . . about 2,000 ministers, members of the Institute for [*sic*] Pacific Relations at Honolulu, Members of the Survey of Relations, Australian newspapers, Consuls and private individuals."[67]

G. H. Blakeslee, a professor of history and international relations at Clark University and a pro-Japanese intellectual who opposed the exclusion movement, worried about the negative effects of Gulick's modification movement. He lectured on the Japanese immigration problem at the Institute of Politics in Williamstown, Mass., arguing that the anti-exclusion movement was harmful to the Japanese already living in California in its potential to arouse the resentment of anti-Japanese Californians. He explained that because Californians considered the immigration issue to be closed, they would try to abolish discriminatory legislation toward Oriental inhabitants. Since the success of the reform movement was questionable, whereas the possibility of its aggravating anti-Japanese sentiment among Californians was great, Blakeslee recommended the discontinuation of all movements to modify the immigration law of 1924. He cited Scharrenberg's statement that California labor would cooperate with the Japanese already living in America if there were no movements to modify the immigration law. In addition to Scharrenberg's statement, Blakeslee also cited a personal communication with a prominent figure in California, who had informed him that if there were no movements to modify the law, Californians would themselves start a movement in the State Assembly to abolish discriminatory laws against the Japanese and Japanese Americans. He declared that Japanese unwillingness to cooperate with American business interests in Asia because of the immigration issue would have "serious and far-reaching results."[68]

Since the FCCCA as an organization had not yet decided whether it should pursue an immigration quota for Japan, Gulick's attitude toward the immigration quota came to be seen as inconsistent. Gulick said he intended to end the pro-quota movement, in letters to San Francisco businessman Robert N. Lynch and the *Japan Times*, for example, but organizations in which he was a leader, such as the CIJG, continued their/his efforts. Because of this inconsistency, it was only natural that McClatchy considered the pro-quota campaign to be still in progress. He advised influential people and members of the CJIC to assume that Gulick was still "interested in approaching Congress for a change in the quota law in favor of Japan," and he argued that while the CJIC "sought to so direct its activities as to make for permanent peace between the two countries," the activities of Gulick and the FCCCA were still "seemingly promoting further misunderstanding with Japan."[69]

McClatchy's anti-quota stand was strongly endorsed by the CJIC's supporting organizations, which might have lost interest in the issue after 1924, but which instead continued to be active in the Japanese exclusion movement. Gulick's modification movement, then, served to consolidate the efforts of exclusion forces. At the seventh annual convention of the California Department of the American Legion, held in September 1925 at Avalon, Catalina Island, McClatchy attacked the pro-quota movement of the FCCCA. Afterward, the convention resolved to support the existing immigration law. McClatchy's speech was printed in a pamphlet entitled *Guarding the Immigration Gates*, which was delivered to the editors of daily newspapers and U.S. congressmen.[70] The Seventh Annual Convention of the Washington Department of the American Legion also passed a resolution to "urge upon Congress that no modification of existing law to place Japan on a quota basis or in any other manner weakening the exclusion provisions, be considered."[71] The executive committee of the Oregon department took similar action.[72]

Organized labor also strongly opposed modification of the immigration law. The 1925 annual convention of the California State Federation of Labor, held in San Diego, resolved that it would oppose any "unpatriotic" efforts to place Japan on the quota system. McClatchy warned the delegates to be careful about pro-Japanese propaganda from the eastern part of the United States. Scharrenberg explained that although the CJIC had intended to disband as soon as it achieved its goals, it had decided to continue its activities because of the modification movement.[73]

The national organizations of both the California State Federation of Labor and the California Department of the American Legion backed the positions of their local divisions. Following upon resolutions of its executive council that declared the pro-quota forces un-American, the forty-fifth annual convention of the American Federation of Labor, held at Atlantic City, warned the delegates that "propagandists are now exceedingly active . . . in attempting to place Japan within the immigration quota law and to otherwise lessen existing immigration restrictions against that country," and recommended that members "guard zealously the barriers [they] have erected against Asiatic immigration."[74] The *New York Times* reported the AFL's claim that "any attempt to modify exclusion of Japanese from the country [will] continue to be resisted by the 'massed strength' of the American Federation of Labor" and that "the action on Japanese exclusion was unanimous."[75] The national convention of the American Legion, held in Omaha that October, also opposed any move to change the existing immigration laws.[76]

By contrast, the forces opposing the exclusion clause were hardly of one mind; relations between the Gulick faction, based in the East, and businessmen on the West Coast were not cooperative. In the face of the exclusionist counterattack, anti-exclusionists took a cautious path. California businessmen were not enthusiastic about the modification movement. Chambers of commerce in California did not support Gulick's pro-quota campaign at all, instead agreeing with the ban on Japanese immigration. According to Robert N. Lynch, who corresponded with McClatchy, the directors of the San Francisco Chamber of Commerce were "in entire harmony with [the CJIC] as to the necessity of regarding the exclusion measure as a closed incident."[77] Businessmen in San Francisco tried to promote cordial U.S.-Japanese relations by focusing their attention on those Japanese already residing within the United States. To that end, the Japanese Relations Committee of the San Francisco Chamber of Commerce designated a special committee to "improve the industrial and agricultural status of Japanese legally resident in California."[78]

Nor were Japanese immigrants in favor of the pro-quota movement led by Gulick and Wickersham. A major Japanese newspaper in San Francisco argued that the movement would eventually cause the Japanese more trouble than it was worth. The article made it clear that the Japanese thought that the risks involved in asking Gulick and Wickersham to start up the pro-quota movement were too great, especially considering that the number of potential immigrants involved would be fewer than two hundred a year. According to the paper, since the anti-Japanese activists earned their bread by agitating on the issue, what they least wanted was to be left without any issue to be agitated. Therefore, if the new movement for the Japanese was started, they would be very pleased. What Japanese immigrants wanted, however, was that the issue remain untouched.[79] Neither did Japanese immigrants appreciate Gulick's pro-quota movement. A major Japanese newspaper in San Francisco accused Gulick of reawakening the McClatchy faction.

In the end, the FCCCA decided not to pressure Congress to give Japan an immigration quota. Instead, as Gulick reported, the Council would promote an educational campaign on U.S.-Japanese relations in an attempt to nurture a healthy public opinion and thus to encourage more cordial relations between the two nations. Gulick maintained that the Council had not succumbed to the opposition groups in California.[80] On December 7, 1925 the *New York Times* published the FCCCA's official statement on the matter:

> The Executive Committee has decided that it is not desirable to carry on any political campaign or make any effort to approach Congress or Congressmen during the present session on the matter of the exclusion law, but . . . we shall continue our quiet educational work to put the facts before the American people and to enlist as members of our committee men and women of influence in all parts of the country who believe as we do regarding the need of reestablishing right relations between America and Japan.[81]

At the end of the day, the Executive Council of the FCCCA attached primary importance not to racial equality but to amicable relations between America and Japan.

Gulick adhered to the new policy by dropping his campaign for the quota. To this end, the stated "purpose" of the NCAJR, as it appeared on official literature, was altered. Rather than promoting the goal of a Japanese quota, the organization now promoted "a general program of education in favor of including Japanese in the quota."[82] The group's monthly newsletter, *International Goodwill*, continued to pay considerable attention to the

Japanese immigration question, but its December 3 issue ignored the issue of a Japanese quota in favor of the aforementioned educational campaign. This brief issue devoted more than three-quarters of its contents to Japan and presented many Japanese views of the United States.[83] After the December 17 issue reported on the "'Declaration' Regarding the Asiatic Exclusion Section of the Immigration Law of 1924" in detail, the magazine ceased to discuss this issue intensively.[84] In an article for the *Annals of the American Academy of Political and Social Science*, Gulick argued that it was "useless to ask Congress to rescind its action until a change of mind [has] taken place on the part of the people generally"; however, he emphasized that it was Americans, not Japanese, who had lobbied for the amendment, and that the purpose of the amendment was "not to please Japan, but to express more adequately the real meaning and significance of the fundamental principles of democracy, liberty and fraternity." He declared that "no question is ever closed and settled that is not settled right."[85]

Despite the executive committee's decision, at the FCCCA's annual meeting that year, held in Detroit from December 9 to 11, the opinions of some members who believed that the FCCCA should work toward obtaining a quota for Japan, were allowed to "go on record for repeal of the present legislation." The executive committee even acknowledged that there existed no "better solution of the problem than the application to Japan, China, and India of the quota law as it comes into force in 1927 which would result in the annual admission of 350 immigrants from these sections of the Orient." However, the committee's earlier decision was upheld, and no concrete plan of realizing this goal was formulated. The executive committee would only "recommend to all right-thinking and peace-loving citizens of the United States, the importance of giving matters earnest study to the end that in due time appropriate steps may be taken to reestablish right relations between the United States and the peoples of the Orient."[86]

Some of the clergymen who had earlier expressed their minority view dissented, even though they believed there would be little hope of success. They argued that clergymen should continue their efforts to modify the immigration law as long as they, as Christians, regarded the law as wrong. The *Christian Century* chastised the FCCCA for its indecisiveness. Although it might not be politically possible to secure modification of the immigration law, the publication argued, "on a question as fundamental as this, it would be better for the churches to fail to accomplish their immediate political ends than for them . . . to lose their testimony."[87]

Gulick's intention to drop his campaign was sincere, as he informed the members of the NCAJR that "it is not desirable to carry on any political campaign, or make any effort to approach Congress or Congressmen." Yet, at the same time, Gulick was under pressure from leading members of the FCCCA, who urged him to be even more aggressive in pursuing the modification of the exclusion clause. He revealed his frustration in a letter to San Francisco businessman Robert Lynch:

> It may interest you to know that prominent church leaders have charged me with not being sufficiently aggressive! They are saying that I am so dominated by timid and conservative interests as not to be competent to do what now needs to be done![88]

Thus, Gulick was forced to take a delicately balanced stand on the modification movement. He declared, "We shall continue our quiet educational work to put the facts before the American people and to enlist, as members of our Committee, men and women of influence in all parts of the country."[89] He may have hoped that by withdrawing his political campaign to place Japan on a quota basis, the anti-Japanese counterfactions would become less aggressive. If that was the case, he would quickly learn how wrong he was.

FOUR

The Long Quiet Battle

The FCCCA's decision to retreat from the immigration quota campaign did not produce the expected results. The McClatchy faction had taken Gulick's educational campaign very seriously, and they refused to acknowledge the policy shift of the FCCCA as a retreat.[1] They weren't the only ones. The *Sacramento Bee* continued to criticize the FCCCA, insisting that it should stop disturbing U.S.-Japanese relations.[2] The NSGW continued to label the FCCCA as "the government of Japan's main propaganda agent" in the United States.[3]

The FCCCA tried to dispel misunderstandings about its policies regarding the Japanese immigration problem. Its 1925 annual report attempted to counter the allegations that it was "carrying on a nationwide campaign to approach Congress."[4] The organization also distributed a policy statement, in which it flatly denied that it was "carrying forward a political campaign . . . to bring Japanese immigration under the quota." However, even this statement, specifically written to dispel misunderstanding, reiterated that the Japanese regarded the immigration law as "a violation of international courtesy" and that the FCCCA would exercise "an educational campaign."[5]

The split within the FCCCA on this issue contributed to the confusion. The statement did not achieve its goals, partly because it was contradicted by a pamphlet the FCCCA had distributed at its Detroit convention, which stated that there was "no better solution . . . than the application . . . of the quota law," and partly because the distinction it made between the "political" and the "educational" campaigns was confusing.[6] Clearly, the activities of the FCCCA were not well-coordinated regarding the issue. For its part, the CJIC felt that "the situation called for renewed efforts in maintaining the exclusion measure,"[7] and McClatchy continued his attacks, warning his followers about the FCCCA's intentions and reminding them of "its determination . . . to press its campaign to secure public support for a demand on Congress for an immigration quota for the Japanese."[8] The *Sacramento Bee* attributed the resurgence of the anti-Japanese movements to the activities of the anti-exclusionists, chiefly clergymen, arguing that "if sentimental Americans will only cease their agitation . . . it will be only a few years until the whole matter is forgotten and the relations between America and Japan become as cordial as they were."[9] The *Grizzly Bear* opined that the missionaries sought to allow the Japanese to "complete their 'peaceful invasion'" of the Pacific Coast in order to improve their own image in Japan, and thus to allow "the Church Federation [to] continue its missionary endeavors in Japan."[10] The *Honolulu Star-Bulletin* commented that the Gulick–Wickersham movement was counterproductive since it was unimaginable that Congress would repeal the law in the near future, and that the only possible reaction the movement could elicit would be counterattacks from the anti-Japanese factions. The newspaper further noted that because Gulick and Wickersham acted through a sizable organization, they gave the Japanese the false impression that there was a great movement demanding repeal of the immigration law. This editorial argued that without Gulick and Wickersham, the exclusion clause would have long before ceased to be a problem.[11]

A reference by Shidehara to the immigration issue in the Imperial Diet in the beginning of 1926 received some negative attention in the United States. Shidehara's speech had contained nothing radical; he had simply reiterated his regret that the immigration issue had not yet been resolved, and he acknowledged that mutual understanding between the countries was increasing.[12] However, the *Sacramento Bee* reported that Shidehara "flay[ed]" the immigration law,[13] and the *Sacramento Union* accused Shidehara of attacking America by criticizing "a domestic statute" whose "exclusive purpose is protection of the American Republic."[14]

By this time, the controversy over the Japanese immigration quota had been reduced to a confrontation between Gulick and McClatchy, since most other parties had dropped the issue. The Hearst newspapers, which had previously devoted considerable space to anti-Japanese articles, now rarely reported on the issue because William Randolph Hearst judged that the Japanese immigration question was no longer attracting his readers' attention.[15]

While McClatchy regarded the FCCCA as an enemy and concentrated on the CJIC response, Gulick naively believed that he and McClatchy might reach a mutual understanding on the Japanese immigration question. Presuming that it would be beneficial to exchange views with McClatchy and with clergymen on the Pacific Coast, Gulick proposed a meeting with McClatchy through George Gleason of Los Angeles. However, McClatchy used Gulick's efforts as fodder for anti-Japanese propaganda.[16]

Gulick later abandoned the idea of meeting with McClatchy, but he still wanted to discuss the "Campaign of Education" with clergymen in California, although several people, concerned about the possible repercussions of his visit, tried to deter him. Dr. Harvey H. Guy informed Gulick that members of the Japanese Relations Committee of the San Francisco Chamber of Commerce feared that his visit would provoke countermovements. Toshihiko Taketomi, the consul general in San Francisco, fearing that Gulick's visit would interfere with other efforts to promote cordial relations between the United States and Japan, informed Gulick that the Church Federation in San Francisco had neither the will nor the resources to launch an education campaign. Discouraged, Gulick cancelled his planned visit to California.[17]

Even though his activities had clearly provoked countermeasures from the McClatchy faction, it seemed that Gulick had not fully learned his lesson. In May of 1926, he released a statement on the Japanese immigration issue, in which although he did not question the basic principle of Asiatic exclusion, he nonetheless labeled the 1924 law as "discourteous" and once again recommended that "an amendment to this law be secured whereby China, Japan and India shall . . . be placed under the quota."[18]

Eventually, both the McClatchy and the Gulick factions suffered from a growing indifference toward their activities among erstwhile supporters. Although Gulick occasionally published anti-exclusion information, he had difficulty raising funds[19] and was forced to ask the members of the NCAJR for a contribution, even though he had "definitely stated that there were no membership dues, nor financial obligations" when he organized this group.[20]

The CJIC also had a hard time raising funds in 1926, with the State Grange discontinuing its financial contributions and the State Federation of Labor contributing a smaller amount than it had in 1925. A concerned McClatchy wrote that "some means should be found for meeting the emergency."[21]

At the same time, Japan was generally calm about the immigration issue. Ambassador Charles MacVeagh reported that "the second anniversary . . . passed without incident."[22] Nevertheless, the calm elapse of time did not necessarily mean that the Japanese had become more tolerant of Japanese exclusion. Although the issue was not mentioned as often as it had been in 1924, Japanese indignation remained deep-seated and occasionally rose to the surface. In Osaka, Kyokutō Renmei Kyōkai was still active in anti-American protests. It distributed anti-American brochures and also small flags on which slogans such as "The anti-Japanese law is against humanity and justice" and "The unity of Asian peoples is a pressing need" were written. About eighteen hundred people were organized by this association on July 2 at Tennōji, Osaka, to protest.[23] The *Osaka Mainichi* published an article entitled "Second Anniversary of Anti-Japanese Law in America," which observed that "the unpleasant memory of the day will not leave the minds of the Japanese, at least for some time yet to come."[24] The *Gaikō Jihō* took a more radical position, calling the immigration law an astonishing declaration which tried to suffocate the have-not nations of the world. The author of this article further stated that in the worst case he was ready to express "resolution" and "righteous indignation characteristic of the Japanese."[25]

While the Gulick–Wickersham movement refrained from conspicuous activities in the late summer of 1926, some intellectuals continued to argue for a Japanese immigration quota, emphasizing the law's effect on U.S.-Japanese relations. At the Institute of Politics, Harry A. Garfield, president of Williams College and the chairman of the Institute, who had recently returned from Japan, said that the United States had already "blundered" in the Pacific by enacting the immigration law. Garfield argued that in order to avoid war in the Pacific, it would be wise to place Japan on a quota system as soon as possible.[26] In the *New York Times*, Merle Davis, secretary-general of the IPR, noted that the immigration law of 1924 was "accepted with outward calm but with inward heart-burning and revolt."[27] Felix Morley, a member of the editorial staff of the *Baltimore Sun*, who had just returned from the Far East, judged that "the passage of this act . . . has been a severe blow to the justified self-esteem of Japan and has unquestionably done lasting injury to America's reputation in Japan."[28]

Gulick, now detached from pro-quota activities, had gotten involved in "the Doll Project," in which more than one thousand American dolls were to be collected to give to Japanese children as gifts. The stated purpose of the project was to improve overall U.S.-Japanese relations, and the specific issue of immigration was never officially mentioned. Concerned about the negative reverberations that his pro-quota campaign had caused, Gulick wrote to Eiichi Shibusawa, the Japanese business tycoon, that it was "unwise to make any very vigorous campaign in favor of placing Japanese immigration under the quota." However, it was clear that the immigration issue was on the minds of the people engaged in the doll project, especially Gulick, who at the same time wrote to Eiichi Shibusawa about his hopes that the project would contribute to cordial U.S.-Japanese relations and eventually solve the immigration issue. He assured Shibusawa that the absence of an aggressive pro-quota campaign in the United States did not mean that his faction was "abolishing [its] educational campaign," and he emphasized, for the benefit of internationalist Japanese, that strong pro-quota opinions still existed in the United States.[29] The American dolls were welcomed enthusiastically in Japan, a fact reported frequently in Japanese newspapers.[30] These articles likely gave the Japanese the impression that the United States had become much more cordial toward Japan than it had been in 1924 when the immigration law was enacted. Schoolchildren in Japan returned the favor by sending Japanese dolls to their American counterparts.

Not all pro-quota supporters embraced the doll project. Henry Atkinson, general secretary of the Church Peace Union, was apprehensive about the project, writing that "in such a serious crisis it seems to me to ask the churches and the League of Women Voters, peace societies and others, to collect a fund to buy dolls to send to Japan is adding insult to injury and belittling the whole cause that [they] represent," and he even felt "ashamed to have my name go out in a letter head connected with such a campaign as this."[31] American diplomats regarded the project as an annoyance. As Assistant Secretary of State William Castle wrote,

> I wish the Federal Council of Churches had never sent their gift of dolls to Japan because the Japanese were sure to respond and it is very difficult for

us to keep out of the picture officially. All the [Japanese] Ambassador wants is to have Mrs. Coolidge see the dolls. . . . I do not quite see how she can graciously refuse to do it.[32]

In the end, Mrs. Coolidge decided not to receive the dolls, and Castle "had to write the Ambassador a letter as pleasant as possible on that subject." For Castle, the doll project represented yet another example of Gulick's imprudent actions, which were unlikely to improve the situation and actually had the potential to aggravate it.[33]

Meanwhile, the supporting organizations of the CJIC, with the exception of the California State Grange, continued to express their approval of the existing immigration law. Claiming that the existing immigration policy was still under threat from "religious organizations," the 1926 convention of the California Department of the American Legion passed yet another resolution supporting it.[34] The September issue of the *Grizzly Bear* published an address delivered by Congressman Albert Johnson of Washington State, in which he argued that Americans were "determined to keep America American by admitting fewer and better of what the Old World has to offer."[35]

Labor concentrated its attack on the FCCCA. *Organized Labor* argued that Japan and its American friends wanted a quota for Japan because they wanted "to establish a precedent which can be enlarged in later years."[36] The convention of the California State Federation of Labor at Oakland, meanwhile, passed the following resolution:

> Whereas, The Federal Council of Churches of Christ in America has prosecuted for a year and is still prosecuting a nationwide campaign for demand upon Congress to admit Japan to quota in 1927 . . . be it
>   Resolved, That the delegate from this Federation to the Detroit convention of the American Federation of Labor be . . . instructed to introduce and use all efforts to secure adoption . . . of a resolution instructing the officers . . . to forcibly present to Congress . . . protest against any modification of the Federal law excluding aliens ineligible to citizenship.[37]

The national convention of the American Federation of Labor endorsed the resolution of its California branch and directed its executive committee to present the protest to Congress.[38]

Even into the fall of 1926, the CJIC continued to believe that the FCCCA had not changed its policy concerning the Japanese immigration issue, as is clear from a CJIC report which noted: "Notwithstanding the attitude of many churchmen in California as to the undesirability of the Gulick policy of forcing the Japanese exclusion matter upon the attention of Congress for revision, the Federal Council . . . is apparently determined to follow his lead." This report was based on a brief reference to the immigration issue in *International Goodwill.*[39]

The McClatchy faction was still attacking the FCCCA as 1926 moved into 1927. In November, McClatchy had reported that "there is no evidence that the leaders of the Federal Council have any intention of abandoning the aggressive policy inspired by Dr. Gulick."[40] The December issue of the *Grizzly Bear* argued that the FCCCA was "pro-Jap and it would sacrifice any interest of the United States to please mikado-worshiping Japs."[41] The January issue urged American churchmen to "clean up their Federal Church by clearing out Sidney L. Gulick, George Wickersham and the other pro-Japs who dominate there."[42] When Paul Scharrenberg surveyed American immigration policy in a speech at the Institute of International Relations at Riverside, California, he concluded by criticizing the clergymen: "Let us pray that the churchmen who have stirred up resentment in Japan against our country's immigration laws will learn to see the error of their ways."[43]

Pro-quota forces continued to publicize the ill-feeling toward the immigration law harbored by Japanese. David S. Spencer, a missionary of the Methodist Episcopal Church in Japan, wrote, "Japan [is] still hurt in spirit because of the Oriental immigration exclusion act." Arguing for modification of the exclusion clause from an international peace perspective, he continued: "The fundamental wrong [the law] did was . . . the destroying of old confidence in America, and in her essential justice."[44] Other anti-exclusion organizations also argued for change in the law mainly from the viewpoint of promoting international peace. The NCAJR distributed a pamphlet entitled *Toward an Understanding of Japan,* which warned of the dangerous nature of the immigration law. The pamphlet stated that "alienation from an old friend, the United States, [has] made it imperative for Japan to turn to China, Russia, or wherever possible," but concluded that "with goodwill on both sides, there is nothing in the relations of the two countries that cannot be adjusted peacefully."[45] In its anti-exclusion movement, the American Friends Service Committee (AFSC) asked for cooperation from influential politicians.[46] In its pamphlet, *Message to the American People on Japan*, the AFSC argued that Japan was "the only Asiatic country that has voluntarily and effectively 'set her house in order' on modern and occidental lines," and that "the Oriental exclusion act, which brings resentment to the boiling point, should be repealed." It recommended that "all means should be used to bring back the old friendship between Japan and the United States."[47]

In early 1927, in line with the policies of its supporting organizations, the CJIC expanded its activities to encompass the issues of Mexican immigration and Filipino immigration, thus making Japanese immigration only one of several issues addressed by this organization. Since countries of the Western Hemisphere, as well as the Philippine Islands, had been exempted from the 1924 exclusion clause, immigrants from those areas continued to arrive after 1924. Although their absolute numbers did not increase rapidly, their numbers relative to total immigration did, and they therefore became much more conspicuous than before. The CJIC declared, "The question of Mexican immigration is really within the scope of the activities of this committee," and also advised Congressman Albert Johnson of the danger of "the rapidly increasing immigration of Filipinos."[48]

Although the CJIC had become relatively less active in the anti-Japanese movement, it did not drop the Japanese immigration question entirely. Among the supporting organizations of the CJIC, the NSGW was still the most interested in the issue of Japanese exclusion. The April 1927 edition of the *Grizzly Bear* cautioned that the Japanese and Chinese might act together against the United States because both were angry at U.S. immigration policy, and suggested that the course of action the United States should take was not the elimination of the exclusion clause, but rather the elimination of pacifism.[49] The May issue published an anti-quota article, by the secretary of the Los Angeles County Anti-Asiatic Association, which proposed that in order to stop the "sweeping away of all barriers against Oriental immigration," Americans should "reverse . . . [the] present onward march in the direction of pacifism and sentimental sympathy with alien and enemy races."[50]

The CJIC constantly monitored the opinions of anti-exclusion figures such as Dr. Harvey H. Guy, an activist in the missionary education movement in California, and Kyūtarō Abiko, a leader of Japanese immigrants there.[51] The CJIC also attached greater importance to the views of the IPR, telling its San Francisco delegates that anti-Japanese "feeling on the part of the whites will entirely disappear . . . unless kept alive by efforts of the Japanese to defeat the law or by the agitation of their Church friends."[52]

The second conference of the IPR was held in Honolulu, from July 15 to 29, 1927, and immigration was one of the major issues discussed. While the Japanese Foreign Ministry was never eager to rehash the exclusion issue, the private sector was determined to keep the issue alive. Japanese delegates to the conference once again expressed deep-rooted resentment of the exclusion clause among the Japanese. Despite the suggestion by Junnosuke Inoue, chairman of the board of directors of the Japanese branch of the IPR, that it was not necessary to bring up the immigration issue, the Japanese delegates, following the advice of Eiichi Shibusawa, the Japanese business tycoon, and Yūsuke Tsurumi, a famous writer and a member of the Lower House, decided to discuss it anyway.[53] In his opening address, Masatarō Sawayanagi, former president of Kyoto Imperial University and a member of Japan's House of Peers, attacked the 1924 immigration law, saying that his government did not question the right of the United States to control immigration but did question "the right of enacting discriminatory laws on the basis of race." He also expressed his hope that "the natural right of all humankind to share the resources of the world on some equitable basis and to enjoy the freedom of movement and residence will be recognized by the thinking leaders of all progressive lands."[54] For Sawayanagi, then, emigration was an important vehicle for Japan to pursue peaceful expansion within the framework of the "Washington Conference System."

Some American delegates were amenable to modification of the immigration law. Ray Lyman Wilbur, president of Stanford University, even stated, "There is sound reason for the hope that the quota basis may eventually be extended to the inhabitants of all countries, including those of Asia."[55] But two American delegates from California firmly opposed bringing Japan into the quota system. Paul Scharrenberg and Chester Rowell argued that Japan would not be satisfied with an immigration quota and would only demand more, such as the right of naturalization.[56] Although most American delegates favored modification, they were nevertheless reluctant to reconsider the immigration issue. The conference proceedings suggest that they feared that giving Japan an immigration quota "would also open the way for China and other Asiatic countries to come under the quota." The overall view of the Americans was that "the time was probably not yet ripe for such a step," and that "failure would entail disappointment and set back the possibility of solution almost indefinitely." Thus, they believed that an intervening period should be used "to promote better understanding of attitudes and interests on both sides and allow the bitterness of controversy to die down."[57]

Although no concrete measures were adopted by the conference, there was one noteworthy incident: Paul Scharrenberg announced that if Japan promised not to protest the land laws and naturalization laws, he would not oppose placing Japan on a quota system.[58] The reasons for his change in opinion are unclear, but the statement came in the form of a casual comment to some of the Japanese delegates, and he committed himself to nothing concrete. When Scharrenberg returned to California, he did not mention this incident but rather emphasized how greatly he had contributed to the cause of Asian exclusion. At a subsequent meeting of the CJIC, he was critical of the general "apologetic attitude" concerning the exclusion clause taken by many American delegates.[59] The August 13, 1927, issue of *Organized Labor* published an article which described how Scharrenberg had defended the exclusion policy at the IPR.[60] Scharrenberg himself wrote an article for the *Labor Clarion* in which he rejected Sawayanagi's point of view and criticized the American delegates to the conference because they "closed their eyes to the sinister truth that Asia is like an overflowing human ocean, always menacing and threatening with inundation the less crowded parts of the world."[61] This should have left little doubt as to Scharrenberg's true views, but the Japanese still placed their hopes on his offhand pro-quota remark.

Discussions at the IPR were widely reported in newspapers. In the eastern United States, the press generally lauded the anti-exclusion attitudes of the American delegates and expressed the hope that public sympathy would eventually embrace an anti-exclusion cause. Though the *New York Times* admitted that the superficial calm in the United States did not necessarily mean there was no anti-Asian feeling, it believed that the discontinuance of Japanese immigration did "presage a new era when those Americans who [have] been most bitterly anti-Oriental [will] consider the problem in a more dispassionate light."[62] On the other hand, exclusionist newspapers in the West attacked the conference's quota supporters. The *San Francisco*

Examiner criticized the Japanese delegates in an article entitled "Japs Want Immigration Ban Ended" and published the opinions of those American delegates who supported the ban.[63] The *Sacramento Bee* argued that since the IPR was an unofficial organization, their "discussion does not mean anything." The *Bee* also suggested that the IPR was ineffective because it tried to mix "a too great idealism with hard facts," and it concluded that "the thing has been settled in the only way it can be settled."[64]

In the summer of 1927, Gulick finally traveled to the West Coast to "learn of the experiences and opinions of Americans and Japanese regarding the problems and conditions of the Japanese." He made "addresses in various places and before various organizations," at the same time making every effort to avoid arousing the anti-Japanese faction in California. Even when he delivered an address before the Immigration Section of the Commonwealth Club, he avoided all references to the exclusion issue. Partly because of his cautiousness and partly because of decreased interest in this issue, the CJIC did not attack him, but only monitored his activities.[65]

During his stay, Gulick noted the confusion that still existed between the FCCCA's former campaign to urge Congress to give Japan a quota and the Gulick faction's continuing educational campaign. He reemphasized that the FCCCA and NCAJR had ceased their attempts to influence Congress and were now focused exclusively on their "educational programs."[66]

When he returned to the East Coast, Gulick submitted a report on his trip to the NCAJR and the FCCCA. While he judged that "anti-Japanese agitation has ceased," he could find "little evidence of any real change [in anti-Japanese prejudice]." Finding "no convincing evidence of any material change in the attitude of California as a whole," he concluded that "those who actively advocated [the law of 1924] are still its strong supporters."[67] The pro-quota faction would need additional momentum to boost its movement.

America's churchmen, however, could not agree on tactics regarding the Japanese issue. At a luncheon to entertain forty Japanese students in New York, the Reverend Samuel McCrea Cavert, general secretary of the FCCCA, preached: "An increase in the acquaintance of East and West with each other will bring about a day when Americans will be heartily ashamed of themselves for having discriminated against Japan in their immigration policies."[68] But not all church organizations followed the policy of conducting an educational campaign. At the Southern California Conference of the

Methodist Episcopal Church, lay members who did not like the idea of the church intervening in political affairs "defeated a resolution to memorialize the general conference at its quadrennial session in Kansas City next May, to protest against Japanese immigration restriction."[69]

Probably because he judged that the pro-quota movement had no hope of success, McClatchy left for Europe for nine months, entrusting the activities of the CJIC to the other executive members, James Fisk, U. S. Webb, James Phelan, and Paul Scharrenberg. Even in Europe, however, he kept an eye on the group's anti-exclusion activities through his secretary in San Francisco.[70] During McClatchy's absence, constituent organizations of the CJIC continued to oppose granting the Japanese a quota, while also monitoring immigration from other areas, particularly the Philippines and Mexico. Fearing the new threat these immigrants posed and finding the Japanese immigration issue less and less of an attention-grabber, the CJIC chose new targets for the anti-immigration movements that were the group's livelihood. Each of the four supporting organizations of the CJIC again took an individual approach. At the ninth annual convention of the California Department of the American Legion, a resolution supporting the existing immigration law was once again passed, but for the first time the problem of Mexican immigration was also discussed. The delegates decided that the issue required further study since Mexican immigrants provided Californian farmers needed cheap labor.[71] The convention of the California State Federation of Labor issued a statement to the effect that "the Japanese exclusion issue is a settled fact" and that "it is clearly the duty of present generation Californians to resist any effort to open the gates to . . . Asiatics." That group also expressed an opinion about Mexicans and Filipinos, stating that "immediate steps ought to be taken by the American Federation of Labor to restrict Filipino and Mexican immigration."[72] The California Federation favored restricting Filipinos because it believed future immigration from the Philippines would fall off dramatically with the arrival of Filipino independence.[73] The *Grizzly Bear* devoted a lot of space that year to Mexican immigration, arguing, "The Mexicans' coming should be stopped."[74]

In 1927, there were a few other shifts in perspectives on the Japanese immigration question, the most important of which was a turnaround on the part of one major newspaper in the United States. On November 4 the *Chicago Daily Tribune*, which had supported the anti-Japanese immigration clause, suddenly reversed course and published an article supporting a quota for Japan. The piece urged Congress to provide "a Japanese quota on exactly the same basis as other nations receive quotas," arguing that the number of Japanese admitted under a quota would be "so small as to be utterly negligible from the standpoint of racial purity," yet "large enough to end forever one of the principal sources of ill feeling between this country and Japan." It also assailed anti-quota Californians, arguing that their protests were "equivalent to a confession that one Japanese immigrant [is] a menace to 15,000 and more California white men."[75]

Though this shift in opinion by one of America's largest newspapers came as a surprise, the paper had been leaning in that direction at least since August 1927, when it published an article by its correspondent in Japan, Roderick Matheson, suggesting that Japanese expansion into Manchuria was justifiable, and was better for the area than rule by China or the Soviet Union. Matheson had written, "Japan needs an outlet for her population and she would bring order and modern progress to Manchuria."[76] On September 7, Matheson again reminded readers that the Japanese were still hurt by the immigration law of 1924.[77]

This paper's shift was warmly received in Japan. The *Tokyo Asahi* reported on the *Tribune*'s pro-quota article and judged that American public opinion had turned to favor Japan.[78] On the other hand, the anti-quota faction in California quickly criticized the Chicago paper. Immediately after Chester Rowell informed members of the CJIC about the article, the *Fresno Bee*, a newspaper under McClatchy's influence, wrote that the *Chicago Tribune* was "badly mistaken," and stated that "no one should be admitted to the United States who cannot become a citizen."[79]

The *Tribune* continued to advocate a quota for Japan, publishing articles in the issues of February 6 and April 21, 1928, entitled "Give Japan a Quota" and "The Just, Courteous Thing to Japan," respectively.[80] The Japanese government was at a loss to explain the paper's change of heart. The move of the Japanese Consulate into a building owned by the *Tribune*, combined with a general improvement in the public image of Japan, especially outside of the West Coast, may have helped turn the *Tribune* pro-quota.[81] Regardless of the reason, this opinion shift by one of the most influential newspapers in the United States gave pro-quota forces a much-needed boost.

In McClatchy's absence, George Burns, a former state senator in Massachusetts, represented the CJIC at the Institute of International Politics at Riverside, California. According to the *Grizzly Bear*, Burns "fired some hot shot among the Japists," saying that "the exclusion of the yellow races was the greatest move the country ever made to avoid international and internal entanglements."[82] Upon learning that vacancies on the House Immigration Committee would occur, members of the CJIC were quick to take action. Phelan wired the Chairman of the House Committee on Committees, expressing his view that "Japanese intrigue never sleeps" and urging him to "put on strong restrictionist members for patriotic reasons."[83] Soon thereafter, Congressman Albert Johnson informed the CJIC that he thought the new members on his committee were "all right" on immigration issues.[84]

The McClatchy faction reacted strongly whenever significant incidents detrimental to the anti-quota cause occurred, but as time went on that happened less and less because of declining public interest. The *Christian Century* noted that California interest in the Japanese question was "abating."[85] Kimpei Sheba [*sic*], a Japanese newspaperman who had been trained in the United States, wrote that the Japanese in San Francisco were not irritated by the exclusion law at all.[86] And when Prime Minister Giichi Tanaka expressed his regret over the immigration law, the *San Francisco Examiner* quoted him without any criticism.[87]

By early 1928, the main targets of the CJIC's efforts were Mexicans and Filipinos. This shift revealed differences of opinion among the CJIC's supporting organizations. Both the California Department of the American Legion and the California Grange withheld their support for a CJIC resolution that "urge[d] . . . that all persons ineligible to citizenship . . . including those from Mexico and the Philippines, be excluded from the territory of the United States." The Legion had been studying the issue since the previous year and wanted to avoid taking any action on Mexican immigration; the Grange simply chose not to ratify the resolution.[88] Unlike Japanese immigrants, who became land-owning farming competitors, Mexican and Filipino immigrants served as valuable manual labor for the California economy. Therefore, some interest groups that opposed Japanese immigration were less adamant about immigrants from Mexico or the Philippines.

The Japanese consul general of San Francisco interpreted the growing indifference to the Japanese immigration issue among anti-quota forces there to mean that public opinion concerning Japan was generally improving. He noted in a report to Tokyo that the *San Francisco Chronicle* and *Bulletin* were generally pro-Japan in their coverage, and that the *Examiner* had not recently published any anti-Japanese articles. He also noted that, increasingly, educated people regarded the immigration law as too radical, and that the Scharrenberg faction was now concentrating on the Mexican issue.[89]

The CJIC now only responded to attacks on its positions concerning Japanese immigration when they appeared in the major media. When Henry S. Pritchett, president of the Carnegie Foundation for the Advancement of Teaching, argued at the IPR and in a series of private meetings that the exclusion of the Japanese had not been the result of "the trend of national thought" but rather was the work of local Californian forces, the CJIC largely ignored him because his statements were not publicized.[90] However, when other remarks of Prichett's were published in *Scribner's Magazine*, the CJIC leapt into action. In the *Scribner's* piece, Pritchett said that the efforts of the U.S. president and the secretary of state to stop Japanese immigration without antagonizing Japan "were defeated by a few politicians, of whom those from the State of California were the most active."[91] Scharrenberg's response was to circulate a new pamphlet, in which he criticized Pritchett, insisting that "the demand for effective Japanese exclusion came from the common people," and that the politicians whom Pritchett attacked did indeed represent those people.[92] Furthermore, in a speech delivered in Sacramento, Scharrenberg declared, "To accept . . . the suggestion to remove all barriers to mankind's movement would be suicidal to the white race."[93] These aggressive anti-Japanese remarks were inconsistent with the views he had expressed at the IPR meeting the previous year, and such inconsistency would continue to characterize Scharrenberg's opinions on the immigration question.

Even with the Gulick faction's relative silence, anti-exclusion sentiment began to strengthen around the country, partly due to a surge of enthusiasm for international peace that developed in connection with the proposed Kellogg–Briand peace treaty. Internationalists and clergymen remained most eloquent in support of the pro-quota cause. Professor Ernest W. Clement of Syracuse University criticized the exclusion act because of its psychological effects on the Japanese.[94] The 1928 convention of the Methodist Episcopal pastors at Kansas City requested the cooperation of all Christians in repealing the exclusion clause.[95] Nicholas Murray Butler, the president of Columbia University, declared at the annual meeting of the trustees of the Carnegie Endowment for International Peace that Japan should be given an immigration quota.[96] The Reverand C. Everett Wagner maintained that America should repeal the Japanese exclusion clause "in return for [Japan's] signing the [Kellogg–Briand] treaty." Wagner also pointed out the difficulty for the Japanese in distinguishing between Americans who supported exclusion and missionaries who were concerned with human welfare, and he hoped that the next Congress would "remove this Japanese exclusion act out of fairness and justice to that nation and gratitude for signing the anti-war pact."[97] Professor Blakeslee continued to take a serious view of the Japanese immigration question. In a report on his trip to Japan as a visiting Carnegie professor, he criticized the exclusion clause, mentioning the immigration issue as one which "particularly affect[s] the Japanese attitude toward America," and expressing his observation of the "sense of wrong and humiliation which [the law] bore in the minds of the students" and occasionally even in the minds of intellectuals, including college professors.[98] Although pro-quota advocates viewed the issue from disparate perspectives, they all agreed that the exclusion clause had a harmful effect on international peace.

After his return to the United States from Europe, it soon became apparent that McClatchy had not lost his interest in the Japanese immigration issue. On June 2, 1928, he appeared before the House Immigration Committee to oppose placing Japan on the quota system, arguing that giving Japan a quota would mean "discriminating against the other Asian races."[99] He also wrote to many quota supporters, including Nicholas M. Butler and even Secretary of State Kellogg, asking them to remain strong in their support of his cause.[100]

When the U.S. ambassador to Japan, Charles MacVeagh, reportedly said that "granting the Japanese a nominal immigration quota . . . would soothe their resentment over the Exclusion act," McClatchy responded quickly.[101] He sent MacVeagh information on the issue prepared by the CJIC and asked him to make clear his view on this question.[102] MacVeagh backed off; in his response to McClatchy, he said that "as an officer of the United States," he had never taken any action in opposition to existing laws.[103]

In early July, as in previous years on the anniversary of the law's implementation, reporting of activities related to the exclusion law increased in

Japanese newspapers and journals. The July 1 issue of the *Gaikō Jihō* argued that unless the exclusion clause was modified, the honor of the Japanese would never be restored.[104] The *Tokyo Asahi* published an article entitled "an unpleasant anniversary" and expressed its hope for modification of the immigration law in the near future.[105] A mass meeting was organized by Kyokutō Renmei Kyōkai, which demanded "the withdrawal of [the immigration] law" and the ending of race discrimination.[106] Probably because American diplomats in Japan were by now accustomed to such protests, Edwin L. Neville, the chargé d'affaires, reported that the "exclusion question does not now seem to evoke the emotions that it once did," and that he was "encouraged to think that the possibility of the exclusion issue leading to a break between the two countries is correspondingly becoming more remote," though he admitted that the immigration law was "a constant factor in [the American] relation with Japan."[107]

But Japanese acceptance of the law was not by any means universal. Kazushige Ugaki, an army leader throughout the interwar years, believed that American exclusionist attitudes made a Japanese–American war unavoidable. He wrote in his diary around this time: "As long as North America and Australia stick to the idea that they make it the basic principle of national life to secure the white man's land by excluding non-white immigrants, I believe that causing a storm in the future will be unavoidable."[108] However, in the entry for the following day, Ugaki reversed his position and insisted on the impossibility of a war, noting instead that it was desirable to establish a profound mutual understanding between Americans and Japanese in order to avoid war.[109]

As has been noted, with less interest in the Japanese immigration issue, the CJIC member organizations began to focus on other issues of individual interest. In particular, labor now targeted immigrants from Mexico and the Philippines. *Organized Labor* repeatedly publicized the danger represented by these immigrants, and Paul Scharrenberg wrote an article, entitled "Exclude the Filipinos!" for the May 12, 1928 issue.[110] In a subsequent article, Scharrenberg declared that although "the influx of Chinese and Japanese has been effectively stopped," labor must continue its fight in order to stem "the third Asiatic invasion of California" by the Filipinos and also to place Mexicans under the quota.[111] Scharrenberg's warnings about the menace of the Mexicans and Filipinos were carried by McClatchy newspapers such as the *Sacramento Bee*.[112] The California Grange, on the other hand, needed the cheap labor of Mexican immigrants as farmhands. They did not view the threat of Mexican and Filipino immigrants in such dire terms. Prompted by labor interests in the American Southwest, the first bill that would have applied a quota to Mexico was introduced in the House Immigration Committee in 1926. The issue of Mexican immigration would continue to be raised until it was eventually resolved through administrative measures.[113] The first bill to exclude Filipinos was introduced by a California representative who was firmly supported by California labor, and that movement would continued until, in 1934, a quota of fifty immigrants per year was applied to the Philippine Islands.[114]

McClatchy continued to engage himself in revitalizing the anti-quota movement. He attended the twenty-ninth annual convention of the California State Federation of Labor, held in Sacramento in 1928, where he spoke to the delegates about "the past three years' activities" of the CJIC. He warned that "Japan is no ordinary adversary," and he also warned of the threat of the campaign by the FCCCA. His warnings were unconvincing, however, as the FCCCA had ceased to be active, particularly in California, and anyway the California State Federation considered the Japanese immigration issue to be settled.[115] The American Federation of Labor, at its annual convention in New Orleans, also shifted its focus towards barring immigration from Mexico and the Philippines.[116]

In September 1928, McClatchy learned that the executive committee of the California State Grange had passed a resolution authorizing the organization's withdrawal from the CJIC.[117] Its reasons were not clear. The State Grange was composed of farmers, most of whom needed cheap labor from Mexico, so it may have been the case that the organization considered that its interests now conflicted with those of the CJIC, especially since another member organization, the California State Federation of Labor, strongly opposed immigration from Mexico. The absence of the perceived menace of Japanese immigration may also have contributed to this decision. The Grange's withdrawal from the CJIC must have dealt a considerable blow to McClatchy, who repeatedly wrote to George R. Harrison, the state grange master, urging him to stay with the CJIC. McClatchy was unable to convince Harrison to reverse his decision, however.[118]

Around this time, Gulick was refraining from conspicuous anti-exclusion activities; indeed, he had learned from his past experiences. When asked for his comments on McClatchy's speech given before the House Immigration Committee, Gulick did not respond, fearing that any answer he might give would be used by McClatchy, as his previous remarks had been three years before. However, his silence did not mean that he had lost interest in the immigration issue. He urged the acting Japanese ambassador to the United States, Setsuzō Sawada, to encourage Japan to keep reminding Americans that the Japanese had not forgotten the issue.[119]

Japanese diplomats were not necessarily standing idly by. They gave speeches concerning the immigration question, explaining the Japanese side of the issue. Toshihiko Taketomi, the consul general at San Francisco, attended the Institute of International Relations at Riverside and explained the Japanese population problem.[120] Minoru Iino, attaché at the consulate in San Francisco, was also an active speaker; he criticized the discriminatory nature of the immigration law in a speech at Mills College and argued for a quota.[121]

Many speakers, Japanese and American alike, expressed pro-quota views throughout late 1928.[122] The most notable of these was Harry Chandler, owner of the *Los Angeles Times*, who expressed the view that an immigration law which restricted a particular nation was unfair and that a solution mutually satisfactory to the United States and Japan should be reached. Although he did not propose anything concrete, the expression of a pro-quota view at a semi-public meeting by the owner of the largest newspaper in Los Angeles was a boon for quota supporters.[123]

Although general concern about the Japanese immigration issue had decreased, it was nevertheless evident that many prominent figures were coming around to the quota argument. Even without benefit of the Gulick faction's conspicuous pro-quota activities, quite a few eminent people were raising their voices in support of the pro-quota cause. With this slow but steady stream of pro-quota support, from newspapers and influential figures alike, support for McClatchy's position began to erode. Toward the end of 1928, McClatchy had to admit that his opponents on the Japanese immigration issue were "steadily gain[ing] a psychological advantage," and he judged that "it perhaps is good diplomacy . . . to be temporarily silent unless [the CJIC] are directly challenged for [their] views [on the Japanese question]."[124] When Prime Minister Tanaka spoke about the immigration law before Japan's Imperial Diet, the McClatchy faction only made a brief mention of it.[125]

However, anti-exclusion forces also had difficulty in finding a way out of the standstill. When, at a convention of the Episcopal Church in Washington, D.C., Wickersham tried to pass a resolution to give Japan a quota, it was rejected by California delegates, who complained that they had not gathered to discuss political matters.[126]

Although pro-quota voices were surely on the rise, both the McClatchy and Gulick factions had reached an impasse by the beginning of 1929. While the McClatchy faction could not arouse the fear of Japanese immigration without the anti-exclusion movement as a target, the education campaign by the Gulick faction had difficulty gaining enough momentum to launch another pro-quota movement because of the lack of a strong catalyst and because of a general indifference toward the Japanese immigration issue.

PART II

The Business Initiative

FIVE

New Movements from the Pacific Coast

Just as the clergy were winding down their campaigns in favor of quotas for Japanese immigrants, another new pro-quota force began to be heard. The movement to modify the immigration law gained new impetus from West Coast businessmen engaged in trade with Japan. The new movement originated in two distinct areas—in California, especially around the Bay Area, where pro-Japanese forces dated back to before 1924, and in the Northwest, where the livelihood of the business community often depended upon trade with Japan, particularly on exports of forestry products. The central figure of the new movement was Wallace M. Alexander of the San Francisco Chamber of Commerce. He was born in Hawaii of missionary parents into a family that had pioneered the sugar business there. After graduating from Yale in 1892, he entered the business world, becoming the president of Alexander & Baldwin Ltd., a huge sugar manufacturing company, and also engaging in the management of numerous other companies including the California and Hawaiian Sugar Refining Company, the Matson Navigation Company, the Honolulu Consolidated Oil Company, Columbia Steel, and the Savings Union Bank and Trust Company.

The first aggressive move by West Coast businessmen to modify the immigration law came from San Francisco, the center of anti-Japanese movements. Since San Francisco controlled the greatest portion of trade with Japan, its chamber of commerce had long held an anti-exclusion position and had petitioned the California legislature on immigration issues as early as 1909.[1] The Japanese Relations Committee of the chamber of commerce, which was established on Alexander's initiative, had opposed the anti-Japanese movement since the committee's establishment in 1915.[2] By the 1920s, Alexander had become an active and influential member of both the chamber of commerce and the Republican Party in San Francisco.[3] Active in promoting trade with Japan, he also served as president of the Japan Society of San Francisco and supported the first conference of the IPR in 1925.[4] Although San Francisco businessmen in the early part of the century were motivated mainly by a desire to develop trade with Japan, their continuing commitment to the Japanese cause, despite economic fluctuations, suggests that their activities were not solely influenced by economic factors.[5]

This was also the case with the appearance of San Francisco business leaders who took up the cause around the winter of 1928–1929, since their activities began long before the economic slowdown of 1929. Furthermore, San Francisco business conditions were not worsening in the period when Alexander began his serious anti-exclusion activities.[6] Other businessmen in the West were optimistic and confident about the future of the economy at the beginning of the Depression.[7] Therefore, the Depression was not a key factor motivating the timing of a renewed anti-exclusion movement in San Francisco, although, as the Depression worsened and exports to Japan from the Pacific Coast drastically decreased, economic factors did tend to increase support for the movement.

Writing in the December 1928 issue of *Nation's Business*, Alexander had implicitly suggested that the immigration question should be solved: "There is no international problem, no Pacific problem, that cannot be solved on the basis of reason and justice to all concerned."[8] Concretely, Alexander sought to resolve the Japanese immigration question not by modifying the exclusion clause but by establishing a treaty that would mutually prohibit immigration between the United States and Japan, which shows that he attached far greater importance to cordial U.S.-Japanese relations than to racial equality in the United States. Since there were few immigrants from the United States to Japan and since the issue for the Japanese was not the number of immigrants they could send to the United States but rather saving Japanese national honor, Alexander's solution seemed satisfactory to both pro- and anti-quota forces.

Alexander's first move to modify the exclusion law occurred in 1929. In early February, he visited Morikazu Ida, the Japanese consul general in San Francisco, and told him that he had the support of Paul Scharrenberg, V. S. McClatchy, and Hiram Johnson for his treaty idea. Meanwhile, some State Department officials were also exhibiting keen interest in the idea of a mutual prohibition treaty. Assistant Secretary of State William Castle expressed support for this idea as early as January 1929, saying that it "might well be worked up."[9] Later in the year, when Castle discussed the possibility of such a treaty with President Herbert Hoover, the president expressed strong approval, telling Castle that "he would be 100 percent behind it."[10] Although Alexander's plan seemed to develop smoothly, in fact, McClatchy had already withdrawn his support by the time Alexander reported it to the Japanese consul general. McClatchy had received confidential information to the effect that Sidney Gulick had revived a pro-Japanese propaganda campaign on the East Coast.[11] Instead of supporting Alexander's treaty plan, McClatchy now decided to resume his fierce attacks on pro-quota movements, arguing that "to grant [a] quota to Japan would destroy . . . the basic policy . . . of excluding aliens ineligible to citizenship."[12] At its 13 February 1929 meeting, the CJIC decided to initiate a letter-writing campaign to members of the California legislature asking them to petition Congress against any amendment of the immigration law.[13] The campaign effectively declared a new war against Japanese quotas.[14]

McClatchy's information was correct. The FCCCA was indeed continuing to express its dissatisfaction (albeit haphazardly) with the exclusion clause. In the January 1929 issue of the *Federal Council Bulletin*, for example, the FCCCA made a clear statement of its position on Japanese immigration: "The Federal Council still believes . . . that the present discriminatory immigration laws of the United States 'are resented by all intelligent Orientals as humiliating and un-Christian.'"[15] In addition, in its 1929 annual report, the FCCCA reaffirmed "the action of the Executive Committee of 1925, urging the importance of so amending our immigration and naturalization laws that they may be applied without discrimination to nationals of all countries now resident in the United States." The report also confirmed that the immigration law was still resented in the Far East.[16] Although it had decided to withdraw from the pro-quota movement for strategic reasons in late 1925, the organization's withdrawal had not been complete: it still occasionally advocated a quota for Japan. This lukewarm, ambiguous attitude, which McClatchy could gauge through their publications, contributed to McClatchy's belief that the FCCCA's original declaration of withdrawal had been a trick. Gulick considered it his duty to remain silent on matters pertaining to the immigration issue, but his conscience was torn between strategic imperatives and his sense of justice. Gulick's lack of diplomacy, coupled with the FCCCA's inability to convince the CJIC of the sincerity of its decision to withdraw from the political campaign, revealed that Gulick had not learned from the FCCCA's mistakes.

While McClatchy fed information about Gulick's alleged campaign to newspapers and magazines, some of his supporters stirred up debate on the immigration question. The *Labor Clarion* published a front-page article about the Japanese immigration issue, warning of the dangers of Gulick's campaign.[17] The *San Francisco Call* headlined one article, "Churches Urge Quota Plan for Japan."[18] At the CJIC's request, California State Senator J. M. Inman submitted a resolution to the State Assembly, which urged that the immigration law be left intact.[19] It passed both houses in California and was sent on to Congress.[20]

Without realizing that his own behavior was damaging the treaty plan, Gulick characterized the idea of a mutual prohibition treaty as an "excellent" plan.[21] In April, on his own accord, Gulick met with the Japanese ambassador, Katsuji Debuchi, and expressed his desire to lobby senators such as William E. Borah in favor of this new proposal, but Debuchi dissuaded him. First, Debuchi felt the proposal would not satisfy the Japanese; and second, there was little hope of such a treaty passing the Senate. The ambassador still hoped that Americans would modify the law voluntarily out of their sense of justice and equity.[22]

Not surprisingly, Alexander took a dislike to Gulick. After visiting Ambassador Debuchi on May 29, he attributed the Japanese rejection of the mutual prohibition treaty proposal to Gulick's lack of tact. Debuchi told him that he had asked Gulick to refrain from engaging in any movement concerning this issue, and that Gulick had agreed to do so. When Debuchi told Alexander that the proposal was unsatisfactory from his personal point of view, Alexander abandoned the treaty proposal entirely.[23]

State Department officials also regarded the involvement of clergymen in the Japanese immigration problem as an annoyance. When William T. Stone of the Foreign Policy Association visited Nelson Johnson, assistant secretary of state, on behalf of "missionary interests" in New York, the assistant secretary asked him to "use any influence he had to persuade these interests to lay off the question of Japanese immigration" because "the slightest evidence of a revival of agitation . . . would be met at once by counter agitation . . . on the Pacific Coast."[24]

McClatchy came to realize the danger of the proposal for a mutual prohibition of immigrants: if immigration came under the control of such a treaty, the issue would be moved "out of the hands of Congress . . . over to the State Department."[25] Even though Congress would have to ratify any such treaty, the mere proposal for a treaty would be a blow to the anti-quota forces. The CJIC was "determinedly opposed to any arrangement under which the control of immigration would pass from the hands of Congress into the hands of the State Department or the Executive."[26] Some sympathizers followed this logic and tried to keep the immigration issue from being reopened. Congressman Arthur M. Free claimed that "continued agitation of the Oriental exclusion issue . . . [would] merely serve to keep open an international wound that otherwise would quickly heal."[27] The *Sacramento Bee* argued that Japanese politicians understood that trade with the United States was "vastly more important . . . than splitting hairs over whether fifty or 100 of their fellow countrymen should be admitted to this country."[28]

While the pro-quota faction concentrated on behind-the-scenes activities, anti-quota forces remained generally inactive during 1929. The annual convention of the California State Federation of Labor focused on Mexican and Filipino immigrants, but mostly ignored the Japanese.[29] The NSGW continued to attack Mexican immigrants, arguing that because of them, "thousands of substantial American citizens in California cannot find employment."[30] The November 1929 issue of the *Grizzly Bear* singled out Mexicans and Filipinos for attack, asserting that it would be excellent to "round up all [ineligible-to-citizenship] Mexican aliens . . . and return them whence they came" and that Filipinos were "not wanted here in California."[31]

In Japan, only a few pro-quota voices could be heard. The *Chūgai Shōgyō Shimpō* argued that it would be useless for the United States to advocate amity with Japan as long as the United States left the immigration issue unattended.[32] Considering the change in the American presidency to be a good opportunity, Representative Yūsuke Tsurumi argued that since the emotional tension between the United States and Japan could never be solved unless the immigration law were modified, the Japanese government should make every effort to rectify the situation. The Japanese government, however, refused to put forth any concrete measures. Explaining that the situation was considered to be a domestic matter by the United States, a counselor to the Foreign Ministry reported that Japan had no recourse other than to hope the United States would modify the law on its own initiative.[33]

The Japanese reserve on the issue was broken at the IPR conference that year, held between October 28 and November 9 in Kyoto. The Japanese delegates all delivered anti-exclusion speeches, which produced strong reverberations in the United States and rekindled debate on the issue. On the first day of the IPR conference, a statement written by Viscount Shibusawa but presented in his absence maintained that "the controversy which arose out of the American immigration legislation of 1924 is not a closed incident. . . . The wound so needlessly inflicted upon [the Japanese] sense of national honour is still open and will remain open until the matter is rightly settled."[34] Professor George Blakeslee helped prompt the Foreign Policy Association to pay close attention to the issue by reporting this statement.[35]

Some leading papers in the United States reported Japan's lingering anger at the immigration law in their coverage of Shibusawa's statement. The *New York Times*, for example, reported on the speech in article subtitled, "Resentment at Immigration Bar Voiced at Opening of Kyoto Conference."[36] The Scripps-Howard newspapers covered Shibusawa's statement and also attacked the immigration law.[37] Hearst papers, however, criticized Shibusawa, arguing that he was overreacting and that Japan seldom complained about exclusion from the British Empire: "United States exclusion laws are no more severe than those enforced by the British Government in Canada, [and] less severe than those in force in Australia and New Zealand."[38] The *Sacramento Bee* also attacked Shibusawa, claiming that the law was not discriminatory against Japan.[39]

Some exclusionist publications took the view that Japanese anger on the issue had subsided. The *Labor Clarion*, for example, noted that "the Japanese are perfectly at ease on our exclusion policy."[40] Scharrenberg claimed that few average Japanese considered the immigration law an insult.[41] At the same time, he suggested that if the Japanese ever achieved the American standard of living, he would not oppose giving them a quota.[42]

Continued anti-exclusion calls from clergymen gave the McClatchy faction an opportunity to publicize what they considered the danger of the clergymen's movement, and that made Scharrenberg waver. The fourteenth annual meeting of the American Division of the World Alliance for International Friendship Through Churches (WAIFTC), for example, passed a resolution attacking the exclusion of Japanese immigration.[43] And the FCCCA's annual report for 1929 quoted Shibusawa and reiterated its support for quotas in East Asian countries.[44] The January 1930 issue of the *Federal Council Bulletin* suggested that the existence of the exclusion clause made missionary work in East Asia more difficult.[45] The result of renewed calls for quotas was that the CJIC came to believe that there was "a determined effort being made and apparently under some sort of understanding between the leaders in Japan and their friends here for a grant of quota." The phrase "friends here" was code for the clergymen of the FCCCA.[46]

McClatchy's answer to the FCCCA was powerful enough to make Scharrenberg reconsider his position. Although Scharrenberg had pleased Japanese delegates in Kyoto with his pro-quota comments, and although he had told a Japanese diplomat that he would not oppose the admission of one hundred or so Japanese immigrants, if clergymen did not raise an uproar, he now ceased to express pro-quota opinions.[47] Alexander and Lynch reported to Castle that Scharrenberg "was just about ready to urge that Japan be included in the quota when that idiot Dr. Gulick got the Federal Council of Churches to start a propaganda on the subject and scared him off."[48]

Privately, Scharrenberg still professed support for pro-quota activists; however, his stance continually wavered in public. For instance, while he manifested his faith in the pro-quota cause to Jerome D. Greene in San Francisco, writing that he would work to end labor's opposition to a quota, he further explained to Greene that his status as a labor leader in California made it impossible for him to take the initiative in such efforts.[49]

Thus, pro-quota supporters in the West were eager to silence their opponents in the East. Recognizing that the modification activities of East Coast clergymen served only to provoke the Californians, Elmer A. Sperry met with Gulick and asked him to call off the pro-quota movement on the East Coast. Gulick, who had never had any intention of doing so, agreed to this request.[50] Alexander also told Consul General Ida of his intention to ask Gulick to keep quiet regarding the immigration issue.[51] On February 21, 1930, James H. Franklin of the CIJG reported to Japanese Consul-General Sawada that the organization had decided to maintain its silence, for the present.[52]

It is unclear whether Gulick fully understood the intent of those who were trying to discourage his pro-quota activities. At the Third Study Conference on the Churches and World Peace, held in Evanston, Illinois, between February 25 and 27, 1930, and organized by the National Committee on the Churches and World Peace (NCCWP), which repre-sented the peace interests of scores of religious bodies and one of whose three secretaries was Gulick, an anti-exclusion resolution was passed which read:

> We are aware that the Exclusion Clause . . . still remains and gives grave
> offense to Asiatic peoples. While Japan keenly resents the humiliation . . .
> she is maintaining an attitude of dignified and restrained protest. We
> earnestly urge that this matter should be set right either by a new treaty
> or by placing Asiatics under the quota provisions of the Immigration
> Law . . . that may be mutually satisfactory.[53]

Gulick was not the only clergyman who was actively engaged in the pro-quota movement. William B. Harvey of the American Friends Service Committee (AFSC) had been behind the pro-quota resolution of the WAIFTC in the fall of 1929, and he now began discussing the idea of a bill to modify the exclusion clause with influential people in the Philadelphia area. When Harvey visited Sawada, however, the consul general argued that such a conspicuous movement at that time would only work to the advan-tage of the anti-Japanese forces in California, and he asked Harvey to refrain from taking such a move.[54] Jerome D. Greene also made an effort to dissuade Harvey from launching a new pro-quota movement, writing that since there were indications of a renewed pro-quota move in California, it would be best for people on the East Coast to "refrain from any public activity that might arouse sectional antagonism on the Pacific Coast."[55] The letter from Greene, and a similar suggestion from Alfred C. Elkinton, the brother-in-law of Japanese intellectual Inazō Nitobe, were apparently successful. Harvey soon wrote to Sawada: "The more I work on the matter, the more I am convinced that it is a case where we must hasten slowly."[56]

Even as pro-quota activists, including businessmen in San Francisco, discouraged clergymen in the East from renewing their efforts for a quota, a new movement arose from among the ranks of businessmen in the Northwest. There were two major stimuli for this new movement: a new Japanese tariff on wood products and the Great Depression. In an effort to increase revenue, the Japanese Imperial Diet had passed a bill, scheduled to take effect on March 30, 1929, that would increase tariffs on several kinds of wood. The aim was to levy heavy import duties on woods which competed with Japanese forestry industry products, and light duties on other types of wood. In practice, this meant heavy duties would be imposed on wood imported from the United States and light duties on imports from Manchuria and Siberia. The bill had passed despite fears that the tariff would aggravate American lumber exporters on the Northern Pacific Coast, where anti-Japanese feeling was already strong.[57]

Since Japan represented the largest outlet for their product, Northwest lumbermen protested soon after the enactment of the law.[58] On October 18, the West Coast Lumbermen's Association passed a resolution requesting the State Department to "exert its utmost efforts . . . to secure removal of the discriminatory features of the Japanese tariff against American woods," and demanding a retaliatory tariff against Japan if efforts to remove the tariff failed.[59] The State Department did not believe that the new law was intended to discriminate against American lumber, but it faced increasing pressure from congressmen who had connections with lumber interests. Finally, the department instructed its embassy in Tokyo to bring the issue to the attention of the Japanese government.[60] Despite this intervention by the U.S. State Department, the Japanese government could do nothing about the offending law until the next session of the Diet.

In the meantime, exports to Japan from the Northwest Pacific declined, and coupled with the effect of the Great Depression, struck a brutal blow to the region's economy. The value of exports from the state of Washington to Japan dropped from $39 million in 1928 to $30 million in 1929, then plummeted to $17 million in 1930.[61] Because of the tariff hike, lumber exporters were severely hurt. The export of cedar logs, for example, one of Washington State's main export commodities to Japan, dropped 56 percent between 1928 and 1930.[62]

Facing this kind of hardship, lumber exporters in the Northwest suddenly developed an interest in the pro-quota movement. In October 1928, F. C. Knapp, president of the Portland (Oregon) Chamber of Commerce and president of the Peninsula Lumber Company, met with the Japanese consul in Portland, and both agreed that the exclusion clause should be modified. Knapp then sent a letter to Julius K. Barnes, president of the New York Chamber of Commerce and an adviser to President Hoover, in which he asked for "assistance in undoing this wrong."[63] Publications in Washington State now advocated a quota for Japan. In November, the *Wenatchee Daily World* insisted that Japan should be given an immigration quota, and, in January 1930, the *Town Crier*, a monthly magazine in Seattle, argued that the exclusion clause was "a blunder" and that it "cannot be too quickly abolished."[64] J. J. Donovan, vice-president of the Bloedel-Donovan Lumber Mills and vice-president of the Chamber of Commerce of Washington, who had earlier supported passage of the immigration law, now appeared before the Japan Society of Seattle to support modification of the law. Donovan became a prolific speaker for the cause of modification; in one speech, he told managers and employers of the Douglas Fir Company that the Japanese, because of their resentment of the immigration law, were "buying goods in Europe today that they should and would like to buy [from Americans]."[65]

When the Japan Society of Seattle asked college presidents and businessmen in Washington and Oregon their views on the immigration law, all of the responses supported modification of the exclusion clause.[66] M. Lyle Spencer, president of University of Washington, responded: "Peace for America can never be assured until [Americans] have a quota for Japan."[67] A. F. Haines, vice-president of the American Mail Line, expressed his view that "as long as a discrimination exists against the Japanese people . . . there will be a resentment which will interfere with the development of amicable relations . . . and lessen . . . [the] volume of trade."[68]

The rise of a pro-quota movement in the Northwest came about independently of Alexander's movement in San Francisco. Alexander would try to take advantage of the rising pro-quota sentiment in the Northwest to suggest that both groups work together to unseat Albert Johnson, the congressman from Washington State who chaired the important House Committee on Immigration.[69] But the pro-quota forces in Seattle declined to cooperate with Alexander; they considered it a better strategy to apply pressure on Johnson through lumber industry leaders and other influential constituents than to confront him directly.[70]

The Seattle Chamber of Commerce was the first chamber of commerce to respond to this pro-quota atmosphere in the Pacific Northwest, passing a pro-quota resolution in 1930. Differing from resolutions passed by clergy-men in the mid-1920s, which had emphasized international goodwill and humanity, the Seattle resolution emphasized the importance of business interests:

> WHEREAS. . . . it is the opinion of many business leaders on the Pacific Coast that our commerce with Japan has suffered as a result of this Exclusion Clause to the extent of seriously crippling some of our industries and thus throwing many thousands of laborers out of employment, and that so long as the United States maintains its present exclusion policy, it will add an unnecessary burden to those commercial interests seeking to upbuild our trade with Japan; it is
> HEREWITH RESOLVED, that the Seattle Chamber of Commerce go on record as favoring a modification of the Immigration Act to admit Japanese under the two per cent quota provisions of the law.

The resolution also invited other major Pacific Coast chambers of commerce to join in an effort to take up the Japanese immigration issue at the National Foreign Trade Council meeting in Los Angeles in May.[71] Pro-quota forces in Washington State lined up J. J. Donovan to speak at the meeting and planned to invite other chambers of commerce to submit pro-quota resolutions directly after Donovan's speech. Consul Suemasa Okamoto, fearing that such a direct act might stimulate anti-Japanese forces, tried to dissuade the pro-quota activists by pointing out that the immigration law was not a direct cause of the declining trade between the United States and Japan, and that Japan's raising of lumber tariffs was not a retaliation against the law. However, K. J. Middleton countered with the argument that appeals to the cause of human equality would not be sufficient to convince businessmen, and that only an appeal to their trade interests would have any chance of pushing them to effect changes in the immigration law.[72]

Portland, as a port city, also suffered from the decline in exports, and its chamber of commerce sought to promote trade with Asia.[73] On April 12,

1930, L. W. Hartman visited the Japanese consul, Hiroshi Ashino, on behalf of the chamber. He informed the consul that the chamber intended to submit a resolution for modification of the exclusion clause at the National Foreign Trade Council meeting. Ashino supported this move, saying that the Japanese government would be glad to see American businessmen submit a resolution voluntarily.[74]

Pro-quota forces on the West Coast were far from monolithic. The San Francisco faction, for example, was unhappy with the aggressive actions of businessmen in the Pacific Northwest. When Alexander visited Portland, he insisted that the pro-quota movement should be headquartered in California, and he asked the Northwest group to refrain from starting conspicuous movements until he judged that the time was ripe. Hartman was disappointed that Alexander did not support his efforts.[75] On their way to the national convention of the chambers of commerce at Washington, D.C., Hartman and Alexander met with Sawada in New York and expressed the opinion that Donovan was too eager for quick success and indicated that they would convince Donovan that an aggressive move would only make matters worse.[76]

The San Francisco pro-quota plan was less aggressive than the Northwest plan. Whereas pro-quota forces in the Pacific Northwest wanted immediate action, the San Franciscans were willing to wait for a more favorable atmosphere. Their plan involved, first, sending a petition to Congress at the end of the year, to be signed by prominent scholars, businessmen, and other influential Californians such as Archbishop Edward J. Hanna, and then to lobby their California congressmen to submit a bill to modify the law, based on this petition.[77] One reason the San Franciscans preached caution was that California was already burdened with the Filipino and Mexican immigration problem, which was not so serious in the Northwest. Due to high unemployment rates, criticism against Mexicans and Filipinos, who were exempt from the exclusion law, showed no signs of subsiding. In an article entitled "Filipinos Unfitted For Citizenship," the *Grizzly Bear* quoted Scharrenberg's comment that Filipinos took jobs away from Americans.[78] The following issue quoted Congressman Albert Johnson: "The Mexis are not alone a menace, but a burden to the taxpayers."[79] The Grand Parlor of the NSGW, at its annual session in May 1930, unanimously adopted a petition to urge

Congress to exclude immigrants from Mexico and the Philippine Islands.[80] Because of all this activity, it was not the right time to begin an aggressive pro-quota movement in California.

The Seattle Chamber of Commerce honored Alexander's request to hold off on a Japanese quota resolution,[81] but businessmen in Portland refused to do so. Hartman had surveyed labor leaders and the local American Legion and learned that they would not strongly oppose his movement, so the Portland Chamber of Commerce passed a resolution in favor of a modification of the immigration law, emphasizing "the furtherance of trade and commerce" between the United States and Japan, and further resolved to send the resolution to the National Foreign Trade Council.[82]

Even before the struggle between California and Northwest business interests concerning pro-activity had been resolved, the convention of the National Foreign Trade Council had been convened in Los Angeles. As planned, Donovan delivered his pro-quota address to a first-day audience of two thousand businessmen. He explained that the Japanese still did not consider the immigration issue to be closed, and that the resulting ill-feelings were damaging trade between the United States and Japan. Donovan attributed the decrease in imports of American wood products to Japanese dissatisfaction with the immigration law, concluding, "We pay a heavy price for excluding 147 Japanese annually."[83] A Japanese diplomat in attendance reported that Donovan's speech was warmly received. The atmosphere at the conference dinner that evening was also strongly pro-quota.[84]

McClatchy, who attended the convention, had earlier submitted a letter to the Resolution Committee of the Council, urging it to "remove any existing feeling on the part of Japanese by promoting a better understanding of the policy and intent of Congress rather than by encouraging them to hope for a change in the law."[85] McClatchy had also advised Consul Toshio Satō that any pro-quota action on the part of the Trade Council would be unwise, in that it would merely rekindle debate but would not result in Congress modifying the law.[86]

McClatchy's efforts were unsuccessful, however. The pro-quota atmosphere predominated to such a degree that even California delegates jumped on the Northwest's bandwagon. A pro-quota declaration was adopted by the convention on its final day.[87] It read:

This National Foreign Trade Convention recognizes the fundamental fact that the only enduring basis for world trade is founded upon the principle of justice and fair play between nations and that international goodwill can only be maintained through the development of friendship and mutual understanding. This convention favors strongly a revision of the Immigration Act 1924 in accordance with these views.[88]

Moreover, the other chambers of commerce along the Pacific Coast agreed to pass their own pro-quota resolutions and send them to Congress.[89]

Meanwhile, the Japanese immigration issue was being raised behind the scenes at a naval conference in London, where U.S. delegates were promising that they would make an effort to modify the immigration law. Lt. Col. Charles Burnett, a member of the conference staff of Secretary of State Henry L. Stimson, tried to persuade Japan to enter into a disarmament agreement by hinting toward cooperation in efforts to modify the immigration law. The lieutenant colonel had his wife write a letter to Inazō and Mary Nitobe, which stated that if Japan accepted the disarmament agreement in London, the United States would abolish the exclusion clause.[90] Burnett also visited Tsuneo Matsudaira, the Japanese ambassador in London, and explained that he had been included in the delegation because Stimson wanted him to explain the Japanese situation, including the immigration issue, to Senators Joseph T. Robinson and David A. Reed, both in attendance at the conference. Burnett told Matsudaira that the senators were sympathetic toward modification of the immigration law.[91] Stimson also acknowledged to Matsudaira that he was sympathetic toward Japan regarding the immigration issue, and that he hoped to be able to resolve the issue during his tenure in office.[92]

Although Japanese officials regarded the London conference as a good opportunity to advance toward a solution of the immigration issue, they refused to link the immigration issue to disarmament. Top officials of the Foreign Ministry, including Shidehara, subscribed to Matsudaira's view that it would be easier to persuade Congress to modify the immigration law if the disarmament conference succeeded. Nevertheless, Shidehara avoided mention of the immigration issue. He did not want to leave delegates with the impression that Japan was willing to compromise on disarmament in exchange for a modification of the immigration law.[93]

After the disarmament agreement was signed in London, Ambassador

Katsuji Debuchi kept in close contact with Japanese consulates in the United States in order to cultivate the pro-quota atmosphere which he believed would arise out of the agreement.[94] Unfortunately, Americans who sympathized with Japan on the immigration issue and who had promised support in influencing Congress lost interest in the immigration issue after the London Conference. Assistant Secretary Castle, who was acting as U.S. ambassador in Tokyo during the conference, predicted that the naval agreement alone could not solve the immigration issue; he recognized that the immigration problem "had no relation to [disarmament] and Congress could not be bound by any agreement made with anybody in Tokyo or London."[95] On November 3, Debuchi met with Castle, only to be informed that the State Department could not intervene in the immigration issue.[96]

When Debuchi visited Castle again on November 28, he took a more aggressive approach. The Japanese ambassador remonstrated that "Senator Reed and Senator Robinson . . . told [Matsudaira] that at the first suitable opportunity they would bring up the question in Congress" and that "at one of the most difficult stages of the Conference Mr. Stimson . . . promised to assist in getting the law changed as much as he could." Castle assured Debuchi that "the Secretary and the two Senators were men who did not promise lightly," and that he was sure they would take action when they regarded the time to be appropriate.[97]

In the meantime, former Ambassador Hanihara suddenly broke his six-year silence concerning the enactment of the immigration law and delivered an anti-exclusion address at a farewell banquet in honor of Ambassador Castle in Tokyo on May 23, 1930. His address came as a complete surprise, even to Castle.[98] Compounding the surprise, immediately following Hanihara's address, Albert Johnson, chairman of the House Committee on Immigration, released a pro-quota statement in Washington. This change of events was heavily reported in the United States. The *Washington Post* noted that "diplomatic circles and the public both were taken by surprise by Hanihara's revival of the slumbering controversy," and that "Johnson [had] made the unexpected announcement . . . that he [would] move for an amendment to the 1924 immigration act."[99]

Most American newspapers took Johnson's statement to mean that he intended to place Japan on the same quota basis as other nations and to admit Japanese as quota immigrants, and pro-quota newspapers applauded the news. The *Christian Science Monitor* headlined the story, "Former Exclusionist Leads in Step to End Friction Over Immigration."[100] The *Philadelphia Public Ledger* said that Johnson's proposition would "be accepted by the Japanese in accordance with the spirit" that would promote conciliation.[101] The *Rafu Shimpō* also believed that Johnson hoped to abolish the exclusion clause.[102] In fact, Johnson was merely in favor of restricting immigration to those eligible for citizenship. Only the *New York Times* presumed that the new quota for Japan "would be restricted . . . to those eligible for naturalization under other provisions of the act,"[103] which meant that no new immigrants of Japanese ancestry would be allowed into the United States, with the exception of the children, born on Japanese soil, to the citizens of nations already eligible for U.S. citizenship.

Japanese newspapers also misinterpreted Jonhson's statement. The *Tokyo Nichinichi Shimbun* gushed "Justice at Last!" and expressed "great joy over the happy news from America."[104] The *Tokyo Asahi* praised Johnson's proposal as the best solution for the present.[105] The *Osaka Mainichi* called the statement "epoch-making," and the *Kokumin Shimbun* regarded it as a sign of a revolutionary transformation in U.S.-Japanese relations.[106] Edwin L. Neville, who had temporarily replaced Castle in Tokyo, reported that the "Japanese have never considered the American Immigration Act of 1924 as a 'closed question.'"[107] Spurred by Johnson's statement, the Japan Mission of the American Presbyterian Church expressed its strong support for placing Japan on a quota basis.[108] And the Kokuryū Kai held a memorial service on the sixth anniversary of the death of the man who had committed suicide immediately following the passage of the immigration law.[109] The Japanese liberal intellectual, Inazō Nitobe, who had proclaimed in 1924 that he would not set foot on U.S. soil until the immigration law was modified, expressed his hope that Albert Johnson was really going to propose an amendment to the law.[110]

Johnson's statement had also been utterly unexpected by the McClatchy faction. McClatchy "call[ed] attention to the fact that such a plan [to give a quota to Japan] was carefully considered by Congress in 1924 and rejected," and he reiterated the CJIC's opposition to quotas for any people ineligible to citizenship.[111] It was natural that McClatchy should regard this series of pro-quota actions (the Foreign Trade Council's resolution, Hanihara's address, and the Johnson statement) as "a preconcerted movement," and the CJIC expressed just such an opinion to its member organizations.[112] As a result, the California divisions of the anti-quota organizations redoubled their opposition to lifting the bar on Japanese immigration.[113] Clarence L. Kincaid, state commander of the American Legion, for example, protested against Johnson's statement with the argument that the present exclusion clause was not discriminatory against Japan because it was applicable to "all the Orientals and colored races of Asia."[114]

Anti-quota newspapers also followed McClatchy's line. The *San Francisco Examiner* wrote about the CJIC's opposition to Johnson's plan.[115] The *Fresno Bee* argued that the "Japanese Immigration Law Should Remain As It Is" because the question had been satisfactorily regarded as settled for six years.[116] The *Sacramento Bee* published a statement by Harry L. Engelbright, representative from California, which said, "It's a rank fallacy to reopen the Japanese immigration question at the same time [as] considering restriction of Mexican immigration and exclusion of Filipinos."[117]

Other anti-quota forces chimed in. The magazine of the state building trades, *Organized Labor*, criticized Hanihara's speech: since Japan had not objected to the Australian policy of maintaining itself as a "white man's country," it was therefore unreasonable for it to criticize the American exclusion of Asians.[118] Contrary to the expectations of pro-quota forces, Scharrenberg made an anti-quota speech at a Central Labor Council meeting, noting that people in the East and Midwest did not understand the immigration problem since "they are not confronted with it."[119] Clarence M. Hunt of the Native Sons wrote an article, entitled "California Threatened by Jap Quota," in which he argued that granting the quota to Japan would signify the Congress's "intention and desire to surrender the territory west of the Rockies to the Yellow race."[120] The Fraternal Order of Eagles, comprised mainly of laborers in Washington State and in British Columbia, resolved to oppose "any change of the Quota Law of the United States of America."[121]

Pro-quota newspapers took advantage of the flurry of interest in the Japanese immigration issue to publish their own propaganda pieces. Sympathetic papers on the West Coast reiterated the desirability of amending the immigration law. The *Los Angeles Times* explained that an amendment of the law was "desirable not because Japan wants it, but because it is ethically just."[122] The *San Francisco Chronicle* maintained that Americans would "lose nothing practical at home, and gain much in friendship, security and opportunity abroad" by amending the immigration law.[123] Other newspapers strongly endorsed the Johnson plan to modify the immigration law. The *Seattle Star* said that although the Johnson plan would not admit Japanese into the United States, it would be accepted as "a friendly gesture toward Japan."[124] The *Seattle Daily Times* lauded Johnson's statement, noting, "Mr. Johnson's bill would remove [the] slur without impairing the usefulness of the act."[125] The Seattle paper also criticized the McClatchy faction for attacking Johnson's statement, arguing that "no reason of race or color [can] be permitted indefinitely to stand in the way of mutual fair dealing."[126] Within Johnson's congressional district, the newspapers were also generally in favor of his statement. According to the *Seattle Daily Times*, both the *Grays Harbor Washingtonian* and the *Olympia Olympian* endorsed it.[127] The *Daily Olympian* said that Johnson's announcement would "get the support of the west, where the strongest objection to Japanese immigration originated."[128]

Although most responses to Johnson's statement were favorable, he was nevertheless astonished at the enormity of the reverberation. Since he had made his announcement without extensive forethought, he was unprepared for the repercussions. Johnson later told Japanese reporters that he had been influenced by influential Americans who had visited Japan, as well as important constituents in his home state, including J. J. Donovan and Frank Lamb; Hanihara's address had merely provided a convenient opportunity for him to make a pro-quota statement.[129] But according to a communication between Undersecretary of State Joseph P. Cotton and IPR chairman Jerome Greene, Johnson asked the State Department not to place too much emphasis on his announcement.[130] When K. K. Kawakami met with Johnson, at the request of Debuchi, Johnson explained that he was not suggesting admitting aliens ineligible for citizenship. The original draft of his statement, which he showed to Kawakami, mentioned only a possible amendment which would "give Japan its proportionate quota." Kawakami was left with the impression that Johnson intended to avoid any clarification of his statement in order to please everybody,[131] and indeed a letter distributed shortly thereafter by Johnson to his constituents concerning the Japanese immigration issue revealed nothing concrete.[132]

When pro-quota activists realized that Johnson's plan, if enacted, would not admit Japanese immigrants, but was only intended for those immigrants eligible for citizenship, they reacted in different ways. Gulick continued to support him, believing that pro-quota activists might later prevail upon Johnson to support a quota plan, if only to maintain his political influence.[133] Alexander, on the other hand, felt that while Johnson's statement was premature, nevertheless Western businessmen had to do something concrete as a group now that the statement had been made. Alexander felt that while it might be hasty to go into action in response to Johnson's statement—the true intention of which was not yet clear—Western businessmen nonetheless ought to seize the opportunity provided by Johnson's statement to take concrete concerted action.[134]

In the meantime, principal chambers of commerce took advantage of the surge of interest in the Japanese immigration quota question. On May 29, the Los Angeles Chamber of Commerce resolved that "the Japanese nation should be placed on a parity with other leading nations of the world in the matter of immigration into the United States."[135] On June 5, the San Francisco Chamber of Commerce passed their own pro-quota resolution, similar to that passed by the National Foreign Trade Council.[136] On June 12, the Honolulu Chamber of Commerce endorsed Johnson's plan and, the following day, warmly applauded Castle, who told them that the Japanese were still hurt by the immigration law.[137]

Pro-quota businessmen in California were optimistic. Robert N. Lynch of the San Francisco Chamber of Commerce wrote to Debuchi that because of recent events, the "time will soon be ripe for action."[138] Alexander believed that since Johnson had "put himself so clearly on record in his first statement to the newspapers, I really do not see how he can back down."[139]

Reports of the diminishing anti-Japanese sentiment and expanding pro-quota activity boosted optimism in Southern California. On June 5, three organizations in Pasadena sent letters to Johnson expressing their support for his statement.[140] On June 15, in an article entitled "West Coast Losing Anti-Japanese Bias," the *New York Times* argued: "A change is coming over the attitude of Southern California toward Oriental exclusion, with special reference to Japan."[141] Four days later, the same paper expressed its opinion that there is no reason to believe that this new friendly sentiment would be diminished by establishing a Japanese quota similar to that for the Europeans."[142] At the end of June 1930, the Southern California annual conference of the Methodist Episcopal Church resolved to "petition . . . Congress to give such reconsideration to the present immigration law as will assign an equitable quota to Japan."[143]

The businessmen's movement, however, did not always proceed smoothly, because of renewed regional disagreement. Southern Californians were eager to send Congress pro-quota petitions from several chambers of commerce on the Pacific Coast, but the San Francisco and Seattle Chambers of Commerce attempted to dissuade these businessmen from engaging in such a drastic plan. In order to iron out their differences, representatives of most chambers of commerce on the Pacific Coast gathered in San Francisco for a secret meeting on July 1. At the meeting, Frank H. Lamb, representing the Washington State Chamber of Commerce, argued that it would be unwise to give the impression that pro-quota businessmen had ceased their activities. He further maintained that since Johnson's constituency seemed not to oppose the pro-quota cause, despite the poor economic situation in the state of Washington, the pro-quota movement should move forward without hesitation. However, opposition from the more cautious Californians was overwhelming.[144] Eventually, it was agreed that publicity should be avoided in order to keep the idea from "being made a political issue," and that a special committee would be formed to covertly· "influence . . . organizations to which anti-Japanese element[s] might look for support." Alexander was elected to chair the committee, and it was decided that "all matters in connection with the quota movement and the Chambers of Commerce be cleared through him."[145] The effective result was that the pro-quota movement of Western businessmen would go underground until Alexander perceived the time to be right.

Alexander's insistence on putting off an aggressive pro-quota campaign did not necessarily imply pessimism about the prospects for the pro-quota cause; on the contrary, he was optimistic. When he met Albert Johnson and learned that Johnson had received five thousand letters endorsing the pro-quota cause, and only about thirty attacking it, Alexander judged that Johnson must have felt "convinced that the proper course for him to pursue is to put the Japanese nation under the quota basis." He concluded, "Thus far the trend of affairs has been most encouraging and if nothing unforeseen develops [pro-quota forces] should be in a position to obtain a strong expression of approval of the quota plan."[146] He wrote to Castle, "As far as

California is concerned, the outlook seems to be improving," whereas the CJIC seemed to be "disintegrating."[147]

Indeed, opposition from the CJIC and other quota adversaries had become less and less prevalent in California, partly because of Alexander's maneuvers. At the annual convention of the California Department of the American Legion, held in Sacramento from August 18 to 20, the Alexander faction succeeded in causing an anti-quota resolution written by McClatchy to be tabled.[148] Moreover, there was no debate about the Japanese immigration issue during that year's California gubernatorial election.[149] Neither did the annual convention of the California State Federation of Labor take up the issue.[150]

Not surprisingly, reverberations from Johnson's statement were also felt in Japan. The *Gaikō Jihō* was full of articles about the immigration issue. In the June 15 issue former Consul General Ujirō Oyama heralded Johnson's statement as a sign that the United States was returning to justice.[151] Although the paper maintained that a mere modification of the immigration law was not enough to achieve harmony between the United States and Japan, it also presumed that Johnson's statement might reflect the American popular conscience. This issue published five articles about the immigration issue. While some cautioned against holding high expectations regarding Johnson's statement, others expressed the hope that change might be realized.[152]

Although some Japanese diplomats always understood the importance of their support and guidance for the pro-quota movement, it had never been easy for them to intervene in the dispute. But stimulated by the growing interest in the pro-quota cause, and fearing that the Alexander faction might move too hastily, the Japanese government finally allowed the diplomats to take an active role in the movement. Consul General Wakasugi, who doubted that the California businessmen could manage a pro-quota movement along with their regular business responsibilities, and who noted that they had no professional knowledge of the law, emphasized restraint and suggested that they be guided, secretly, by the Japanese government.[153] No record exists, however, of any such activity on the part of Japanese diplomats. It is interesting to note that despite the great emphasis they placed on restoring the national honor, tarnished by the exclusion clause, Japanese diplomats attached little importance to the welfare of their fellow countrymen living in the United States. When the wife of a Japanese migrant worker was admitted into the country by the U.S. circuit court of appeals, expectations swelled for other Japanese immigrants who hoped to bring their wives to the United States. Although he admitted this case might prove to be "a gospel" for Japanese workers engaged in business in the United States, Wakasugi deemed discussion on the issue inadvisable, especially since such discussion might prove harmful to the developing pro-quota movements.[154] Japanese Consul Satō, in Los Angeles, also believed that allowing the entrance of Japanese spouses was inappropriate at a time when pro-quota movements were expanding, and that pro-quota activists should refrain from publicizing the case, even though to do so meant sacrificing the welfare of Japanese in the United States.[155]

There was disagreement within the State Department as to what role it should play in the affair. The Division of Far Eastern Affairs, led by Stanley K. Hornbeck, considered a repeal of the exclusion clause favorable for U.S.-Japanese relations, but concluded that "the Department of State should not . . . take any initiative in this matter."[156] Hornbeck thought that he would "have to keep as tight a hold as possible on [the Alexander faction] lest their enthusiastic optimism get in the way of the connection between their feet and the ground."[157] On the other hand, Castle was very sympathetic to the pro-quota movement of the Alexander faction. Although the State Department was unable to overtly support the pro-quota movement, he told Alexander, "If that move comes from the Pacific Coast, you can be sure that the Department of State would back it up to the limit."[158] Castle was optimistic as to "the possibility of putting Japan on the quota," and he thought Scharrenberg's expression of support for the cause was important.[159] In an interview with the *New York Times*, Castle once again emphasized how the Japanese were still hurt by the immigration law.[160]

Secretary of State Stimson agreed with Hornbeck's cautious approach, noting, "Mr. Alexander is at times inclined to be somewhat too sanguine."[161] As a general policy, Hornbeck believed that the Japanese immigration issue should not be publicized. When Ambassador W. Cameron Forbes was criticized by the Japanese public for attempting to stifle Japanese requests for a resolution of the immigration question,[162] Hornbeck reassured Forbes that officials of the State Department had "a feeling that the less the subject is made a matter of public discussion the better for all concerned."[163]

By this time, Alexander had come to realize that events would not turn out as he had expected, and he had lost his earlier optimism. He was disappointed by Representative Johnson's assurances to the CJIC that he would oppose any change in the immigration law.[164] As to the situation in California, when Alexander learned of McClatchy's success in winning Ulysses S. Webb, the California state attorney general, and the American Legion back to his side, he confessed that the current picture was not "as bright as I [had] painted."[165]

High unemployment rates caused by the Great Depression made prospects even dimmer. At the request of President Hoover, in September 1930 the State Department began to curtail the number of all immigrants to the United States by broadly interpreting a clause in the 1917 immigration act that prohibited the admission of persons "likely to become a public charge." In his annual message to Congress that December, Hoover proposed that all immigration should be temporarily halted. Since Congress was already busy discussing two bills submitted separately by Albert Johnson and David Reed to restrict immigration generally, it did not take up the issue of a quota for Japan in that session.[166]

Alexander had become increasingly cautious in his pro-quota activities, causing Japanese diplomats to consider the necessity of bold action. Frustrated by Johnson's indecision, Reed's noncommittal attitude, and Stimson and Castle's ineffectiveness,[167] Japanese diplomats decided to urge the pro-quota faction to take more aggressive action. Consul General Wakasugi pressed Alexander to take a more aggressive approach with Congress, noting that if he didn't take his chance now, he would have to wait several years before he could try again. Alexander promised to take concrete measures at the Western Division meeting of the U.S. Chamber of Commerce, scheduled to be held in Portland that December.[168] At the meeting, Alexander engaged in a flurry of behind-the-scenes negotiations. He was able to persuade Representative Florence Kahn to submit a pro-quota bill if no other congressmen were forthcoming, but Kahn later reneged on his promise. The pro-quota faction voted against submitting a pro-quota resolution at the convention, deciding instead to expand their educational efforts.[169] Although Alexander's efforts had been ineffective, Consul Ashino continued to urge him and Robert Lynch to take bold measures. Lynch explained that there were anti-Japanese elements even in the chambers of commerce, and he reiterated that they must be all the more careful now that American attitudes toward Japan were becoming more favorable.[170] In the end, Alexander and Lynch were only able to tell the consul that one could not be too cautious in this matter.[171]

Meanwhile, the differences between Northwesterners and Californians resurfaced. In the state of Washington, businessmen tended to be more aggressive than Californians. While J. J. Donovan was confident of his ability to persuade Representative Albert Johnson to the cause, Californians had no confidence in their prospects of persuading Senator Hiram Johnson. On the other hand, although businessmen in Oregon were also pro-quota, there was some variation in Northwestern businessmen's attitudes toward the pro-quota cause. When Californians asked if Oregon businessmen could take on the responsibility of embarking on aggressive measures, they could not give an explicit answer.[172]

Still, Northwestern businessmen were generally pro-quota, and they continued their pro-quota activities. The Chamber of Commerce of Tacoma, the largest city in Albert Johnson's constituency, passed a pro-quota resolution which praised Johnson's statement and urged Congress to modify the immigration law.[173] The Portland Chamber of Commerce passed a resolution on the Japanese immigration issue to submit to the National Foreign Trade Convention. It also urged the U.S. Chamber of Commerce to include the Japanese immigration issue as one of the subjects to be discussed at its annual convention and to recommend modification of the law to Congress.[174]

Yet again, Alexander's forces asked the Portland Chamber of Commerce to suspend its plan. Although they were not eager to do so, the Portland chamber complied, because of an earlier agreement that all Pacific Coast chambers should act in unison.[175] At the convention of the National Foreign Trade Council, there was hardly any discussion of the issue, except that the former governor of Hawaii, Wallace R. Farrington, included a brief mention of the desirability of a quota system in his speech to the delegates.[176] To keep the Northwestern businessmen in line, Alexander visited Seattle and met with chamber leaders in the region. They agreed that Northwesterners should maintain a cautious attitude until Californians could be sure of the success of their movement.[177]

Because of the increasingly active West Coast community of businessmen, in 1931 the U.S. Chamber of Commerce finally showed some interest in the Japanese immigration problem. Throughout the 1920s, the U.S. Chamber had ignored the issue, with the exception of a single recommendation to modify the law that appeared in the group's 1929 annual report.[178] But on June 5, 1931, F. Stuart Fitzpatrick, representing the U.S. Chamber of Commerce, visited Hugh Cumming, of the Visa Division of the U.S. State Department, to obtain "information and advice" about the exclusion problem. Fitzpatrick was told that any move should be initiated on the Pacific Coast and that it was imperative to acquire the support of local congressmen and the public before any action was initiated.[179] Members of the Immigration Committee of the U.S. Chamber of Commerce then made an inquiry to William Green of the American Federation of Labor soliciting labor's views, and Green in turn sent an inquiry to the Federation's California members. In his reply, Scharrenberg reiterated that he was not anti-quota, presumably because he considered the CJIC to be crumbling.[180] The Immigration Committee consequently passed a pro-quota resolution on July 31:

> The Committee . . . believes the time has now come to apply to Japan and other far eastern countries similarly situated the quota law which has been in successful operation for seven years in respect to the entrance into the United States of European nationals.

The resolution was sent to the board of directors of the U.S. Chamber of Commerce, and they also approved it.[181]

This resolution rekindled discussion of the immigration issue. Opinions in California remained divided. Traditionally anti-quota activists and media viewed the resolution negatively: on the day the resolution was released, James K. Fisk of the American Legion protested, as did McClatchy.[182] In an article entitled, "State Opens Fight Against Move To Lift Oriental Ban," the *San Francisco Examiner* reported on the opposition of the American Legion, labor, and the Native Sons to the Chamber's resolution.[183] The Native Sons bitterly criticized the latest turn of events. "Governmental interests have joined hands with the Federation of Churches of Christ in America, the group of pacifist societies and other influences," the group declared. If the Native Sons were not vigilant, then "California and the Pacific Coast will within a generation or two pass largely under Japanese domination."[184] The *Labor Clarion* criticized Alexander as "the head of the agitation," arguing that he was "swayed by a desire for cheaper labor on [his] Hawaiian plantations, trans-Pacific steamships and other activities."[185] The *San Francisco*

Chronicle remained neutral, reporting on the anti-quota opinions of Fisk and Senator Shortridge, but also on the pro-quota views of Representative Florence P. Kahn and Alexander.[186] Pro-quota activists attached importance to the effects on trade. The *San Francisco News* argued that the Japanese ban should be removed because "trade in the Pacific is languishing, and in these times any trade is precious," and the *Los Angeles Times*, publishing excerpts of the resolution, regarded the likelihood of Congress's paying attention to the issue as high.[187]

Newspapers outside the Pacific Coast area were generally supportive of the resolution. The *New York Times* regarded it favorably, arguing that the moment was opportune for the change, because American trade with Asia was suffering from the Depression, whereas European countries had strengthened their trade with Asia.[188] The *Christian Science Monitor* regarded the exclusion clause as a "needless affront to a friendly power."[189] The *Chicago Daily Tribune* supported the resolution, asserting that since Americans would "live a long time with their neighbors across the Pacific, it should be the national policy to do everything consistent with the nation's vital interests to foster good feeling and active cooperation with them."[190]

Japanese newspapers were generally pleased with the news of the resolution of the U.S. Chamber of Commerce. The *Tokyo Asahi* published an article with the headline, "Signs of the relaxation of the anti-Japanese law appearing in the United States." The article predicted that ordinary Americans suffering from the effects of the Depression would support quotas if they understood that doing so would lead to the promotion of U.S.-Japanese trade.[191] The *Jiji Shimpō* noted that prospects for the abrogation of the anti-Japanese immigration law had become promising.[192] The *Gaikō Jihō*, in an article entitled "New trend for the modification of the anti-Japanese immigration law," argued that pro-quota businessmen would help improve American public opinion of Japan.[193] The *Rafu Shimpō* claimed that a signal fire for justice had been lit by the U.S. Chamber of Commerce.[194] Japanese diplomats, however, were not sanguine. Ambassador Debuchi said he did not expect too much of the pro-quota movement because, in the end, action would have to be taken by Congress, and efforts for this issue would not contribute to any popularity on the constituent level.[195]

Alexander, who feared publicity, was surprised by the sensation created by the resolution. As he might have expected, anti-Japanese voices in California bellowed long and loud after the resolution's passage. Senator Samuel Shortridge announced before the Rotary Club that he supported "the complete exclusion of Oriental peoples from California and the United States," adding that they should "remain where God placed them."[196] McClatchy, in a *Labor Clarion* article, declared that the immigration law of 1924 had been a success.[197] He published yet another of his anti-quota pamphlets, which circulated for a long time. This pamphlet, in the form of an open letter to Wallace R. Farrington, attacked the pro-quota arguments of Farrington and Alexander.[198] Alexander later acknowledged that the resolution "had on the whole a rather unfortunate effect on the Pacific Coast."[199] Despite these sporadically aggressive anti-quota activities, the McClatchy faction was not financially sound. According to the minutes of a CJIC meeting which Scharrenberg showed secretly to Wakasugi, more than three-quarters of the operating funds for the CJIC came out of McClatchy's pocket.[200]

Originated by businessmen in San Francisco and led by Wallace Alexander, later promoted by Northwestern businessmen who were suffering from a shrinking trade with Japan, the pro-quota movement by Western businessmen emerged at the end of the 1920s to pick up the banner of the disheartened church movement. The businessmen proceeded cautiously so as not to provoke anti-Japanese factions in California, partly because they benefited from knowledge of the experiences of the clergy, and partly because their main priority was the restoration of good trade relations with Japan, and not human justice. They focused on restoring cordial U.S.-Japanese relations, which, from a commercial perspective, would strengthen an American economy weakened by the Great Depression. Although their activities proceeded well at first, the division of opinion among San Franciscans, Northwesterners, and Japanese diplomats had the effect of diminishing their already insufficient power, and made concerted action difficult. Although the Great Depression prompted West Coast businessmen to advocate the pro-quota cause, it also made that cause look less attractive because of the high unemployment rate. Nevertheless, the group's steady, behind-the-scenes activities had a positive influence on Albert Johnson, whose remarks brought about a near state of euphoria among pro-quota supporters. One result was that the U.S. Chamber of Commerce finally began paying attention to the Japanese immigration issue. Although the action of the U.S. Chamber of Commerce brought the McClatchy faction once again into the fray, the Chamber's work represented a great step forward because it was a national organization powerful enough to influence Congress. Although the organization's immigration resolution remained at the level of its Immigration Committee, and pro-quota businessmen still needed time to promote a more favorable pro-quota atmosphere, the cause of Japanese quotas seemed to be in its most promising position since the enactment of the law in 1924. Noting the rise of favorable opinion concerning quotas, the U.S. secretary of state, Henry L. Stimson, expressed his hope for a resolution of the issue. After a meeting with the Japanese ambassador, Katsuji Debuchi, on September 17, 1931, Stimson wrote:

> American opinion towards Japan had become so kindly that I was encouraged to hope that before I left office I might be able to take up for successful solution the long standing source of irritation arising out of our immigration laws of nearly ten years before, and to put them upon a basis which, while conforming to our own requirements, might be not offensive to the sensibilities of the Japanese people.[201]

Whatever window of opportunity that may have existed for changing the law, however, would be closed by the onset of Japanese military activities in China, which would influence American opinion about Japan and further complicate the Japanese immigration issue.

SIX

Japanese Imperialism and the Immigration Question

The Manchurian Incident

On the night of September 18, 1931, following a bomb explosion on the Japanese-controlled South Manchurian Railway near Mukden, the Japanese Kwantung Army invaded the Chinese province of Manchuria, claiming that the bomb had been set by the Chinese. The invasion had been scripted by the top officials of the Kwantung Army, and the bomb explosion was a part of the plot. Since this invasion was started without the Japanese government's knowledge, there was some difficulty in gathering information about the incident, even inside the Japanese government in Tokyo.

American public opinion was initially unaffected by Japan's invasion of Manchuria, partly because information was slow to reach the United States and partly because Americans did not fully understand the intentions of the Japanese army. Even State Department officials were at a loss to explain what had happened. On September 29, William R. Castle, the undersecretary of state, wrote in his diary, "The situation is very obscure. Even how it started is not clear."[1] The information received by Secretary of State Henry Stimson did not differ much. At a press conference, he stated that the Japanese army had begun to withdraw.[2] The U.S. ambassador to Japan, W. Cameron Forbes, had set sail to the United States for a vacation on September 19, even though he had been informed about the incident. Castle recorded the ambassador's explanation in his diary: "As the [Japanese Foreign Ministry] said it was only an incident, soon remedied, he saw no reason for changing his plans," adding, "Why he was such an idiot the Lord knows."[3]

Even Far East specialists at the State Department did not initially criticize Japan, including Stanley K. Hornbeck, chief of the Division of Far Eastern Affairs and a China expert.[4] Mahlon F. Perkins, counselor of the American legation at Beijing, reacted favorably to Japan's aggression. He attributed the cause of the Manchurian incident to the "cumulative effect of a long series of Chinese irritations," and was convinced that if one could "take an x-ray picture of the brains of the Chinese in Manchuria, . . . [one] would find an overwhelming sentiment in favor of Japanese control of the region. . . . Even outside of Manchuria, there would be large numbers of thinking Chinese who would agree that it was fortunate for China to have at least one province where somebody kept order." Castle considered Perkins's account credible because of Perkins's long familiarity with China and the Chinese.[5]

The Japanese army's unwillingness to withdraw from Manchuria, however, gradually stiffened the attitude of the U.S. government. Stimson and Hornbeck leaned toward taking a harder line through such measures as an embargo. However, Hoover and Castle opposed a hard-line policy for fear of causing a war. As a result, the Stimson note declaring the non-recognition policy was presented to Japan on January 8. Although some in the U.S. government opposed a hard line, they all eventually agreed that Japan was in the wrong. But they considered U.S.-Japanese relations only within the framework of the Nine Power Treaty that had been signed at the Washington Conference of 1921–1922 and had no intention of trying to improve relations bilaterally.[6]

While the U.S. government in Washington criticized the Japanese action, a favorable atmosphere for the various movements working to create a quota for Japan persisted throughout the initial phase of the Manchurian crisis. In the eastern U.S., where the pro-quota forces were traditionally prominent, pro-quota support had not diminished, despite the Manchurian incident. Thomas Lamont of the J. P. Morgan Company, for example, showed no sign of opposition to Japan's military action.[7] On October 2, the board of directors of the U.S. Chamber of Commerce approved the recommendation for a quota for Japan suggested by its Immigration Committee. Excluding the actions of the FCCCA, this was the first time a nationwide organization of this size had ever recommended a quota for Japan. The decision was supported by many publications. For example, the *New York Evening Post* said, "Congress should heed the opinion of American business as expressed in the attitude of our national Chamber of Commerce."[8] It is particularly noteworthy that pro-quota opinions were at this time influential in major cities on the West Coast, such as San Francisco and Seattle, which were centers of the anti-Japanese movement. When W. Cameron Forbes stopped in Seattle on his way to the East Coast, several pro-quota Americans visited him to discuss the quota issue. They agreed that it was best to focus on educating the public. When Forbes revealed that he maintained his pro-quota views,[9] the *Seattle Daily Times* published Forbes's opinion in favor of Japan with the headline, "Exclusion Hurts Pride Of People."[10] The *New York Times* mentioned Forbes's comment: "It would be a gracious and timely move on the part of the U.S. to place Japan under the quota system."[11] Also, in Hawaii, Wallace R. Farrington, the ex-governor, fell in with the pro-quota opinion by publicly criticizing V. S. McClatchy, a long-standing exclusionist, in the *Honolulu Star-Bulletin.*

Pro-quota activists on the West Coast were not daunted by the Manchurian incident. Since many of them were engaged in trade with Japan, they attached great importance to the maintenance of cordial U.S.-Japanese relations for their own business interests. A hard-pressed economy made them more than serious about the quota issue. Exports and imports from the West Coast customs districts had greatly decreased. For example, the value exports from the San Francisco district had dropped from $206 million in 1929 to $147 million in 1930. This figure had sunk even further, to $112 million in 1931. Exports from the Washington district dropped from $154 million in 1929 to $67 million in 1931. While the tonnage of vessels traveling to and from Japan remained steady in California, it greatly decreased in the Northwest.[12] Because Japan was the major market for wood exports from the Northwest, it was reasonable that exporters in that area would be willing to exchange an immigration quota for more amicable relations with Japan. It was highly likely that traders there were also eager to increase the amount of trade at the time of the Great Depression.

The pro-quota faction monitored the traditionally anti-Japanese organizations carefully and, whenever it was feasible, they tried to intervene through behind-the-scenes maneuvers. They worked to deter resolutions against placing Japan on the quota basis. At the convention of the California State Federation of Labor in September 1931, although it was resolved that immigrants from the Philippines should be excluded, a resolution against granting a quota to Japan did not appear. The reasons for this were not clear. On the one hand, Consul Satō in Los Angeles obtained rather reliable information from J. F. Dalton, former president of the State Federation of Labor and his personal acquaintance, that the organization was most interested in the recent increase of Filipino seamen in terms of the immigration issue. On the other hand, it was the belief of Consul General Wakasugi in San Francisco that the failure to mention the Japanese immigration issue at the convention should be solely attributed to the mediation of Scharrenberg.[13] The national body of the labor organization must not have had time to spare for consideration of the tiny quota for the Japanese. The report of the executive council to the national convention of the American Federation of Labor in Vancouver did not mention any particular country when discussing immigration. Wallace Alexander, a longtime pro-quota activist in the San Francisco Chamber of Commerce, naively attributed the failure to mention the Japanese immigration issue at the council in Vancouver to Scharrenberg's efforts. It is, however, likely that, regarding the immigration question, the council was simply preoccupied with a general restriction on immigration.[14]

Pro-quota forces also worked on another traditionally anti-Japanese organization. Wallace Alexander sent a friend to the national convention of the American Legion in Detroit. McClatchy's party had been successful in its attempt to reaffirm the anti-quota position of the American Legion during its California state convention at Long Beach, and Alexander was "not very hopeful as to the results" at the upcoming national convention. However, in spite of McClatchy's maneuvers, making any resolution concerning the quota for Japan at this convention was prevented.[15]

Major newspapers on the Pacific Coast continued to support the movement for a Japanese quota. The *San Francisco Chronicle* published an article by Chester Rowell, a well-known editor and columnist, who had attended the Institute of Pacific Relations meeting in Shanghai. Rowell argued that Congress should enact a quota for Japan, by mentioning two Japanese, Eiichi Shibusawa and Inazō Nitobe, who endeavored to promote cordial U.S.-Japanese relations and who were shocked by the 1924 immigration law.[16] The *Los Angeles Times* also mentioned the advisability of giving quotas to Japan and China.[17] In an article entitled "Quotas For Friends," the *Seattle Daily Times* argued, "Friendships would be strengthened and trade greatly stimulated by the suggested change in our immigration policy."[18]

There were two distinct points of view concerning the relationship between Japanese military activities in China and the immigration issue. One argued that because Japan had invaded Manchuria, it was not qualified for a quota, while the other maintained that placing Japan on the quota system would somehow make Japan less aggressive in Manchuria. Those who held the latter opinion generally did not criticize Japan for the Manchurian incident. In fact, the Manchurian crisis tended to work in favor of a quota for Japan. The *New York Times* announced in a headline, "Our Part In Far Eastern Crisis Renews Interest At Capitol On Idea Of Ending Exclusion."[19] At a luncheon of the Seattle Chamber of Commerce, on his way back to Tokyo on October 23, Ambassador Forbes argued that Japan had a right by treaty to station its army in the land owned by the Manchurian Railway Company and, moreover, that it had to protect the two hundred thousand Japanese and one million Koreans in Manchuria. On this occasion, he reiterated his opinion that the United States should modify the anti-Japanese clause of the immigration law.[20] The *Philadelphia Record* asserted that the anti-Japanese clause would hinder the United States's effort to contribute to the maintenance of world peace, because that clause might appear incompatible with the American peace-loving spirit.[21] Others traditionally uninterested in the quota issue were aware that the Manchurian conflict might benefit the pro-quota movement. Senator George Higgins Moses of the Senate Committee on Foreign Relations anticipated that the conflict between Japan and China in Manchuria would promote efforts to give an immigration quota to Japan.[22] Senator William E. Borah, chairman of the Senate Foreign Relations Committee, who was critical of Japanese expansion, considered that if Japan showed great discretion, the administration should urge the Senate to modify the immigration law.

Toward the end of 1931, the pro-quota movement by West Coast traders made significant progress, as efforts were made by traders in California, Washington, and Oregon to establish new organizations to promote the quota.[23] A retired lieutenant colonel of the American Legion, Joseph W. Sutphen, visited the Japanese consul in Los Angeles, Toshio Satō, to request

financial assistance from Japan to develop a new idea for a pro-quota organization. Satō discouraged him, partly because this kind of conspicuous
action would stimulate the anti-Japanese movement and partly because the
consul feared that Sutphen could not be trusted.[24]

At this time, just as Satō was asking for guidance from the Foreign
Ministry, a new organization called the Pacific Oriental Trades Association
came into being. It was established "by Pacific Coast business interests to
support the movement for repeal of the Japanese exclusion act." Sutphen
wrote letters to influential people in Southern California and encouraged
them to join his new organization.[25] The list of the supporters of this organization included William M. Garland, chairman of the 1932 Olympic Games
Committee; William Lacy, former president of the Los Angeles Chamber of
Commerce; E. C. Moore, a director of the University of California at Los
Angeles; Lee A. Phillips, vice-president of the Pacific Mutual Insurance
Company and the owner of a vast amount of land in the San Joaquin Delta;
and Ernest Moore, the mayor of Santa Cruz.[26]

In late November, the Foreign Ministry in Tokyo advised Satō to avoid
any commitment to this sort of movement because it would probably be
ineffective and redundant. The Foreign Ministry response, however, also
mentioned that if the movement proved to be powerful, discouraging it
would be inappropriate.[27] This response reflects the difficult position of the
Foreign Ministry regarding this issue. While officials in Tokyo wanted to
work toward resolving the immigration issue, at the same time they did not
want to be regarded as interfering in American domestic affairs, which might
arouse the anti-Japanese movement. There is no record of this association
being engaged in serious pro-quota activities after 1932. However, the quick
response to the pro-quota movement by an obscure individual like Sutphen
revealed that there was an atmosphere greatly favorable to the pro-quota
movement among influential people in California.

In late 1931, another organization for the initiation of a quota was
formed in Berkeley, California: the California Council on Oriental Relations
(CCOR), whose objectives included "the modification of the 1924 Immigration Law, the removal of the discriminatory clause, and the placing of
Japan, China, and other Asiatic countries on a quota basis."[28] The CCOR
was essentially a continuation of previous Bay Area–based businessmen's
movements, but it included intellectuals as well as businessmen. Samuel

Hume, who was well known in the small theater movement and who was supported by Wallace Alexander, was chosen as the leader of this new organization. It was vital to have a leader like Hume in order to appeal to the intellectuals. The membership list included Robert G. Sproul, president of the University of California at Berkeley; Aurelia H. Reinhardt, president of Mills College; Clinton E. Miller, a real estate businessman; and Fred W. Kiesel, the president of the California National Bank.[29]

The anti-Japanese faction was on the defensive. When the *New York Times* stated that public opinion in California toward Japan was favorable and even declared in a headline that a "Move To Place Japan And China On Quota Would Not Be Seriously Opposed,"[30] J. K. Fisk, chairman of the CJIC, had to make haste to deny it by sending a letter to the newspaper, maintaining that Californian anti-Asian sentiment was as strong as ever.[31] McClatchy, seeing growing public support for a Japanese quota, once again became interested in the idea of a reciprocal ban on immigrants. Although he had abandoned this idea two years earlier, he now suggested it to Stanley Hornbeck of the State Department.[32] The atmosphere was so favorable to giving a quota to Japan that McClatchy might at this time have resorted to an attempt to push through a reciprocal agreement.

The Manchurian incident, however, had some negative effects on the pro-quota atmosphere. As early as the beginning of October 1931, Upton Close visited the Japanese consul general in Harbin to explain that the Manchurian incident had compelled him to stop arguing for a quota for Japan, and to say that he was going to attack the Japanese militarists over this incident.[33] Roy W. Howard, the chairman of the board of Scripps-Howard newspapers, visited Ambassador Debuchi to say that he could no longer support the movement for the rectification of the anti-Japanese clause because of the Japanese activities in Manchuria. The ambassador reported to Tokyo that it would be very difficult to change Howard's mind because he was such a strong advocate of world peace.[34] Because Howard controlled more than twenty newspapers in the United States and had been a pro-quota advocate, the change in his opinion was a heavy blow to the Japanese cause. Naturally, McClatchy also jumped on the Manchurian incident as an argument against a quota for Japan. He warned that Japan would coerce the United States into modifying the immigration law with the same covert tactics it had used in Manchuria.[35]

Another blow was that Chester Rowell, who had expressed opinions in favor of a quota for Japan and had published an article to that effect, also changed his attitude around this time. Through lectures and essays, he began to argue strongly against the Japanese cause, possibly as a reaction to the Japanese censorship of a telegram he had tried to send to America about the bombing of Jinzhou. Another possible explanation for Rowell's change of opinion was revealed by Scharrenberg to Wakasugi. According to Scharrenberg, who was on the same ship as Rowell on a return trip from China, when Rowell was invited to the house of Chiang Kai-Shek in Shanghai, he was offered a position as adviser in charge of publicity for China and was told that the salary would be as high as he wanted. In light of this story and other information about Rowell's having spent time in China with John Powell of the pro-China *China Weekly Review*, the consul general reported to Tokyo that he believed Scharrenberg's story must be true.[36] This story is another example of Japanese diplomats believing Scharrenberg. It is probable that Scharrenberg was trying to damage Rowell's credibility and enhance his own value to the Japanese diplomats. Unaware of Scharrenberg's secret communication with Wakasugi, Rowell wrote to Wakasugi, "I am friendly to Japan, and hope to continue to be of service in promoting a better understanding of Japan." Of his work to place Japan on a quota, he stated that he expected "to continue that activity." However, he suggested that the movement for a quota should be postponed because, "at the moment, there would be danger of stirring up too much agitation by our own jingoes [anti-Japanese activists]."[37] Because there is no evidence indicating that Rowell received money from China and because his opinion, that the time was not opportune for pro-quota activities, proved to be accurate, it is impossible to know whether he accepted Chiang Kai-Shek's alleged offer.

The fact that the Commonwealth Club of California was turning its attention to the Japanese quota question at this time reflects the growing interest in the Japanese immigration issue on the West Coast in the 1930s. The organization's section on immigration, which had devoted most of its meetings up to September of 1931 to the issues of alien registration and deportation, began to choose the issue of the Japanese immigration quota as a topic of its biweekly meetings. The organization seemed to remain neutral on the issue. It usually called upon opposing sides to give their positions. On October 1, Dr. E. P. Dennett of the *Christian Advocate* spoke in favor of the quota in a lecture entitled "A Study of Advisability of Placing the Japanese

Under the Quota." He argued that nothing was more absurd than hurting the friendship between the United States and Japan by the refusal of a mere two hundred immigrants per year. According to a report by Consul General Wakasugi, a large majority of the Commonwealth Club's Immigration Section thought the 1924 immigration law was unjust. On the other hand, anti-quota opinions were strongly voiced by both V. S. McClatchy, who spoke on October 15 and November 5, and by U. S. Webb, attorney general of California, who, on November 15, compared the Japanese in Hawaii to wolves and the Caucasians in Hawaii to sheep. He claimed that if they were allowed in the same cage, the wolves would eat the sheep. On November 19, E. Clemens Horst, president of the E. C. Horst Company, and McClatchy argued the pro- and anti-quota viewpoints, respectively.[38]

The deepening nationwide economic depression hindered the pro-quota shift. Not directly related to pro- or anti-Japanese sentiments, many bills regarding immigration were submitted to the 72nd Congress, most of which were aimed at curtailing the number of immigrants. Representative John W. Moore of Kentucky submitted a bill (H.R. 10602) which would have reduced the number of quota immigrants to 10 percent of the current number. He explained that "the migration of immigrants under existing law would . . . only tend to further aggravate the unemployment situation." This kind of bill had been frequently submitted from the time of the previous Congress on account of the high unemployment caused by the Great Depression, and was intended to replace the immigration restrictions which had been in force since September 1930.[39]

At the State Department's request, Representative Samuel Dickstein of New York submitted a bill (H.R. 7801) to limit the number of permissible immigrants who came to "carry on trade" by defining the category more strictly. By restricting "trade" to "trade between the United States and the foreign state of which he [the immigrant] is a national," the State Department tried to prevent immigration by people who intended to "carry on trade" as, say, street vendors. The bill that Congress finally considered (H.R. 8766) was practically identical to the Dickstein bill.[40] But, because the word "trade" was also used in Article 1 of the U.S.-Japanese commercial treaty, and because "trade" had been interpreted more widely by the courts in the United States, Japanese diplomats pointed out that this bill might be in conflict with the treaty. However, the Department of State avoided arguing this point directly and asserted that it would be impossible to limit immigrants if "trade" was interpreted broadly. The Department of State promised that it would be responsive to those Japanese who had already resided in the United States for a long time when they wanted to bring their family members over from Japan.[41] President Hoover signed the bill into law on July 6, 1932.[42] Without knowing that the president had already signed this bill, Leland W. Cutler, the president of the San Francisco Chamber of Commerce, wired Hoover and his secretary, Lawrence Richey, who was a personal friend of Cutler's. He implored Richey to use his influence to obtain a veto for H.R. 8766 in the "Interest of Cultivation of Friendly International Relations," since the bill might be in conflict with Article 1 of the U.S.-Japanese commercial treaty.[43] Richey replied that prohibiting entry to Japanese who were engaged in local, not international trade, would not hurt friendly international relations.[44]

While American businessmen on the West Coast aggressively pursued the modification campaign, there is no record that Japanese immigrants supported the modification movement with any enthusiasm. Some, like Kyūtarō Abiko, a Japanese immigrant leader in San Francisco, who regarded himself as a cultural bridge between America and Japan, did tend to mention the exclusion clause, but most others including ordinary Issei (first-generation Japanese immigrants) and Nisei (second-generation Japanese immigrants) leaders seemed relatively uninterested in the exclusion clause. All of them hoped for the modification of the exclusion clause, but their perspective on the immigration issue differed from that of the Japanese in Japan. Although the Japanese in the United States regarded an immigration quota as essential for their national honor, they also considered it to be tangential to their own lives in the United States. They were more likely to act on matters which directly affected them. For example, a Japanese organization in Los Angeles sent representatives to Washington to support a bill which would have granted entry to U.S. citizens' parents who were over fifty-five years old and to the husbands of U.S. citizens. This focus resulted in part from the fact that the Japanese thought it would be next to impossible to modify the immigration law after the U.S. Supreme Court's decision in the Ozawa case, which clearly stated that the Japanese were ineligible for U.S. naturalization.[45]

Japanese American newspapers reflected their readers' concerns, devoting a large amount of space to news directly related to their daily lives, such as the deportation of Japanese, the entry into the United States of husbands of U.S. citizens, and the anti-alien land law. The *Rafu Shimpō* reported energetic activity by American women demanding entry for husbands of U.S. citizens.[46] The *Tairiku Nippō* reported an incident in which a Japanese man, working for a company different from the one he had indicated upon entering the United States, was ordered deported.[47] For most ordinary Japanese Americans, the national pride which would be maintained by obtaining a quota for fewer than two hundred Japanese immigrants per year to the United States was less important than such daily issues as deportation and land ownership.

Although the Japanese in the United States placed more importance on their daily lives than on the national honor of Japan, it is also true that they strongly supported the Japanese army's actions in China. In part, this support was in reaction to U.S. anti-Japanese propaganda. Immediately after the outbreak of the Manchurian incident, the *Nichi Bei* criticized Japan for its aggressive actions and argued that since Japanese advocated co-prosperity for all Asian nations, it should make a greater effort to respect China's point of view.[48] However, aggressive anti-Japanese propaganda by Chinese in the United States quickly pushed the Japanese in the United States into supporting Japan's action. Just three days after its initial article, the *Nichi Bei* argued that it was natural for Japan to act militarily in China, in order to protect its rights, because the Chinese were continuing to harass Japanese and insult the Japanese empire.[49] This support for Japanese hostility in China from Japanese papers in the United States would continue throughout the initial phases of the invasion of China. Not only the Issei, who had spent their formative years in Japan, but also many Nisei, especially leaders of the newly formed Japanese American Citizens League (JACL), whose core members consisted mostly of businessmen and professionals, backed the Japanese invasion in Manchuria. For example, James Y. Sakamoto, a key figure of the JACL in the 1930s, who had argued for the Americanization of Japanese immigrants, forcefully defended the Japanese action in Manchuria. There were some progressive-minded Nisei, such as the editors of the *Dōhō*, a progressive bilingual weekly newspaper, who regarded the Japanese action in Manchuria as dangerous because it might intensify white Americans' discrimination against Japanese Americans. They were very critical of the

JACL's sympathetic attitude toward Japanese militarism in China. However, these progressives formed a small minority within Japanese American communities. The Japanese military victories in China provided an opportunity for the recovery of national pride for those immigrants who had once hoped to assimilate into white society and who had earlier denied identification with their homeland. While Japanese immigrants tended to keep some distance from their homeland's government, which had not shown interest in the betterment of the immigrants in the 1920s, the excitement generated by Japanese military activities in China helped improve the relations between the immigrants and their homeland government by creating in the immigrants a greater sense of loyalty.[50]

The Shanghai Incident

Partly to put an end to a Chinese boycott of Japanese goods, the Japanese navy landed troops at Shanghai on January 28, 1932. The troops met with stubborn resistance from the 19th Route Army under General Tsai Ting-Kai, and the clash resulted in fierce street fighting.

In contrast to the American public's indifference to the Manchurian incident, the Shanghai incident of 1932 caused American public opinion to turn against Japan. In part, this shift can be attributed to the fact that in Shanghai, unlike in Manchuria, there were more than 3,500 American residents and many reporters.[51] They reported the Japanese military activities directly to the American audience. On January 30, the internationalist *New York Times* headline read, "Great Area In Ruins, Hundreds Slain; League Acts, U.S. And Britain Protest."[52] The next day, a reporter in Shanghai wrote,

> At 11:30 o'clock this morning the Japanese inexplicably began firing machine guns down Broadway past the Astor House Hotel. . . . The streets were then filled with milling masses of frightened, homeless Chinese, some of them wearily sitting on bundles of household goods. Immediately there was the wildest panic. . . . Chinese women with their bound feet and with babies in their arms were attempting to run to safety as their faces streamed in tears.[53]

The isolationist and traditionally anti-Japanese *San Francisco Examiner*

claimed, "Jap Bombardment Perils 25,000 Americans And Other Foreigners."[54] It did not hesitate to call the Japanese army "invaders" and the
Japanese airplanes "enemy planes."[55] According to a top-secret report to
Tokyo by Consul General Wakasugi in San Francisco, even those Americans
who had not criticized the Manchurian incident came to hate Japan; they
were moved by stories of civilian suffering which were reported both by U.S.
Chinese nationalists, who made every effort to publicize this suffering, and
by American journalists. The Japan Society in San Francisco reported a drop
in membership. Some Americans refused to shop in Japanese-owned stores,
and some wholesale dealers stopped buying Japanese goods. Wakasugi concluded his report by saying that, although there were no large-scale
repercussions yet, the number of Americans who would hold anti-Japanese
sentiments might increase if the incidents in China lingered.[56] George
Wickersham, ex-chairman of the pro-Japan National Committee on
American-Japanese Relations, could not be unconcerned about the Shanghai
situation, wondering whether the Japanese army leaders had "lost their heads
just . . . as the German militarists in 1914."[57] On February 4, Castle wrote in
his diary: "During the last week the United States has become definitely
anti-Japanese."[58]

Not all sectors in the United States became anti-Japanese in response to
the Shanghai incident. While pro-quota pacifists were shocked and
expressed grave concern about the incident, many businessmen in both the
eastern and western parts of the United States remained pro-Japan, asserting
that Japan was simply protecting foreigners from the Chinese army. At the
convention of the National Foreign Trade Council, held in Honolulu in
May 1932, the leadership said that it would not take sides in the controversy
between Japan and China and maintained that it regarded both China and
Japan as friends.[59] Alexander delivered an address at the convention in which
he emphasized the importance of Asia in terms of trade by insisting that "all
the figures indicate clearly the decline of the predominance of the Atlantic
and the rise of the Pacific." While he asserted that "it would be inappropriate for any of [the members] to align [themselves] with either of the parties
to this regrettable controversy," Alexander devoted considerable time to discussing Japan's economy in order to underscore the significance of trade with
Japan for the United States. He even pointed out how much Japan had contributed to the development of Manchuria, and he also insisted that the

United States give immigration quotas to Japan and China.[60] The American Asiatic Association was reluctant to change its neutral stance on the Sino-Japanese conflict.[61] Though they were not overtly pro-Japan, a great number of American businessmen did not want the United States to intervene in the conflict.[62]

Nor did the Shanghai incident dissuade the CCOR from continuing its pro-quota activities. Hume, working actively in his capacity as executive secretary, lectured throughout California in an effort to make Californians understand the importance of giving quotas to Asian countries. He referred to the address which he delivered before the Commonwealth Club of California under the title "The Square Deal in the Pacific," as "a presentation of the arguments in favor of a modification of the United States Immigration Act of 1924, the elimination of the discriminatory exclusion clause . . . and the extension of the quota system to China, Japan, and other Asiatic countries." While he admitted the necessity of strictly restricting immigration, he argued that discriminatory exclusion was not the best way and insisted further that it went against "International Justice and Fair Play." He also emphasized the importance of the quota issue in terms of business, maintaining that trade with the Far East, especially with Japan, was suffering as a result of the 1924 law. In short, his argument combined the arguments that had been made by businessmen and clergymen during the 1920s: excluding Japanese immigrants was unwise from both an ethical and an economic viewpoint.[63] He did not pay much attention to the morality of Japanese military activities in China.

Hume delivered addresses at many other places. At a meeting of the California Chamber of Commerce in Sacramento on March 25, he emphasized that the issue was a matter of international justice and argued that, since California was the most important state in terms of relations with the Far Eastern markets, it should be the one to advocate modification of the immigration law.[64] On April 15, he addressed a Los Angeles Rotary Club luncheon regarding international relations at the Baltimore Hotel that was attended by more than three hundred influential people. He argued that the United States should endeavor to maintain good relations with Japan because Japan was the only developed and stable country in the region, which could be a barrier against Communism. Because of his eloquence and logical approach, his address was received with warm applause. Toshio Satō, the Japanese consul in Los Angeles, was intrigued that the argument for a Japanese quota had met with a favorable response despite the deterioration of the general American attitude toward Japan.[65]

In addition to making speeches, Hume kept in personal contact with many important people in California, trying to convince them to join his pro-quota movement. On April 8, he met with David P. Barrows, professor of political science at the University of California at Berkeley, and explained the importance of his movement. In a letter thanking Barrows for the meeting, Hume wrote that "the California Council on Oriental Relations needs the interest and active cooperation of leaders like yourself."[66] He also outlined the purpose of the CCOR in a letter to A. Dana Hodgdon, chief of the Visa Division of the Department of State, in which he defended Japanese military activities in China, maintaining that the United States should make allowance for these activities and suggesting that the United States should view Japan's position "a little more realistically."[67]

Naturally, the CJIC's criticism centered upon the profit-seeking motives of the pro-quota movement. McClatchy distributed to the members of the Commonwealth Club a brief about an immigration quota for Japan, which he had prepared for the CJIC in December 1931. Explaining that the membership of the CCOR consisted of capitalists who would benefit from trade with Japan, and owners of Hawaiian sugar plantations and rich farmers in California who would gain from the entrance of cheap labor from Asia, he maintained that the organization represented the interests of a small, exclusive upper class.[68] The *Grizzly Bear* more succinctly asked its readers whether Californians desired to "sacrific[e] this White man's paradise for a few Jap-dollars."[69]

The pro-quota faction continued its behind-the-scenes activities. Although it was difficult to push organizations that were not considered pro-Japan into supporting a quota for Japan, they worked hard to prevent anti-Japanese organizations from succeeding in their counterefforts. Prior to the national convention of the American Legion in Portland, Alexander wrote to A. E. Holden of the Japan Society of Seattle, inquiring about the attitude of the delegates from Seattle on the quota issue.[70] In his response, Holden explained that in Washington State, "no mention was made of Japan or the quota," partly because the chairman of the Resolutions Committee of the Washington American Legion, John O'Brien, was a good friend of the

Japanese. Since one of the commanders of the Legion of Washington State was his personal friend, Holden promised that he would "use [his] influence with him to prevent any agitation . . . [in] support of the quota by the Washington delegation to the Portland Convention."[71] In order to facilitate cooperation, Alexander mentioned O'Brien by name to his American Legion friends who would be attending the national convention.[72]

In contrast to the pre-1924 period, Western states were not overwhelmingly anti-Japanese. Several organizations became more interested in the quota issue, but they had difficulty reaching a consensus. At the International Business Practice Conference, held during the annual convention of Rotary International in Seattle, Rotarians were not in accord. Although Almon E. Roth, a past president of the group, was in favor of giving a quota to Japan, some members disagreed. When W. D. D. Agnew of Vancouver said, "Let us populate Canada with Anglo-Saxon blood," there was applause equal to that heard when Roth had argued for a quota. Because the purpose of this discussion was not the making of a resolution, no organizational opinion was decided upon in this matter.[73]

The Section on Immigration of the Commonwealth Club of California, which concentrated on the issue of Japanese immigration throughout 1932, was not able to reach a consensus on the matter, either. Both pro- and anti-quota speakers were invited to meetings, including most of the principals in the debate, such as Consul General Kaname Wakasugi, Secretary of the California Federation of Labor Paul Scharrenberg, State Attorney General U. S. Webb, and Samuel J. Hume. On March 3, speaking in a non-official capacity, Scharrenberg delivered a speech entitled, "Japan, the Quota, and Labor," in which he supported a quota for Japan in principle. He suggested that the 1924 immigration law should be tailored more carefully in order not to aggravate foreign countries, and explained that Japan's and China's complaints about the law stemmed not from their desire to send immigrants to the United States but from the desire to be treated equally with other countries. He concluded that although the general sentiment in California was anti-Japanese, and the moment was not propitious for modification of the law, this source of trouble would be removed someday if pro-quota supporters continued to exert themselves.[74] At a luncheon meeting on April 21, Arthur H. O'Conner of the Australian National Travel Association presented an anti-quota viewpoint, arguing that the United States should never give a quota to Japan because most Japanese were ideologically different from whites and because giving a quota would mean treating the Japanese as equals.[75] And on July 7, M. A. Goldstone, a merchant and a member of the Commonwealth Club, presented pro-quota views in his speech, "Race Mixture and Selective Immigration in Their Relation to a Quota for Japan." Quoting scientific arguments about intermarriage, he recommended only "minimum quotas to at least the three countries of India, China, and Japan." He believed that immigration would have favorable effects on American society only if "above-average," or "exceptionally endowed Asiatics" were admitted. He also pointed out some of the merits of granting a quota: it "might strengthen our friendship with that country [China] and prove valuable in the event of trouble in our relations with Japan.[76]

The Commonwealth Club arranged a "head-on battle" between McClatchy and Hume for its monthly dinner meeting on November 17.[77] Paul Stinchfield, chairman of the club's section on immigration, reported the results of a postcard vote taken among committee members on the issue. Asked whether they favored "granting an immigration quota to Japan," twenty-eight members had answered in the affirmative and twenty-nine had answered in the negative. To the question of whether they favored "the repeal of the Naturalization law which now disqualifies certain races from United States citizenship," only thirteen members responded that they did, while thirty-seven answered that they did not. Some members of the section also did not like the idea of giving a quota to Japan while excluding other Asian countries. The chairman concluded his report on the poll by saying that the section was "evenly divided on the question of granting a quota to Japan."[78] Hume then took the floor to argue in favor of a Japanese quota, explaining that the "exclusion law [had] passed solely through resentment." He went on,

> Whether 185 Japanese or none enter our country each year is of no practical importance to either government. This is a question of feelings, and yet good will among nations is determined, to a large extent, by a nice consideration for our neighbor's feelings. . . . This spirit of friendship, justice, and fair play . . . should animate all our relations with the Orient.[79]

McClatchy disputed Hume's claim, arguing that even if the United States were to give a quota to Japan, "any 'good will' gained could only be temporary," and positing "there [is] no foundation for the statement that Japan, if granted a quota, would interpose as a buffer between Communist Russia and western civilization." He criticized Japan's attitude in Manchuria, accusing Japan of closing the Manchurian market to American goods. He also said that Japan would eventually cease to criticize the United States, just as it had ceased to criticize Australia, which had also banned Japanese immigration. He attacked the pro-quota faction's upper-class stance and concluded, "Our first consideration . . . should be the permanent welfare of this nation, notwithstanding the desires of foreign nations or the interest of class, section or group in this country."[80]

The participants presented their various opinions from the floor. When Wakasugi tried to refute McClatchy's arguments, a dispute between the two ensued. Howard C. Rowley, publisher of the *California Fruit News*, argued against a quota for Japan because "the only means of avoiding an oriental or colored population . . . [is] through exclusion." Both pro- and anti-quota people discussed the issue in connection with the possibility of a war with Japan. Harry Kingman, secretary of the YMCA of the University of California, who had lived in Japan, warned, "To maintain our present discriminatory attitude toward the Japanese we must prepare and expect to fight Japan." However, as a method of appeasing Japan, Gerrard T. January, master mariner of California, proposed that no immigration be allowed from any country. Carlos B. Lastreto, a trader, suggested that the reason why Japan continued to complain about the immigration issue was that it intended to use this issue as a pretext to begin a war against the United States. Since both sides were equally matched, it was decided that "a postcard vote of the entire Club membership upon the questions involved in the report of the Immigration Section" should be taken.[81] Prior to the vote, the CJIC did not fail to put forth its arguments against the movement to amend the immigration law.[82]

In the meantime, the non-conciliatory attitude of the United States toward Japan reminded the Japanese of the humiliation of 1924. Provoked by the American non-recognition policy toward Japanese activities in China, the Ajia Renmei Kyōkai (Asia Allies' Association), a rightist organization, attacked the U.S. attitude toward China, arguing that the United States was "a wolf in sheep's clothing" that would soon cast off that clothing to devour China. When these anti-American organizations attacked the United States, they always referred to the exclusion clause as evidence of American racial prejudice against the Japanese. The Ajia Renmei Kyōkai argued that all Asians should unite against the United States, and warned that "the waves of the Pacific were about to break their permanent tranquillity." The organization also made a declaration criticizing the United States, especially its 1924 immigration act:

> The enforcement of the immigration act on July 1, 1924, destroyed good-will between Japan and the United States, violated the splendid honor of Japan which has never been insulted in history, and defamed our Asian ally, the Republic of China, and other nations by American inhumane racial discrimination. However, the United States has never regretted it from a perspective of human love, tries to interfere with our diplomacy towards China by manipulating the League of Nations, and defies the empire of Japan by concentrating the U.S. fleet in the Pacific and by laying military administration in Hawaii.

The association also organized a mock battle between "the Asian allied forces" and "the North American allied forces," using model airplanes, and substituting the Shin Yodo River in Osaka for the Pacific Ocean.[83]

As it had done every year, the *Gaikō Jihō* published an article on the anniversary of the implementation of the 1924 law, but this time the paper argued that July 1 was National Humiliation Day, not for Japan but for the United States, because the United States had humiliated itself by violating international justice. The purpose of this article was to "correct the mistakes of the United States and to promote cordial relations between Japan and the Untied States."[84]

American diplomats were not necessarily unconcerned about the immigration issue. They had often reported how strongly the Japanese people felt about the law. Ambassador Grew warned that the absence of the immigration issue from the opening speeches of the Imperial Diet, for the first time since 1924, and the apparent lack of interest in this issue did not necessarily mean that "to the Japanese the issue is closed."[85] Laurence E. Salisbury, who had served as a second secretary at the embassy in Tokyo, from whence he had just returned in May, supplemented Grew's report by describing the gravity of the effect of the immigration law for the Japanese. He added that "children in school are being taught to regard America as a land of injustice to the Japanese people," and he concluded that "modification would have far-reaching effects on the Japanese attitude toward America."[86] Thomas G. Cranford, Jr., the assistant military attaché at the American embassy, attributed the lack of Japanese response to Japanese sensitivity:

> This anti-American feeling is due to the excessive pride and sensitiveness of the Japanese which springs from a real racial inferiority complex. . . . After the immediate excitement over the Immigration Act of 1924 had subsided it looked as though their feelings towards America were improving, because the Japanese and many Americans as well were working assiduously to have the discriminatory clause in the Act revised.[87]

Officials in the State Department did not necessarily ignore these reports from Japan. They recognized the favorable impact an amendment to the immigration law might have upon Japanese opinion of the United States, and judged that business interests were in favor of such an amendment. In a note to legal adviser Green H. Hackworth, his assistant, Richard W. Flournoy, Jr., expressed the view that "this Department should lend its support to the movement to eliminate from the Immigration Act of 1924 the discriminatory provisions of Section 13 (c) which are so distasteful to the Japanese Government and people."[88]

However, no pro-modification efforts were authorized by high-ranking State Department officials. Although A. Dana Hodgdon, chief of the Visa Division, acknowledged in a report that the amendment would be desirable, he doubted "whether the Sino-Japanese developments during the past year have resulted in the creation of an attitude among the general public . . . that Japan has lost prestige in the United States because of its military activities in the Far East . . . and whether as a result suggestions for a change in the immigration laws to provide quotas for Japan and other Oriental countries would have an unfavorable reception."[89] Although the Division of Far Eastern Affairs did not oppose the amendment, a memorandum of the division addressing the Hodgdon report recommended an attitude of "passive receptivity": "In case efforts toward raising this question are made and the opinion of this Department is sought, we should discreetly advise the authors of efforts to avoid making the question a legislative issue," unless they were pretty sure of passage of the amendment in Congress.[90]

In the meantime, helped by the fact that the chairman of the Immigration

Section was against giving quotas, the majority of the postcard vote of the Commonwealth Club, which occurred in January 1933, turned out to be against the modification of the exclusion clause. Two-thirds of the members answered "No" when asked whether they favored "granting an immigration quota to Japan." Fewer than 10 percent answered "Yes" to the question "Do you favor granting an immigration quota to Japan exclusive of other Asiatic countries?"[91] Anti-quota people recognized the significance of this vote. The CJIC was overjoyed, of course, and made sure that the anti-quota results of the postcard vote were well publicized across the country.[92] McClatchy reported the results of the vote to Hornbeck,[93] and Paul Stinchfield, chairman of the Immigration Section of the Commonwealth Club, sent them to the State Department. Stinchfield added a personal statement to the report of the vote results, remarking that: "America's vital interests now and for the future lie in maintaining the complete bar against permanent Japanese Immigration which Congress adopted in the Quota Law of 1924."[94]

Japanese diplomats continued to pay attention to the immigration issue. They tended to regard the issue in the same light as other political issues. When Ambassador Debuchi met with Eugene Hoffman Dooman, first secretary at the American embassy in Great Britain and a longtime acquaintance, the ambassador mentioned Japanese exclusion and argued that the United States should not interfere in the Manchurian issue. Debuchi said that since Japan had not pressed hard for a repeal of the exclusion law, "the United States should leave its account open with Japan over Manchuria as Manchuria did not affect the vital interests of the United States."[95] Japanese diplomats thus made the immigration problem more intractable by linking the issue to the Manchurian question.

On the other hand, American diplomats regarded the immigration issue as separate from other issues. As of the beginning of 1933, the Division of Far Eastern Affairs, for example, characterized the immigration issue and the Manchurian situation as the "two important issues in relations between Japan and the United States."[96] The Division of Far Eastern Affairs examined the relationship between the two issues. The result was a memorandum entitled "Manchuria Situation—The Effect of a Revision of the Immigration Act on Present Relations Between the United States and Japan," which concluded that the Japanese conflict with China over Manchuria and the exclusion issue were two totally different issues. According to the report, the former was "a conflict over concrete and fundamental interests," whereas the latter was "a conflict over a principle or an ideal."

> An offer on our part at this time to them of a concession the chief value of which would be sentimental could scarcely be expected to contribute substantially toward reconciling them to our opposition to their course in relation to a matter which they feel to be of vital importance and in a different connection . . . there could be little to gain and might be much to lose by the suggestion at this time by this Department of any action in reference to the immigration question.[97]

The secretary of state himself placed importance on the Japanese immigration issue. In a memorandum to Hornbeck on February 1, written before he had read the division's memorandum, Stimson suggested making a gesture toward amending the immigration law. He expected "an ameliorating influence on Japanese opinion, which might offset some of the propaganda of their militaristic clique." However, after reading the section's memorandum, Stimson seems to have changed his opinion on the idea that the immigration issue could be used as a tool to appease Japan in Manchuria.[98] Grew concurred that the State Department should do nothing regarding the immigration issue,[99] and submitted a report to Stimson's successor, Cordell Hull, to this effect one month later. "As long as the so-called Exclusion Act remains in force, the Japanese will continue to regard the relations between our two countries as 'strained,' " he concluded. "This habit of mind is a chronic one and not acute."[100]

From this time forward, although State Department officials placed considerable importance on the Japanese immigration issue, they never deviated from their neutral stance. Believing that confronting the Japanese quota issue would do more harm than good, the State Department wanted to avoid it entirely. J. W. Mailliard, Jr., president of the San Francisco Chamber of Commerce, believed that Hornbeck, during a private talk with Dr. Henry F. Grady, a trade adviser to the San Francisco Chamber of Commerce, had shown support for a Japanese immigration quota, and he wrote to Hornbeck, "It is indeed comforting to be reassured that our own liberal attitude [toward the Japanese immigration quota] is shared by officials in the State Department . . . inasmuch as there seems to be agreement between us on the question of grant of quota." It was true that when he met Grady, Hornbeck said to him, "This Department is not unsympathetic toward efforts to put the immigration question right as between the United States and Japan." But he had added, "There has been enough of 'mess' over this immigration question already; we do not want to see the 'mess' made even 'messier.'"[101] It seemed to Hornbeck that Mailliard did not understand the subtleties of the issue, and the letter from Mailliard was the beginning of a widespread misuse of Hornbeck's comments. It might be dangerous, he thought, if this was publicized as the formal statement of the State Department regarding the immigration issue. Hornbeck devoted most of his reply to Mailliard to explaining that he had "at no time committed . . . either for or against the principle of granting a quota."[102]

While news about the Sino-Japanese conflict in the Far East had ceased to attract widespread attention among the American public by the summer of 1932, pro-quota voices among Western citizens remained strong. Since its foundation, the CCOR had been vigorously continuing its activities. By the end of June 1933, Hume had spoken at more than one hundred locations in California, including chambers of commerce, Rotary clubs, Kiwanis clubs, Lion's clubs, and women's clubs. More than three thousand prominent people sympathized with his opinion.[103] Harry Chandler of the *Los Angeles Times*, one of the most influential members of the CCOR, succeeded in convincing the journalist Walter Lippmann that "the sentiment in favor of a change in our exclusion law was progressing very satisfactorily."[104] On June 16, in a letter to the president, Clinton Miller argued that the time of anti-Oriental agitation had passed and that California now strongly favored a rectification of the immigration law. He also argued that the recognition of Russia would have to be accompanied by the modification of the anti-Japanese clause, in order to "counterbalance the possible unfortunate results in the mind of Japan of a recognition of Russia."[105]

Although many pro-quota activists regarded international relations realistically, some tended to regard them in a light favorable to Japan's position. Professor George H. Blakeslee of Clark University provides an example of this tendency. He believed that "Japan look[s] forward to ages of prosperous and friendly cooperation between the two peoples [Chinese and Japanese]."[106] Such attitudes made the pro-quota forces seem less realistic in the eyes of the State Department officials.

Although Hume understood that even greater efforts were necessary to effect a modification of the act, the pro-quota voices helped keep American attitudes from turning anti-Japanese. While the State Department kept silent and Japanese immigrants focused on their day-to-day affairs, it was only the pro-quota people in the private sector who continued their tenacious efforts to promote cordial U.S.-Japanese relations. At the time of the Great Depression, in a national atmosphere that was generally unfavorable toward immigrants, it is important to note there still existed strong voices for the pro-quota cause on the West Coast, the center of the anti-Japanese movement.

SEVEN

Howard's Pro-Quota Campaign

In mid-1933, the pro-quota forces found the additional strength they had needed. Upon his return from a survey trip to the Far East, Roy Howard of the Scripps-Howard newspaper chain reversed his position on Japanese immigration quotas. Although his devotion to world peace required that he take a position opposed to Japanese military activities in China, he now maintained that the United States should give an immigration quota to Japan in order to make Japan less aggressive militarily. He began his campaign for friendlier U.S.-Japanese relations even before his arrival in San Francisco by publishing the report of his interview with Emperor Hirohito in about twenty of the Scripps-Howard newspapers. Typical headlines were "Japanese Emperor Seeks American Friendship."[1]

On July 7, some Scripps-Howard newspapers published Howard's article about American–Far Eastern relations, which proposed a movement, originating in California, to repeal the anti-Japanese clause of the 1924 immigration act. Since the dark cloud hanging over U.S.-Japanese relations was due not to conflicts regarding their basic interests but rather to psychological conflicts, Howard argued, the repeal of the clause would serve to reestablish cordial relations.

The *San Francisco News*, one of the most important newspapers in the Scripps-Howard chain, whose geographic reach encompassed ground-zero for anti-immigration forces, had significant influence among its readers. The paper reported that Bay Area leaders favored Howard's efforts to improve relations with Japan. The *News* kept the issue before the public, publishing articles for more than ten days following the appearance of Howard's first piece. Concerning the immigration quota, one of these appealed to the conscience of Californians by maintaining, "We of the Pacific coast carry a heavy responsibility for bad feeling because of an immigration problem that has been handled none too tactfully." Headlines such as "Nippon Should Be Accorded Like Privileges With Other Nations To Preserve Peace In Pacific" also appeared.[2] On July 11, the paper wrote that many influential people in California were pro-quota, such as Theodore Kreps, professor in the graduate school of business of Stanford University, and Robert Sproul, president of the University of California at Berkeley. The work of the CCOR was also featured prominently.[3] So as to appear bias-free, the anti-quota views of McClatchy and the Native Sons of the Golden West were also published.[4]

Howard's pro-quota arguments differed from the earlier arguments of clergymen, who had emphasized international justice, and West Coast businessmen, who had focused on commerce. Whereas pro-quota activists in the 1920s had generally advocated disarmament, the changed mood of the 1930s was reflected in Howard's recommendation that what was needed was a military buildup coupled with a Japanese quota. Since "the Japanese public has been convinced that America, inclining toward pacifism [as a] consequence of female suffrage, is facing military impotence," he argued, only a strong military force would prevent war and thereby lead to peaceful U.S.-Japanese relations.[5] Howard believed that a military buildup would be viewed, not as a preparation for war, but rather as a warning to countries trying to resist peace efforts.[6] Even the Native Sons supported this argument.[7]

Howard, even though his pro-quota rationale differed from that of other pro-quota groups, nevertheless immensely helped their cause. Hume, the new head of the CCOR, was invited to speak in favor of quotas for Japan at the Twentieth World-News Symposium, sponsored by the *San Francisco News*.[8] In his talk, he stressed the importance of the Far East as a market, and argued, "There is nothing we could do which would bring about a warmer response from the Chinese and Japanese and create more good feeling than to rectify this unfortunate legislation, remove the discrimination and extend quota to the countries of the Far East."[9] The Japanese consul general, Kaname Wakasugi, attended the evening session of the symposium, and remarked that the "exclusion act's rectification was something to be decided solely by the opinions of the American people," while at the same voicing his appreciation to the *San Francisco News*.[10]

Howard used his influential position in California to further his cause, through newspaper editorials and personal letters to other influential Californians. In a letter to Senator Hiram Johnson on July 17, Howard emphasized the importance of the repeal of the exclusion law and explained that this was for the sake not of his newspapers but of "our country."[11] On the same day, Howard wrote to Alexander recommending that he coordinate activities to repeal the exclusion act with the CCOR, and stating that "the combined attack and a synchronizing of our efforts might be more productive of results than would result from uncorrelated efforts."[12] Howard also talked with Harry Chandler of the *Los Angeles Times* and asked him to add his efforts to the campaign to repeal the exclusion law. Chandler agreed. W. N. Burkhardt, editor of the *San Francisco News*, tried to obtain a pro-quota statement from Senator Hiram Johnson, but found that Johnson would not "take any chances unnecessarily" until his reelection in November 1934. The suicide of the senator's son, Archie, on August 1, made Burkhardt's task more difficult.[13]

Some groups in California reacted quickly and favorably to the *News's* pro-quota campaign. The most enthusiastic were business people. The San Francisco Chamber of Commerce, long a supporter of quotas, "reaffirmed its position . . . favoring grant[ing] of [an] immigration quota to Japan and other countries of the Far East," and requested that other chambers of commerce coordinate their pro-quota efforts with them.[14] The *San Francisco News* and the *San Francisco Chronicle* both supported the chamber. The *Chronicle* noted that the chamber's action represented "the common-sense view to which American opinion is swinging."[15] The board of directors of the California Chamber of Commerce followed suit, resolving it, too, would work for a quota for the East Asian countries. The Board of Rabbis of Northern California passed a similar resolution on August 5.[16] On August 6, the San Francisco Congregation Bethlehem Israeli Church chimed in, arguing that the exclusion policy of the United States would tend to make Japanese militarism and economic imperialism more and more keen.[17]

Consul General Wakasugi continued to be active and made steady educational efforts to disseminate the pro-quota opinion. Speaking at the

International House at Berkeley, he reiterated that Japan protested against the immigration act not because it excluded Japanese immigrants but because it excluded them unequally. Wakasugi responded to many opposing arguments from the audience, many of whom were students.[18]

Both sides used the *News*'s articles as propaganda. Hume purchased three thousand copies of the issue that contained Howard's pro-quota argument and sent them to the members of the CCOR and other influential Californians. He also distributed one thousand copies of an issue that contained his own interview with the paper.[19] McClatchy attributed Howard's change of opinion to the fact that "he had the honor—unprecedented for a newspaper man—of a personal audience with the Emperor of Japan."[20]

The *San Francisco Chronicle* also supported the pro-quota stand of the chambers of commerce. It claimed that giving a quota to Japan would be timely, because the United States was "in sharp disagreement with Japan" on the Manchurian issue. The newspaper argued that although modification of the immigration law would admit only a negligible number of Japanese immigrants, "the Japanese [will] regard this as very important indeed," and since the modification "mean[s] much to them and little to us, we would well afford to do it."[21]

Japanese newspapers in the U.S. also reported Howard's pro-quota opinions. The *Nichi Bei* mentioned Howard's observation that while probably less than one out of every thousand Americans living east of the Rocky Mountains knew of the act, a great many Japanese believed that their national honor was injured by it. The *Nichi Bei* also reported that Howard believed the exclusion act to be the biggest issue threatening relations across the Pacific.[22] In light of Howard's campaign and the activities of the CCOR, the *Nichi Bei* expressed a growing expectation for modification of the law.[23]

The speedy coverage, in Japan, of Howard's pro-quota move, by such periodicals as the *Gaikō Jihō* and the *Tokyo Asahi*, showed that the Japanese had not stopped paying attention to the immigration issue.[24] The Japanese media also reported on the efforts of the California State Chamber of Commerce and the San Francisco Chamber of Commerce regarding modification. This favorable coverage of the pro-quota movement in California by Japanese newspapers was reported to the State Department by the American embassy in Tokyo, and it was interpreted to indicate an increase in Japanese friendliness toward the United States.[25]

The Japanese also continued to express their dissatisfaction with the exclusion clause at international gatherings. The Japanese delegates to the 1933 conference of the IPR argued that the exclusion policy should be removed. On August 23, in a closed session, the Japanese and Chinese delegates together argued for a more equal immigration policy toward their countries. However, this kind of private internationalist organization, which had been influential in the 1920s, possessed increasingly less influence in the 1930s. Scharrenberg strongly opposed the joint argument, and the discussion went nowhere.[26]

McClatchy responded to the reactivated pro-quota movement by resuming his own movement against a quota on August 9. The *San Francisco Call-Bulletin* supported McClatchy and argued that it would be not just difficult but actually impossible to persuade Californians that Japanese exclusion had been a mistake. McClatchy had met with Hearst to ask him to support the anti-quota forces shortly after Howard's views had been reported in the Scripps-Howard newspapers.[27] The upshot was that the struggle became a conflict between the pro-quota faction composed of Hume and the Scripps-Howard newspapers, and the anti-quota faction composed of McClatchy and the Hearst newspapers.[28] Hume and McClatchy exchanged open letters attacking one another's positions.[29]

The flow of anti-quota propaganda was torrential. The state convention of the American Legion held in Pasadena between August 14 and 18 passed a resolution supporting the maintenance of the existing immigration law, despite the efforts of Hume, who was in Pasadena at that time. The drafters of the resolution said that their intention was to fight movements that would have increased European immigration quotas in order to aid those trying to escape Nazi persecution, and even though Japanese diplomats gave credence to this explanation, anti-Japanese newspapers reported on the resolution as if it were directed solely at the Japanese.[30] The *Los Angeles Herald Express*, a Hearst newspaper, supported the resolution on August 17, arguing that the exclusion law had already proven to be a wise law.[31] The *San Francisco Examiner* of August 18 argued that the resolution reflected the opinions of most Americans and attacked Roy Howard by saying that he had come to favor a quota for Japan only because he had visited the country and spoken with the Japanese emperor.[32] The same day, the *San Francisco Call-Bulletin* criticized Japan for excluding Koreans and Chinese. On the following day, the *Examiner* published an article by McClatchy that argued that Japan would not be satisfied with a quota.[33] Despite the optimistic interpretation of the Legion's actions by Japanese diplomats, California members proposed an anti-quota resolution at the group's national convention in Chicago.[34] The Native Sons of the Golden West asserted that "the yellow-dollar, in the guise of goodwill, is the real impelling motive behind" them and expressed its unchanged support for McClatchy.[35]

Howard responded to McClatchy's and Hearst's criticisms in the *San Francisco News*. Although Howard agreed with the restriction of immigration from Asia, the newspaper explained, he also believed that it should not be done by any antagonistic and unfriendly method.[36] Howard himself wrote to Hiram Johnson in an attempt to persuade the senator to support a quota. Although Scharrenberg thought that the senator had not changed his anti-quota position, Alexander believed that Johnson had become at least neutral in this matter as a result of Howard's letter. For Johnson, who was thinking more about his next senatorial campaign than anything else, the letter, from the owner of a huge newspaper chain in his home state, could not be ignored.[37]

Revitalized interest in the quota movement soon spread to the Northern Pacific Coast. The *Seattle Post-Intelligencer* began a serious anti-quota campaign. On August 21, it published an article by McClatchy arguing that giving a quota to Japan would be regarded as American weakness.[38] A few days later, the paper reported that labor and the American Legion were both in favor of exclusion of Asians. Henry H. Lewis, former head of the American Legion of Washington State, said that he would continue to oppose modification of the immigration law. Sam Gibbony, president of the Seattle Central Labor Council, and William M. Short, ex-president of the Washington State Federation of Labor, also publicly opposed quotas for Asians.[39] John F. Dore, the mayor of Seattle, and Ewing D. Colvin, a leader of the Anti-Japanese League, agreed that Japanese immigration should not be resumed. Colvin said that he was prepared to mobilize an anti-Japanese body. Dore said that the pro-quota people had chosen the most inopportune time for reactivating their movements because there were more than a million unemployed people in the country.[40]

In this charged atmosphere, the Japanese vice-minister for foreign affairs, Mamoru Shigemitsu, was reported to have said:

It is most welcome news that a campaign has been inaugurated in the United States for the admission of Japanese immigrants under the quota system on equal footing with immigrants from other countries, and is receiving the support of an increasing number of Americans. . . . We feel the exclusion regulations at present in force are an affront to Japanese national honor.[41]

Shigemitsu's statement was an example of exactly what pro-quota activists and Japanese diplomats in the United States had made every effort to avoid in order not to stimulate unnecessary anti-Japanese propaganda. The *New York Herald Tribune* published an article entitled "Japanese Urge U.S. To Modify Exclusion Act," which emphasized that the Foreign Ministry in Tokyo considered the immigration law an "Affront to Honor."[42] The *Providence (Rhode Island) Journal* argued that the United States did not discriminate against Japan since it treated Japan like "other nations of the Orient."[43] This prompted the *Seattle Daily Times*, which had earlier argued for a quota for Japan, to break its silence to note that Shigemitsu's comments came to Seattle "out of the sky." The *Times* had supported pro-quota movements, but it now questioned whether the resumption of the controversy over the immigration issue, which would inevitably arouse opposition on the Pacific Coast, would be welcomed by current Japanese residents of the United States.

When Toshihiko Taketomi, now counselor of the Japanese embassy, met with Hornbeck to discuss other issues, he had Shigemitsu's statement in mind and asked about the prospects for repeal of the anti-Japanese clause. Both bureaucrats agreed that the statement had represented Shigemitsu's intention to support pro-quota efforts at the IPR conference, but Hornbeck noted that it was not the most opportune moment for the Japanese government to take action.[44]

Shigemitsu's comments were not popular in Japan, where some newspapers criticized them as irresponsible. The *Jiji Shimpō* complained that American opinion toward the immigration issue had been improving and that Shigemitsu's comments would increase American distrust of Japan.[45] A Japanese newspaper in the United States was much more critical. The *Nichi Bei* characterized Shigemitsu as "a diplomat who did not know diplomacy."[46]

Hornbeck would later ask Ambassador Debuchi to suggest, unofficially, to Shigemitsu that the moment was not opportune for a campaign to modify the anti-Japanese clause. Taketomi tried to defuse the controversy by suggesting to Hornbeck that Shigemitsu had little experience in the United States and that there was only one senior officer in the Foreign Ministry in Tokyo who had extensive experience in the United States.[47]

In any event, the Department of State wanted to avoid any response that implied a commitment to the pro-quota movements. When W. A. Simpson, president of the Los Angeles Chamber of Commerce, asked the Department for advice, it was suggested that he "seek guidance on this subject from Senators and Representatives of your state and nearby states." Furthermore, the Department requested that "no publicity be given, in particular, to this exchange of letters."[48] When a vice-president of the Guaranty Company of New York, which "had a good many relationships with Japan," suggested "placing Japan on the quota system," Hornbeck explained that very careful consideration was needed regarding this matter and did not commit himself to anything.[49]

Perhaps encouraged by the atmosphere favoring quotas in the early part of 1933, Ryōhei Uchida wrote an essay entitled "Encouraging the U.S. Authorities and Thinking People to Think Hard about Japanese-American Relations." Uchida may also have been inspired by the inauguration of Franklin Roosevelt as president, whose surname was the same as former president Theodore Roosevelt, a man Uchida felt had understood U.S.-Japanese relations particularly well. Uchida explained how deeply the Japanese had been hurt by the American treatment of Japan, invoking the naval disarmament agreements and the immigration act. He then cited the 1930 pro-quota resolution of the San Francisco Chamber of Commerce to suggest that more and more thinking people in the United States regarded the modification of the immigration act as desirable.[50] Uchida's essay shows that the modification movement in the United States helped Japanese understand that the exclusion act was not supported unanimously in the United States and that more and more Americans regarded it as undesirable.

In the meantime, the CCOR expanded its pro-quota efforts by starting a monthly bulletin entitled *Quota*. In order to impress upon readers that the pro-quota movement was broadly supported, the first issue excerpted articles from various pro-quota newspapers such as the *San Francisco Chronicle* and the *San Francisco News*, and the speeches and public pronouncements of other influential Californians such as past presidents of the State Chamber of Commerce and Rotary International. By arguing that the United States

Fig. 4. "Let Sleeping Dogs Lie." Cartoon published in the *San Francisco Examiner*, 28 August 1933, after a renewed campaign to admit Japanese immigrants under a quota system reinvigorated anti-quota forces in the state. Reprinted by permission.

should give quotas not only to Japan but also to China, the bulletin tried to show the more general purpose of this movement.[51] Although pro-quota forces in the 1920s had occasionally sought quotas for other Asian countries besides Japan, this tendency intensified in the 1930s. The deterioration of the American image of Japan due to Japanese military activities in China made it difficult for the pro-quota people to ask for a quota only for Japan. Hume kept in touch with B. W. Fleisher of the *Japan Advertiser* in order to inform the Japanese of developments in the pro-quota movement.[52]

Hume's aggressive move intensified the anti-quota campaign by the Hearst newspapers and some other newspapers that were in close communication with McClatchy.[53] The *Fresno Bee* argued, "The only thing that keeps it [the exclusion issue] alive is the misguided and misdirected agitation of a group of Californians who ought to know better."[54] The *San Francisco Examiner* published a cartoon (see Figure 4) entitled "Let Sleeping Dogs Lie," in which "meddling publicists" used their "quota talk" to try to awaken the huge "sleeping dog" of the "Asiatic Exclusion Controversy." The same issue of the *Examiner* reported that Herman C. Lichtenberger of Los Angeles, past grand president of the NSGW, had restated California's opposition to placing Japan on the quota list.[55] Pacific Parlor No. 10 of the NSGW later wired "a telegram of congratulations to Mr. William Randolph Hearst on the splendid stand taken by the Hearst newspapers against the proposed Japanese quota." The *Pacific Bulletin* published the telegram and Hearst's reply,[56] as did the *San Francisco Call-Bulletin*.[57]

The situation in the Pacific Northwest was the same as that in California. The *Seattle Star* on August 31 argued that different races were not able to live together as peaceful neighbors.[58] The *Seattle Post-Intelligencer* published three articles against a quota for Japan within one week: a report of the agricultural interests of Washington State that was against a quota for Japan; a McClatchy article; and a quote from U.S. District Attorney Pierson Hall, who opposed any change in the immigration law.[59] In addition, the *Post-Intelligencer* published many articles regarding Japan as a military menace to the United States, such as one entitled "Why Japan Is Preparing To Seize Hawaii And The Philippines."[60] It also reported on the arguments of workers who opposed giving a quota to Japan, for instance, workers in the restaurant industry.[61]

Despite such fierce attacks by the rival newspaper chain, Howard remained optimistic. He wrote Burkhardt that they would "be able to get results [in the] Fall."[62] He also wrote to Alexander, "This time . . . we've got a chance to win, despite Mr. Hearst, Mr. McClatchy, et al."[63] However, Alexander wrote, he was "fearful that if the matter is brought up in Congress and . . . defeated, with all the attendant newspaper publicity, that the reverse effect in Japan would be serious."[64] Alexander and Howard also held differing opinions about Scharrenberg. Alexander regarded Sharrenberg's occasional anti-quota attitudes as "more or less camouflaged" because of his "difficult position" as "an employee of the California Federation of Labor," but Howard argued that Scharrenberg "flopped over to the anti-quota side" whenever he felt "that [this was] better for him from the standpoint of labor politics."[65]

McClatchy remained alert to any move against the anti-quota cause. When the *Literary Digest* reported that Californians had changed their anti-quota position, and that "California civic organizations now seem to agree that the quota system represents a scientific method of immigration control," McClatchy fired back a response immediately. He reviewed the vote of the Commonwealth Club at the beginning of the year, and he accused the *Literary Digest* of "accepting without investigation statements inspired by interests which for many years past had sought to open the gates to Orientals." The *San Francisco Call-Bulletin* and the *Seattle Post-Intelligencer* supported McClatchy's argument. Albert Johnson, who had retired from Congress the previous March and become an editor of the Hoquiam *Grays Harbor Washingtonian*, wired the *Digest* to say that giving a quota to people without the right of naturalization would be meaningless. The *Grizzly Bear* also attacked the article, calling it a "falsehood, deliberate, or due to ignorance of the situation in the state!"[66] The *Literary Digest* reversed itself by subsequently publishing an article entitled, "California Opinion Split on the Japanese Quota Question."[67]

Not all newspapers in the Pacific Northwest were anti-quota. Indeed, general public opinion had become less anti-Japanese, and those newspapers located in cities whose economic well-being was tied to Japanese exports advocated for cordial U.S.-Japanese relations. For example, the *Seattle Daily Times* criticized the *Post-Intelligencer* for suggesting that a war between the United States and Japan was unavoidable.[68] Around Portland, a city which was not enthusiastic about the anti-Japanese movement, the *Hood River News* wrote that although it was against granting a quota to Japan, this was only because such a campaign might open up old wounds and cause relations to deteriorate.[69] The *Helena Daily Independent*, however, supported the Japanese position and criticized the arguments of anti-Japanese newspapers.[70] The *Long Beach Press Telegram* also supported modification of the immigration act.[71]

The Portland Chamber of Commerce was strongly pro-quota and unanimously passed a resolution favoring a quota for Japan. It was also willing to cooperate with the pro-quota faction in the Bay Area. When Hume asked the Portland chamber to consult with the San Franciscans so as to avoid unnecessary provocation of the anti-quota people, the Portland Chamber agreed.[72] There continued to be some disarray, however, among chambers of commerce on the Pacific Coast. Partly because they had previously been forestalled by the anti-quota people, some businessmen on the Pacific Coast hesitated to reactivate their pro-quota movement. According to the explanation K. J. Middleton gave to Consul Uchiyama of Seattle, the most significant concern of business was its relationship with labor. Since these relations were already strained as a result of a conflict concerning the National Recovery Administration, businessmen were reluctant to bring up another sensitive issue, especially one that had little bearing on immediate vital interests.[73] The Los Angeles Chamber of Commerce was discontented with the handling of the quota issue by the San Francisco Chamber of Commerce, which publicly announced its pro-quota stance without waiting for the approval of pro-quota forces outside the Bay Area.[74]

Although they agreed to follow the guidance of Californians, the chambers of commerce on the Pacific Northwest, such as those in Tacoma and Seattle, held a grudge against the Californians because they had stood idly by when the chambers of commerce in Tacoma and Seattle had passed pro-quota resolutions. Unaware of this animosity, San Franciscans now asked the chambers of the Pacific Northwest to take action. In a letter to Holden, Alexander asked the Tacoma and Seattle chambers along with the numerous smaller chambers in the region to begin a concerted action in favor of quotas. Uchiyama suggested to Alexander that he should first gauge the opinion of the Seattle chamber about these activities.[75] Alexander accordingly sent a telegram to J. W. Spangler, one of the board members of the Seattle Chamber of Commerce, and asked him to make every effort to reaffirm the pro-quota resolutions.

Although Spangler and other chamber members still favored giving a quota to Japan, the full chamber was less enthusiastic about the pro-quota movement than before, primarily because of the unemployment situation in Seattle. Uchiyama also believed commercial relations between Seattle and East Asia had changed; China had become a better customer of wheat and lumber from Seattle, and Japanese fishing products were becoming a threat to local area fishermen.[76] Although the total volume of Northwestern exports to Japan was still greater than that to China, changes were occurring. A closer look at U.S. exports of Douglas fir, which originated mostly in Washington and Oregon, is revealing. As of 1934, about 80 percent of lumber exports in Washington were unmanufactured Douglas fir; for Oregon, the figure was about 60 percent. Between 1932 and 1934, however, the percentage of U.S. exports of Douglas fir going to Japan had steadily decreased, whereas the percentage of such exports to China had risen, so that the difference between the two percentages had narrowed to as little as 3 percent. One result of these economic changes in the export of Douglas fir was that

Alexander decided to refrain from participating in any new aggressive pro-quota activities.[77]

Awakened by the recent revived activities concerning the quota issue, but unaware of the Alexander faction's decision, pro-quota activists continued their fight. On September 14, the Foreign Trade Club of Southern California passed a resolution favoring a quota for "the Orientals."[78] Edward B. De Groot, newly elected district governor of the second district of the Rotary International, also expressed his willingness to support the pro-quota movement. The second district was the largest Rotary district in the world and included California, Nevada, and Hawaii. In his monthly letter to Rotary, De Groot argued that the immigration law should be modified:

> Time and events have demonstrated that the U.S. Immigration Act of 1924 . . . was a political, economic and social blunder. The intangible ingredients of the 1924 immigration act have become the 1933 tangible factors of an alarming international situation practically out of control. . . . The first step in the restoration and maintenance of happy political, social and economic relations with Japan waits upon our prompt and whole-hearted rectification of the act of 1924.

According to the *San Francisco News*, De Groot's argument was supported by more than fifty presidents of Rotary clubs in California.[79] The September issue of *Quota* printed De Groot's remarks on the front page. Hume obtained similar support from past governors of the Lions and Kiwanis clubs, as well as from other Rotarians.[80]

Hume continued his educational campaign, engaging in every possible opportunity to promote his cause. On September 20, he participated in a well-attended debate against the former senator from California, Samuel M. Shortridge. According to one Japanese report, while Hume repeated his familiar arguments, Shortridge sought to arouse the fear of the audience by describing how strong the loyalty of the Japanese toward the emperor was and how rapidly the Japanese could multiply. Shortridge called Japan a "stuck-up, proud, vain little empire." Both speakers were applauded by the audience. The debate ended with no vote being taken.[81]

Hume even placed a full-page advertisement for the pro-quota cause in the October issue of *California Legionnaires*, a publication of the traditionally anti-Japanese California Department of the American Legion. His

CCOR and the San Francisco Chamber of Commerce tried to convince readers that the pro-quota forces favored the exclusion of the Asian immigrants from the United States, and that what they wanted was simply that the United States show courtesy toward Japan through nominal quotas which would admit fewer than two hundred Japanese immigrants per year.[82] Hume's advertisement generated a negative response from prominent members of the California Legion, implying that there must have been differences of opinion as to its immigration policy. The Legion's official publication accepted the pro-quota advertisement, but it generated a negative response from prominent members of the organization, which suggests that the California Legion, which had been insistently anti-quota, was not monolithic in its opinions on the quota issue.[83]

Although the American Legion was seemingly less anti-Japanese than earlier, high unemployment rates necessitated an emphasis on general immigration reduction. On October 2, the national convention of the American Legion took place in Chicago, with the president of the United States in attendance. Although the convention voted against a proposal "favoring the quota basis for all immigration into the United States," it did not pass crude anti-Japanese resolutions. The Legion was more concerned about a general restriction of immigration rather than with simply "Oriental" exclusion. The convention passed a resolution that supported a 90 percent reduction in the numbers of all immigrants.[84] The attitude of California's delegates was criticized by the *Honolulu Star-Bulletin*, which wrote, "Hawaii may well join in the mainland chorus adding its voice to the voices of those who are endeavoring to place oriental immigration on the same basis as that from occidental countries."[85] On the other hand, the *Nichi Bei* of San Francisco merely reported that the convention had decided not to take up the "Oriental" quota question.[86] Japanese newspapers in the United States, which did not want to see another flare-up of emotions pro and con, seemed to be satisfied with this result.

It appears that Howard accomplished little at the American Legion convention, but he tried again at the national convention of the American Federation of Labor, which took place in Washington on October 2. Howard wrote to Lowell Mellett of the Scripps-Howard newspaper alliance in Washington, urging him to discuss quota prospects when he met with the AFL's secretary. Alexander expressed optimism about the possible outcome of Mellett's meeting in a letter to Howard, in which he wrote that William Green, the president of the AFL, was not "particularly adverse to granting a quota for the Japanese." Alexander also hoped that Scharrenberg would be able to exert some influence on the labor leader.[87]

These hopes, however, ended in disappointment. The report of the AFL's executive council to the convention focused on the recent "most vigorous campaign . . . in favor of placing Japan under the quota law,"[88] but a proposal to make a motion specifically addressing the exclusion clause was not taken up. Instead, the convention passed a resolution against the relaxation of existing immigration laws. The resolution, drafted by Scharrenberg, provides a perfect example of how he sought to avoid conflict from all sides.[89]

Despite pressure from pro-quota forces, Scharrenberg maintained a noncommittal attitude. When he had returned from the IPR meeting at Banff, Burkhardt had tried to enlist his help in the pro-quota campaign. However, Scharrenberg had not wanted to commit himself.[90] On October 15, Scharrenberg visited Debuchi to explain his difficult position as a labor leader who favored modification of the immigration act, and he tried to impress on Debuchi that it would be better to be silent on the quota issue for the moment.[91]

Meanwhile, Howard contacted Senator Hiram Johnson. Acknowledging the importance of the Japanese immigration issue, the senator concluded that "to change the immigration law at the present time would be a very sad blunder on our part." He reiterated his opinion that Japan would not be satisfied with just a quota and would demand other concessions.[92] Howard thought that Johnson had neither "deep convictions [nor] soundly grounded opposition to putting Japan on the quota basis," and he felt that Johnson's views on this issue were dependent on "the political considerations of the situation and . . . a feeling that popular sentiment in California had not yet crystallized in favor of a repeal."[93] In his reply to Johnson, Howard agreed to disagree about the Japanese immigration issue. Although he acknowledged that the exclusion act might "never work any direct breach of our relations with Japan," he doubted that Johnson would "admit that [failure to repeal the exclusion clause] might in time be provocative of trouble."[94] While Howard understood Johnson's difficult political position, the optimistic Alexander still placed a great deal of faith in his personal relationship with Johnson, with whom he felt he was "on quite a friendly basis."[95]

Much like Senator Hiram Johnson, President Roosevelt showed no positive interest in the Japanese immigration issue. Alexander wanted the upcoming convention of the Western Division of the National Chamber of Commerce to pass a pro-quota resolution to the effect that the subject should be taken up in the next Congress.[96] Since the success of this plan depended upon the views of the administration, Alexander tried to learn whether the administration would support such a move. He and Hume both wrote to F. Stuart Fitzpatrick, manager of the National Chamber of Commerce, and asked him to investigate. Fitzpatrick met with State Department officials, having brought the letters from Alexander and Hume with him. On November 2, Hornbeck told Fitzpatrick "the Administration did not intend to take a position or give a lead in reference to this question," and he repeated that the matter belonged to Congress. Fitzpatrick had to inform Alexander and Hume that they should not expect any support from the administration.[97] Meanwhile, Howard went to see the president and found Roosevelt's attitude toward this question to be "rather inactive and disinterested." According to Howard, Roosevelt displayed neither hostility nor a "very keen interest in, or knowledge of, the matter." The president's "interest at the moment . . . [is] centered in getting action on those matters on which he has been given authority to act, rather than having any part of his attention diverted to movements" which needed new legislation. As a result, Howard advised Alexander to work to soften the attitudes of the anti-quota people in California.[98]

In the meantime, Hume was very active on his lecturing tour, emphasizing the positive effect of the pro-quota cause on transpacific trade, and trying to extend his pro-quota activities outside of California. In a swing through the Northwest, on November 15 he lectured at the Seattle Rotary Club, whose members included several hundred influential businessmen. Hume attacked not exclusion itself, but the method of exclusion.[99] Hume then visited Portland, where he engaged vigorously in pro-quota activities. He made speeches before the board of directors of the Portland Chamber of Commerce and also before the International Club. He emphasized the importance of Japan and China as markets, and the need for cordial relations with these nations. At a dinner for the mayor, hosted by Toyokazu Nakamura, the Japanese consul, the president of the Chamber of Commerce, presidents of universities, and several powerful members of the American

Legion, Hume presented a summary of his arguments and responded to questions from the audience. Influenced by Hume's statements, the Portland Chamber of Commerce began to work toward creating an organization similar to the CCOR.[100]

Anti-quota activists responded vigorously to the upsurge in Hume's pro-quota movement. Several politicians, including Representative John F. Dockweiler, protested that the movement was harmful to the employment situation.[101] The CJIC attempted to refute every argument the pro-quota faction had made. McClatchy described the act of giving an immigration quota to Japan as a "suicidal policy" which would contribute to unemployment in the United States.[102] He also refuted Hume's argument about the Gentlemen's Agreement,[103] and distributed press releases to explain labor's position on Japanese immigration and U.S. unemployment.[104] The Native Sons suggested that college presidents who supported CCOR were motivated by the prospects of "increased enrollments of Jap students in their institutions."[105]

On December 2, the convention of the Western Division of the United States Chamber of Commerce took place in Sacramento. Alexander and Hume, with the assistance of several chambers of commerce that had passed resolutions in favor of quotas, advocated modification of the immigration law. However, since Robert H. Fouke, secretary of the Immigration Section of the Commonwealth Club, strongly opposed Hume, the convention did not take a vote on the issue. Hume and Fouke debated this issue in Palo Alto a few days later. When a vote was taken at the request of the pro-quota side, nine people favored a quota, and twelve opposed it.[106]

Not all chambers of commerce on the Pacific Coast were enthusiastic about the idea of giving a quota to Japan. For instance, the Seattle and San Diego Chambers of Commerce did not favor it, and the Los Angeles Chamber regarded the moment as inopportune for pro-quota action. After hearing the arguments of Hume and McClatchy, the Sacramento Chamber of Commerce decided to oppose "any effort to repeal or modify the present exclusion law."[107] This decision was highly praised by the Native Sons.[108]

Publications that were not affiliated with either the Hearst or Scripps-Howard chains, or the McClatchy faction, were generally neutral or supported a quota for Japan. The *Chicago Daily Tribune*, far from the eye of the storm, argued calmly that the United States should give quotas to Japan and

China because the exclusion clause was "one of the chief elements of discord in our relations with Japan and one which can be removed without substantial injury to our fellow citizens of the Pacific coast."[109] Unaffiliated publications on the Pacific Coast were also generally in favor of a quota. *Saturday Night*, a monthly magazine in Los Angeles, argued that exclusion was "a gratuitous affront that might . . . prove costly, and, certainly, was unnecessary."[110] The *Oregonian* argued that the exclusion clause should be removed because the "mutual interest of the United States and Japan in the Pacific area are so close that they must co-operate, . . . which [requires] mutual respect as between equals."[111] The *Honolulu Advertiser* said that the exclusion law had been a "plenteous source of irritation against [the] USA in Japan" and that giving quotas would "allow an enormous amount of 'face'" and prevent illegal entries.[112] Pro-quota opinions were also prevalent in Texas, whose export economy was linked to Japan. Statistics for 1933 show that, after the United Kingdom and France, vessels cleared from the Galveston customs district ranked third in total amount of cargo tonnage destined for Japan.[113] In 1934 exports to Japan from the Galveston district were equivalent to the total exports to Japan from the four Pacific states. Galveston and New Orleans exported about 70 percent of U.S. raw cotton in 1933, and since 1931 Japan had been the largest importer of raw cotton from the United States.[114] The *Atlanta Constitution* suggested that public opinion on the Pacific Coast was now in favor of a quota system for Japan.[115] It regarded the activities of the CCOR as a harbinger of a "sweeping reversal of public opinion." It argued that placing Japan on a quota basis was "a step of international justice and decency which this country should take at the earliest possible moment."[116] These newspapers and magazines were the exception, however. In general, U.S. newspapers and magazines were indifferent to the Japanese immigration issue, and even those which had covered the issue in mid-1933 increasingly lost interest in it.

By the end of 1933, the pro-quota impetus created by Howard's campaign had weakened, and Howard himself gradually lost interest in the issue. The *San Francisco News* stopped calling for a Japanese immigration quota. Due to a lack of support from the Roosevelt administration, the Alexander faction also abandoned its plans to submit a modification proposal to Congress. With pro-quota forces in hibernation, the CCOR also decided to retreat, and lay in waiting.[117]

EIGHT

The Declining Impetus of the Pro-Quota Forces

The anti-quota movement, reactivated by the pro-quota movement in 1933, continued its efforts even after Howard halted his active campaign. The December 1933 progress report of the CJIC, distributed only to CJIC members, reveals that the CJIC had followed the pro-quota movement carefully, and had gathered much information along the way. It had charted the activities of the CCOR, the Rotary clubs, the chambers of commerce, the Scripps-Howard newspapers, and the Roosevelt administration.[1] Whenever the CJIC had noted the slightest sign of a pro-quota action, it had made every effort to nip it in the bud. When the CJIC learned that Roosevelt was creating a committee whose task would be to recommend "revision of the nationality laws of the United States 'particularly with reference to removal of certain existing discriminations,'" for example, it sent the committee's members letters outlining its "point of view" in order to forestall any approval of a quota for Japan.[2]

The anti-Japanese movement became active as a result of the conspicuous pro-quota campaign. Washington State representative Nelson B. Neff of Port Angeles submitted a house joint memorandum to urge "the Congress of the United States to refrain from permitting the immigration of Orientals into the United States." Although his memo was shelved, it showed that Asian immigration had once again become a popular issue. The Japanese consul in Seattle, Kiyoshi Uchiyama, confessed that there was no knowing what would happen next.[3] McClatchy used various channels to spread anti-quota propaganda. He reported to Hornbeck every possible scrap of information which could be used to promote anti-quota sentiments. When he found that K. K. Kawakami had written that "the average Japanese . . . is not concerned with the question of national 'face,'" McClatchy used the quote to show that Japan "has only been 'pretending' in being interested in the immigration issue."[4]

Meanwhile, there were encouraging developments for the pro-quota movement in the Northwest. Influenced by Hume's tour, people in Portland decided to create the Oregon Council on Oriental Relations (OCOR), an organization similar to the CCOR, to work for a quota in cooperation with the CCOR. The membership core consisted of members of the Portland Chamber of Commerce. L. W. Hartman, former president of the chamber, was chosen as the chairman of this new organization. The founders succeeded in persuading many influential Oregonians to join their organization, including Joseph K. Carson, Jr., the mayor of Portland; Norman F. Coleman, president of Reed College; and A. W. Norblad, a former governor of Oregon.[5] In the state of Washington, the Washington Council of Oriental Relations (WCOR) was established. After Hume's visit to Seattle, Alexander asked A. E. Holden, a former president of the Seattle Japan Society, to promote the pro-quota cause. Holden visited twenty-six cities in the state and gave more than sixty lectures to groups such as chambers of commerce and Rotary clubs.[6]

Still, the pro-quota movement in the Northwest was weakened by distrust of the movement's presumed allies in California. Some pro-quota activists in the Northwest continued to be frustrated by the self-centered behavior of pro-quota activists in San Francisco. For example, representatives of the Washington State Chamber of Commerce had tried to advance the pro-quota movement at a secret meeting on July 1, 1930, but they encountered opposition from California. The Seattle group suspected that their pro-quota movement was seen by the Californians as nothing more than a way of restraining the anti-Japanese opposition in California. The *Seattle Daily Times* held a similar view, and argued that the pro-quota movement in Seattle should remain quiescent until a majority of California's congressmen had became pro-quota. Consul Uchiyama voiced the same opinion.[7]

The CCOR, WCOR, and OCOR soon established the Pacific Coast

Council on Oriental Relations (PCCOR) to coordinate all of their pro-quota efforts, with Hume as executive secretary of the new organization. The January issue of *Quota* then changed its description from "The Bulletin of the CCOR" to "The Bulletin of the PCCOR," and reported, "All Pacific Coast University Presidents Urge Quota and Denounce Exclusion Clause."[8]

In addition to the commercial advantages of better ties with Japan, Hume emphasized the humanitarian nature of his movement. In a letter to B. W. Fleisher of the *Japan Advertiser*, he wrote that he believed it would be possible to "neutralize" the American Legion and organized labor, and that he sought a quota system for Japan for humanitarian reasons. Since some Japanese would only be able to rejoin their family members in the United States through a quota system, Hume argued, "the quota becomes a humanitarian act."[9]

Partly because of these campaigns, public interest in the issue increased. On January 7, 1934, the *New York Times* published a letter from a reader that argued for modification of the exclusion clause: "This is the psychological moment to repeal the exclusion clause as a first step toward strengthening relations with Japan."[10] Letters requesting modification of the immigration act from the viewpoint of international peace poured into the Roosevelt administration. The Mount Holyoke Peace Club, a student organization, sent a telegram to Roosevelt urging "A Rectification of the United States Immigration Act of 1924."[11] A resident of Philadelphia sent a letter in a similar vein.[12] Thirteen young residents of Philadelphia demanded, "The Japanese Exclusion Act Must Be Repealed to Promote Friendship with Japan."[13]

Any effect these pro-quota letters from common citizens might have had, however, was completely overshadowed by a single letter from a group of California congressmen. On January 22, twenty members of the California delegation wrote President Roosevelt to express their "earnest hope that [the] Administration will not become responsible for renewal of an agitation [for a quota]." They believed that the Japanese exclusion policy was a "wise policy to be maintained."[14] In light of the administration's sensitivity to Congress's views on immigration, this letter dealt a great blow to the pro-quota movement.

Secretary of State Hull told Roosevelt that the administration's best policy would be simply to explain that it could do nothing because the matter belonged in Congress. Pro-quota groups should try to influence not the administration, but members of Congress. For Hull, any attempt at modification was out of the question. He advised Roosevelt to "call in some member of the signatory group and inform him . . . that it is no part of your intention under existing circumstances to take any step with regard to the matter." Roosevelt asked his assistant secretary, Marvin McIntyre, to invite "the most responsible of California Congressmen to come and see [him]."[15]

In sync with the congressmen's letter, Representative Charles Kramer of California, who was one of the signatories, submitted his own resolution opposing modification of the exclusion clause.[16] Roosevelt sent a message to Kramer through James C. Dunn, chief of the Division of Protocol and Conferences, to reassure him "there will be nothing done about Japanese immigration at this session of Congress."[17] Hornbeck then met with Kramer in order to dissuade him from "pressing for action upon his resolution." Hornbeck expressed the administration's view that it "did not wish to take any sort of an initiative toward discussion of the question involved," and Kramer agreed that "the less there is of public discussion of the questions at this time the better the situation for all concerned."[18]

Before Roosevelt was able to meet with the California congressmen, a similar letter arrived from eight representatives from the states of Washington and Oregon. They were "vigorously opposed to the abolition of the Exclusion policy." This coordination between the California congressmen and those of Washington and Oregon had been orchestrated by the California Department of the Veterans of Foreign Wars, with the assistance of the congressmen.[19]

McIntyre forwarded the second letter to Hull for advice. Undersecretary William Phillips answered on Hull's behalf, saying, "It is the understanding of this Department that the President intended to . . . inform [some representatives] in confidence that it was no part of the intention of the Administration to bring this question up." Finally, Charles H. Martin of Oregon and Clarence F. Lea of California were called to the White House on February 26 to speak with the president about the issue.[20] Thus ended any possibility that the Roosevelt administration would take a pro-quota initiative.

Although Alexander understood that he had failed to win Californian politicians over to his side, he maintained the hope that the president might still be in favor of enacting a quota. He explained to the Japanese consul general in San Francisco his belief that since Roosevelt had recognized the Soviet

Union despite much opposition, it might still be possible that he would also repeal the exclusion policy. Alexander was, however, basically pessimistic about public reaction to the Manchurian and Shanghai incidents. He even hinted at the possibility of his quitting the pro-quota movement, noting that he would decide whether to continue his financial support for Hume after returning from a trip to Hawaii.[21]

In Oregon, the situation was not so gloomy for the pro-quota people. Toyokazu Nakamura, the Japanese consul in Portland, after analyzing the situation in the state, believed that neither the pro- nor the anti-quota activists had a decisive influence in the state. According to his analysis, although the major newspapers were pro-quota, public opinion was generally indifferent to the issue and people tended to be anti-foreign due to the "recent recession." He concluded, however, that there would be no strong opposition if opinions in California became more pro-quota or if the president decided to support the pro-quota movement.[22]

The apparent expansion of pro-quota forces in the Northwest aroused their opponents, and since Oregon was relatively pro-quota, attacks by the anti-quota forces there were particularly intense. McClatchy wrote a letter to all members of the newly established OCOR urging "careful investigation" before they proceeded any further with the issue. He tried to discredit the pro-quota movement by bringing to the public's attention the result of the vote at the Commonwealth Club, the letters to the president from some congressmen, and the votes of some chambers of commerce against a quota system.[23]

Meanwhile, letters requesting the repeal of the exclusion clause continued to reach the administration. Elmer T. Thompson, director of the International Students House at the University of Pennsylvania, regarded the exclusion clause as "one of the contributing factors at the present, disturbing the relations of our two peoples." He urged Roosevelt to "request the legislature to remove by repeal this restriction and place the Japanese on the quota basis."[24] William L. Mudge, executive secretary of the Pennsylvania Council of Churches, informed the president that his organization had passed a resolution which said: "We are very earnestly of the opinion that our Government ought not longer to defer placing Japan and other Oriental Nations on a quota basis."[25] Members of the Central Methodist Episcopal Church of Stockton, California, petitioned the president to "do everything in [his] power to cancel said act of unfair discrimination."[26] A survey of Cleveland citizens revealed their "belief that the immigration law of the United States should be amended so as to put Japan upon the quota basis."[27] These letters show that there were strong voices advocating peaceful U.S.-Japanese relations in the mid-1930s. The State Department's response was usually to send only a bureaucratic acknowledgment.

In the meantime, the American Bar Association began to investigate the possibility of a modification of the immigration law. Edward W. Everett, chairman of the ABA's Committee of Jurisprudence and Law Reform, told the Japanese consul in Chicago that his committee was considering reform of the immigration law, including the addition of a quota for Japan. This action was taken independently of other pro-quota movements and was instigated strictly from a legal perspective. Everett was the lawyer for the Japanese delegation to the Chicago World's Fair and a member of the Japan America Society of Chicago.[28]

Letters to the administration were not always in favor of a quota, although those who supported exclusion wrote in far smaller numbers. The Women's Club of San Bernardino sent Secretary of State Hull a resolution which strongly supported "total exclusion of unassimilable Asiatics." A Los Angeles resident wrote, "Under any circumstances as long as you can say no do not agree to make any changes in the immigration laws to allow any more—rats—into this country."[29]

Japanese immigrants still would not aggressively support the pro-quota movement. The Japanese American Citizens League, which seemed uninterested in the pro-quota movement since its founding in 1930, had a different perspective on the issue. It requested that Congress "admit alien wives, husbands and/or parents of American citizens of Japanese ancestry into the United States as non-quota immigrants." Tokutarō Slocum, an immigrant activist, made a strenuous effort to obtain U.S. citizenship for those Japanese who had fought for the United States in the First World War.[30] Japanese Americans preferred to focus their energies on issues they deemed possible to resolve, rather than on the larger question of naturalization for all Issei.[31]

Japanese diplomats still concerned themselves with the immigration issue from the perspective of national honor. Ambassador Tsuneo Matsudaira told Maxwell Hamilton, assistant chief of the Division of Far Eastern Affairs at the State Department, "at the appropriate time something should be done to adjust the immigration question so as to remove this wound to Japanese pride and sensibilities." However, when Hamilton asked whether Japan would be satisfied with a quota or whether it would instead request a change of the naturalization law, the ambassador could not make a "clear-cut reply."[32] In an interview with Constantine Brown of the *Washington Evening Star*, Hiroshi Saitō, who replaced Ambassador Matsudaira, spoke about the Japanese immigration issue. Saitō "consider[s] this question of endeavoring to liquidate this question as one of the most important things in [his] career," wrote the *Star*'s reporter, explaining that he believes that a change in the immigration law "would do more toward an improvement of relations between the two countries than anything that has been done in the last decade."[33] In New York, Saitō spoke at a dinner to honor of Sidney L. Gulick, who planned to retire that July. Saitō said he was happy to note that "there are now signs in evidence in this country that it may, in the not too distant future, contrive to place the Japanese and other Asiatic peoples on the same basis as Europeans in the matter of immigration." In response, Gulick emphasized the necessity of "nation-wide education and unceasing devotion to the task of peace." While the *New York Times* reported only on what Saitō and Gulick said, many newspapers in the South, where there were few Japanese immigration problems and whose cotton was exported to Japan in large quantity, supported a quota to Japan. During the early 1930s, Japan was mostly the largest importer of raw cotton from the United States.[34] The *New Orleans Tribune*, the *New Orleans Item*, and the *Houston Post* also recommended a quota.[35] The *New Orleans States* argued that giving a quota to Japan would decrease the "possibility of war between Japan and the United States."[36] However, anti-Japanese publications did not overlook Saitō's statement and extended a warning to their readers.[37]

Even though the pro-quota cause remained in evidence throughout the United States, Roy Howard seemed to lose interest in it. His paper, the *San Francisco News*, began to show less sympathy toward Japan than it had during 1933. In an article about the exchange of letters between Secretary Hull and Foreign Minister Kōki Hirota, the paper harshly criticized the Japanese attitude toward the Nine Power Treaty and America's naval buildup, and it identified the immigration law as only one of the causes of U.S.-Japanese friction.[38]

McClatchy continued to pay close attention to developments concerning Japanese immigration and kept in constant touch with Washington about his anti-quota movement. When the *San Francisco Chronicle* reported Secretary Hull's remarks on March 29, saying that "if the Japanese exclusion act were canceled, it would not affect the United States," and that "giving Japan the same status as other nations would make a great dent in the armor of the Japanese jingoes," McClatchy immediately insisted in a letter to Hornbeck that "Secretary Hull never made such a statement." Although it is not clear whether or not Hull made the statement, Hornbeck graciously agreed with McClatchy's assessment.[39]

Samuel Hume also alluded to the *Chronicle* article in a letter to Hull one month later. John Simmons, chief of the Visa Division, responded to Hume in a pro-forma manner, acknowledging his concerns but not addressing any of them substantively. Apparently, the anti-quota people were better connected with the State Department than the pro-quota factions.[40]

McClatchy also continuously denounced the activities of the OCOR. He distributed anti-quota releases intermittently, and he emphasized the threat of "a flood of immigrants from all the colored races of Asia."[41] He criticized what he called OCOR's ignorance of the possibility that allowing entry for about two hundred immigrants under a quota would cause the entry of thousands of Japanese wives into the United States as non-quota immigrants.[42] Using a similar argument, McClatchy criticized Professor E. K. Strong of Stanford University, who claimed that a quota would actually restrict the number of Japanese immigrants to 185 a year.[43] The CJIC stated that because of a liberal immigration policy of Brazil, "Japan has regarded Brazil as her most promising field for colonization on the Western Hemisphere."[44] However, newspapers in Oregon generally favored modification of the exclusion clause and did not report McClatchy's activities.[45]

In the state of Washington, A. E. Holden, who had been placed in charge of the pro-quota movement, succeeded in gathering some six hundred supporters, but he also encountered strong racial hatred. The views of Albert Johnson, who had retired from Congress and who was interviewed by Holden, were typical. Johnson said that his ideas had not changed at all from the time when he supported the enactment of the 1924 immigration act. He argued that slavery had produced the greatest threat to whites in the United

States. He preferred the maintenance of the exclusion policy even if it caused war between the United States and Japan. Holden concluded that the anti-quota people in his state were usually from the South or California, and they generally regarded the Japanese as "treacherous."[46]

The pro- and anti-quota movements in San Francisco, which had remained calm in 1934, were roused to life by a United Press story that said Japan would accept the existing naval ratio if the United States were to (1) revise the exclusion law, (2) recognize Manchukuo, the new name for China's Manchurian province, and (3) abandon U.S. naval and air bases in the Philippines. Although the Foreign Ministry in Tokyo "categorically" denied the report, their denial did not put an end to the story. K. K. Kawakami, the Japanese writer, who was in Washington at the time, wrote in *Hōchi* that there would be a renewed discussion among Californians interested in U.S.-Japanese relations of a "non-aggression pact, an arbitration pact, the question of Manchukuo, naval problems and immigration." *Time* magazine reported Kawakami's remarks and commented, "Such revision would kindle California into political flame hotter than any which burned last week at Hakodate."[47]

Frederick J. Koster of the San Francisco Chamber of Commerce reacted to Kawakami's comments by saying, "There is a very widespread recognition of the fact that such a revision would be desirable and should be made and the initiative to bring about that end originates in California."[48] The anti-quota faction launched a concentrated attack against Koster's remarks. The McClatchy faction and the Hearst papers quickly criticized Koster's comment and the pro-quota movements as a whole. The *Sacramento Bee* argued that the earlier letter of the twenty congressmen to the president proved the pro-quota supporters' defeat. The *San Francisco Examiner* criticized Koster as "a self-appointed spokesman for California," and argued that his statement was "entirely wrong." "California will not, without protest, submit to laws permitting Japanese to enter this country." The *Examiner* said that because of immigration's direct influence on the living standards of American labor, the issue should be discussed apart from other issues such as naval ratios and the neutrality of the Philippines.[49] McClatchy argued forcefully against a change of the law at the Fifty-Seventh Grand Parlor of the Native Sons of the Golden West in Ukiah, California, on May 22. He attacked the campaign by the CCOR on the grounds that it was supported by people who "have been induced to approve the plan . . . in belief that international good will be promoted . . . without detriment to national welfare."[50] According to McClatchy, the pro-quota people attached more importance to international goodwill than to American welfare. He also attacked the demands of the Japanese American Citizens League for the "entrance of alien Japanese wives," because such a policy would be inclined to "develop an unassimilated hyphenated group subordinating national interest to racial ambitions." McClatchy's arguments were backed by organized labor in California. The *Labor Clarion* supported all of his arguments.[51] The Grand Parlor recommended the deportation of Filipino, Mexican, Japanese, and Hindu laborers to their respective homelands.[52] McClatchy also pointed out the factual mistakes which he said the pro-quota people had made.[53] For instance, he criticized Hume for continuously quoting Hull's pro-quota statement, which Hull himself had denied. The pro-quota side was put on the defensive.[54]

Although many letters which insisted on the modification of the exclusion clause continued to reach the administration, the State Department made every effort to appear neutral. This position was again confirmed in a strictly confidential memorandum crafted by Hornbeck for Hull. Entitled "Problem of Japanese-American Relations: Considerations Relating to the Immediate Future; Estimate of Policy and Suggestions of Strategy," it stated: "The real problems of Japanese-American relations arise out of and revolve around the facts and factors in the Far East." However, Hornbeck regarded the immigration issue as an exception, one that had its roots in Japanese pride and honor, not in practical national interest. He examined this issue as one of the ten "particular proposals which may be made." He evaluated the capacity of the anti-quota faction, and judged that "any proposal in this connection would bring upon the administration a vigorous attack."

> The net result of making this subject one of official discussion and consideration would be to create a new increment of criticism of the Administration and to inject new and inflammatory irritants into the situation as between the United States and Japan.
>
> It therefore is believed that we would need to prepare a very carefully phrased reply the substance of which would be that in our opinion the present is not an opportune time to attempt to do anything with regard to the Japanese immigration question.[55]

The pro-quota movement evidenced a lack of enthusiasm in mid-1934. Despite the efforts of Edward W. Everett, the pro-quota efforts of the American Bar Association did not come to fruition. Everett had submitted a pamphlet entitled *Resolution as to Placing Japan upon the Quota System, and Arguments in Support Thereof* at the group's annual meeting, which suggested that the association "recommend to Congress that it pass the necessary laws to permit the citizens of Japan to enter the United States." However, his resolution was not adopted, on the grounds that it was a "political issue."[56]

Without a conspicuous pro-quota movement, anti-quota forces also paid less attention to the Japanese immigration issue. The annual state convention of the American Legion for the Department of Washington, which took place between August 22 and 25 at Spokane, was not anti-quota. According to Holden, "No effort was made to introduce any resolutions against the quota movement nor opposing Japanese immigration." He judged that there was "very little real anti-Oriental feeling" and that two issues—the election of a new commander and the threat of communism—occupied the delegates. He recommended using the question of communism as a leverage to mount an educational campaign about the quota movement among the Legionnaires. He also recommended cooperation between the WCOR and the American Legion.[57] He judged that if his pro-quota movement got "in ahead of McClatchy," he could win the support of the Legions in Oregon and Idaho. He also recommended that the pro-quota people should point out "the position of Japan as an ally with the United States in opposition to the forces of radicalism."[58]

Meanwhile, Japanese intellectuals and diplomats stuck to the immigration issue, and the exclusion question was still frequently mentioned in Japanese publications. In the early part of 1934, the *Gaikō Jihō* published a series of articles written by Jikichirō Kawahara, a prominent political scientist, entitled "Review of the History of the Anti-Japanese Movement in the United States." Nothing had hurt Japanese feeling and pride more than the enactment of the anti-Japanese exclusion act, the author wrote. He wondered whether the sense of justice of the American people, who proudly hailed the Statue of Liberty, was so cheap that they could do so and still practice racial discrimination.[59] He also asserted that the most convenient way to establish a true peace between Japan and the United States was the modification of the immigration act.[60] "Improvement of U.S.-Japan relations," an article in the April 1 issue of the *Gaikō Jihō*, argued that the immigration issue was one of the two causes that injured U.S.-Japanese relations. The Japanese foreign policy elite now placed much more importance on the issue than they had ten years earlier after the enactment of the immigration law. Kiichi Kanzaki, who wrote the article, expected that the Roosevelt administration would do something to remove the exclusion law.[61] The July 1 anniversary issue of the *Gaikō Jihō* published its customary article by Ujirō Ōyama, who repeated his argument that the exclusion law was a national dishonor to the United States. He mentioned the disarmament talks in London, and stated that Japan would recognize neither racial nor military discrimination.[62] Prominent Japanese never failed to mention the immigration question when they talked about U.S.-Japanese relations. When Chairman of the Upper House Fumimaro Konoe visited the United States, he surveyed American opinions about the principal problems of U.S.-Japanese relations. Konoe concluded that the immigration question was one of the major issues between the two countries and concluded that public opinion in the United States on the pro-quota cause was not yet ripe for action.[63] When he made speeches in Japan about U.S.-Japanese relations, former Ambassador Katsuji Debuchi did not fail to mention the immigration issue, although he never directly attacked the United States in his speeches and spoke ostensibly with the goal of promoting friendship between the two countries. On October 10, Debuchi delivered an address entitled "America–Japan Relations" at the Hokkaido Imperial University, in which he argued that the "immigration act does not represent the public opinion of the United States." He delivered similar addresses in various parts of Japan.[64]

Japanese diplomats tried to prevent the immigration question from becoming dormant. In a conversation with Edward Bell, a correspondent for the *Literary Digest*, Eiji Amau, head of the Information Bureau of the Japanese Foreign Ministry, attributed the Japanese expansion into Korea and Manchuria to the exclusion of the Japanese by countries like United States, Canada, and Australia.[65] Asked by another foreign correspondent about the possible effect on U.S.-Japanese relations of giving a quota to Japan, Amau answered that it would greatly improve the relationship.[66] In London, Ambassador Matsudaira said the real cause of the trouble on the naval issue was the immigration law of 1924. To Norman H. Davis, chairman of the American delegation at the London Naval Conference, Matsudaira proclaimed:

The real cause of the hostility in Japan to the naval ratio originated in their resentment at the Immigration Act of [your] Congress, which they considered to be a deliberate effort to brand them as an inferior race, and which they feel is reflected in the inferior naval ratio.[67]

Roosevelt did not take this argument seriously. He considered such references to the immigration issue by Japanese diplomats "nothing more or less than a smoke screen."[68] Roosevelt was perhaps right, because Japanese officials tended to compartmentalize diplomatic issues into two categories: real political issues and ideological issues, and they included immigration in the latter category.

For American clergymen, no such division existed, and they consequently felt justified in discussing their opposition to exclusion regardless of the political climate. A few clergymen still advocated the pro-quota cause. At a meeting of the National Committee on the Churches and World Peace, held at Dayton, Ohio, it was recommended that the exclusion clause "be repealed and Orientals placed upon the same quota as that accorded to the nationals of other countries."[69] The Reverend Charles S. Reifsnider, Suffragan Bishop of North Tokyo and president of St. Paul's University in Tokyo, initiated a lecture series to support the Japanese stand in America. He argued that "the blow to her national self-respect still rankles as deeply as it did the day the news reached her that America . . . had given notice to the world that . . . the Japanese were an inferior people." Without the abrogation of the law, he said, "there can never be the trust and confidence in our mutual relations that is necessary for a peaceful solution of the many problems affecting us." As a few pro-quota missionaries in the 1930s had done, Reifsnider also supported the Japanese cause in Manchuria, arguing that "Japan has done in Manchukuo what the French did in Morocco, the Italians in Tripoli and what America did in Panama."[70]

In Washington, Reifsnider visited William Castle, who was known to be "pro-Japanese." But Reifsnider's argument that Japan's actions in China came not from a militarist clique but from a nationwide idea "astonished and deeply disappointed" Castle, who regarded U.S.-Japanese relations from a more realistic perspective. While the bishop said that the absolute Japanese control of Manchukuo was "for the good of the Chinese in Manchuria," Castle argued that Japan would benefit little from it in the long run.[71]

Nevertheless, Castle arranged a meeting between Secretary of State Hull and the bishop. Although Castle accompanied Reifsnider to the State Department, he avoided going up to Hull's office because Castle thought Reifsnider would "make a better impression alone than with a damned Republican" and because Castle "did not want very much to be associated with" his "very pro-Japanese stuff." Reifsnider later argued to Hull that "the 'racial equality' question was at the bottom of much of the difficulty which we encounter in connection with relations with Japan." Castle also arranged a meeting between the bishop and Hornbeck. The bishop described "a brief historical outline," and then confidently observed that "just now we could accomplish much if we would amend the Immigration Act of 1924 and put Japan on a quota basis as regards immigration." He also believed that Roosevelt could force passage of any bill that he might propose at the next session of Congress. The bishop's self-assured argument did not get through to cool-headed State Department officials. Hornbeck noted, "I could not but feel that Bishop Reifsnider was utterly convinced of the soundness of his thesis but that he had little or no understanding of the practical political processes and the complex of international political facts and factors involved."[72]

Sidney Gulick, who had stayed in the background in the early 1930s, tried to contribute to the pro-quota cause in a way that would be less likely to stimulate the anti-Japanese factions. He wrote directly to Roosevelt and argued for revision of the immigration law. He said the true reason for Japan's desire to "have the West admit her right to a navy equal to that of the United States and Great Britain" was "her insistence on equality of race status and race treatment." He reemphasized the importance of the "race humiliation to which Japan felt herself subjected" when her request for the insertion of a race equality clause into the League of Nations Covenant was rejected and when the immigration act had been passed in 1924. Gulick predicted that modification of the exclusion clause "would at once help create a favorable atmosphere for further naval conversations and fresh proposals on the naval situation." He even recommended that the State Department and the British Foreign Ministry accept "Japan's hegemony in East Asia." Gulick's support of Japanese militarism in East Asia made his argument even less convincing. Considering that Roosevelt did not take seriously the reference to the immigration issue in Matsudaira's conversation with Davis, it is doubtful that the president paid any attention to Gulick's opinions.[73]

Nevertheless, Gulick continued to support the pro-quota cause. He published a book entitled *Toward Understanding Japan*, which he said offered "constructive proposals for removing the menace of war." One of the constructive policies offered was the "repeal of our Asiatic exclusion law." Gulick regarded modification of the exclusion clause as "the most immediately obvious step that the United States could take in relieving the anti-American tension in Japan and in promoting good neighborliness." Gulick's book was full of his sympathy for Japan. He urged readers to make allowances for Japan's problems such as overpopulation and her economic difficulties. Gulick also expressed his support for the Japanese Manchurian policy and recommended that the United States recognize Manchukuo.[74] Although Gulick was recognized as a Japan expert, his pro-Japan argument defending Japanese militarism was found wanting, even by his fellow churchmen.

Some intellectuals also continued to engage in pro-quota activities from the perspective of international justice and goodwill. Charles E. Martin, professor of international law and political science at the University of Washington, reprinted one of his lectures, entitled *Who Shall Enter Our Gates?* as a pamphlet. Martin criticized exclusion from every conceivable perspective, noting, among other things, that exclusion was "a deliberate discrimination against a region and a race with which the United States has enjoyed close and friendly relations in the past," and that it had "offended unnecessarily a proud and sensitive people."[75] David Brewer Eddy of the ABCFM delivered a radio address in Honolulu on January 6, 1935, in which he insisted improved U.S.-Japanese relations could be achieved through abrogation of the exclusion clause of the 1924 immigration act. He argued that showing American friendship by placing Japan on a quota basis would make Japanese demands at the disarmament talks in London less aggressive.[76]

In the meantime, on January 6, 1935, probably due to a lack of conspicuous anti-quota activities in California, the *New York Times* reported that Californians were moving toward favoring a quota for Japan. Although the *Times* acknowledged that the exclusion of Japanese immigrants was still favored by some Californians such as Senator Johnson and McClatchy, it suggested that the "feeling in California against the Japanese has abated." "It is unquestionable that Mr. Alexander's organization [the CCOR] has mobilized the intelligence, wealth and good-will of California behind a more liberal policy and that it has made great headway in the past few years in its campaign for extension of the quota system to the Orient," the *Times* concluded.[77] McClatchy hastened to send an opposing article, arguing that "there has been no change in general sentiment [in California]."[78]

Sporadic and uncoordinated pro-quota movements continued around the country. On February 16, 1935, the *Houston Post* once again advocated modification of the exclusion clause. A meeting of the ministers of the Methodist churches in Oregon and Washington passed a pro-quota resolution. The Presbyterian Church of Cincinnati hoped that "the exclusion law of 1924 . . . may be rescinded." The Student Cabinet of the YMCA of the University of California passed a resolution opposing "discriminatory exclusion of Orientals and urg[ing] the Congress of the United States to put Orientals on a quota basis."[79] The Women's Missionary Council of the Methodist Episcopal Church, South, worked toward the repeal of the immigration law. In its session in St. Louis, the group recorded "its protest against the Exclusion Act and its earnest desire to strive in every way to bring about the reversal of this action at the earliest possible date." The council also passed a similar resolution at its session in Nashville on April 11. The Little Rock Conference of the Women's Missionary Society of the Methodist Episcopal Church, South, and the Kentucky Society also passed similar resolutions.[80] Professor Blakeslee still advocated the desirability of the modification of the immigration act. At the Mid-West Institute of International Relations at Northwestern University, he argued, "The United States can and should place Japan on the quota basis."[81]

Occasional anti-Japanese incidents in the United States, such as one in Arizona in mid-1934, kept the Japanese sensitive to American racial prejudice. There, a series of violent incidents, mostly instigated by European immigrant farmers and local politicians, were intended to drive out Japanese farmers. Unsuccessful in these attempts, anti-Japanese activists then tried to pass a stricter anti-foreigner land law at the state legislature, but when the bill failed to pass, the turmoil finally subsided. In Japan, public opinion of America was adversely affected. In the Lower House of the Japanese Diet, two representatives posed questions to the Minister for Foreign Affairs about the anti-Japanese situation in the United States. The minister replied that U.S.-Japanese relations were becoming increasingly amicable. When Representative Takeo Tanaka asked what kind of position the government was going to take toward the anti-Japanese movements in Arizona and California, Foreign Minister Hirota answered that since the anti-Japanese question had adversely affected U.S.-Japanese relations before, it would be best for the Japanese government to watch the situation calmly.[82]

The outbreak of anti-Japanese violence in Arizona rekindled anti-American discussion outside the Diet. The *Gaikō Jihō* reported on the Arizona events and warned that Japan would not ignore these problems, even though they were regional issues.[83] Ujirō Ōyama regretted that the movement for modification still had so far to travel before reaching its destination.[84]

Representative Mamoru Kishi argued that since Americans possessed a sense of superiority and looked down on Japan as an inferior nation, Japan should fight this discriminatory treatment. According to Kishi, an improvement in Japan's status would mean an improvement in the status of all of Asia. The foreign minister should negotiate firmly with the United States in order to have the unjust legislation abolished. He concluded that the first step of diplomacy should be the clearing away of the American sense of racial discrimination. This was a difficult issue for Kōki Hirota because he knew that he could do little about the anti-Japanese movement in the United States and that taking any action would surely bring negative consequences. He explained that he was doing everything possible, and apologized for the fact that there had been no result so far. He also said that he, like Kishi, strongly believed that every effort should be made to solve the problem when the proper opportunity arose.[85]

On July 1, Ajia Renmei Kyōkai (the Asia Allies Association) prayed for the abrogation of the immigration law and the realization of Pan-Asianism. Ajia Renmei Kyōkai regarded the first of July as the day when Asians had suffered an unbearable insult by American racial discrimination. It also maintained that the United States continued to insult and reject the Empire of Japan, which was a first-class power, and should not be treated as a much lesser power by the immigration law. This organization firmly opposed the law and urged its swift abrogation, and warned that if the United States did not agree, Japan would destroy the United States as a public enemy. Kunizō Kimoto, the group's leader, sent these opinions to the Foreign Minister and urged him to take a firmer stand against the United States. There is no evidence that the Foreign Minister lent any credence to the organization's point of view, however.[86]

In the meantime, McClatchy was busy publishing CJIC releases. He now shifted his main thrust from the quota issue to issues such as Japanese propaganda in American public schools, "Mexican Indians," and statehood for Hawaii. He asserted that the Japanese government distributed textbooks prepared in Japan to public schools in the United States, especially in Hawaii, in order to give "the Japanese point of view on matters national and international." Although there was no evidence that this actually occurred,[87] he declared: "Imagine the reaction in Japan if the United States announced preparation by it of text books for use in Japan's public schools to 'properly inform' Japanese pupils on subjects of concern to us!"[88] McClatchy also distributed copies of a protest which was made by the Sino-Korean People's League to the Hawaiian Commissioners of Education.[89]

McClatchy appeared before a meeting of the superintendents of education in California, where he attacked Walter G. Hoffman's textbook, *Pacific Relations*. He argued that the text deceived students and made them lean toward the Japanese side. He also warned that the textbook offered a "careful presentation of Japan's point of view," and he urged that the "use or recognition in the public should be refused to any text book which misrepresents known facts concerning matters of grave import to the United States." Chester Rowell criticized McClatchy, noting that the decision as to whether or not a book was a good textbook was not one to be made by an amateur like McClatchy. On November 11, 1936, the superintendents decided that Hoffman's book did not represent Japanese propaganda.[90]

At the beginning of 1937, Representative Samuel Dickstein of New York, chairman of the House Immigration Committee, brought up the possibility of giving quotas to China and Japan. His statement created a great sensation in Japan, where it was reported in the major newspapers. *Tokyo Asahi* reported on its front page, "The chairman of the House immigration committee stated that he is ready to examine modification of the U.S. immigration law." *Yomiuri* even published the congressman's picture and said, "At the very beginning of Congress, the chairman of the House committee expressed his decision to abrogate the anti-Japanese immigration law."[91] The Japanese Foreign Ministry responded quickly to Dickstein's statement. It ordered its embassy in Washington to examine Dickstein's true intentions for this plan and judge the prospects for its realization.[92] The embassy soon ascertained that Dickstein was actually referring to a general review of immigration laws, and that the quota issue would be included only because the review would cover a wide range of issues. The report from the embassy warned the Foreign Ministry not to expect much.[93]

Although pro-quota debates continued to be aired all over the United States, a pro-quota surge could not reach a critical mass, given the mood of the 1930s, when the unemployment rate was high and internationalism was not popular. Hume was pessimistic about the prospects for the Dickstein plan. He thought that if the quota issue was raised, McClatchy and California labor would try to block it through Senator Hiram Johnson and Representative John Dockweiler, both proponents of the exclusion clause. Furthermore, there were no members of the California delegation in Congress who had clear pro-quota views. All Hume could hope to do was influence Senator William Gibbs McAdoo and Representative Frank Buck, both from California, who were considered to be neutral on the Japanese immigration issue. Consul General Shiozaki reported to Tokyo that it seemed that the San Francisco Chamber of Commerce and the CCOR had recently lost their enthusiasm for pro-quota activities.[94]

NINE

The Final Collapse: Toward Pearl Harbor

As the pro-quota movement on the West Coast gradually lost impetus, so did the countermovement. However, the immigration question remained alive in Japan, as in the March 1937 discussions in the Budget Committee of the Lower House of the Imperial Diet.

On March 23, Representative Hirotoshi Nakamura asked Foreign Minister Naotake Satō about his plans for resolving the immigration issue. Nakamura felt that because of the discriminatory immigration law of the United States, other countries looked down upon Japan. Since Roosevelt was beginning his second term, Nakamura requested that the foreign minister immediately make an effort to solve this problem. Satō did not explicitly answer Nakamura's question, merely indicating that there were movements in the United States to give Japan a quota. Although he acknowledged that the immigration law was the most deplorable barrier between Japan and the United States, he simply said that the government would continue to pay close attention to American efforts to solve the problem.[1] *Tokyo Asahi* printed a brief report of Satō's rather noncommittal remarks.[2] In its report, however, the *Los Angeles Times* exaggerated Satō's comment, quoting him as having said: "Japan will make every effort for an amicable settlement of issues arising from the Asian Exclusion Act of the United States government."[3]

At about the same time, Kennosuke Satō, a well-known journalist at the *Osaka Mainichi*, departed for a tour of the United States. According to the

Honolulu Advertiser, Satō believed that "the one great barrier to perfect harmony between the two nations and undisturbed peace in the Pacific . . . is America's immigration law that bars Japanese from entering the country." Kennosuke Satō had come to America "with a mission" to "present in the kindliest light possible the Japanese attitude toward America's exclusion laws." He believed that "when the American Congress realizes the injustice of the law, the humiliation it heaps upon [the Japanese], the international ill-feeling it has created, American wisdom and common sense will correct a wrong."[4] Japan should be given an immigration quota just like the European powers, he argued, since Japan was one of the strongest nations in the world. According to an editorial supporting a quota for Japan in the *Oregonian*, Satō had also said, "I would like to interest American statesmen in the injustice of the immigration law in the way it treats Japan," and argued that "it is slander to a proud nation to be refused the same treatment that is given the other powers." Emphasizing the fact that "Japan is [America's] biggest overseas customer," Satō had maintained that "it would be a very wise move upon the part of American statesmen" to place Japan on the quota basis.[5] The *Oregonian* made a distinction between Japan and other Asian countries whose people were also excluded from the United States, and argued that the Japanese "whose nation was rapidly becoming one of the strongest" should not be treated in like manner with the other "Orientals." The editorial concluded by urging the Roosevelt administration to take up the issue.[6] The *New York Herald Tribune* also reported on Satō's trip in an article whose headline read "Japanese Seek To Modify Law On Immigrants."[7]

Ken Satō's trip and the foreign minister's statement were taken by the anti-quota forces to be a coordinated pro-quota effort by the Japanese and the result was another series of anti-Japanese activities. As the CJIC later explained, it broke its silence to respond to these pro-quota moves.[8] The *Sacramento Bee* criticized the two prominent Japanese, noting that the Pacific states were still against the rectification of the act of 1924 and that Japan itself discriminated against its own race by banning immigration from other Asian countries.[9] The *San Francisco Examiner* asked why Japan, which "placidly accepts exclusion from Australia and also applies exclusion from its own territory of any alien settlers," demanded rights of immigration to the United States.[10] The newspaper declared that the exclusion act was the "permanent policy of America."[11]

Californian labor, which had been supportive of McClatchy, regarded Satō's trip as a direct challenge. The *Labor Clarion* wrote: "Japan has already inaugurated a general campaign to force the United States to admit alien Japanese as immigrants by grant of quota," and then argued that the attempt would be futile.[12]

The CJIC wrote to the secretary of state that the Japanese foreign minister was "misinformed." Other countries which excluded Japanese immigrants had "denied to Japan what she demands of the United States and the firm adherence to such policies prevented constant repetition of the demand . . . on Japan's part."[13] In a letter to the president, the CJIC referred to Satō's trip as the "'Ken Satō mission' to 'American editors, Congressmen and the President'" in order to request publicly "the admission of Japanese immigration." The CJIC argued that the exclusion act was "necessary in [the] national interest" and that the exclusion policy "offer[ed] no reflection on the Japanese, as race or nation, and that it [was the American] desire to set with Japan in friendly cooperation . . . for the preservation of peace of the Pacific."[14] McClatchy did everything he could to obstruct Satō's activities, including an effort to cancel a scheduled lecture of Satō at the Commonwealth Club by maintaining that the lecture was merely more propaganda of the Japanese government. Since there is no extant record of Satō's lecture in the records of the club's Friday luncheons, monthly dinner meetings, or section meetings, McClatchy's maneuver must have been successful.[15]

In addition to politicians and journalists, Japanese officials at the Foreign Ministry attached importance to the immigration problem. A 1937 report prepared by the Japanese Foreign Ministry for a Japanese economic mission to the United States and Europe reveals the official Japanese view regarding the immigration issue at that time. The report noted that since the exclusion clause of the 1924 immigration act had left a blemish on traditionally cordial U.S.-Japanese relations, the mission should remind the Americans that the Japanese had not forgotten the issue, regardless of the topics they were to discuss at the forthcoming meetings. The report also recommended that the mission contact influential individuals in California to convince them to take up the cause of the immigration issue. It is clear that the Japanese Foreign Ministry still considered the settlement of the immigration issue extremely important.[16]

Japan's actions in the Far East, however, continued to compromise its image in America. A skirmish between Chinese and Japanese troops at the Marco Polo Bridge near Beijing on July 7, 1937, which came to be known as the Marco Polo Bridge incident, soon expanded into a full-scale undeclared war between the two nations. This and subsequent Japanese military activities had devastating effects on American public opinion. As Japanese forces attacked Chinese cities, Chinese intellectuals and pro-Chinese Americans began denouncing the Japanese government. They asked for American help, describing the brutality of the Japanese forces and how dangerous they were, not only to China but also to all peace-loving nations. Chinese intellectuals in Shanghai immediately began publishing propaganda materials in English to send to the United States. One of these pamphlets, entitled *Japan: The World Enemy*, proclaimed an "Urgent Need For Coordinated International Action Against [a] Common Foe." H. C. Wu, the editor of the pamphlet, argued, "You should cooperate to crush Japan's arrogance in order to make world peace a reality." These pieces usually carried sensational photographs, such as, in one instance, a picture of the bloody corpse of a dead baby.[17] The China Information Committee distributed a pamphlet entitled *Destruction of Schools by Japanese Invaders*, which was signed by more than one hundred Chinese college professors.[18] Another pamphlet, *The Indiscriminate Aerial Bombing of Non-Combatants in China by Japanese*, criticized the Japanese for the killing of Chinese civilians.[19]

In the United States, Chinese and pro-China Americans became active. On October 1, a Chinese intellectual pleaded on CBS radio for American help. The Chinese Cultural Society in New York published a pamphlet, written by W. W. Willoughby, which argued that China was "resisting the advance of forces which, if unchecked, threaten the continued existence of factors essential to the maintenance of international law and order."[20] These anti-Japanese movements were extremely detrimental to pro-quota forces who had argued for the Japanese quota from the viewpoint of international peace.

The Japanese did not remain silent. They also published propaganda, in which they maintained that the Chinese had begun the war. One publication of the Japanese Chamber of Commerce of Los Angeles argued that Japan fought in China because Chinese people were "goaded into war against Nippon . . . by a highly systematized anti-Japanese educational campaign fostered by the Communist elements."[21] The Foreign Affairs Association of

Japan insisted that the Chinese army was brutally attacking Japanese civilians.[22] The Japanese Chamber of Commerce of New York argued: "Japan, in short, is the aggrieved party in this unfortunate conflict which she did everything to avoid. She is grieved because her endeavors of 16 years for peace and friendship with China have been greeted with taunting rebuff by the other side."[23]

Few Americans, however, including those who had been pro-Japanese, now defended Japan. Thomas Lamont, who had been sympathetic to the Japanese cause, was skeptical about the effectiveness of Japan's efforts to defend its Far Eastern policy. In a series of letters to Kaname Wakasugi, consul general in New York, he warned that Japan's attempts to justify their military actions would be "quite fruitless and if anything [would] do more harm than good" since it was "very doubtful as to whether you will find one American in one hundred thousand who is not shocked and distressed beyond measure at the manner in which the Japanese military have conducted their operations in and around Shanghai."[24] Lamont warned that the Japanese bombings "made an impression on the American people that no explanation by words can eradicate."[25] Even the Federal Council of the Churches, which had been a driving force in the pro-quota movement, condemned the Japanese aggression in China.[26]

Japanese immigrants and Japanese Americans, especially Issei and JACL Nisei, strongly supported Japanese aggression in China. Japanese newspapers in the United States were enthusiastically pro-Japan and reported details of the battles in the Far East. Issei organized committees to explain the Japanese cause to Americans and to help Japanese soldiers in China by sending money and *imonbukuro* (packages for soldiers in the battlefields). After the Marco Polo Bridge incident, Nisei leaders like James Y. Sakamoto argued in defense of Japan. But some Nisei began to worry that their pro-Japan attitudes might not be compatible with their loyalty to America. As time went by, more and more Nisei became unwilling to participate in Japanese patriotic activities, and by the end of the 1930s Japan had lost the support of most Nisei.[27]

The face of the quota battle was completely changed at this time, not only by the shift in American public opinion, but also by the deaths of key leaders of both the pro- and anti-quota causes. McClatchy died of a heart attack at the age of eighty on May 15, 1938. Even the pro-quota *San Francisco News* published a respectful obituary for him, reporting that although his assertions about Japanese immigration ran counter to those of the *News*, what he had done for California was far from negligible.

In the following year, on November 22, 1939, Alexander died in Honolulu at the age of seventy. His death was seen as real loss by those Japanese who believed in cordial U.S.-Japanese relations. In a December 13 memorial service, under the joint auspices of the America Japan Society, the Chamber of Commerce and Industry of Japan, the IPR, and the Japan America Relations Committee, Alexander was remembered as "instrumental in many ways in promoting understanding and improving relations between the two countries." Many political and military leaders such as Admiral Kichisaburo Nomura, Japan's minister for foreign affairs, Viscount Kikujirō Ishii, and the American ambassador to Japan, Joseph Grew, attended and delivered words of tribute.[28] Grew concluded his remarks by saying: "Let us all pray to Almighty God that . . . the enlightened work of Wallace Alexander will not have been in vain."[29] Although his PCCOR had already ceased to exist at least a year earlier,[30] Alexander's death dealt a final blow to the pro-quota movement of West Coast businessmen, and they ceased to appear in the reports of the Japanese Foreign Ministry.

As Japanese atrocities in China gradually ruined the American image of Japan, Americans came to have a more favorable image of China. China was now depicted as the victim of Japanese brutality. This transformation helped the anti-Japanese cause. The CJIC continued its anti-Japanese activities even after McClatchy's death. A release dated October 18, 1938, warned of the "Japanese Threat to Dominate Hawaii," and suggested that American citizens of Japanese descent would "use their political power" for Japan if Hawaii were to become a state.[31] James K. Fisk, chairman of the CJIC, wrote to Senator Hiram Johnson about "the impossibility of granting statehood to Hawaii and the utter unwisdom of perpetuating such conditions by extension of the immigration quota privilege to Japan."[32] Labor continued to vigorously oppose a quota for Japan. When the historians Charles and Mary Beard characterized the exclusion clause as an "insult" to Japan, the *Labor Clarion* defended the 1924 act, arguing that "there [is] no racial hatred of the Japanese," and that the Beards were ignoring facts. This article concluded with the late McClatchy's words: "The American nation cannot permit its permanent welfare to be jeopardized by conceding a demand which . . . has no foundation in fact or in justice."[33] Some obstinate anti-Asianists remained unaffected by the general improvement of the American image of China. A report of the executive council of the American Federation of Labor defended the "Asiatic Exclusion Law" and opposed any bill that would extend the right of naturalization to natives of India and the Philippines. It argued, "The natives of Japan, China, and other Asiatic countries would have justifiable cause for complaints of discrimination."[34] The *Grizzly Bear* not only opposed any modification of immigration laws excluding Asians but also blasted Japanese aggression in China by calling the Japanese "fascist murderers." For the Native Sons of the Golden West, advocating Asian exclusion was compatible with being on the side of China in the Far Eastern conflict.[35]

While American public opinion swayed toward the Chinese side, a few Americans remained in favor of Japan, including some former missionaries to Japan and several intellectuals. But business people on the West Coast, most of whom had taken the side of Japan in the pro-quota movement, withdrew from the movement. Since they had been motivated chiefly by trade interests, it was relatively easy for them to halt their pro-quota activities when the public perception of the movement's merit dwindled. Some clergymen, however, continued to express pro-Japanese views. William Axling published a booklet, entitled *Toward An Understanding of the Far Eastern Crisis*, in which he argued: "The passage of the discriminatory immigration legislation . . . left an unhealed wound in the hearts of the Japanese people." The immigration act was one of the "milestones that mark[ed] the trail along Japan's decision to work out her future in Eastern Asia." Axling was also sympathetic to Japanese expansion on the Asian continent. He argued that the Western "have" nations should not interfere with the efforts of "have-not" nations such as Japan to reform "existing injustices in the distribution of the earth's area and resources."[36]

Such voices were stifled by those of numerous former missionaries and teachers to China, including Harry B. Price and Thomas A. Bisson. They were not only more numerous than their pro-Japanese counterparts but also much better connected with influential business interests and politicians in the United States. They organized an American Committee for Non-Participation in Japanese Aggression against China, whose chief objective was to stop the sale of war materials to Japan. *America's Share in Japan's War Guilt*, a pamphlet published by the committee, argued that the United States should play its role in world peace "by refusing to give economic support for war purposes to [Japan]." Although the committee failed in its effort to shift the administration's attention from Europe to East Asia, its massive campaign did influence American public opinion. Pro-Japanese people in the United States must have felt that they could not hold their heads high under such circumstances.[37]

Nevertheless, a few intellectuals continued to agitate on the immigration issue. For example, in New York, Hachirō Yuasa, a professor at Dōshisha University in Kyoto, advocated the abrogation of the exclusionist policy, asserting that the exclusion act "clashes with Christian pleas." Rajah Manikam of the National Christian Council of India agreed: "The way to amend the Exclusion Law 'in the Christian way' would be to set up quotas for India and other Eastern countries."[38] Jean Pajus, a lecturer at the University of California, published *The Real Japanese California*, which surveyed the immigration issue in a very sympathetic manner. Japanese diplomats regarded it as an ideal book which would contribute to laying the groundwork for modification of the exclusion clause. But the author's integrity was questioned. When he was writing his book, Pajus had visited the Japanese consul general in San Francisco to ask for financial assistance. He had even offered to modify the content or the title of his book in accordance with the wishes of the Japanese side. Consul General Shiozaki requested permission for the Foreign Ministry to purchase one thousand copies of this book.[39] No documents showing the decision of the Foreign Ministry exist. Although it is unlikely that this pro-Japanese book sold well, it was still valuable to the Japanese side at a time when the atmosphere in the United States had turned increasingly anti-Japanese.

As the clash of interests between the United States and Japan in Asia intensified, a new viewpoint, that the solution of the immigration question would not necessarily improve U.S.-Japanese relations, emerged among Japanese diplomats. On March 10, 1939, when Professor William C. Johnstone, Jr. of George Washington University met with the chief of the Treaty Affairs Bureau of the Japanese Foreign Ministry in Shanghai, Johnstone asked whether an amendment of the 1924 immigration act would improve U.S.-Japanese relations. The Japanese official was pessimistic. He told Johnstone in confidence that unless the United States made a concession to Japan concerning China or the Philippines, the modification of the 1924 act "would not help to put American Japanese relations on a better basis."[40]

Nevertheless, although those Japanese interested in foreign relations realized that the immigration question had nothing to do with the China question, they continued to be emotionally engaged in the issue. For instance, the *Gaikō Jihō* did not cease to mention the immigration issue. It maintained that the recent deterioration in U.S.-Japanese relations was caused not by Japan but by the United States. "Japan is not an assailant but a victim," the *Gaikō Jihō* argued, "beginning with the exclusion clause to the immigration law and the naval ratio. . . . There are too many examples to enumerate." Ōyama's annual essay, published in the July issue, was more confrontational than in the previous years. The Japanese government had waited patiently and prudently for the right time, refraining from official action in order not to be regarded as interfering with American domestic politics, Ōyama wrote, but now the government should pay renewed attention to this issue. Too much patience would be worse than hasty action. He concluded that Japan should not leave this problem in a vague situation.[41]

Educated Japanese continued to view the U.S.-Japanese confrontation as a racial issue. The *Gaikō Jihō* attributed the real cause of the "persistent" exclusion of Japanese by the United States and the British Empire to racial prejudice. Shigeo Suehiro, the author of this article, considered that since decades would pass before the situation would change if Japan failed to actively press the issue, and since a true peace could not coexist with racial discrimination, Japan should make every effort to resolve the immigration problem in a timely fashion. Suehiro also felt that the decline of the British Empire presented a golden opportunity for Japan, an emerging world power, to settle the immigration issue with the United States.[42]

Some officials in the Foreign Ministry shared the same view. Immediately after the tripartite alliance was signed in Berlin on September 27, 1940, Chūichi Ōhashi, a vice minister for foreign affairs, who had observed anti-Japanese movements around 1924 when he was consul in Seattle, explained the alliance in the context of the U.S. immigration policy. As he said, the alliance was "specifically directed against the United States. . . . Ever since 1924, the date on which Japanese exclusion was embodied in the American immigration laws, the United States has been hampering Japan in its inevitable necessity for expansion."[43]

This tendency to attribute the source of U.S.-Japanese confrontation to American racial prejudice intensified as the conflict of interest between the two countries intensified. Ōhashi stuck to the immigration issue. During a conversation with Eugene H. Dooman, counselor at the American embassy in Tokyo, he once again mentioned the 1924 immigration act. Ōhashi said that the immigration act was one of the incidents that made the Japanese believe that they were "prevented from expanding into areas which could use their industry and initiative."[44]

Even as late as early 1941, both the U.S. and Japanese governments were still working to reach a compromise on the issue, although the situation was very unpromising. The notion that military power was the only possible means of eradicating racial discrimination against the Japanese in the United States pervaded the Japanese Foreign Ministry. A key document, prepared by the information bureau of the Foreign Ministry in February 1941, described the anti-Japanese movement in the United States from three perspectives: the immigration issue, the treatment of Japanese who were already in the United States, and diplomatic relations. After outlining the historical background, this report attributed the causes of the anti-Japanese movement to six factors: "(1) The Japanese question being utilized as . . . political football, (2) The economic argument, (3) Race prejudice as such, (4) The fear and suspicion of Japan and the Japanese, (5) The deliberate and otherwise misunderstanding and ignorance, and (6) The increase in [the] number of Japanese." The report was very pessimistic about the prospects of future U.S.-Japanese relations. As for the immigration law, it concluded that there was little "hope for a favorable revision of the immigration law in the near future." It also predicted "some sort of a concentration camp" might be created in the event of war, though it thought that this camp would be primarily for Issei.[45] This report came to a gloomy conclusion:

> The conclusion is firmly drawn in so far as this author is concerned that the so-called economic basis for the anti-Japanese agitation is merely a pretense. Fundamentally, today, it is a question of racial antagonism pure and simple. The Japanese, physically, can be distinguished so easily from the whites. . . . The only solution to the fundamental question of the racial superiority complex of the white Americans is by a demonstration of the actual power and ability of Japan as a nation, ultimately, of course in our present world condition, by force of arms.[46]

Although this report was originally prepared for reference purposes for officials stationed abroad, it was circulated to the heads of all sections of the Foreign Ministry in May 1941.[47] It is interesting to note that the Japanese Foreign Ministry, which did its best to soothe the Japanese people's anger against the exclusion clause in 1924 so as to keep peaceful U.S.-Japanese relations undisturbed, now concluded that the only solution could be obtained "by force of arms."

Probably because some Japanese officials attached so much importance to the immigration issue, American officials tried to give the impression that they also took this issue seriously. When Secretary Hull talked with Nomura about U.S.-Japanese relations at the beginning of March 1941, he told him, "When I came to the State Department, one of my greatest ambitions was to work out a mutually satisfactory arrangement with respect to the Quota Limitation Act of 1924."[48] This statement basically repeated the American side's "willingness" to work on the immigration issue, often heard in places such as the London Disarmament Conference in 1930. When Nomura referred to this statement at a different meeting, Hull simply replied that immigration was a domestic issue.[49] Partly because he was used to hearing this kind of statement, Nomura revealed no disappointment in his report to Tokyo, which only said that little could be expected concerning the immigration issue because Hull said that the issue was difficult.[50]

In the spring of 1941, in an effort to iron out the differences between the two countries, Ambassador Nomura and Secretary Hull, with help from private citizens of both Japan and the United States, set to work on a common statement of East Asian policies. On April 9, two Maryknoll priests, Bishop James E. Walsh and Father James M. Drought, along with Tadao Wikawa (Ikawa), an officer of the Cooperative Bank of Japan, and Hideo Iwakuro, the Japanese assistant military attaché, submitted a draft proposal to the State Department.[51] It included a clause, Section 7, dealing with "the policies of both nations affecting political stabilization of the Pacific," which read: "Japanese immigration to the United States and to the Southwestern Pacific area shall receive amicable consideration on basis of equality with other nationals and freedom from discrimination."[52] In response, on April 16 Hull presented Nomura with a list of four basic U.S. policies on the issue. Recognizing that their present work was only preliminary, Hull reiterated to Nomura that they "both agree[d] that [they had] in no sense reached the stage of negotiations; that [they were] only exploring in a purely preliminary and unofficial way what action might pave the way for negotiations later." At a subsequent meeting with Hull, Nomura asked how the immigration problem was to be addressed, but Hull avoided the issue, reminding Nomura that immigration was a domestic question.[53] The immigration issue had already been omitted from a proposal draft, prepared "as a tentative basis for a possible counter-draft to the Japanese draft of April 9" by Maxwell M. Hamilton, chief of the State Department Division for the Far East, and Joseph W. Ballantine, a foreign service officer.[54]

In transmitting the proceedings of his meetings to Tokyo, Nomura distorted the information. He did not convey Hull's feeling that both sides had yet to reach the stage of negotiation, and he left the impression that the American side had basically agreed to the draft proposal of April 9. He also failed to transmit Hull's list of U.S. policies until May.[55] Regarding the immigration question, Nomura told Tokyo that Hull's opinion was that, because of tenuous relations with the state governments, the federal government was having difficulty solving this question, despite Hull's flat denial of any possibility of solving the immigration question.[56] Japanese officials worked on the draft proposal of April 9 and inserted into the draft Nomura handed to Hull on May 12 a sentence about the immigration issue, identical to that of the April 9 proposal, with the exception of the reference to the Southwestern Pacific area.[57] Hull, rejecting any possibility of solving the Japanese immigration issue, deleted this clause from the American draft that was handed to Nomura on May 31.[58] According to a verbal explanation of the American draft, the immigration issue was "omitted in view of the established position of the United States that the question of immigration is a domestic matter."[59] Neither the oral statement nor the draft proposal of the American side delivered on June 21 referred to the immigration issue.[60]

The Japanese counterproposal restored the reference to the immigration issue. A report from Japan's Foreign Minister to Nomura explaining the Japanese changes indicated that the changes were based upon the belief that the draft proposal of April 9 was the official American proposal, and announced that the reasons for adhering to the immigration issue were that the clause was originally in the American draft, and further that it would be impossible to negotiate U.S.-Japanese relations without addressing national honor.[61] The omission of the immigration issue was declared as one of seven reasons why the Japanese government found it difficult to accept the

American draft proposal of June 21 at the Japanese governmental liaison conference.[62] Although the Japanese government understood that the immigration issue had no practical value, as was revealed at the liaison conference, the flat refusal of the American side to address what was still an emotional issue for the Japanese contributed to Japan's growing sense of estrangement toward the United States. The mere mention of the issue in the draft proposals, even without serious governmental efforts to realize the clause, would have eased this emotional estrangement to some extent, though by this point it was probably too late to have had any bearing on the impending American-Japanese war.

As late as November 26, when Hull met with Nomura and Kurusu at the State Department, Hull made an effort to show that he paid serious attention to the immigration issue. Hull referred to his earlier comment that he had intended to solve this problem when he became secretary of state, and he explained that "the situation had so far prevented him from realizing that ambition." He probably sought to impress the Japanese delegates by showing that he still had intentions of modifying the immigration law. However, the Japanese delegates remained unimpressed.[63]

At this point, businessmen engaged in foreign trade, who had avoided attacking Japan directly, finally started to do so. James A. Farrell, chairman of the National Foreign Council, declared in the introduction to the report of the annual convention of the National Foreign Trade Convention, "Japan has treacherously made undeclared war upon the United States while her envoys at Washington were deceiving America by talking peace."[64]

There were still a few voices calling for cordial U.S.-Japanese relations. Letters from Americans who believed that amendment of the 1924 act would make Japanese forces less aggressive continued to reach the State Department. For example, a Californian wrote to Hull and argued that the amendment of the 1924 immigration act would "greatly ease the threatened menace in the East." Usually, the department responded to this sort of letter by noting that the immigration act could only be changed by Congress.[65]

A small number of intellectuals also continued to promote amity between the United States and Japan. In an essay entitled "Is There a Peaceful Solution of American-Japanese Issues?" Professor Blakeslee argued that although it was difficult, a peaceful settlement was still "distinctly possible," and he enumerated seven requirements for the settlement, one of which was the modification of the exclusion clause.[66]

In a letter to Sumner Welles, an undersecretary of state, dated December 4, 1941, Henry M. Hart, Jr., a professor at Harvard Law School, argued that the State Department should "give serious consideration to urging . . . the repeal of all the provisions of the immigration and naturalization laws discriminating against Orientals," because he could not imagine "a subtler or more effective way of undermining anti-American feeling in Japan, or of doing so at less cost." Professor Hart also argued for a quota for China. His letter was received too late, at least for the Japanese. Welles wrote to Hart two weeks later, "Events which have occurred since the date of your letter have, as I feel sure you will agree, made the question to which you call attention no longer of current import."[67]

Since the war in China dragged on and the American image of Japan became less and less favorable and since business with Japan became less important for them, West Coast businessmen who had advocated the pro-quota cause in the early half of the 1930s had grown silent. A few clergymen and intellectuals continued to believe in the pro-quota cause, but they were far outnumbered by their pro-Chinese counterparts. While pro-quota Americans came to be much less active, some Japanese stuck emotionally to the immigration issue, though they knew the issue was completely divorced from Japanese material interests in world politics. Taking pride in having become one of the great powers of the world, educated Japanese could not sit idly by while their dignity was tarnished by exclusion due to race. When the political and strategic interests of the United States and Japan collided intensely in the Far East, the exclusion issue amplified antagonisms across the Pacific and the prospect of the modification of the immigration act became increasingly dim. Finally, the attack on Pearl Harbor obliterated the last hope.

Conclusion

The exclusion clause in the immigration act of 1924 was one of the few factors to significantly disturb U.S.-Japanese relations during the two decades before the Pacific War. Although the issue had little connection with the material interests of either Americans or Japanese, the Japanese public regarded it as clear evidence of racial discrimination. Japanese reaction to the enactment of the exclusion clause was characterized by a split in attitudes. The Japanese regarded the clause with indignation and some even militantly advocated declaring war against the United States. At the same time, most of them realized that the United States was far more powerful than Japan, and so vowed to remain patient and maintain good relations with the United States. Similarly, while the Japanese Foreign Ministry ostensibly dealt calmly with the immigration issue, it allowed the *Gaikō Jihō*, a semi-official journal, to loudly denounce the law. This split psychology was sometimes even evident at the individual level. For example, Kazushige Ugaki, an army leader, felt great indignation at the exclusion clause. He wrote in his diary that as long as North America and Australia stuck to the idea of barring the immigration of colored people, making it a national principle, discord would be unavoidable in the future. He added that it was quite unreasonable for those countries to ask East Asia to open their doors while closing their own doors at home. On the other hand, he also concluded that it was useful and necessary for Japan and the United States to keep and to promote mutual friendship.[1] This split psychology was typical among educated Japanese during the interwar period, from the leaders of rightist organizations to top officials and generals. In the immediate aftermath of the enactment of the act in 1924, such opinions were widely expressed in Japan, but the issue gradually subsided, at least in terms of public discussion. Nonetheless, this characteristically split attitude formed the basis of the Japanese mindset toward the United States until the split psychology was finally resolved at Pearl Harbor. The impact of the exclusion clause on the Japanese mind was so great that the clause became a symbol of American racial discrimination against the Japanese and considerably weakened those internationalist voices in Japan which advocated peaceful U.S.-Japanese relations.

Despite the deep-seated Japanese antagonism towards the U.S. immigration law, neither the Japanese nor the U.S. government made any serious attempt to disentangle the issue. The Foreign Minstry in Tokyo did not want to appear to be interfering in U.S. domestic affairs, and the Department of State did not want to appear to be infringing on the will of Congress. While the U.S. government was unwilling to make serious efforts to abrogate the exclusion clause, and while most Americans outside of the Pacific Coast knew little about the issue, there were some private citizens—clergymen and businessmen, in particular—who came to the fore.

Immediately after the law's passage, clergymen, along with peace activists, commenced efforts to have it modified. They were motivated chiefly by a Christian sense of justice and by a desire to maintain international peace. They believed that excluding immigrants on account of race was morally unjustifiable and would debase peaceful U.S.-Japanese relations, and thus they demanded that the Japanese be allowed to enter the United States on the same quota basis that existed for European immigrants. A majority in this group emphasized international relations over justice, asserting that the exclusion clause had ruined the previously amicable relationship between the United States and Japan. They failed to address the pervasive strain of racial discrimination that underlay the quota system itself, concentrating their efforts instead on establishing a token immigration quota for Japan of fewer than two hundred immigrants per year. Even such a minimal quota, they believed, would remove the stigma of exclusion and would restore cordial U.S.-Japanese relations.

Although the pro-quota activities of the clergymen had ground to halt, for the most part, by the late 1920s, partly due to negative reverberations caused by an anti-Japanese counterfaction, the pro-quota cause was not unpopular in the 1920s, when a spirit of internationalism was enjoying some currency in the United States. At about the time when the clergymen fell silent, West Coast businessmen picked up the pro-quota campaign. They were motivated mainly, though not exclusively, by economic concerns. In the 1920s, when the clergymen and peace activists were forcefully pursuing their cause, businessmen had made little effort to modify the immigration law, and had even accused clergymen of aggravating the anti-Japanese activists in California through their aggressive campaign. They did not care about the immigration question as long as cordial U.S.-Japanese commercial relations were not disturbed. In the economic euphoria of the mid-1920s, they were content to let the Japanese immigration question gradually fade from view, and anyway, they believed the question had been closed with the implementation of the 1924 act. But by the end of the 1920s Pacific trade with Japan had deteriorated substantially, and business leaders now initiated a serious pro-quota movement in the hope that cordial U.S.-Japanese relations would promote trade between the two countries. Having learned from the clergymen's mistakes, and with business interests overriding any ethical concerns, they acted to remove the exclusion clause in a more practical and meticulous manner, proceeding with scrupulous care so as not to irritate the anti-Japanese factions. To this end, they carefully surveyed the anti-Japanese landscape and concentrated on behind-the-scenes negotiations.

The worsening economy on the 1930s complicated the situation. On the one hand, the Great Depression motivated businessmen to support the pro-quota cause out of an ever-increasing need to improve trade with Japan. On the other hand, the sluggish economy also provided fodder for the exclusionists, who argued that the United States should not reopen its gates to Asians when so many Americans were out of work. For a while, the former argument prevailed, both because a quota would have permitted fewer than two hundred Japanese immigrants per year and because internationalism had not yet lost its influence. Thus, the pro-quota campaign by West Coast businessmen was progressing smoothly around the turn of the decade.

In the summer of 1931, the pro-quota movement by businessmen in the West Coast was going well. The atmosphere favorable to the pro-quota cause did not change easily, even after the Manchurian incident, due to the usual indifference of the American public to Far Eastern affairs and a lack of reliable information concerning the Manchurian situation. In contrast, the well-documented reports of atrocities in Shanghai shocked the American public, and some American pro-quota intellectuals ceased to advocate the pro-quota cause in protest against Japanese military activities. Pro-quota businessmen remained unconcerned about the situation in the Far East, however, and their pro-quota movement did not lose its impetus. Indeed, the pro-quota forces established a new organization, whose main purpose was to modify the exclusion clause. While the mainstay of this organization were Californian businessmen who gave priority to commerce, many West Coast intellectuals joined as well, believing that giving a quota to Japan would appease Japan and, as a result, restore amity between the United States and Japan. It is interesting to note that while intellectuals outside the Pacific Coast, who recognized the unethical nature of Japanese military activities, ceased to be pro-quota after the Manchurian and Shanghai incidents, West Coast intellectuals remained pro-quota. Japanese internationalists were encouraged by these pro-quota activities, and the Japanese often cited the pro-quota movement when they argued that not all Americans were exclusionists.[2] By emphasizing the promotion of trade with East Asia, pro-quota businessmen presented not only an alternative way to counteract the economic slump but also a vision of coexistence based upon trade relations between the United States and Japan. Essentially ignoring the immorality of Japanese military actions in China, they expanded their pro-quota activities in the early 1930s and maintained a neutral stance on the Sino-Japanese conflict in China throughout the 1930s. It is important to note that even during the early 1930s, when Americans were increasingly isolationist, strong voices advocated cordial U.S.-Japanese relations with an emphasis on commercial relations. The pro-quota movement weakened drastically after 1937, when the Sino-Japanese war began and the pro-Chinese atmosphere in the United States destroyed any hope for the pro-quota cause for Japan.

The surge in pro-quota activities by businessmen and the continuation of their activities even after the Manchurian incident of 1931 suggest that their motives were strongly influenced by the economic slump, which meant that they would not hesitate to withdraw from the pro-quota movement once trade with Japan became less important. The clergymen, on the other hand, did not cooperate with the efforts of the businessmen in the 1930s. Some were reacting all too late to criticism that their actions in the 1920s had been counterproductive, in that they repeatedly reawakened the otherwise dormant anti-Japanese forces in California. Others refused to take up the cause because they attached greater importance to the unethical nature of the Japanese military activities in China. The clergymen's silence during the 1930s did not necessarily mean that they had lost interest in the Japanese immigration issue. A few, especially Sidney L. Gulick, continued to advocate cordial U.S.-Japanese relations throughout the 1930s. However, China missionaries, who defended China and criticized Japan, were far more numerous than the supporters of Japan, and the former group had close connections with important government figures and were able to secure the sympathy of those officials in Washington. Moreover, Gulick's tolerance for Japanese militarism in China was unacceptable, even to most of his fellow churchmen.[3]

The pro-quota activities of both the clergymen and businessmen did not include cooperation with Japanese immigrants, although some contact was maintained with leaders of Japanese immigrant communities who were sensitive to Japanese national honor. For those pro-quota activists who regarded the maintenance of cordial U.S.-Japanese relations as the most important issue, the daily lives of ordinary Japanese living in the United States were relatively unimportant. In general, Americans opposed to the exclusion clause were acquainted only with highly educated Japanese from the upper echelons of society and had no contact with the ordinary Japanese immigrants who suffered directly from the anti-Japanese movement on the Pacific Coast. At the same time, Japanese immigrants had their own reasons for not engaging in the pro-quota movement; they were convinced that it would be difficult to modify the immigration law, especially after the Ozawa case in 1922, and they concentrated on their own affairs in America. Those Japanese community leaders in the United States who maintained close connections with the Japanese consulates followed their policy of not becoming actively engaged in the pro-quota movement.

The narrow-minded attitudes of the pro-quota forces, focusing solely on the Japanese, limited their effectiveness. Most importantly, they did not cooperate with pro-China forces. Although they added China to the list of countries for which they pursued quotas, this decision was primarily for the strategic reason of appearing to be impartial. In actuality, they sought amicable bilateral relations with Japan alone, not with East Asia as a whole. This meant that the Japanese tendency toward their own form of racism, differentiating themselves from other Asian peoples, was also observed in pro-quota Americans. Japanese discrimination against Chinese and Koreans in Japan also contributed to dissuading Chinese and Koreans from cooperating with pro-Japanese forces in the United States. Such attitudes limited the influence of pro-quota forces, and the outbreak of the Sino-Japanese military confrontation completely dispelled any hope of cooperation.

The movement to repeal the Chinese exclusion law during World War II shared some characteristics with the movement to repeal the anti-Japanese exclusion clause of the 1920s and 1930s. While Chinese American interests were ignored and Chinese Americans were mostly kept out of the movement, American diplomatic relations with China were considered important during World War II. But the pro-quota movement that was started after the Pearl Harbor attack was not extended beyond the Chinese. The post–World War II pro-quota movement differed greatly from the pro-quota movements that took place before and during World War II. The later movement was initiated and conducted primarily by Japanese Americans. In a major change from the earlier two movements, the well-being of Japanese Americans was emphasized.

It is apparent that there were regional variations in opinion on the exclusion legislation. A close look at the history of the Japanese immigration issue reveals that most Americans outside the Pacific Coast area were indifferent to the problem. The strongest anti- and pro-quota forces existed along the Pacific Coast, and especially in California, where residents had to face the issue daily. Outside of California, the only opinions that appeared in the media were pro-quota, reflecting the economic interests of trading with Japan. In the Northwest, where the economy was greatly dependent on lumber exports to Japan, lumbermen were eager pro-quota advocates. In the South, cotton growers favored cordial U.S.-Japanese relations because Japan was ranked as at least the third most important importer of raw cotton from the American South. In the East, only some pacifists, clergymen, and businessmen, including traders and bankers, were interested in the issue. In general, then, only pro-quota opinions tended to appear in the media outside of California, and we may conclude that any regional variations in this pattern were mostly influenced by economics.

In terms of class and ethnicity, whereas labor unions, agitated by local politicians and newspapers, tended to support the anti-quota cause, wealthy businessmen in the West and pacifists and intellectuals in the East tended to be pro-quota. The fact that the anti-quota force derived its main support from the laboring class would explain the phenomenon of the CJIC easily switching its focus from Japanese immigrants to Mexicans and Filipinos. It is also safe to say that the majority of the anti-quota activists were either non-British immigrants themselves, or the children of such immigrants. James Phelan's father and V. S. McClatchy's father were both immigrants from Ireland, and Paul Scharrenberg was himself an immigrant from Germany.

While most organizations actively engaged in the pro-quota movement in the United States were single-issue organizations established solely to promote an immigration quota for Japan, the majority of the anti-quota organizations were not. Likewise, in Japan, there were a few single-issue organizations, but most of the groups which strongly criticized the United States for enacting the exclusion law were not single-issue organizations. This suggests that while pro-quota sentiments were limited in the United States, anti-American sentiments were widespread in Japan, in terms of both regional and class variations.

In the 1930s, even if all the pro-quota factions had cooperated in their efforts to win a quota for Japan, it is unlikely they would have succeeded, given the skyrocketing unemployment that accompanied the Great Depression. However, if the pro-quota forces had cooperated in the 1920s, a period characterized in the United States by a comparative openness to internationalism, it might have been possible for them to succeed. At the time, Japan tended to be seen in the West as the only hope in East Asia. Even in California, the center of the anti-Japanese movement, anti-Japanese forces gradually lost public support due to a growing indifference toward the Japanese immigration question. Even the CJIC, which had been the driving force behind the Japanese exclusion movement, focused most of its attention on the problem of immigrants from Mexico and the Philippines. Meanwhile, prominent Americans who advocated the pro-quota cause for Japan greatly increased in number in the late 1920s, in an atmosphere favoring international cooperation. If that atmosphere had continued well into the 1930s, the resistance to the pro-quota movement would have crumbled.

As the record shows, the issue remained a high priority for Japanese diplomats, who continually raised it in their meetings with American diplomats, from the time of the law's passage in 1924 all the way up to the bombing of Pearl Harbor in 1941. As a number of recent studies have shown, the immigration act of 1924 played a significant role in discouraging people from advocating peaceful U.S.-Japanese relations, and thus contributed to the final corrosion of the link between the United States and Japan.[4] Had Japan been given a quota, the Pearl Harbor attack would in all probability not have been prevented; a quota, however, would have provided people advocating cordial U.S.-Japanese relations with substantial support. The Japanese interested in U.S.-Japanese relations carefully observed the development of the pro-quota movement in the United States.

The pro-quota movement in the 1920s and 1930s shows that private Americans held strong opinions with regard to American relations with Japan. At this time, when the U.S. government did not generally express firm opinions about U.S.-Japanese relations, private citizens were the only ones who revealed their views to the public and championed amicable U.S.-Japanese relations. While clergymen and peace activists regarded U.S.-Japanese relations from a perspective of international peace and justice, businessmen understood cordial U.S.-Japanese relations to mean sound trade relations between the two countries. The argument that promotion of mutual understanding between nations would decrease the possibility of war became influential in the 1920s, championed by the pro-quota clergymen. The pro-quota businessmen's argument, that close commercial ties between the nations would contribute to peace, was also cogent in the 1920s. The activities of businessmen acquired more significance in the 1930s, at a time when other internationalist voices became less influential in the United States. Yet, due to the high unemployment rate and despite their strenuous efforts, their views did not convince the American public.

Despite the fact that the efforts of pro-quota activists did not come to fruition, it is still important to note that there were strong voices advocating cordial U.S.-Japanese relations, with an emphasis on international peace and justice and commercial relations, in the 1920s and in the 1930s. There was a possibility for peaceful U.S.-Japanese relations, at least in the thinking of the nonofficial sector, up until the late 1930s. Those internationalist views did not perish during the war; they reappeared immediately after the war, greatly facilitating the restoration of amicable relations with a defeated Japan. Within the traditional framework of study, focusing on intergovernmental relations, one might miss these important alternative visions of international relations in the nonofficial sector, a sector whose roles greatly expanded in the field of international relations in the interwar period. The examination of the nonofficial sector's attitudes toward diplomatic issues thus sheds new light on American diplomatic history during the turbulent decades of the early twentieth century through World War II.

Epilogue: The Japanese American Initiative

The Pearl Harbor attack decimated Americans' image of Japan and dealt a fatal blow to the pro-quota cause.[1] Although Protestant organizations issued a message the day after the attack calling on Americans "to maintain a Christian composure and charity in their dealing with the Japanese among us," few people heard it. Anti-Japanese forces triumphantly declared that their warnings about the "Jap's peaceful invasion" had been proved right. Indeed, Japanese and Japanese Americans living in the United States were greatly affected by the declaration of war between Japan and the United States. On February 19, 1942, President Roosevelt signed Executive Order 9066, which authorized the evacuation of all "enemy aliens" from designated areas within the United States. Although "enemy aliens" included alien Germans and Italians, the order was enforced only on people of Japanese ancestry.

Some traditionally anti-Japanese organizations desired even harsher treatment for people of Japanese origin, including the divestiture of citizenship for Japanese Americans who were legal American citizens by birth.[2] The Native Sons of the Golden West, for example, sought "to bring about a reversal of the case . . . which held that Orientals born in the United States are citizens of the United States,"[3] even claiming that if all Japanese were not removed, the Pacific coast states would "be lost to the White race."[4]

On the other hand, the war with Japan brought about a most vigorous movement, whose primary impetus was strategic as well as humanitarian, for modification of Chinese exclusion. Long before Japanese immigration had been curtailed, Chinese immigration had been barred by a nineteenth-century immigration law enacted expressly for that purpose. Now that China was an important ally in the fight against Japan, the discriminatory treatment of Chinese in the immigration laws was embarrassing, and, it was feared, might potentially dampen Chinese morale in the fight with Japan. The law also handed Japan a convenient weapon in the propaganda war for Asian supremacy.[5] A Tokyo radio station, broadcasting in Mandarin, claimed that the United States had "drafted innumerable single Chinese and put them in the army . . . in the Japanese-occupied territories of East Asia," whereas the Japanese had "never forced the Chinese into [the] army."[6] The *Japan Times and Advertiser*, an English-language newspaper, urged the Chinese to remember "how cruelly [the U.S.] excluded [Chinese] from that country," and proclaimed that "the War of Greater East Asia [presented] a golden opportunity for the Asiatic peoples to redeem themselves from such injustice and humiliation."[7] The Japanese-controlled media in Hong Kong broadcast to Chungking in Mandarin: "The United States abolished extra-territorial rights because she wished to ingratiate East Asia. She is not doing it because she wants to liberate China. From her immigration laws, you see her real intentions." While Japan tried to make the conflict in Asia into a race war using the slogan, "Asia for the Asians," U.S. media advocated democracy. But democracy could not be dissociated from "all that it implies as to equality," wrote *Newsweek*, and so the U.S. government risked "impairing the propaganda value of democracy" by relocating the Japanese Americans.[8]

The major impetus for the repeal of the Chinese exclusion act came from the private sector. Similar to the pro-Japanese anti-exclusion movement, it consisted of business interests, clergy organizations, and peace organizations. The most effective of them was the Citizens Committee to Repeal Chinese Exclusion (CCRCE), a body organized solely for this purpose. Its membership was comprised primarily of Americans who had spent time in the Far East, including Richard J. Walsh, editor of *Asia and the Americas*, Charles Nelson Spinks, an authority on the Far East, and Ronald Dunham, a former diplomat in Hong Kong. This organization was very useful in coordinating the repeal movements and played a decisive role in the realization of the repeal of Chinese exclusion.[9]

Business interests supported the anti-exclusion cause, not because they wanted cheap Chinese labor but because they thought the repeal would be necessary for better trade relations with China after the war. While the major national organizations such as the U.S. Chamber of Commerce did not offer the repeal movement strong support, business organizations on the Pacific Coast backed the movement. The national chamber believed that all Asians should be treated in the same way. On the other hand, West Coast businessmen who had extensive interests in East Asia focused on the repeal of Chinese exclusion as a feasible end. Many chambers of commerce on the Pacific Coast including those of Seattle, Portland, Tacoma, San Bernardino, and San Francisco aggressively supported the movement to repeal the Chinese exclusion law. While West Coast businessmen did not go beyond expressing their pro-quota view, it was the CCRCE that had its voice heard in Washington.[10]

Clergymen and pacifists also supported the repeal of exclusion through their belief in the brotherhood of man. Protestant organizations were most active in advocating the anti-exclusion cause. At first, some organizations pursued revision of the exclusion law for all Asians. In February 1943, the FCCCA's agenda to revise the exclusion law included not only China but also Japan. By May of that year, the FCCCA had removed Japan from the agenda and finally asked its constituent bodies to support the repeal of Chinese exclusion.[11]

Chinese Americans were not quiet on this issue. The *China Daily News*, a Chinese newspaper published in New York's Chinatown, advised Chinese Americans and their organizations to express their support for the repeal of the Chinese exclusion act. Some organizations such as the Chinese Consolidated Benevolent Association expressed their willingness to support the repeal and send letters to congressmen urging them to support the movement.[12] However, these conspicuous pro-repeal voices from Chinese Americans were exceptional. In cooperation with American activists, Chinese Americans refrained from noticeable movements in order to create the impression that the repeal movement came from the indigenous interests. The CCRCE not only restricted its membership to Americans but also tried to keep Chinese Americans from speaking out on this issue.[13] Chinese officials did not make public comments supporting the moves to repeal the Chinese exclusion act.[14]

The CCRCE's educational campaign stressed the benefits to Americans of a repeal for the Chinese.[15] For example, in the February 1942 issue of Walsh's *Asia and the Americas*, Charles N. Spinks, a member of the CCRCE, argued, "Now that we are fighting side by side with the Chinese as our Allies to destroy the Axis menace to the fundamental principles of justice for all mankind, it is more imperative than ever that we put our relations with the peoples of Asia on a basis of equality."[16] Chairman Walsh himself warned that the Japanese government was publicizing American exclusion of Chinese and argued for removing the exclusion and for naturalization rights for Chinese in the United States.[17] Reprints of his article were distributed to those who were interested in the Asian exclusion issue. Letters about Chinese exclusion were sent to interested parties, including newspapers and magazines, and radio programs advocating repeal were broadcast. After receiving a favorable public response to these campaigns, the CCRCE finally sent letters to all congressmen showing that the American people were in favor of repeal of exclusion.[18]

Meanwhile, bills to repeal the Chinese exclusion act and to offer Chinese the right to be naturalized were proposed in Congress in February and were discussed throughout the year. Members of the executive branch, which had refrained from mentioning the exclusion issue in public before Pearl Harbor, perceived that Congress was generally in favor of the repeal and now spoke out. Although the State Department proceeded cautiously, fearful that bitter debate in Congress about the issue would be counterproductive, it finally made an open move in October 1943, when Undersecretary of State E. R. Stettinius, Jr., wrote to Senator Richard B. Russell recommending a repeal of the Chinese exclusion law. At the same time, President Roosevelt sent a message to Congress, saying:

> I regard this legislation as important in the cause of winning the war and of establishing a secure peace. . . . China's resistance does not depend alone on guns. . . . It is based as much in the spirit of her people and her faith in her allies. . . . By the repeal of the Chinese exclusion laws, we can correct a historic mistake and silence the distorted Japanese propaganda.[19]

Traditionally exclusionist organizations such as the American Federation of Labor and the American Legion continued to support Chinese exclusion. Lewis G. Hines, legislative representative of the American Federation of Labor, voiced concern that if the United States permitted the entrance of

107 Chinese, it would not take much time until "107 shall be extended to 5,000."[20] S. E. Wilkins of the Veterans of Foreign Wars maintained, "It is difficult to see how the admission into the United States . . . of a few Chinese subjects would be a contribution to their war effort."[21] The Native Sons of the Golden West also expressed strong opposition to the repeal of the law.[22]

However, their anti-quota voices were lost in the pro-China roar during the war. Supported by the activities of the CCRCE and the general pro-China sentiment in the United States that had emerged after the outbreak of the Sino-Japanese war in 1937, and boosted by the visit of Madame Chiang Kai-Shek to the United States in the winter of 1942–1943, the bill to remove Chinese exclusion and allow naturalization of Chinese passed in Congress and was signed by Roosevelt on December 17, 1943.[23]

The *Nippon Times*, the English-language Japanese propaganda newspaper which continuously criticized the United States as a racist nation, regarded this American move to modify the Chinese exclusion law as "nothing but a political expediency aimed at keeping Chungking from dropping out from the military lineup against Japan." Regarding the move as "a wartime measure," the paper predicted that "Americans . . . [would] not hesitate to shut the doors again to Chinese after the war [was] over."[24] The Japanese propaganda assault was not restricted to the issue of Chinese exclusion. The *Nippon Times* also criticized American attitudes toward Filipinos, arguing that while praising the Filipino soldiers in their fight against Japanese forces, Americans "made no hesitation in putting the Filipinos . . . in the same class with the Negroes."[25] The *Nippon Times* also pointed to Australian racial discrimination against Asians as evidence of Anglo-American racism. The paper argued that despite the fact that Australia was located in Asia, it excluded Asians, including "allied Chungking Chinese as well as fellow subjects of Indian extraction." It denounced the Allied principles of humanity and justice as "empty lip-service."[26] The paper shifted the focus of its attack from Chinese exclusion to American discrimination against African Americans.[27]

After the war, when it had become evident that the removal of Chinese exclusion had caused no great influx of immigrants, the case of India, a British colony fighting on the side of the allies in World War II, was taken up. Both the White House and the State Department supported a quota bill for India, which was passed with little fanfare in 1946.[28] Within months, another bill to allow Filipinos to be naturalized also passed the Congress.[29]

The Japanese case was, of course, totally different from that of China, or India, or the Philippines, three nations that had fought alongside the United States during the war. The ban on Japanese immigration would finally be lifted, but only after an extended and tenacious effort. Emerging as the driving force in this battle to modify the immigration and naturalization laws was the Japanese American Citizens League (JACL), whose membership was composed only of Nisei. To achieve this end, the Anti-Discrimination Committee was established as a lobbying branch of the JACL. Mike Masaoka, a World War II veteran who had just come back from Europe, flew to Washington, D.C., to head the lobbying.[30]

Financial support for the lobbying effort came primarily from Issei, although they were ineligible for membership in the JACL. They established organizations to support the lobbying financially in cities where Japanese Americans were clustered. In Los Angeles, Rafu Kikaken Kakutoku Kisei Dōmei (Naturalization Committee of Los Angeles) was organized by Gongorō Nakamura and others on February 22, 1947.[31] A similar organization named Hokka Kikaken Kisei Dōmei (Naturalization Committee of Northern California) was established in San Francisco around the same time.[32] Stimulated by a visit of representatives of the JACL, a Hawaiian counterpart of the Naturalization Committee was created in March 1947.[33] Although the Issei's fundraising goals were not impressive, their support of the JACL's lobbying was very generous, considering that the wartime relocation had deprived them of most of their assets.[34] In their struggle, the JACL was aided by the Committee for Equality in Naturalization, a private organization established under the auspices of the American Civil Liberties Union. The committee represented the first American citizens' group to be organized in support of the claims of Japanese Americans.[35]

In the meantime, discussion of the immigration issue had not died out in Japan. At the Far East War Crimes Trial in Tokyo, Kiyose Ichirō, deputy chief of the Japanese defense counsel, directly attributed Japanese military preparation to Western racism. Hideo Yamada, a Japan Communist Party member, demanded the right of free emigration overseas in an agenda submitted to General Douglas MacArthur. The newly established Kaigai Ijū Kyōkai (Oversea Emigration Association) also advocated free overseas emigration. However, these arguments concerned with immigration were not liked by the SCAP and were sometimes censored. For example, when the

Yomiuri tried to publish an interview with Roger Baldwin, director of the American Civil Liberties Union, the part in which he mentioned the possibility that the Japanese exclusion clause would soon be modified was censored.[36] Partly due to the fact that Japan was under the strict control of the occupation forces, it seems that these Japanese voices did not have much of an influence on the situation in the United States at this time.

The initial legislative attempt to modify the immigration law was made during the first session of the 80th Congress in 1947, when two bills were submitted to the Senate. However, neither bill was addressed before the end of the session. Another bill was submitted at the beginning of the second session, which led to hearings before the House Subcommittee on Immigration and Naturalization of the Judiciary Committee. In the hearings, many influential people from various backgrounds supported modification of the immigration and naturalization laws, and a loosening of regulations on Japanese immigration was linked to the fight against Communism. Joseph R. Farrington, a delegate from Hawaii, testified that the enactment of a bill removing racial discrimination on naturalization would be "of very practical value in carrying on the ideological work that . . . will win the people of the Far East to our side in our contest with Soviet Russia."[37] The bill even garnered the support of many former exclusionists such as George P. Miller, representative from California. Broad-based support of a Japanese quota from such a broad range of citizens only a few years after the end of the war was indicative of the startling transformation of public opinion that had occurred. Although the immigration bill did not come to a vote in the 80th Congress, the hearings helped congressmen understand that there was broad support for modification of the immigration law.[38]

In the 81st Congress, the same bill was introduced and proceeded smoothly through the House, passing on March 1, 1949, by a vote of 336 to 39. In the Senate, a subcommittee of the Judiciary Committee held public hearings. Representing the State Department at the hearings, Deputy Undersecretary Dean Rusk testified that the Department had "complete sympathy with and fully support[ed]" the bill, also raising the specter of world Communism, which was "trying throughout Asia to identify in the minds of Asiatic people communism with their own national aspirations."[39] Unfortunately, the Senate could not agree on language for the second portion of the bill, dealing with Caribbean and Chinese immigration issues, and it was not reported out of committee. The second session of the 81st Congress took up the naturalization bill once again, but the two houses could not agree either on the bill's scope or on the language of certain security clauses that would have given the government more power to deport certain undesirable immigrants. In the end, this bill, too, went down to defeat.[40]

After several failed attempts, an immigration bill was finally passed by the 82nd Congress in mid-1952. The McCarran–Walter Act was sent to the White House for the president's signature on June 13. It seemed that the long fight was finally over. But on June 25, Truman vetoed the act and sent it back to Congress with a lengthy message in which he attacked the act's retention of the quota system, which Truman considered equivalent to racial exclusion. The president also argued that the new grounds for deportation written into the act were "unnecessarily severe" against immigrants.[41] But McCarran rejected Truman's comments, stating, "The basic principles upon which the national origins quota system is founded are fair and just."[42] Representative Walter Judd argued that the Cold War necessitated passage of the bill as written:

> We have lost a good part of continental Asia to Communist control. Everybody knows what we have done in the last year to try to keep on our side what can be a bulwark of freedom in that part of the world—Japan. Racial discrimination in our dealings with other peoples is the weakest spot in America's armor. We must make clear to [the] watching millions that the representatives of the people of the United States believe in trying to correct things that are inequitable."[43]

Congress was not to be denied. On June 26, the House overrode the president's veto 278 to 112, and the Senate followed the next day, with a vote of 57 to 26.[44]

Whatever its faults, the McCarran–Walter Act realized the goal that pro-quota forces had pursued since 1924. By the time of its passage, however, in 1952, the relationship between the United States and Japan had been drastically changed; Japan had become one of the United States's most important partners in the Far East in the fight against Communism. Japanese were not excited about the news of the passage of the bill. *Mainichi Shimbun* briefly reported the passage of the law.[45] *Asahi Shimbun*, formed by the merger of *Tokyo Asahi* and *Osaka Asahi Shimbun*, both of which had fervently attacked the 1924 law, showed no enthusiasm about the bill's passage; it merely noted that the McCarran–Walter Act had become law and that Japan was to be given a quota of 185 immigrants a year, while the naturalization right would be given to first-generation Japanese immigrants.[46] It looked as if the Japanese had forgotten how vehemently they had pursued an immigration quota for Japan before the Pacific War. Perhaps the quota of only 185 looked insignificant to Japanese who were still busy rebuilding their country, but it was a historical moment when the U.S. Congress granted the right of naturalization to the Japanese for the first time and placed Japan on the same quota system as European countries.

Notes

Introduction

1. See, e.g., Miwa, "Tokutomi Sohō no rekishizō to nichibei sensō no genriteki kaishi." According to records kept by Hidenari Terasaki, a close adviser to Emperor Hirohito, the emperor said that a remote cause of the Pacific War was the Great Powers' refusal to accept the race-equality clause at the peace conference following World War I, that the sense among the yellow people of having been discriminated against by white people remained, and that the rejection of Japanese immigrants in California caused resentment among the Japanese (see Terasaki and Terasaki Miller, *Shōwa tennō dokuhakuroku/Terasaki Hidenari goyōkakari nikki*, 19–21).

2. "Fujita Kikuichi nisshi" [The Diary of Kikuichi Fujita], December 1941. MS., Department of War History, National Institute for Defense Studies, Tokyo.

3. Iriye, "Tenkanki," 52–54; May, *American Imperialism*.

4. Iriye, "Tenkanki," 56–57.

5. Iriye, "Japan as a Competitor."

6. Miller, *War Plan Orange*.

7. Ichioka, *The Issei*.

8. Iriye, "Tenkanki," 61; my 1991 master's thesis, "Nijusseiki shotō san furanshisuko ni okeru han nikkeijin undō" [Anti-Japanese Movements in San Francisco in the Early Twentieth Century], uses labor publications in San

Francisco to examine the transformation of American labor's views on Japan and Japanese immigrants around the years of the Russo-Japanese War.

9. Daniels, *Prejudice*, 27–28.

10. Ibid., 52.

11. Ibid., 79.

12. Shimazu, *Japan, Race and Equality.*

13. Minohara, "The Road to Exclusion," 51–55.

14. Daniels, *Prejudice*, 91.

15. Ibid., 97.

16. Ichioka, "The Early Japanese Immigrant Quest for Citizenship," 2.

17. *Congressional Record*, 68th Cong., 1st sess., 1924, 65, pt. 6:6073–74.

18. Gaimushō gaikō shiryōkan nihon gaikōshi jiten hensan iinkai, *Nihon gaikōshi jiten*, 837.

19. Daniels, *Prejudice*, 102.

20. Minohara, "Kariforunia ni okeru hainichi undō to 1924 nen iminhō no seiritsu katei," esp. chap. 5.

21. Although the bill was passed in the Senate on April 15, two senators who were absent on that day complained and a second vote was taken on April 16. The Joint Conference of the House and Senate then combined the two bills into one, deciding that the law would become effective on July 1, 1924. The bill was finally passed in both houses on May 15 and sent to President Coolidge on May 17. The Japanese public, with no interest in the complexities of the legislative process, simply reacted to the fact that the U.S. Congress had passed the bill with the exclusion clause.

22. Although it examines the pre-1924 period, Roger Daniels's *The Politics of Prejudice* is essential for studies of both exclusionist and anti-exclusionist forces in California. Bruce A. Abrams's "A Muted Cry: White Opposition to the Japanese Exclusion Movement, 1911–1924" should be mentioned because of its focus on the anti-exclusion point of view. There are also several exceptional studies which deal with the post-1924 period, including John Roger Stemen's "The Diplomacy of the Immigration Issue: A Study in Japanese-American Relations, 1894–1941," although the post-1924 period takes up only 36 of the dissertation's total 347 pages. Gladys Henning's "Antiforeign Movements in California, 1919–1929" covers the entire decade of the 1920s and focuses on the exclusionist point of view. Lee Arne Makela's "Japanese Attitudes towards the United States Immigration Act of 1924" details the immediate aftermath of exclusion in Japan, although it depends mostly upon English-language sources. Eleanor Tupper and George McReynolds's *Japan in American Public Opinion* is a contemporary survey of opinions appearing in

periodicals. Sadao Asada's *Ryō taisen kan no nichibei kankei* [Japanese American Relations between the Wars] devotes a chapter to the racial aspects of U.S.-Japanese relations, providing insightful analysis of the immigration issue.

23. Hunter, *Gospel of Gentility*.

24. Taylor, *Advocate*.

25. Rosenberg, *Spreading the American Dream*.

26. Wilson, *American Business and Foreign Policy*.

27. For the Japanese side during the interwar years, see Fletcher, *The Japanese Business Community*.

28. Most of these small rightist organizations were obscure, and there is little information available about them. According to reports of the Foreign Ministry, Kyokutō Renmei Kyōkai was established in Osaka around the time of the enactment of the immigration bill in 1924. It was active in the mid-1920s, but disappeared from the records thereafter. According to reports by the Ministry of Interior, Ajia Renmei Kyōkai was founded in Osaka in 1927 by Kunizō Kimoto and consisted of about twenty members.

29. The effects of the immigration act on those who were neither pro-America nor anti-America in Japan, such as young bureaucrats in the Foreign Office who became important figures in the 1930s, cannot be ignored. The enactment of the immigration act must have contributed to the formation of their image of the United States; however, since they did not discuss U.S.-Japanese relations often, it is difficult to trace those effects.

30. California State Federation of Labor, *Proceedings of the Twenty-Seventh Annual Convention*, 1926, 91.

31. Lopez, "History of the California State Federation of Labor," 4.

32. Chambers, *California Farm Organizations*, 9–30, 205.

33. Chapman, *The Native Son Fellowships*.

34. Conmy, *Origin and Purposes*, 20–24.

35. Daniels, *Prejudice*, 86.

36. Smith, *History, Department of California*, 10, 66–67.

Chapter 1

1. Woods to Hughes, 1 May 1924, 711.945/1074, in U.S. Department of State Files, Record Group 59, decimal file, National Archives (hereafter cited as SD).

2. *Tokyo Nichinichi Shimbun*, 19 April 1924.

3. *Teikoku Daigaku Shimbun*, 23 May 1924.

4. For example, *Tokyo Asahi Shimbun*, 23 April 1924, and *Kokumin Shimbun*, 25 April 1924.

5. *Osaka Asahi Shimbun*, 16 April 1924.

6. *Chūgai Shōgyō Shimpō*, 14 April 1924.

7. *Tokyo Asahi Shimbun*, 21 April 1924.

8. Woods to Hughes, 17 April 1924, 711.945/1078, SD.

9. *Tokyo Asahi Shimbun*, 26 April 1924; *Kokumin Shimbun*, 26 April 1924; Beikoku hainichi iminhō ni taisuru honpō ni okeru undō jōkyō chōsa [Survey of Movements in Japan against the United States Exclusion Immigration Law], 23 June 1924, and Iminhō seiritsu ni taisuru naigai hantaiundō jyōkyō chōsa [Survey of Protests against the Immigration Law at Home and Abroad], both in Diplomatic Record Office, Tokyo, Japan (hereafter cited as JDRO).

10. Hata, *Kankeishi*, 154.

11. Uchida Ryōhei bunsho kenkyūkai, *Uchida*, 9:292–94.

12. *Kokumin Shimbun*, 23 April 1924; Superintendent-General of the Metropolitan Police to Saburi, 12 July 1924, in Beikoku ni okeru hainichi mondai ikken: 1924 nen iminhō seiritsu ni taisuru naigai no hantai undō [Documents Relating to Anti-Japanese Problems in the United States: Domestic and Foreign Movements against the Enactment of the Immigration Law of 1924], JDRO (hereafter cited as BHNG).

13. Okamoto, *Jūdai naru kekka*, 1–5.

14. Tatsukichi Minobe, "Taibei zakkan" [Miscellaneous Thoughts on the United States], *Kaizō*, May 1924, 29–30.

15. *Kaizō*, May 1924, 92.

16. *Nihon oyobi nihonjin*, 1 and 15 May 1924.

17. Makela, "Attitudes," 127–28.

18. Ibid., 128–29; *Osaka Mainichi Shimbun*, 24 April 1924.

19. *Manshū Nichinichi Shimbun*, 18 April 1924.

20. Ibid., 2 May 1924.

21. Eliot to MacDonald, 10 April 1924, Foreign Office 410, document no. 76, Public Record Office, London (hereafter cited as FO with class and document numbers).

22. Eliot to MacDonald, 25 April 1924, FO 115/2899; Eliot to MacDonald, 16 May 1924, FO 371/9586; Eliot to MacDonald, 16 May 1924, FO 371/9586; Ito and Hirose, *Makino Nobuatsu nikki*, 126.

23. "Hainichi mondai no sekininsha" [The Person Responsible for the Japanese Exclusion Problem], *Gaikō Jihō*, 15 May 1924, i–ii.

24. "Hainichi mondai no kyōkun" [The Lessons of the Anti-Japanese Problem], *Gaikō Jihō*, 1 June 1924, 1–9.

25. Japan, Bōeichō Bōeikenshūsho Senshishitsu [Department of War History,

National Institute of Defense Studies, Defense Agency], *Daihon'ei Kaigunbu: Rengōkantai*, 1:112.

26. Ibid., 1:197–98.

27. Japan, Gaimushō [Ministry of Foreign Affairs], *Nihon gaikō bunsho* [Documents on Japanese Foreign Policy], 1924, 1:293–95 (hereafter cited as *NGB* with year).

28. *NGB*, 1924, 1:302–3.

29. *Yomiuri Shimbun*, 23 April 1924.

30. Kaigun Rōdō Kumiai Maizuru Kyōritsukai to Matsui, 29 April 1924, in Beikoku ni okeru hainichi mondai zakken: Beikoku iminhō ni taisuru haibei jōhō [Miscellaneous Documents Relating to Anti-Japanese Problems in the United States: Anti-American Information Relating to the United States Immigration Law], JDRO (hereafter cited as BIHJ).

31. Eliot to MacDonald, 16 May and 5 June 1924, FO 371/9586.

32. Wada to Addams, 18 April 1924, Jane Addams Papers, series 1, Swarthmore College Peace Collection, Swarthmore College, Swarthmore, Pa.

33. Ladies' Association to Addams, 28 April 1924, Records of the Women's International League for Peace and Freedom, Swarthmore College Peace Collection, Swarthmore College, Swarthmore, Pa.

34. *New York Times*, 16 April 1924.

35. *Osaka Mainichi Shimbun*, 28 May 1924.

36. *Tokyo Asahi Shimbun*, 28 May 1924.

37. *Chūgai Shōgyō Shimpō*, 28 May 1924.

38. *Tokyo Asahi Shimbun*, 1 July 1924.

39. *Foreign Relations of the United States*, 1924, 2:396 (hereafter cited as *FRUS* with year).

40. Asada, *Ryō taisenkan*, 302, 308–9; Ōshiro, *Nitobe Inazō*, 182–83.

41. *Kokumin Shimbun*, 8 June 1924.

42. *Seisho no kenkyū*, 10.

43. Caffery to Hughes, 15 October 1924, 711.945/1230, SD.

44. Kaneko to the Executive Committee of the America-Japan Society, 711.945/1269, SD.

45. Asada, *Ryō taisenkan*, 310–11.

46. For example, Shibusawa to Lamont, 22 May 1924, box 189, Thomas W. Lamont Collection, Baker Library, Harvard Business School (hereafter cited as Lamont Collection).

47. Kimura, *Shibusawa Eiichi*, 163–67.

48. Shibusawa to his American friends, 25 December 1924, 711.945/1266, SD.

49. Dan to Lamont, 25 June 1924, box 188, Lamont Collection.

50. *Tōyōkeizai Shinpō*, no. 1095, 26 April 1924, 10–11; Eliot to MacDonald, 16 May 1924, FO 371/9586.

51. Caffery to Hughes, 5 October 1924, 711.945/1230, SD; Shiozaki, "Gaimushō kakushinha no genjōdaha ninshiki to seisaku," 165–66.

52. Report by Philip R. Faymonville, June 16, 1924, U.S. Military Intelligence Reports, Japan, 1918–1941 (microfilm [1985], available from University Publications of America, Frederick, Md.).

53. Eliot to MacDonald, 20 June 1924, FO 371/9586.

54. An open letter on the American-Japanese problem by the Bishop of the Japan Methodist Church, 18 June 1924, box 5, John Caldwell Calhoun Newton Papers, William R. Perkins Library, Duke University (hereafter cited as Newton Papers).

55. Robert E. Speer et al. to the Churches of Christ in Japan, 14 July 1924, box 5, Newton Papers.

56. *Chūō Shimbun*, 17 April 1924.

57. Japan, Sūmitsuin [The Privy Council], *Sūmitsuin kaigi gijiroku* [Proceedings of the Privy Council], 35:238–64.

58. Woods to Hughes, 28 May 1924, 711.946/1113, SD.

59. Appendix to Japan, Gaimushō [Ministry of Foreign Affairs], *Nihon gaikō bunsho: Taibei imin mondai keika gaiyō* [Documents on Japanese Foreign Policy: Summary of the Course of Negotiations between Japan and the United States concerning the Problems of Japanese Immigration in the United States] (hereafter cited as *NGBTIM*), 760–67.

60. Eliot to MacDonald, 5 June 1924, FO 410/77.

61. *New York Times*, 1 June 1924; *Tokyo Asahi Shimbun*, 1 June 1924; *Kokumin Shimbun*, 1 June 1924.

62. *New York Times*, 2 June 1924.

63. *Tokyo Asahi Shimbun*, 2 June 1924.

64. *New York Times*, 5 and 9 June 1924; *Tokyo Asahi Shimbun*, 5 and 8 June 1924.

65. *Kokumin Shimbun*, 5 June 1924.

66. Uchida Ryōhei kankei bunsho kenkyūkai, *Uchida*, 7:58, 154; Kokuryū kurabu, *Kokushi Uchida Ryōhei den*, 619; *Osaka Asahi Shimbun*, 6 June 1924; *Kokumin Shimbun*, 6 June 1924; Superintendent-General of the Metropolitan Police to Saburi, 12 July 1924, BHNG.

67. Kinoshita, *Nihon kokkashugi undōshi*, 1:32–44.

68. Hata, *Kankeishi*, 154–55; Makela, "Attitudes," 167–68; *Tokyo Asahi Shimbun*, 8 June 1924; *Kokumin Shimbun*, 8 June 1924.

69. Satō, "Kumakō no gensetsu," 41–43.

70. *Kokumin Shimbun*, 6 June 1924. Kanji Ishiwara, the army officer who

planned the Manchurian incident, wrote in a letter dated 18 July 1924 that he regarded the exclusion of American films desirable for the Japanese national ideology (see Ishiwara, 2:245).

71. *Tokyo Asahi Shimbun,* 9 June 1924; *Kokumin Shimbun,* 9 June 1924.

72. Governor of Hyōgo to Reijirō Wakatsuki, Minister of Interior, 5 July 1924, in Beikoku ni okeru hainichi mondai ikken: 1924 nen iminhō seiritsu ni taisuru naigaino hantai undō [Documents Relating to Anti-Japanese Movements in the United States: Protests against the 1924 Immigration Law at Home and Abroad], Diplomatic Record Office, Tokyo (hereafter cited as BHNG).

73. *Kokumin Shimbun,* 14 June 1924.

74. *Tokyo Asahi Shimbun,* 10 June 1924.

75. Ibid., 11 June 1924.

76. Dokuritsu Haibei Dan to American Embassy, Tokyo, 16 June 1924, 711.945/1152, 1181, SD.

77. Eugene H. Dooman Interview, Columbia University Oral History Collection, Columbia University.

78. Governor of Osaka to Wakatsuki, 10 June 1924, BIHJ.

79. Governor of Osaka to Wakatsuki, 18 June 1924, BIHJ.

80. Beikoku jin shozaichi no hogo keikaku [The Plan for Protection of American Residences], BIHJ.

81. Governor of Kanagawa to Shidehara, 24 June 1924, BIHJ.

82. Eliot to MacDonald, 2 July 1924, FO 371/9586.

83. Caffery to Hughes, 24 June 1924, 711.945/1152, SD.

84. *(Japan Society of New York) News Bulletin,* October 1924, 7.

85. *FRUS,* 1924, 2:403–8.

86. *Kokumin Shimbun,* 20 June 1924.

87. *Osaka Asahi Shimbun,* 20 June 1924.

88. *Kokumin Shimbun,* 21 June 1924.

89. Eliot to MacDonald, 27 June 1924, FO 371/9587; Shidehara, *Gaikō gojūnen,* 28–44.

90. Caffery to Hughes, 19 June 1924, 711.945/1146, SD.

91. *Kokumin Shimbun,* 1 July 1924; *Tokyo Asahi Shimbun,* 2 July 1924.

92. Uchida Ryōhei bunsho kenkyūkai, *Uchida,* 7:83–84, 141–42.

93. Uesugi, *Nichibei shōtotsu no hisshi to kokumin no kakugo* [Necessity of Japan–U.S. Clash and National Determination].

94. Governor of Osaka to Wakasugi, 2 July 1924, BHNG.

95. *Kokumin Shimbun,* 2 July 1924.

96. *Tokyo Nichinichi Shimbun,* 2 July 1924.

97. Governor of Osaka to Wakatsuki, 1 July 1924, BIHJ.

98. Eliot to MacDonald, 11 July 1924, FO 371/9587.

99. Claudel to Herriot, 2 July 1924, Asie-Océanie, Japon: Politique étrangère, vol. 67. Archives du Ministère des Affaires Étrangères, Paris (hereafter cited as AMAE).

100. *Yomiuri Shimbun*, 26 May 1924.

101. Governor of Osaka to Wakatsuki, 2 July 1924, BIHJ.

102. Governor of Osaka to Wakatsuki, June 20, 1924, BIHJ.

103. Governor of Nagano to Wakatsuki, 1 July 1924, BHNG; Governor of Saitama to Wakatsuki, 2 July 1924, BHNG.

104. Kunishige Tanaka to Yūsaku Uehara, 29 July 1924, in Uehara Yūsaku kankeibunsho kenkyūkai, *Uehara*, 267.

105. "Taibei mondai ni tsuki zaigō gunjinkai shidō ni kansuru ken" [Guidance for Veterans' Associations Regarding U.S.-Japanese Questions], Dai nikki, kō, eizonshorui kōshū, dainirui [General Files, Permanent Records], vol. 13 (1924): 668–70, Department of War History, National Institute of Defense Studies, Tokyo (hereafter cited as DWH).

106. Mitsu dai nikki [Confidential General Files], 25 April 1924, vol. 5 (1924): 1428–39, DWH.

107. Kunishige Tanaka to Yūsaku Uehara, 29 July 1924, in Uehara Yūsaku kankei bunsho kenkyūkai, *Uehara*, 268.

108. "Nichibei kankei to teikoku no kokubō" [Japan-U.S. Relations and the Defense of the Empire], Mitsu dai nikki [Confidential General Files], vol. 5 (1924): 1841–75, DWH.

109. "Beikoku shin iminhō to teikoku kokuun no seisui" [The New U.S. Immigration Law and the Future of Japan's Prosperity], Mitsu dai nikki [Confidential General Files], vol. 5 (1924): 1538–1623, DWH.

110. Ishimaru, *Nichibei Sensō: Nihon wa makenai*.

111. Governor of Kyoto to Wakasugi, 22 August 1924, BHNG.

112. Honganji, *Hainichi mondai to kokumin no kakugo* [The Japanese Exclusion Question and National Determination] (pamphlet).

113. *Manshū Nichinichi Shimbun*, 2 July 1924.

114. *Tokyo Nichinichi Shimbun*, 2 July 1924.

115. Caffery to Hughes, 1 July 1924, 711.945/1165, SD.

116. Japan, Teikoku Gikai Shūgiin [House of Representatives of the Imperial Diet], *Shūgiin tsūjōkai giji sokkiroku* [Proceedings in the Imperial Diet of Japan, House of Representatives], 1 July 1924 (hereafter cited as *STGS*).

117. Japan, Teikoku Gikai Kizokuin [House of Peers of the Imperial Diet], *Kizokuin tsūjōkai giji sokkiroku* [*Proceedings in the Imperial Diet of Japan, House of Peers*], 1 July 1924 (hereafter cited as *KTGS*).

118. *KTGS*, 2 July 1924; *Tokyo Asahi Shimbun*, 3 July 1924.

119. *Tokyo Asahi Shimbun*, 2 July 1924.

120. Ibid., 3 July 1924.

121. *NGB*, 1924, 1:270–71.

122. *Bungei shunjū*, July 1924, 22–23, 41–43.

123. Yasaka Takagi, "Beikoku shin'iminhō no hihan" [The Criticism of the New American Immigration Law], *Chūō kōron*, July 1924, 41–54.

124. *Chūō kōron*, August 1924, 79–106.

125. Makela, "Attitudes," 234.

126. *Nihon oyobi nihonjin*, 1 September 1924.

127. Makela, "Attitudes," 195–203; *New York Times*, 13 July 1924.

128. Ichioka, *Issei*, 247–48.

129. *NGB*, 1924, 1:218–21.

130. Ibid., 1:218–21.

131. Ichioka, *Issei*, 247.

132. *Rafu Shimpō*, 18 April 1924.

133. *Rafu Shimpō*, 2 May 1924.

134. Togawa Diary, 1 July 1924, Japanese American Research Project Collection, University of California, Los Angeles.

135. *Rafu Shimpō*, 29 May 1924.

136. *Nichi Bei*, 29 April 1924.

137. Ariyama, "1924 nen iminhō to *Rafu Shimpō*," 181.

138. *Nichi Bei*, 29 May 1924.

139. Ibid., 23 June 1924.

140. Modell, *Racial Accommodation*, 66.

141. *Rafu Shimpō*, 30 May 1924.

142. *Nichi Bei*, 17 April 1924.

143. Ichioka, "A Study in Dualism," 57; Ichioka, *Issei*, 252–54.

144. Hayashi, *"For the Sake of Our Japanese Brethren,"* 127–47.

145. *Chung Sai Yat Po*, 22 and 23 April 1924.

146. *Stockholms Dagblad*, 25 April 1924, quoted and translated in Minister to Sweden to Hughes, 25 April 1924, 711.945/1088, SD.

147. Minister to the Netherlands to Hughes, 1 and 20 May 1924, 711.945/1092, 1125, SD.

148. Claudel, *Correspondence Diplomatique*, 251–57, 273–76; Claudel to Lefèbure du Prey, 13 June 1924, Asie-Océanie, Japon: Politique étrangère, vol. 67, AMAE.

149. Eliot to MacDonald, 3 May 1924, FO 371/10318; Eliot to MacDonald, 16 May 1924, Colonial Office 532, document no. 287, Public Record Office, London (hereafter cited as CO with class and document numbers).

150. Thomas to MacDonald, 9 June 1924, CO 532/287; Thomas to Governor of Southern Rhodesia, 6 June 1924, FO 371/10302.

151. *Parliamentary Debates*, Commons, 5th ser., vol. 174 (1924): 2122.

152. Register No. M.I. 2/3103, 23 July 1924, War Office 106, document no. 5477, Public Record Office, London (hereafter cited as WO with class and document numbers).

153. *Russki Golos*, May 1924, quoted and translated in Consul at Harbin to Hughes, 15 May 1924, 711.945/1122, SD.

154. *Harbin Dawning*, 29 April 1924, quoted and translated in Consul at Harbin to Hughes, 2 May 1924, 711.945/1122, SD.

155. *Shanghai Times*, 15 April 1924.

156. *Chen Pao*, 4 May 1924, summarized in Schuman, Minister to China, to Hughes, 5 May 1924, 711.945/1076, SD.

157. *China Weekly Review*, 14 June 1924, 35.

158. Koria kenkyūsho, *Kesareta genron, seiji hen*, 182–84, 197–99, 209–11.

159. Maxwell Blake, consul general in Melbourne, to Hughes, 19 May 1924, Confidential U.S. Diplomatic Post Records, Japan: 1919–1929, U.S. Department of State Files, Record Group 59, National Archives; *Melbourne Herald*, 19 May 1924; Macleay to MacDonald, 5 June 1924, FO 371/958b.

160. Consul general at Tientsin to Hughes, 15 May 1924, 711.945/1133, SD.

161. *Daily Commercial News*, 16 May 1924.

162. Ibid.; *Los Angeles Times*, 28 May 1924; *San Francisco Examiner*, 21 April 1924; *Seattle Post-Intelligencer*, 21 April and 14 June 1924.

163. *NGB*, 1924, 1:279–83.

164. *Organized Labor*, 17 May 1924.

165. *Labor Clarion*, 9 May 1924.

166. California State Federation of Labor, *Proceedings of the Twenty-Fifth Annual Convention*, 1924, 56.

167. *NGB*, 1924, 1:279–83.

168. *New York Times*, 13 June 1924.

169. *Christian Science Monitor*, 21 May 1924.

170. *Philadelphia Evening Bulletin*, 15 April 1924.

171. *Washington Post*, 29 May 1924.

172. *Chicago Daily Tribune*, 15 April 1924.

173. *Foreign Commerce and Navigation of the United States*, 1921, 379–80; 1922, 239–40; 1923, 236; 1924, 62; 1925, 1:59–60; and 1926, 1:59 (hereafter cited as *FCN* with year, volume number, and page numbers, as applicable).

174. *Atlanta Constitution*, 15 April 1924.

175. *Atlantic Monthly*, July 1924, 124–33.

176. The editors of *LIFE* to Coolidge, 3 May 1924, 711.945/1083, SD.

177. *Asia*, March 1917; *Asia*, August 1924, 627–31.

178. *Outlook*, 16 April 1924, 640–41.

179. Shankman, "'Asiatic Ogre'," 580–87; *Chicago Defender*, 28 June 1924; Kearney, *African American Views*, 65–66.

180. *Kansas City Call*, 6 June 1924.

181. *Negro World*, 7 June 1924.

182. *Chicago Defender*, 19 April 1924.

183. Kearney, *African American Views*, 70–71; *Chicago Defender*, 31 May 1924.

184. *New York Times*, 3 June 1924.

185. Ibid., 1 and 2 June 1924; *Seattle Post-Intelligencer*, 1 June 1924; *San Francisco Examiner*, 1 June 1924.

186. Garner to Hoover, 17 April 1924, box 348, Herbert Hoover Papers, Herbert Hoover Presidential Library, West Branch, Iowa (hereafter cited as Hoover Papers).

187. *Tokyo Nichinichi Shimbun*, 19 April 1924.

188. *New York Times*, 6 July 1924.

189. Condict to Hoover, 26 April 1924, box 348, Hoover Papers.

190. Shibusawa to Lamont, 21(?) April 1924, box 188, Lamont Collection.

191. *NGB*, 1924, 1:234; Egan to Lamont, 23 April 1924, and Lamont to Shibusawa, 24 April 1924, box 188, Lamont Collection.

192. Morris to Kabayama, 12 June 1924, Roland S. Morris Papers, container 3, Library of Congress.

193. Griggs to Hoover, 18 April 1924, box 348, Hoover Papers.

194. Knox, American Exporters' and Importers' Association, to Boylan, House of Representatives, 28 April 1924, and Knox to Hoover, 29 April 1924, box 348, Hoover Papers.

195. *New York World*, 8 May 1924; *New York Times*, 8 May 1924.

196. *New York Times*, 9 May 1924.

197. "Second California State Conference" (leaflet), 9, 10, and 11 May 1924; and Miller to Hoover, 12 May 1924; both in box 349, Hoover Papers.

198. *NGB*, 1924, 1:276.

199. *Transactions of the Commonwealth Club* 19, no. 11 (January 1925): 665, 728–29.

200. Wilson, *American Business and Foreign Policy*, 220.

201. *New York Times*, 18 April 1924.

202. *NGBTIM*, 855.

203. *NGB*, 1924, 1:273–74.

204. Cavert to Geistweit, 23 April 1924, Record Group 18, box 12, National

Council of the Churches of Christ in the United States Papers, Presbyterian Department of History, Philadelphia (hereafter cited as NCCCA).

205. *NGB*, 1924, 1:273.

206. *New York Times*, 21 April 1924.

207. Finley to Borah, 21 April 1924, container 154, William E. Borah Papers, Library of Congress, Washington, D.C.

208. Minutes of the Administrative Committee of the FCCCA, 9 May 1924, Record Group 18, box 2, NCCCA.

209. CIJG, *A Statement of Our Relations with Japan, 1924*, National Committee on American-Japanese Relations Papers, Swarthmore College Peace Collection, Swarthmore College, Swarthmore, Pa. (hereafter cited as NCAJR Papers).

210. Taylor, *Advocate*, 153–54; FCCCA, *Annual Report 1921*, 107. These organizations included the FCCCA, the World Alliance for International Peace, the Council on Foreign Relations, the Bible Society, the YMCA, the New York Peace Society, the Foreign Policy Association, and the Japan Society. This committee was composed mainly of peace movement activists and clergymen, and membership was restricted to American citizens in order to avoid the criticism that it was acting on behalf of Japan. Sidney L. Gulick played a major role in establishing this committee.

211. Gulick to Members of the Committee, 24 April 1924, NCAJR Papers.

212. Wickersham to Lamont, 12 May 1924, box 186, Lamont Collection.

213. *NGB*, 1924, 1:264–68.

214. William R. Castle Journals (MS Am 2021), 19 April 1924, Houghton Library, Harvard University, Cambridge, Mass. (hereafter cited as Castle Journals with date). Houghton Library materials are cited by permission of the Houghton Library, Harvard University.

215. Ibid., 7 June 1924.

216. Ibid., 19 June 1924.

217. Joseph C. Grew, Diary (MS Am 1687–1687.9), 30 April 1924, Grew Papers, Houghton Library, Harvard University, Cambridge, Mass. (hereafter cited as Grew Diary with date).

218. Castle Journals, 18 January 1924.

219. Grew Diary, 3 May 1924.

220. Johnson to MacMurray, 28 June 1924, container 3, Nelson T. Johnson Papers, Library of Congress, Washington, D.C.

221. *Missionary Review of the World*, August 1924, 589.

222. *Chicago Daily Tribune*, 2 June 1924.

223. Reports of the Japan Mission, 16.4.1., vol. 24, no. 10, ABCFM Papers, Houghton Library, Harvard University, Cambridge, Mass.

224. *Christian Century*, 7 August 1924, 1028.

225. Acts of the Fifty-Second Annual Meeting of the Japan Mission, 4–10 June 1924, 16.4.1, vol. 41, no. 100, ABCFM Papers, Houghton Library, Harvard University, Cambridge, Mass.

226. Learned to Barton, 16.4.1, vol. 49, no. 115, ABCFM Papers, Houghton Library, Harvard University, Cambridge, Mass.

227. *New York Times*, 3 July 1924.

228. Northern Baptist Convention, *Race Prejudice: Part of the Annual Address of Corwin S. Shank. May 28–June 3, 1924* (pamphlet).

229. *NGB*, 1924, 1:286; *New York Times*, 15 August 1924.

230. Moore to Shidehara, 30 July and 6 August 1924, Kakkoku ni okeru hainichi kankei zakken: Beikoku no bu [Miscellaneous Documents Relating to Anti-Japanese Movements in Foreign Countries: The United States], JDRO (hereafter cited as KHZB).

231. Conversation with Saburi, 22 August 1924, 711.945/1212, SD.

232. Shidehara to Yoshida, 11 September 1924, KHZB.

233. Tupper and McReynolds, *Japan*, 203.

234. Ibid., 204–5.

235. *New York Times*, 1, 2, 3, 4, 5, 7, and 11 October 1924.

236. *San Francisco Chronicle*, 27, 29, and 30 September 1924.

237. Caffery to Hughes, 3 October 1924, 511.3 B 1/214, SD; *New York Times*, 4 October 1924.

238. *San Francisco Examiner*, 9 October 1924.

239. Ibid., 11 October 1924.

240. *New York Times*, 14 October 1924.

241. *Chūgai Shōgyō Shinpō*, 1 October 1924.

242. *Tokyo Asahi Shimbun*, 1 October 1924.

243. *Seattle Post-Intelligencer*, 14 October 1924.

244. *New York Times*, 19 December 1924.

245. Ibid., 21 December 1924.

Chapter 2

1. Hughes to Bancroft, 19 February 1925, 711.945/1215, SD.

2. Hughes to Bancroft, 17 January 1925, 711.945/1215, SD.

3. *New York Times*, 3 July 1924.

4. CIJG, *A Statement of Our Relations with Japan, 1924*, NCAJR Papers; Taylor, *Advocate*, 153; DeBeneditti, *Modern American Peace Movement*, 99.

5. NCAJR, *National Committee on American-Japanese Relations* (pamphlet). Several versions of this pamphlet exist for this title.

6. DeBeneditti, *Modern American Peace Movement*, 3–113.

7. NCAJR, *National Committee on American-Japanese Relations* (pamphlet).

8. Gulick, *New Factors in American Japanese Relations and a Constructive Proposal* (pamphlet).

9. Axling, *Japan Wonders Why?* (pamphlet).

10. Gulick to Friend, 15 September 1924, NCAJR Papers.

11. NCAJR, *America and Japan* (pamphlet).

12. Gulick, *The Proposal: The Reestablishment of Right Relations between America and Japan* (pamphlet).

13. National Foreign Trade Convention, *Official Report of the Eleventh National Foreign Trade Convention*, 1924, viii, 191.

14. Ōhashi to Shidehara, 6 December 1924, KHZB.

15. Daniels, *Prejudice*, 91, 147.

16. *Grizzly Bear*, May 1924.

17. McClatchy to Phelan, 29 February 1924, box 72, James D. Phelan Papers (BANC MSS C-B 800), Bancroft Library, University of California, Berkeley (hereafter cited as Phelan Papers).

18. McClatchy to Saburi, 20 June 1924, KHZB.

19. McClatchy to Phelan, 19 June 1924, box 72, Phelan Papers.

20. Ichioka, "Private Japanese Diplomacy," 16–18.

21. "Meeting of the CJIC," 13 August 1924, box 72, Phelan Papers.

22. Smith, *History: Department of California*, 10.

23. *Grizzly Bear*, May 1917.

24. "Meeting of the CJIC," 13 August 1924, box 72, Phelan Papers.

25. McClatchy to Fisk, 19 February 1925, carton 20, Phelan Papers.

26. CJIC, *Congress and Japan* (pamphlet).

27. CJIC, *Japan, Geneva, and Congress* (pamphlet), 20 October 1924, box 28, Hiram Johnson Papers (BANC MSS C-B 581), Bancroft Library, University of California, Berkeley (hereafter cited as Hiram Johnson Papers).

28. *NGB*, 1924, 1:272–76.

29. CJIC to members of the women's clubs, 18 October 1924, box 28, Hiram Johnson Papers.

30. "Progress Report of the CJIC," 30 October 1924, box 72, Phelan Papers; CJIC, Report of Meetings, 3 November 1924, carton 20, Phelan Papers.

31. "Progress Report of the CJIC," 30 October 1924, box 72, Phelan Papers.

32. Ibid.

33. Stanford University Survey of Race Relations, *Tentative Findings*, 18.

34. *Nichi Bei*, 1 July 1925.

35. "Progress Report of the CJIC," 8 November 1924, carton 20, Phelan Papers.

36. CJIC, *An Appeal to the Japanese Vote* (pamphlet), 12 November 1924, box 28, Hiram Johnson Papers.

37. CJIC, *Japan's Cure for Dual Citizenship* (pamphlet), 17 November 1924, box 28, Hiram Johnson Papers.

38. CJIC, *Tourist Brides from Japan* (pamphlet), 18 November 1924, box 28, Hiram Johnson Papers.

39. Bancroft to Martin Egan, 6 November 1924, Edgar A. Bancroft Papers, Special Collections and Archives, Knox College Library, Galesburg, Ill. (hereafter cited as Bancroft Papers).

40. American Federation of Labor, *Report of Proceedings of the Forty-Fourth Annual Convention,* 1924, 186.

41. CJIC, "Meeting of Committee," 1 December 1924, carton 20, Phelan Papers.

42. CJIC, "Minutes of Meeting," 29 December 1924, carton 20, Phelan Papers.

43. Abrams, "Cry," 350.

44. "Progress Report of the CJIC," 25 November 1924, carton 20, Phelan Papers.

45. CJIC, "Meeting of Committee," 1 December 1924, carton 20, Phelan Papers.

46. *Welcome and Christian Fellowship by Migrating People* (pamphlet), box 3a, World Alliance for International Friendship Through Churches Papers, Swarthmore College Peace Collection, Swarthmore College, Swarthmore, Pa. (hereafter cited as WAIFTC Papers).

47. *Resolutions Adopted at the Ninth Annual Meeting of The World Alliance for International Friendship Through Churches at Buffalo, N.Y., November 11–13, 1924* (pamphlet), box 2, WAIFTC Papers.

48. McClatchy to McLafferty, 25 November 1924, carton 20, Phelan Papers.

49. *Washington Evening Star,* 2 December 1924.

50. *Philadelphia Inquirer,* 4 December 1924.

51. Cavert, *United in Service,* 5, 47–51; MacFarland, *Christian Unity in the Making,* 257; *New York Times,* 6 December 1924.

52. "The 1925 Program of The Federated Churches for a Warless World" (Atlanta, 8 December 1924), box 19, Sidney L. Gulick Family Papers (accession no. *65M-183), Houghton Library, Harvard University, Cambridge, Mass. (hereafter cited as Gulick Family Papers); *Washington Post,* 9 December 1924; *Christian Century,* 18 December 1924, 1645–46.

53. Yoshida to Shidehara, 11 December 1924, KHZB.

54. Memorandum from Moore to Yoshida, 5 February 1924, KHZB.

55. *Collier's*, 17 January 1925, 24; CJIC, *McClatchy to the Editor of Collier's* (pamphlet), 29 January 1925, carton 20, Phelan Papers.

56. CJIC, "Minutes of Meeting," 9 February 1925, carton 20, Phelan Papers.

57. CJIC, "To Members of the Committee," 10 February 1925, carton 20, Phelan Papers.

58. CJIC, *Japanese Immigration Drops*, 20 February 1925, box 28, Hiram Johnson Papers.

59. McClatchy to Fisk, 19 February 1925, carton 20, Phelan Papers.

60. *Grizzly Bear*, June 1924.

61. Ibid., September 1924.

62. Ibid., January 1925.

63. *Organized Labor*, 21 March 1925.

64. *Labor Clarion*, 3 June 1925.

Chapter 3

1. Caffery to Hughes, 15 October 1924, 711.945/1230, SD.

2. *Japan Times*, 1 October 1924.

3. CJIC, *California's Answer to Japan* (pamphlet).

4. *Tokyo Asahi Shimbun*, 29 December 1924.

5. *STGS*, 22 January 1925; *KTGS*, 22 January 1925.

6. *Nichi Bei*, 24 and 29 January 1925.

7. *STGS*, 23 January 1925.

8. *KTGS*, 30 January 1925.

9. Wickersham to Benton, 13 January 1925, NCAJR Papers.

10. Gulick to Friend, 3 Apr. 1925, NCAJR Papers.

11. *International Goodwill*, 12 March 1925.

12. Gulick to Atkinson, 25 January 1925, box 240, Council on Religion and International Affairs Papers (now called the Carnegie Council on Ethics and International Affairs Papers), Butler Library, Columbia University, New York (hereafter cited as CRIA).

13. CJIC, "Minutes of Meeting," 5 March 1925, carton 20, Phelan Papers; *NGB*, 1925, 1:305.

14. *NGB*, 1925, 1:311.

15. Ibid., 1:310.

16. Ibid., 1:310–11.

17. McClatchy to Gleason, 23 April 1925, carton 20, Phelan Papers.

18. *NGB*, 1925, 1:305–6.

19. *San Francisco Bulletin*, 18 April 1925.

20. *NGB*, 1925, 1:308; *San Francisco Examiner*, 4 May 1925.

21. *Seattle Post-Intelligencer*, 5 May 1925.

22. CJIC, "The Wickersham Japanese Movement," 5 May 1925, carton 20, Phelan Papers; *San Francisco Examiner*, 5 May 1925.

23. *NGB*, 1925, 1:307–8.

24. CJIC, "Congress and the Council of Churches," 11 May 1925, carton 20, Phelan Papers.

25. McClatchy to Burbank, 14 May 1925, carton 20, Phelan Papers.

26. McClatchy to Gulick, 19 May 1925, box 72, Phelan Papers; CJIC, "Minutes of Meeting," 27 May 1925, carton 20, Phelan Papers.

27. CJIC, Release #203, carton 15, Phelan Papers.

28. McClatchy to the members of the NCAJR, 20 May 1925, carton 20, Phelan Papers.

29. *Grizzly Bear*, June 1925.

30. Scharrenberg, "Japanese Exclusion by Law," 423.

31. *NGB*, 1925, 1:311.

32. *Christian Century*, 15 and 29 January 1925, and 16 April 1925.

33. *Japan Times*, 28 April 1925; CJIC, "Japanese Views of the Wickersham Movement," box 20, Chester H. Rowell Papers (BANC MSS C-B 401), Bancroft Library, University of California, Berkeley (hereafter cited as Rowell Papers).

34. Bancroft to Secretary of State, 9 June 1925, 711.945/1304, SD.

35. Bancroft to Secretary of State, 7 July 1925, 711.945/1305, SD.

36. *Osaka Mainichi Shimbun*, 3 July 1925.

37. Lockhart to Secretary of State, 11 June 1925, 711.945/1303, SD.

38. Secretary of State to Bancroft, 12 June 1925, 711.945/1304, SD.

39. Bancroft to Hughes, 5 January 1925, Bancroft Papers.

40. *Rafu Shimpō*, 22 Apr. 1925.

41. *Nichi Bei*, 24 April 1925.

42. *NGB*, 1925, 1:313.

43. In Toyohashi, west of Tokyo, a regional branch of the veterans' association distributed brochures, one of which admonished, "Do not forget July 1." In Hiroshima, an anti-American gathering took place on July 1 (Governor of Aichi to Shidehara, 1 July 1925, and governor of Hiroshima to Shidehara, 2 July 1925, 1924 nen iminhō ni taisuru ippan yoron: Shūsei undō [Public Opinion Relating to the 1924 Immigration Law: The Modification Movement], JDRO.

44. Bancroft to Secretary of State, 7 July 1925, 711.945/1305, SD.

45. *NGB*, 1925, 1:314; *San Francisco Examiner*, 1 July 1925.

46. *New York Times*, 1 and 2 July 1925.

47. "The Foundation of the American Anti-Japanese Immigration Law," *Seiyū*, May 1925, 19–24, and June 1925, 37–43.

48. *Tokyo Asahi Shimbun*, 28 June 1925.

49. *Chūgai Shōgyō Shinpō*, 1 and 2 July 1925.

50. *Kokumin Shimbun*, 1 July 1925.

51. *Tokyo Asahi Shimbun*, 3 July 1925.

52. *Chūgai Shōgyō Shinpō*, 13, 14, and 16 July 1925.

53. Eliot to Chamberlain, 23 April 1925, FO 371/10634.

54. Inoue, *Taiheiyō*, 3–7; *NGB*, 1925, 1:344–45.

55. Institute of Pacific Relations, *Institute of Pacific Relations*, 77–78; *Honolulu Advertiser*, 15 July 1925.

56. *San Francisco Daily News*, 17 August 1925.

57. *San Francisco Bulletin*, 7 July 1925.

58. *NGB*, 1925, 1:340–41.

59. *Organized Labor*, 4 July 1925.

60. *Honolulu Star-Bulletin*, 14 July 1925; *San Francisco Examiner*, 14 July 1925.

61. *Nichi Bei*, 1 July 1925.

62. *Rafu Shimpō*, 1 July 1925.

63. *Nippu Jiji*, 15 July 1925; *Be Patient, Neighbor Japan* (pamphlet), no. 8, Takagi Collection, Center for American Studies, University of Tokyo, Tokyo (hereafter cited as Takagi Collection).

64. CJIC, Release #211, 17 July 1925, carton 20, Phelan Papers.

65. CJIC, *America and Japan* (pamphlet).

66. McClatchy to Members of Women's Clubs, 24 June 1925, and McClatchy to Members of State Federation of Farm Bureaus, 3 July 1925; McClatchy to Department Adjutant, American Legion, 3 July 1925; all in carton 15, Phelan Papers.

67. "Progress Report of the CJIC," 8 July 1925, carton 20, Phelan Papers.

68. *NGB*, 1925, 1:325–26; *San Francisco Bulletin*, 12 August 1925; *Sacramento Bee*, 12 August 1925.

69. CJIC, "Encouraging Ill Will in Japan," Release #217, 20 August 1925, box 34, Phelan Papers.

70. American Legion of California, *Summary of Proceedings of the Seventh Annual Convention*, 10–11; Smith, *History, Department of California*, 25; Waldron, "Antiforeign Movements," 231; McClatchy, *Guarding the Immigration Gates* (pamphlet); McClatchy to editors, Release #222, 7 October 1925, and McClatchy to Congressmen, Release #223, 8 October 1925, both in carton 15, Phelan Papers.

71. Department of Washington, American Legion, "Resolution," carton 15, Phelan Papers; CJIC, "Minutes of Meeting," 25 August 1925, carton 20, Phelan Papers.

72. *Pacific Legion*, November 1925.

73. California State Federation of Labor, *Proceedings of the Twenty-Sixth Annual Convention of the California State Federation (1925)*, 21–25, 31–32, 77–78; Taketomi to Shidehara, 3 December 1925, KHZB.

74. *San Francisco Examiner*, 6 August 1925; American Federation of Labor, *Report of Proceedings of the Forty-Fifth Annual Convention*, 1925, 170.

75. *New York Times*, 9 October 1925.

76. Tupper and McReynolds, *Japan*, 218.

77. CJIC, "Minutes of Meeting," 25 August 1925, carton 20, Phelan Papers.

78. Shibusawa to Wickersham, 3 October 1925, box 240, CRIA.

79. *Shinsekai*, 10 and 11 October 1925.

80. *NGB*, 1925, 1:326–27.

81. *New York Times*, 7 December 1925.

82. NCAJR, *National Committee on American-Japanese Relations* (1925 pamphlet), NCAJR Papers.

83. *International Goodwill*, 3 December 1925.

84. Ibid., 17 December 1925.

85. Gulick, "American-Japanese Relations," 186.

86. Cavert, *Twenty Years*, 183–84; Tupper and McReynolds, *Japan*, 219; *Fresno Republican*, 10 December 1925.

87. *Christian Century*, 26 November 1925.

88. Gulick to Lynch, 16 November 1925, box 240, CRIA.

89. Gulick to Lamont, 4 December 1925, box 186, Lamont Collection.

Chapter 4

1. "Progress Report of the CJIC," 17 December 1925, carton 20, Phelan Papers.

2. *Sacramento Bee*, 25 December 1925.

3. *Grizzly Bear*, December 1925.

4. FCCCA, *Annual Report*, 1925, 47.

5. FCCCA, "A Statement of the Policy of the Federal Council of the Churches in America Regarding Japanese Immigration," end of 1925, Record Group 18, box 35, NCCCA.

6. FCCCA, "Declaration Regarding Asiatic Exclusion," 1925(?), Record Group 18, box 35, NCCCA.

7. CJIC, "Minutes of Meeting," 29 December 1925, carton 20, Phelan Papers.

8. McClatchy to Editor of the *Pacific Legion*, 25 January 1926, carton 20, Phelan Papers.

9. *Sacramento Bee*, 20 January 1926.

10. *Grizzly Bear*, February 1926.

262   *Notes to Chapter 4*

11. *NGB*, 1926, 1:166–68.

12. *STGS*, 21 January 1926.

13. *Sacramento Bee*, 21 January 1926.

14. *Sacramento Union*, 2 February 1926.

15. *NGB*, 1926, 1:164–65.

16. Ibid., 1:165–66.

17. Ibid.

18. "Statement by Sidney L. Gulick," 10 May 1926, Record Group 18, box 33, NCCCA.

19. *International Goodwill*, 8 April 1926.

20. Gulick to Members of the NCAJR, 20 January 1926, box 19, Gulick Family Papers.

21. CJIC, "Minutes of Meeting," 2 July 1926, carton 20, Phelan Papers.

22. Governor of Osaka to Shidehara, 15 and 26 June and 2 July 1924, 1924 nen iminhō ni taisuru ippan yoron: Shūsei undō [Public Opinion Relating to the 1924 Immigration Law: The Modification Movement], JDRO.

23. MacVeagh to Secretary of State, 2 July 1926, 711.945/1306, SD. Although the day of protest ceased to be observed nationwide, isolated anti-America gatherings still took place. For example, Kyokutō Renmei Kyōkai organized a gathering in Osaka on July 1 (Governor of Osaka to Minister of Interior, 9 July 1926, Zai naigai kyōkai kankei zakken: Zainai no bu [Miscellaneous Documents Relating to Organizations at Home and Abroad: Organizations at Home], JDRO).

24. *Osaka Mainichi Shimbun*, 2 July 1926.

25. *Gaikō Jihō*, 1 July 1926, 1–9.

26. *New York Times*, 24 August 1926.

27. Ibid., 14 November 1926.

28. Tupper and McReynolds, *Japan*, 219.

29. *International Goodwill*, 12 September, 14 October, 11 November, 23 December 1926 and 3 March 1927; Gulick to Shibusawa, 15 April 1926, in Shibasawa seien kinen zaidan ryūmonsha, *Shibusawa Eiichi denki shiryō*, 38:6–9; Yoshimura, "Ningyō shisetsu kara ningen shisetsu he," 40–45.

30. For example, *Tokyo Asahi Shimbun*, 18, 20, and 27 January, 22 February, and 4 March 1927; *Chūgai Shōgyō Shinpō*, 8 and 18 January and 4 March 1927.

31. Atkinson to Gulick, 19 June 1926, box 241, CRIA.

32. *Castle Journals*, 21 December 1927.

33. Ibid., 22 December 1927.

34. Waldron, "Antiforeign," 231; *San Francisco Call*, 6 September 1926.

35. *Grizzly Bear*, September 1926.

36. *Organized Labor*, 18 September 1926.

37. California State Federation of Labor, *Proceedings of the Twenty-Seventh Annual Convention, Oakland, Calif.,* 1926, 18, 94–95; Taketomi to Shidehara, 28 September 1926, KHZB.

38. American Federation of Labor, *Report of Proceedings of the Forty-Sixth Annual Convention,* 1926, 214.

39. "Progress Report of the CJIC," 24 September 1926; *International Goodwill,* 16 September 1926.

40. "Progress Report of the CJIC," 19 November 1926.

41. *Grizzly Bear,* December 1926.

42. Ibid., January 1927.

43. Paul Scharrenberg, "America's Immigration Problem: A Chronological Review of the Principal Legislative Enactments Restricting Immigration with Comment Emphasizing the Pacific Coast Viewpoint," carton 2, Paul Scharrenberg Papers (BANC MSS C-B 906), Bancroft Library, University of California, Berkeley (hereafter cited as Scharrenberg Papers).

44. *International Goodwill,* 3 February 1927.

45. NCAJR, *Toward an Understanding of Japan* (pamphlet).

46. O. E. Janney to Hoover, 2 May 1927, box 289, Hoover Papers.

47. American Friends Service Committee, *Message to the American People on Japan* (pamphlet).

48. CJIC, "Minutes of Meeting," 15 January 1927, and Progress Report, 24 March 1927, carton 20, Phelan Papers.

49. *Grizzly Bear,* April 1927.

50. Ibid., May 1927.

51. CJIC, "Response from Dr. H. H. Guy," 2 July 1927; Abiko to McClatchy, 5 July 1927; both in carton 20, Phelan Papers.

52. CJIC, "Conference Luncheon for San Francisco Delegates to the Institute of Pacific Relations," 13 July 1927, carton 20, Phelan Papers.

53. Katagiri, "Taiheiyō mondai chōsakai (IPR) to imin mondai: Dainikai hawai kaigi o chūshintoshite," 161.

54. Condliffe, *Problems,* 32.

55. Ibid., 58; *New York Herald-Tribune,* 17 July 1927.

56. Inoue, *Taiheiyō,* 155–57.

57. Condliffe, *Problems,* 156–58.

58. Inoue, *Taiheiyō,* 157.

59. CJIC, "Minutes of Meeting," 11 August 1927.

60. *Organized Labor,* 13 August 1927.

61. *Labor Clarion,* 2 September 1927.

62. *New York Times,* 15–19, 21, 22, 29, and 31 July 1927.

63. *San Francisco Examiner*, 29 July 1927.

64. *Sacramento Bee*, 13 August 1927.

65. *Trans-Pacific*, 5 November 1927; Taylor, *Advocate*, 165; "Progress Report of the CJIC," 27 July 1927, carton 20, Phelan Papers.

66. "Weekly Report of the CJIC," 11 October 1927, carton 20, Phelan Papers.

67. Ibid.; Matsudaira to Tanaka, 26 October 1927, KHZB.

68. *New York Times*, 12 August 1927.

69. "Weekly Report of the CJIC," 11 October 1927, carton 20, Phelan Papers.

70. McClatchy to Phelan, 11 August 1927, box 72, Phelan Papers.

71. Waldron, "Antiforeign," 231.

72. California State Federation of Labor, *Proceedings of the Twenty-Eighth Annual Convention, San Bernardino, Calif.*, 1927, 26–27.

73. *Oakland Tribune*, 29 September 1927.

74. *Grizzly Bear*, December 1927.

75. *Chicago Daily Tribune*, 4 November 1927.

76. Ibid., 5 August 1927.

77. Ibid., 7 September 1927.

78. *Tokyo Asahi Shimbun*, 8 November 1927.

79. "Weekly Report of the CJIC," 15 November 1927, carton 20, Phelan Papers; *Fresno Bee*, 19 November 1927.

80. *Chicago Daily Tribune*, 6 February and 21 April 1928.

81. Tamura to Tanaka, 16 February and 1 May 1928, KHZB.

82. *Grizzly Bear*, January 1928; CJIC, "Weekly Report," 6 December 1927, carton 20, Phelan Papers.

83. Phelan to Madden, 10 December 1927, carton 16, Phelan Papers.

84. "Weekly Report of the CJIC," 14 December 1927, carton 20, Phelan Papers.

85. *Christian Century*, 5 January 1928.

86. *San Francisco Bulletin*, 13 January 1928.

87. *San Francisco Examiner*, 21 January 1928.

88. Kaltenbach to Gentlemen of the CJIC, 7 February 1928, box 34, Phelan Papers; "Weekly Report of the CJIC," 16 February 1928, carton 20, Phelan Papers.

89. Ida to Tanaka, 21 February 1928, KHZB.

90. *Santa Barbara News*, 2 September 1927.

91. *Scribner's Magazine* 83 (January 1928): 62–71.

92. Scharrenberg, *An Answer to Dr. Henry S. Pritchett Who Insists that a Few California Politicians Are Solely Responsible for Excluding the Japanese* (pamphlet).

93. *Sacramento Bee*, 4 February 1928.

94. *New York Times*, 30 March 1928.

95. Tamura to Tanaka, 9 May 1928, in Beikoku ni okeru hainichi mondai zakken: Iminhō shūsei kankei [Miscellaneous Documents Relating to Anti-Japanese Problems in the United States: Documents Relating to the Amendment of the Immigration Law], JDRO (hereafter cited as BHZIS).

96. *Tokyo Asahi Shimbun*, 12 May 1928; CJIC, "Notes for Information of Committee," 30 July 1928, box 72, Phelan Papers.

97. *New York Times*, 23 July 1928.

98. Report of George H. Blakeslee on his Trip to Japan as Visiting Carnegie Professor of International Relations, 21 February 1928, George Hubbard Blakeslee Papers, Goddard Library, Clark University, Worcester, Mass. (hereafter cited as Blakeslee Papers).

99. *San Francisco Chronicle*, 3 June 1928.

100. McClatchy to Butler, 7 July 1928, box 72, Phelan Papers; McClatchy to Kellogg, 2 August 1928, 150.946/201, SD.

101. *New York Times*, 13 July 1928; *San Francisco Chronicle*, 12 July 1928.

102. McClatchy to MacVeagh, 14 and 30 July 1928, 150.946/202, SD.

103. MacVeagh to McClatchy, 30 August 1928, 150.946/202, SD.

104. Gyokujō Hanzawa, "Nichibei kankei no kinjyō" [The Recent Situation of U.S.-Japanese Relations], *Gaikō Jihō*, 1 July 1928, 1–12.

105. *Tokyo Asahi Shimbun*, 6 July 1928.

106. Declaration of the Mass Meeting of the People of the Far East, 1 July 1928, 150.946/200, SD.

107. Neville to Kellogg, 11 July 1928, 711.945/1309, SD.

108. Ugaki, *Nikki*, 1:674.

109. Ibid., 1:675.

110. *Organized Labor*, 12 May 1928; see also *Organized Labor*, 30 June and 16 July 1928.

111. *Organized Labor*, 1 September 1928.

112. *Sacramento Bee*, 3 September 1928.

113. Divine, *American Immigration Policy*, 54–68.

114. Ibid., 68–75.

115. California State Federation of Labor, *Proceedings of the Twenty-Ninth Annual Convention, Sacramento, Calif.*, 1928, 28–29, 48–52; *Sacramento Bee*, 18 September 1928; CJIC, "Activities of the CJIC," 18 September 1928, box 72, Phelan Papers; *San Francisco Examiner*, 19 September 1928; Ida to Tanaka, 19 September 1928, KHZB.

116. American Federation of Labor, *Report of Proceedings of the Forty-Eighth Annual Convention*, 1928, 217, 257; *Organized Labor*, 1 December 1928.

117. CJIC, "Minutes of Meeting," 5 September 1928, carton 20, Phelan Papers.

118. McClatchy to Harrison, 22 September and 30 October 1928, box 72, Phelan Papers; Harrison to McClatchy, 27 October 1928, box 72, Phelan Papers.

119. Sawada to Tanaka, 17 September 1928, KHZB.

120. *Tokyo Asahi Shimbun*, 11 December 1927.

121. *San Francisco Chronicle*, 23 August 1928.

122. For example, *Selma Enterprise*, 6 September 1928; *Washington Post*, 19 October 1928; and *Selma Irrigator*, 27 December 1928.

123. Mizusawa to Tanaka, 8 October 1928, BHZIS.

124. McClatchy to Phelan, 12 October 1928, box 72, Phelan Papers.

125. Shakai mondai kenkyūkai, ed., *Teikoku gikai shi*, series 1, 2:10–11; CJIC, "Progress Report," 1 February 1929, carton 20, Phelan Papers.

126. Debuchi to Tanaka, 26 October 1928, BHZIS; *Organized Labor*, 10 November 1928; *Tokyo Asahi Shimbun*, 28 October 1928.

Chapter 5

1. Daniels, *Prejudice*, 48. According to *Foreign Commerce and Navigation of the United States* (hereafter cited as *FCN* with year, and volume number, if applicable), for the fiscal year ending 30 June 1909, Japan was the heaviest merchandise trade partner for San Francisco; almost half of the imports there came from Japan and about a quarter of the exports went to Japan (146–47).

2. *NGB*, 1924, 1:275.

3. Issel and Cherny, *San Francisco*, 40–41.

4. *New York Times*, 23 November 1939.

5. For example, when businessmen in California opposed the immigration bill in 1923 and 1924, exports to Japan from both San Francisco and Los Angeles increased (*FCN*, 1923, 16; *FCN*, 1924, 12).

6. Exports of merchandise from San Francisco to Japan increased more than 30 percent from 1927 to 1928, and slightly increased from 1928 to 1929 (*FCN*, 1927, 1:11; *FCN*, 1928, 12; and *FCN*, 1929, 1:12).

7. Mullins, *The Depression and the Urban West Coast*, 10, 12.

8. *Nation's Business*, December 1928.

9. Castle Journals, 25 January 1929.

10. Ibid., 11 December 1929.

11. *NGBTIM*, 1017–18; Ida to Tanaka, 14 February 1929, KHZB; CJIC, "Progress Report," 1 February 1929, carton 20, Phelan Papers.

12. *Washington Evening Star*, 6 February 1929.

13. CJIC, "Minutes of Meeting," 13 February 1929, carton 20, Phelan Papers.

14. McClatchy to members of California State Legislature, 14 February 1929, box 72, Phelan Papers.

15. *Federal Council Bulletin* 12, no. 2 (January 1929): 20.

16. Cavert, *Twenty Years*, 259.

17. *Labor Clarion*, 1 March 1929, 1.

18. *San Francisco Call*, 26 February 1929.

19. *Sacramento Bee*, 27 February 1929.

20. *NGBTIM*, 1019.

21. Gulick to Alexander, 21 February 1929, KHZB.

22. Conversation between Debuchi and Gulick, 8 April 1929, KHZB; *NGBTIM*, 1020.

23. Debuchi to Yoshida, 14 June 1929, KHZB; *NGBTIM*, 1021–22.

24. Conversation between Stone and Johnson, 20 March 1929, container 49, Nelson T. Johnson Papers.

25. McClatchy to Phelan, 25 March 1929, box 72, Phelan Papers.

26. McClatchy to Phelan, Webb, and Scharrenberg, 28 March 1929, box 72, Phelan Papers.

27. *Sacramento Union*, 15 April 1929.

28. *Sacramento Bee*, 27 April 1929.

29. California State Federation of Labor, *Proceedings of the Thirtieth Annual Convention*, 1929, 77.

30. *Grizzly Bear*, May 1929.

31. Ibid., November 1929.

32. *Chūgai Shōgyō Shinpō*, 14 March 1929.

33. Shakai mondai kenkyūkai, *Teikoku gikai shi*, series 1, 5:960–62; *Tokyo Asahi Shimbun*, 24 March 1929.

34. Shibusawa, "Peace on the Pacific," 273–77.

35. "Oriental Affairs in Light of Kyoto Conference," 7 December 1929, CZ BLAK 3–5, Blakeslee Papers.

36. *New York Times*, 29 October 1929.

37. *San Francisco Daily News*, 30 October 1929.

38. *San Francisco Examiner*, 30 October 1929.

39. *Sacramento Bee*, 1 November 1925.

40. *Labor Clarion*, 20 December 1929.

41. *Commonwealth* 5, no. 51 (17 December 1929); report by Ida, 24 December 1929, KHZB.

42. McClatchy to Phelan, 24 December 1929, box 72, Phelan Papers.

43. *New York Times*, 13 November 1929.

44. FCCCA, *Annual Report*, 1929, 47–48.

45. *Federal Council Bulletin*, January 1930.

46. "Preliminary Report of the CJIC," 24 December 1929, carton 20, Phelan Papers.

47. Debuchi to Shidehara, 14 January 1930, BHZIS.

48. Castle Journals, 1 January 1930.

49. Sawada to Shidehara, 13 February and 25 March 1930, BHZIS.

50. Debuchi to Shidehara, 14 January 1930, BHZIS.

51. Ida to Shidehara, 19 January 1930 (rec'd), KHZB.

52. Sawada to Shidehara, 21 February 1930, BHZIS.

53. NCCWP, *The Churches and World Peace* (pamphlet), 13, in National Committee on the Churches and World Peace Papers, Swarthmore College Peace Collection, Swarthmore College, Swarthmore, Pa. (hereafter cited as NCCWP Papers).

54. Sawada to Shidehara, 17 January 1930, BHZIS.

55. Greene to Harvey, 10 January 1930, BHZIS.

56. Harvey to Sawada, 16 April 1930, BHZIS.

57. Shakai mondai kenkyūkai, *Teikoku gikai shi*, series 1, 5:282–88. This question was solved in 1931 when the Japanese Diet raised the tariff on various woods, imported mainly from Manchuria and Siberia.

58. Memorandum attached to Dickover to Stimson, 2 May 1929, 694.113 Lumber/94, SD.

59. *West Coast Lumberman*, November 1929, 85; *American Lumberman*, 26 October 1929, 48.

60. Neville to Stimson, 15 June 1929, 694.113 Lumber/105, SD; Secretary of State to Embassy in Tokyo, 22 March 1929, 694.113 Lumber/26, SD.

61. *FCN*, 1928, 12; *FCN*, 1929, 1:12; *FCN*, 1930, 11.

62. *FCN*, 1928, 84; *FCN*, 1930, 346.

63. Inoue to Saitō, 30 October 1928, BHZIS; Knapp to Barnes, 26 October 1928, BHZIS.

64. Okamoto to Shidehara, 20 January 1930, BHZIS; *(Seattle) Town Crier*, January 1930.

65. Okamoto to Shidehara, 6 March 1930, BHZIS; *West Coast Lumberman*, February 1930, 49.

66. Okamoto to Shidehara, 15 March 1930, BHZIS.

67. Spencer to Holden, 16 December 1929, BHZIS.

68. Haines to Holden, 3 January 1930, BHZIS.

69. Alexander to Holden, 13 February 1930, BHZIS.

70. Holden to Alexander, 26 February 1930, BHZIS; Okamoto to Shidehara, 15 March 1930, BHZIS.

71. "Resolution, Seattle Chamber of Commerce," about 10 April 1930, KHZB.

72. Okamoto to Shidehara, 16 April 1930, BHZIS.

73. Total exports from Oregon to Japan declined from $13,869,102 in 1929 to $7,153,875 in 1930 (*FCN*, 1929, 1:12; *FCN*, 1930, 11).

74. Ashino to Shidehara, 12 April 1930, BHZIS.

75. Ashino to Shidehara, 15 May 1930, BHZIS.

76. Sawada to Shidehara, 30 April 1930, BHZIS.

77. Sawada to Shidehara, 3 May 1930, BHZIS.

78. *Grizzly Bear*, Apr. 1930.

79. Ibid., May 1930.

80. Ibid., June 1930.

81. Okamoto to Shidehara, 16 May 1930, BHZIS.

82. "Resolution, Portland Chamber of Commerce, May 7, 1930," KHZB; Ashino to Shidehara, 15 May 1930, BHZIS.

83. National Foreign Trade Convention, *Official Report of the Seventeenth National Foreign Trade Convention*, 1930, 34–35.

84. Satō to Shidehara, 21 May 1930, BHZIS.

85. CJIC to the Resolution Committee, 21 May 1930, carton 20, Phelan Papers.

86. Satō to Shidehara, 22 May 1930, BHZIS.

87. *Los Angeles Times*, 24 May 1930.

88. National Foreign Trade Convention, *Official Report of the Seventeenth National Foreign Trade Convention*, 1930, viii; Satō to Shidehara, 24 May 1930 (rec'd), BHZIS.

89. Satō to Shidehara, 23 May 1930, BHZIS.

90. Castle Journals, 3 April 1930; note from Castle to Stimson, 4 April 1930, 150.946/215, SD.

91. Matsudaira to Shidehara, 8 March 1930, BHZIS.

92. Matsudaira to Shidehara, 17 March 1930, KHZB.

93. Shidehara to Matsudaira, 1 April 1930, KHZB.

94. Debuchi to Shidehara, 25 April 1930, BHZIS.

95. Castle Journals, 31 May 1930.

96. *FRUS*, 1930, 3:315–16; Japan, Gaimushō [Ministry of Foreign Affairs], *Nihon gaikō bunsho: Shōwa-ki* [Documents on Japanese Foreign Policy: Shōwa Era] (hereafter cited as *NGBSK*), series 1, pt. 2, 4:167.

97. *FRUS*, 1930, 3:316–17; *NGBSK*, series 1, pt. 2, 4:167–68.

98. Castle Journals, 28 May 1930. When Castle saw an early draft of the speech, he was displeased; the Japanese foreign minister and vice-minister were also totally unprepared for Hanihara's speech (see Tilley to Henderson, 30 May

1930, FO 371/14295). A British official stationed in Tokyo also paid close attention to Hanihara's speech (see Sir J. Tilley, 26 May 1930, WO 106/5477).

99. *Washington Post,* 24 May 1930.

100. *Christian Science Monitor,* 24 May 1930.

101. *Philadelphia Public Ledger,* 25 May 1930.

102. *Rafu Shimpō,* 28 May 1930.

103. *New York Times,* 24 May 1930.

104. *Tokyo Nichinichi Shimbun,* 25 May 1930.

105. *Tokyo Asahi Shimbun,* 27 May 1930.

106. *Osaka Mainichi Shimbun,* 27 May 1930; *Kokumin Shimbun,* 28 May 1930.

107. Neville to Stimson, 3 June 1930, 150.946/217, SD.

108. Brokaw to State Department, 27 May 1930 (rec'd), 811.111 Quota 94/78, SD.

109. "Taibei mondai ni kansuru mumei resshi hōyō ni tsuite [About the Memorial Service for Anonymous Person concerning U.S.-Japanese Problems]," 29 May 1930, KHZB.

110. *Osaka Mainichi Shimbun,* 4 June 1930.

111. McClatchy to Johnson, 23 May 1930, carton 20, Phelan Papers; CJIC, "Released, 23 May 1930," carton 20, Phelan Papers.

112. CJIC, "Important," 26 May 1930, carton 20, Phelan Papers.

113. Kaneko to Shidehara, 5 June 1930, BHZIS.

114. *San Francisco Call,* 6 June 1930.

115. *San Francisco Examiner,* 25 May 1930.

116. *Fresno Bee,* 26 May 1930.

117. *Sacramento Bee,* 5 June 1930.

118. *Organized Labor,* 7 June 1930.

119. *Labor Press,* 6 June 1930.

120. *Grizzly Bear,* June 1930.

121. *Victoria Times,* 10 June 1930.

122. *Los Angeles Times,* 27 May 1930.

123. *San Francisco Chronicle,* 29 May 1930.

124. *Seattle Star,* 24 May 1930.

125. *Seattle Daily Times,* 27 May 1930.

126. Ibid., 16 July 1930.

127. Ibid., 8 June 1930.

128. *Daily (Olympia, Wash.) Olympian,* 2 June 1930.

129. Debuchi to Shidehara, 30 May 1930, BHZIS.

130. Sawada to Shidehara, 27 May 1930, BHZIS.

131. Debuchi to Shidehara, 30 May 1930, BHZIS; Debuchi to Shidehara, 31 May 1930, BHZIS.

132. Okamoto to Shidehara, 10 June 1930, BHZIS.

133. Sawada to Shidehara, 31 May 1930, BHZIS.

134. Kaneko to Shidehara, 28 May 1930, BHZIS.

135. "Resolution, Los Angeles Chamber of Commerce, May 29, 1930," KHZB.

136. Kaneko to Shidehara, 6 June 1930, BHZIS.

137. William Castle, "Japanese Relations," 13 June 1930, KHZB.

138. Lynch to Debuchi, 9 June 1930, BHZIS.

139. Alexander to Holden, 6 June 1930, BHZIS.

140. First Friends Church of Pasadena to Johnson, 5 June 1930, BHZIS; Central Committee of Pasadena Federated Church Brotherhoods to Johnson, 5 June 1930, BHZIS; Japanese Committee of the Council of International Relations of Pasadena, 5 June 1930, BHZIS.

141. *New York Times*, 15 June 1930.

142. Ibid., 19 June 1930.

143. "Resolution," 30 June 1930, BHZIS.

144. Wakasugi to Shidehara, 2 July 1930, BHZIS.

145. Holden to Okamoto, 21 July 1930, BHZIS.

146. Alexander to Castle, 26 September 1930, 150.946/222, SD.

147. Alexander to Castle, 15 October 1930, 150.946/225, SD; see also Alexander to Holden, 16 October 1930, BHZIS.

148. Alexander to Castle, 21 August 1930, 150.946/220, SD; Wakasugi to Shidehara, 3 September 1930, BHZIS.

149. Wakasugi to Shidehara, 23 September 1930, BHZIS.

150. California State Federation of Labor, *Proceedings of the Thirty-First Annual Convention*, 1931.

151. Ōyama Ujirō, "Hainichi iminhō no shūsei ni tsuite" [Regarding the Modification of the Anti-Japanese Immigration Act], *Gaikō Jihō*, 15 June 1930, 1–10.

152. *Gaikō Jihō*, 1 July 1930.

153. Wakasugi to Shidehara, 23 September 1930, BHZIS.

154. Wakasugi to Shidehara, 17 July 1930 (rec'd), BHZIS.

155. Satō to Debuchi, 16 July 1930, BHZIS.

156. Hornbeck to Castle, 3 July 1930, 150.946/219, SD.

157. Memo by Hornbeck to Castle, 4 November 1930, 150.946/229, SD.

158. Castle to Alexander, 8 July 1930, 150.946/219, SD.

159. Castle to Hornbeck, 8 July 1930, 150.946/219, SD.

160. *New York Times*, 10 August 1930.

161. Stimson to Forbes, 29 November 1930, 150.946/231, SD.

162. *NGBSK*, series 1, pt. 2, 4:163–65.

163. Hornbeck to Forbes, 9 October 1930, 150.946/226, SD.

164. Alexander to Castle, 29 September 1930, 150.946/222, SD; Alexander to Holden, 30 September 1930, BHZIS.

165. Alexander to Greene, 31 October 1930, 150.946/229, SD.

166. Divine, *American Immigration Policy*, 77–84.

167. Debuchi to Shidehara, 4 December 1930, BHZIS.

168. *NGBSK*, series 1, pt. 2, 4:169–71.

169. *NGBSK*, series 1, pt. 2, 4:173–74.

170. Wakasugi to Debuchi, 16 December 1930, BHZIS.

171. *NGBSK*, series 1, pt. 2, 4:174–75.

172. Ibid.

173. Okamoto to Shidehara, 6 January 1931, BHZIS.

174. Ashino to Shidehara, 17 March 1931, BHZIS.

175. Ashino to Shidehara, 6 April 1931, BHZIS.

176. National Foreign Trade Convention, *Offical Report of the Eighteenth National Foreign Trade Convention*, 1931, 37; Horiuchi to Shidehara, 29 May 1931, BHZIS.

177. Uchiyama to Shidehara, 14 July 1931, BHZIS.

178. Chamber of Commerce of the United States, *Seventh Annual Meeting*, 1929, 66–67.

179. "Conversation: Fitzpatrick and Isaacs of the U.S. Chamber of Commerce; Cumming, Miller, and Dooman, 5 June 1931," 811.111 Quota 94/95, SD.

180. *NGBSK*, series 1, pt. 2, 4:182–86.

181. Chamber of Commerce of the United States, "Immediate Release," BHZIS.

182. Wakasugi to Shidehara, 2 August 1931 (rec'd), BHZIS.

183. *San Francisco Examiner*, 1 August 1931.

184. *Grizzly Bear*, October 1931.

185. *Labor Clarion*, 7 August 1931.

186. *San Francisco Chronicle*, 1 August 1931.

187. *San Francisco Daily News*, 5 August 1931; *Los Angeles Times*, 1 August 1931.

188. *New York Times*, 4 August 1931.

189. *Christian Science Monitor*, 1 August 1931.

190. *Chicago Daily Tribune*, 7 August 1931.

191. *Tokyo Asahi Shimbun*, 2 August 1931.

192. *Jiji Shimpō*, 2 August 1931.

193. "Hainichi iminhō kaisei no kiun" [Trend to the Modification of the Anti-Japanese Immigration Law], *Gaikō Jihō*, 15 August 1931, 179–80.

194. *Rafu Shimpō*, 2 August 1931.

195. *NGBSK*, series 1, pt. 2, 4:183–84.

196. *Sacramento Bee*, 6 August 1931.

197. *Labor Clarion*, 14 August 1931.

198. CJIC, *Quota for Japan: Conflicting Views of Hawaii and California* (pamphlet).

199. Alexander to Castle, 17 August 1931, 150.946/260, SD.

200. *NGBSK*, series 1, pt. 2, 4:184–86.

201. Stimson, *Far Eastern Crisis*, 3. At this point, the State Department had already evolved a plan to deal with Asian immigration questions. However, it was of the opinion that the initiative should not come from the State Department itself. Although the process of the development of the plan and the extent to which Stimson was actively involved is unclear, it is certain that Stimson himself paid a great deal of attention to the matter. Although it is uncertain whether or not he really thought it possible to modify the exclusion clause, he considered it desirable to show to the Japanese a positive attitude at the State Department toward the pro-quota cause, and clearly tried to do this in 1933 (see Chapter 6).

Chapter 6

1. Castle Journals, 29 September 1931.

2. Castle Journals, 10 October 1931; Japan, Gaimushō, *Nihon gaikō bunsho: Manshū jihen* [Documents on Japanese Foreign Policy: The Manchurian Incident], series 1, 3:19.

3. Castle Journals, 1 October 1931.

4. Doenecke, *Diplomacy of Frustration*, 16.

5. Castle Journals, 6 October 1931.

6. Ibid., 9 and 20 November 1931.

7. Cohen, *Chinese Connection*, 180.

8. Debuchi to Shidehara, 3 October 1931, KHZB; *New York Evening Post*, 6 October 1931.

9. Uchiyama to Shidehara, 30 September 1931, BHZIS.

10. *Seattle Times*, 28 September 1931.

11. *New York Times*, 29 September 1931.

12. *FCN*, 1929, 1:12; 1932, 11; 1932, s4.

13. Wakasugi to Shidehara, 24 September 1931 (rec'd), BHZIS; Satō to Shidehara, 6 October 1931, KHZB.

14. American Federation of Labor, *Report of the Executive Council*, 1931, 89; Alexander to Castle, 23 September 1931, 150.946/261, SD.

15. Wakasugi to Shidehara, 8 October 1931, BHZIS; Alexander to Castle, 23 September 1931, 150.946/261, SD.

16. *San Francisco Chronicle*, 12 October 1931; *NGBTIM*, 1146–47.

17. *Los Angeles Times*, 12 October 1931; *NGBTIM*, 1147–48.

18. *Seattle Times*, 22 October 1931.

19. *New York Times*, 15 October 1931.

20. Uchiyama to Shidehara, 24 October 1931, BHZIS, 2393; *NGBTIM*, 1148–59.

21. *Philadelphia Record*, 25 October 1931.

22. *New York Times*, 14 November 1931; Tupper and McReynolds, *Japan*, 227.

23. *Rafu Shimpō*, 2 October 1931.

24. Satō to Shidehara, 2 November 1931, BHZIS.

25. For example, Sutphen to Harvey L. Laughlin Company, BHZIS.

26. V. S. McClatchy, "Brief: In the Matter of Immigration Quota for Japan," December 1931, carton 1, Scharrenberg Papers; Satō to Shidehara, 9 November 1931, BHZIS.

27. Shidehara to Satō, 20 November 1931, BHZIS.

28. Tupper and McReynolds, *Japan*, 227; Hume to Barrows, 8 April 1932, box 19, David P. Barrows Papers (BANC MSS C-B 1005), Bancroft Library, University of California, Berkeley (hereafter cited as Barrows Papers).

29. Wakasugi to Yoshizawa, 28 March 1932, BHZIS.

30. *New York Times*, 18 November 1931.

31. Ibid., 27 October 1931.

32. McClatchy to Hornbeck, 18 December 1931, 711.945/319, SD; Hornbeck answered in the negative on 8 January 1932.

33. *NGBTIM*, 1143.

34. *NGBSK*, series 1, pt. 2, 4:187–88; *NGBTIM*, 1143–44.

35. *Washington Evening Star*, 16 October 1931; *NGBTIM*, 1144.

36. Wakasugi to Inukai, 31 December 1931, BHZIS; *NGBTIM*, 1145.

37. Rowell to Wakasugi, 1 January 1932, box 7, Rowell Papers.

38. Wakasugi to Shidehara, 10 October 1931, BHZIS; *Hokubei Jiji*, 7 November 1931; Wakasugi to Shidehara, 24 November 1931, BHZIS; *Transactions of the Commonwealth Club* 26, no. 10 (29 March 1932): 555–57.

39. Debuchi to Yoshizawa, 13 April 1932, KHZB; Debuchi to Yoshizawa, 10 May 1932, KHZB.

40. Debuchi to Uchida, 16 July 1932, BHZIS.

41. Debuchi to Uchida, 10 July 1932, BHZIS.

42. Debuchi to Uchida, 16 July 1932, BHZIS.

43. Cutler to Richey, 15 July 1932, BHZIS; Cutler to the President, 15 July 1932, BHZIS.

44. Wakasugi to Uchida, 29 July 1932, BHZIS.

45. *Rafu Shimpō*, 18 January 1932.

46. *Rafu Shimpō*, 20 January 1932. In the first session of the 72nd Congress, the bill concerning husbands of U.S. citizens passed; the bill concerning parents of U.S. citizens and the Moore Bill were carried over to the next session (KHZB).

47. *Tairiku Nippō*, 30 January 1932.

48. *Nichi Bei*, 22 September 1931.

49. Ibid., 25 September 1931.

50. Takahashi, *Nisei/Sansei*, 48–72; Hayashi, *"For the Sake of Our Japanese Brethren,"* 127–30.

51. Doenecke, *When the Wicked Rise*, 53.

52. *New York Times*, 30 January 1932.

53. Ibid., 31 January 1932.

54. *San Francisco Examiner*, 30 January 1932.

55. Ibid., 31 January 1932.

56. Wakasugi to Yoshizawa, 1 March 1932, KHZB.

57. Herzberg, *A Broken Bond*, 46.

58. Castle Journals, 4 February 1932.

59. National Foreign Trade Convention, *Official Report of the Nineteenth National Foreign Trade Convention and Ninth Pacific Foreign Trade Convention*, 1932, 23.

60. Alexander, *The United States's View of Trade Relations with Japan* (pamphlet).

61. *Bulletin of the American Asiatic Association*, December 1932, 2.

62. Doenecke, *When the Wicked Rise*, 57.

63. Hume, *The Square Deal in the Pacific* (pamphlet).

64. *Rafu Shimpō*, 26 March 1932; *Nichi Bei*, 28 March 1932.

65. Satō to Yoshizawa, 20 April 1932, BHZIS.

66. Hume to Barrows, 8 April 1932, box 19, Barrows Papers.

67. Hume to Hodgdon, 9 July 1932, 150.946/275, SD.

68. Wakasugi to Uchida, 31 October 1932, BHZIS; McClatchy, "Brief"; *NGBTIM*, 1159.

69. *Grizzly Bear*, July 1932.

70. Alexander to Holden, 8 August 1932, KHZB.

71. Holden to Alexander, 15 August 1932, KHZB.

72. Alexander to Holden, 18 August 1932, KHZB.

73. Rotary International, *Proceedings*, 1932, 432–36.

74. *Transactions of the Commonwealth Club* 27, no. 9 (7 February 1933): 421–23; Wakasugi to Yoshizawa, 22 March 1932, BHZIS.

75. Wakasugi to Yoshizawa, 6 May 1932, KHZB.

76. M. A. Goldstone, "Race Mixture and Selective Immigration in Their Relation to A Quota for Japan," paper read before the Commonwealth Club Section on Immigration, in carton 2, Scharrenberg Papers.

77. *The Commonwealth* 8, no. 46 (15 November 1932): 209.

78. *The Commonwealth* 8, no. 51 (20 December 1932): 285–95.

79. Ibid., 296–308.

80. Ibid., 309–20.

81. Ibid., 321–36.

82. CJIC, Release #307, 6 January 1933, CJIC Collection, 1924–1936 (BANC MSS 88/202c), Bancroft Library, University of California, Berkeley (hereafter cited as CJIC Collection).

83. Ajia Renmei Kyōkai to Saitō, 1 July 1932, KHZB.

84. Ujirō Ōyama, "Hainichi iminhō dai kyūshūnen" [The Ninth Anniversary of the Anti-Japanese Immigration Law], *Gaikō Jihō*, 1 July 1932, 1–13.

85. Grew to Stimson, 14 July 1932, 150.946/276, SD.

86. Memo by L. E. Salisbury, 12 August 1932, 150.946/276, SD.

87. *FRUS*, 1932, 4:706–15.

88. R. W. Flournoy, Jr., to Hackworth, 3 August 1924, 150.946/276, SD.

89. Hodgdon, 8 August 1932, 150.946/276, SD.

90. Memorandum by the Division of Far Eastern Affairs, 27 August 1932, 150.946/276, SD.

91. *Transactions of the Commonwealth Club* 29, no. 12 (25 June 1935): 350–51.

92. CJIC, Release #312, 13 February 1933, and Release #314, 21 March 1933, both in Hiram Johnson Papers.

93. McClatchy to Hornbeck, 29 March 1933, 150.946/286 1/2, SD.

94. Stinchfield to Stimson, 28 February 1933, 811.111 Quota 94/124, SD.

95. *FRUS*, 1932, 4:459–62.

96. "Manchurian Situation," 31 January 1933, 711.94/769, SD.

97. *FRUS*, 1933, 3:758–65.

98. Memorandum for Hornbeck, 1 February 1933, 711.98/770, SD.

99. Grew to Secretary of State, 9 March 1933, 150.946/36, SD.

100. *FRUS*, 1933, 3:700–702.

101. Conversation between Grady and Hornbeck, 2 May 1933, 150.946/290, SD.

102. Mailliard to Hornbeck, 2 June 1933, BHZIS; Hornbeck to Mailliard, 12 July 1933, BHZIS.

103. Wakasugi to Uchida, 21 July 1933, BHZIS.

104. Memorandum of Conversation with Walter Lippmann, 13 April 1933, 150.946/288, SD.

105. Miller to the President, 15 May 1933, 150.946/293, SD.

106. George H. Blakeslee, "Observations of the Japanese Government on the Report of the Commission of Inquiry," 20 November 1932, Blakeslee Papers. Blakeslee approved of the China policy of Japan's liberal government and also continued to believe that the U.S. immigration law should be modified. But he drew a sharp distinction between the policies of Japan's liberal government and the actions of Japan's military in China, and especially their application of so-called Japanese Monroe Doctrine (Blakeslee, "The Japanese Monroe Doctrine," *Foreign Affairs* 11 (July 1933): 671–81.

Chapter 7

1. *Albuquerque Tribune*, 23 June 1933; the Scripps-Howard newspapers which published this interview included the *Baltimore Post, Cincinnati Post, Denver Rocky Mountain News, Houston Press, San Diego Sun*, and *Washington Daily News*. The sudden beginning of Howard's pro-quota activities was partly due to the vigorous persuasion of Alexander, with whom he spent time in Hawaii on his return trip.

2. *San Francisco Daily News*, 8 July 1933; *New York Herald-Tribune*, 8 July 1933; Horiuchi to Uchida, 8 July 1933, BHZIS.

3. *San Francisco Daily News*, 11 July 1933.

4. Ibid., 13 July 1933; Wakasugi to Uchida, 20 July 1933, BHZIS.

5. *San Francisco Daily News*, 7 July 1933; *Washington Daily News*, 7 July 1933; *(New York) World Telegram*, 7 July 1933; Wakasugi to Uchida, 8 July 1933, BHZIS; Horiuchi to Uchida, 8 July 1933, BHZIS; Debuchi to Uchida, 10 July 1933, BHZIS.

6. *San Francisco Daily News*, 8 July 1933.

7. *Grizzly Bear*, August 1933.

8. *Nichi Bei Jiji*, 15 July 1933.

9. *San Francisco Daily News*, 17 July 1933.

10. Ibid., 17 July 1933.

11. Howard to Johnson, 17 July 1933, box 84, Roy W. Howard Papers, Library of Congress, Washington, D.C. (hereafter cited as Howard Papers).

12. Howard to Alexander, 17 July 1933, box 84, Howard Papers.

13. Burkhardt to Howard, 22 July and 2 August 1933; Howard to Alexander, 7 August 1933; both in box 84, Howard Papers.

14. San Francisco Chamber of Commerce, "Release," 18 July 1933, box 84, Howard Papers.

15. *San Francisco Chronicle*, 19 July 1933; Hume to Ben Foster, Jr., 22 July 1933, box 84, Howard Papers.

16. Wakasugi to Uchida, 15 August 1933, BHZIS.

17. *Nichi Bei*, 8 August 1933.

18. Ibid., 20 July 1933.

19. Burkhardt to Howard, 22 July 1933, Inter-Company Correspondence, box 84, Howard Papers.

20. CJIC, Release #319, 28 July 1933, Press Releases and Documents of the CJIC (BANC fJV6920.A2.C3), Bancroft Library, University of California, Berkeley (hereafter cited as Press Releases and Documents of the CJIC).

21. *San Francisco Chronicle*, 17 August 1933; Wakasugi to Uchida, 17 August 1933, BHZIS.

22. *Nichi Bei*, 9 July 1933.

23. Ibid., 12 July 1933.

24. Ujirō Ōyama, "Hainichi iminhō dai jisshūnen" [The Tenth Anniversary of the Anti-Japanese Immigration Law], *Gaikō Jihō*, 1 July 1933, 1–6; "Hawādo shi no nichiman ron" [Howard's Argument about Japan and Manchuria], *Gaikō Jihō*, 1 August 1933, 191–93; *Tokyo Asahi Shimbun*, 8 and 16 July 1933.

25. *FRUS*, 1933, 3:706–9; *Tokyo Asahi Shimbun*, 20 July 1933.

26. *Nichi Bei*, 24 August 1933.

27. Conversation between Debuchi and Scharrenberg, 15 October 1933, BHZIS. Since there would have been no advantage in lying on this point and from circumstantial evidence, what Scharrenberg told Debuchi regarding the point is likely to be true.

28. Wakasugi to Uchida, 12 August 1933, BHZIS.

29. CJIC, Release #323, 11 August 1933, CJIC Collection.

30. Wakasugi to Uchida, 25 August 1933, BHZIS; *Nichi Bei*, 19 August 1933.

31. Satow to Uchida, 18 August 1933, BHZIS.

32. *San Francisco Examiner*, 18 August 1933; Wakasugi to Uchida, 18 August 1933, BHZIS.

33. *San Francisco Examiner*, 19 August 1933; Wakasugi to Uchida, 19 August 1933, BHZIS.

34. *Nichi Bei*, 23 August 1933.

35. *Grizzly Bear*, August 1933.

36. *San Francisco Daily News*, 19 August 1933; Wakasugi to Uchida, 22 August 1933, BHZIS.

37. Alexander to Howard, 17 August 1933, box 84, Howard Papers.

38. Nakamura to Uchida, 16 August 1933, BHZIS; Uchiyama to Uchida, 21 August 1933, BHZIS.

39. Uchiyama to Uchida, 24 August 1933, BHZIS.

40. Uchiyama to Uchida, 25 August 1933, BHZIS; *Seattle Post-Intelligencer*, 25 August 1933.

41. 28 July 1933, BHZIS. Although this statement to the United Press, which

was filed in the Japanese diplomatic documents, was dated July 28, the document of the Department of State said that Shigemitsu made this kind of statement on August 23 (see Memo to Hodgdon, 30 August 1933, 811.111 Quota 94/130, SD). Considering the fact that most newspaper coverage occurred around the end of August, it is possible that the date on the Japanese diplomatic document was a mistake. However, it is also conceivable that Shigemitsu made this kind of statement more than once.

42. *New York Herald-Tribune*, 24 August 1933.

43. *Providence (Rhode Island) Journal*, 26 August 1933.

44. *Seattle Daily Times*, 25 August 1933; conversation between Taketomi and Hornbeck, 25 August 1933, 150.946/300, SD.

45. *Jiji Shimpō*, 26 August 1933.

46. *Nichi Bei*, 27 August 1933.

47. Conversation between Taketomi and Hornbeck, 25 August 1933, 150.946/300, SD; see also 711.94/845, SD.

48. Hornbeck(?) to Simpson, 29 September 1933, 150.946/296, SD.

49. Walker to Hull, 13 September 1933, and Hornbeck to Walker, 3 October 1933, 150.946/302, SD.

50. Uchida Ryōhei bunsho kenkyūkai, *Uchida*, 10:247–51.

51. *Quota*, August 1933; Tupper and McReynolds, *Japan*, 230–239.

52. Hume to Fleisher, 1 September 1933, BHZIS.

53. Wakasugi to Uchida, 28 August 1933, BHZIS.

54. *Fresno Bee*, 25 August 1933.

55. *San Francisco Examiner*, 28 August 1933.

56. *Pacific Bulletin*, September 1933, box 241, Stanley K. Hornbeck Papers, Hoover Institute on War, Revolution, and Peace Archives, Stanford, Calif.

57. *San Francisco Call-Bulletin*, 20 September 1933; Wakasugi to Hirota, 21 September 1933, BHZIS.

58. Uchiyama to Uchida, 31 August 1933, BHZIS.

59. Uchiyama to Uchida, 1 September 1933, BHZIS.

60. *Seattle Post-Intelligencer*, 3, 4, and 7 September 1933.

61. Ibid., 14 September 1933.

62. Howard to Burkhardt, 7 August 1933, box 84, Howard Papers.

63. Howard to Alexander, 28 August 1933, box 84, Howard Papers.

64. Alexander to Howard, 17 August 1933, box 84, Howard Papers.

65. Alexander to Howard, 11 September 1933, and Howard to Alexander, 6 September 1933, box 84, Howard Papers.

66. *Grizzly Bear*, October 1933.

67. *Literary Digest,* 2 and 30 September 1933; *Seattle Post-Intelligencer,* 12 September 1933; Wakasugi to Hirota, 14 September 1933, BHZIS; Uchiyama to Hirota, 14 September 1933, BHZIS.

68. *Seattle Daily Times,* 5 September 1933; Uchiyama to Uchida, 5 September 1933, BHZIS.

69. Nakamura to Uchida, 2 September 1933, BHZIS.

70. *Helena (Montana) Daily Independent,* 29 August 1933; Uchiyama to Uchida, 6 September 1933, BHZIS.

71. Satow to Uchida, 8 September 1933, BHZIS.

72. Nakamura to Uchida, 26 August 1933, BHZIS.

73. Uchiyama to Uchida, 24 August 1933, BHZIS.

74. Satow to Uchida, 8 September 1933, BHZIS.

75. Uchiyama to Uchida, 8 September 1933, BHZIS.

76. Uchiyama to Uchida, 12 September 1933, BHZIS.

77. Uchiyama to Uchida, 13 September 1933, BHZIS.

78. Satow to Hirota, 26 October 1933, BHZIS.

79. *San Francisco Daily News,* 15 September 1933.

80. *Quota,* September 1933.

81. Wakasugi to Hirota, 22 September 1933, BHZIS.

82. *California Legionnaire,* October 1933.

83. *Grizzly Bear,* November 1933.

84. Mutō to Hirota, 6 November 1933, BHZIS; Okada to Hirota, 9 November 1933, BHZIS; American Legion, *Proceedings of the Fifteenth National Convention,* 1934, 51; Alexander to Howard, 3 October 1933, box 84, Howard Papers.

85. *Honolulu Star-Bulletin,* 6 October 1933.

86. *Nichi Bei,* 6 October 1933.

87. Alexander to Howard, 2 October 1933, box 84, Howard Papers.

88. American Federation of Labor, *Report of the Executive Council,* 1933, 77–78.

89. *Nichi Bei,* 14 October 1933.

90. Burkhardt to Howard, 29 August 1933, box 84, Howard Papers.

91. Conversation between Scharrenberg and Debuchi, 15 October 1933, BHZIS.

92. Johnson to Howard, 19 October 1933, box 84, Howard Papers.

93. Howard to Alexander, 21 October 1933, box 84, Howard Papers.

94. Howard to Johnson, 21 October 1933, box 84, Howard Papers.

95. Alexander to Howard, 26 October 1933, box 84, Howard Papers.

96. Wakasugi to Hirota, 20 October 1933, BHZIS.

97. Conversation between Fitzpatrick and Hornbeck, 2 November 1933, and Fitzpatrick to Hume, 2 November 1933, 150.946/308, SD.

98. Howard to Alexander, 9 November 1933, box 84, Howard Papers.

99. Uchiyama to Hirota, 16 November 1933, BHZIS.

100. Nakamura to Hirota, 24 November 1933, BHZIS; "Progress report of the CJIC," 12 December 1933, carton 2, Scharrenberg Papers.

101. *Nichi Bei*, 23 October 1933.

102. CJIC, Release #349, 13 November 1933, carton 1, Scharrenberg Papers.

103. CJIC, Release #356, 13 November 1933, carton 2, Scharrenberg Papers.

104. CJIC, Release #349, 13 November 1933, carton 1; Release #366, 27 November 1933, carton 1; and Release #367, 2 December 1933, carton 2; all in Scharrenberg Papers.

105. *Grizzly Bear*, December 1933.

106. Tomii to Hirota, 11 December 1933, BHZIS; "Progress Report of the CJIC," 12 December 1933, carton 2, Scharrenberg Papers.

107. "Progress Report of the CJIC," 12 December 1933, carton 2, Scharrenberg Papers.

108. *Grizzly Bear*, January 1934.

109. *Chicago Daily Tribune*, 27 October 1933.

110. *(Los Angeles) Saturday Night*, 28 October 1933.

111. *(Portland) Oregonian*, 16 November 1933.

112. *Honolulu Advertiser*, 17 November 1933.

113. FCN, 1933, 546–47.

114. FCN, 1930, 63, 335; FCN, 1931, 63, 326; FCN, 1932, 62, 308; FCN, 1934, 52–53, 294–95.

115. FCN, 1934, 446.

116. *Atlanta Constitution*, 21 November 1933.

117. Tomii to Hirota, 11 December 1933, BHZIS.

Chapter 8

1. "Progress Report of the CJIC," 12 December 1933, carton 2, Scharrenberg Papers.

2. Ibid.

3. Uchiyama to Hirota, 22 December 1933, and 27 February 1934, BHZIS.

4. McClatchy to Hornbeck, 19 January 1934, 150.946/315 1/2, SD; Kawakami, *Manchukuo*, 40–41.

5. Nakamura to Hirota, 18 January 1934, BHZIS.

6. Tomii to Hirota, 14 February 1934, BHZIS; Uchiyama to Hirota, 27 February 1934, BHZIS.

7. Uchiyama to Hirota, 27 February 1934, BHZIS.

8. *Quota*, January 1934.

9. Hume to Fleisher, 21 December 1933, KHZB.

10. *New York Times,* 7 January 1934.

11. Mount Holyoke Peace Club to the President, 11 January 1934, 150.946/313, SD.

12. Hanna to the President, 5 February 1934, 150.946/318, SD.

13. Mary Bishop to the President, 13 February 1934, 150.946/319, SD.

14. Members of the California Delegations in Congress to Roosevelt, 22 January 1934, quoted in Nixon, *Roosevelt,* 1:597–98.

15. Nixon, *Roosevelt,* 1:620–21, 639; Hull to Roosevelt, 31 January 1934, 150.946/315A, SD.

16. Saitō to Hirota, 15 February 1934, KHZB; Saitō to Hirota, 20 February 1934, BHZIS.

17. LeHand to Dunn, 24 February 1934. 150.946/328, SD.

18. Memo by Hornbeck, 2 March 1934, 150.946/328, SD.

19. Nixon, *Roosevelt,* 1:639; CJIC, "For Attention of Members," 2 March 1934, carton 2, Scharrenberg Papers.

20. Nixon, *Roosevelt,* 1:639; McIntyre to Hull, 19 February 1934, and Phillips to McIntyre, 24 February 1934, 150.946/321, SD.

21. Tomii to Hirota, 14 February 1934, BHZIS.

22. Nakamura to Hirota, 9 March 1934, BHZIS.

23. CJIC, Release #373, 1 February 1934, Scharrenberg Papers.

24. Thompson to the President, 31 January 1934, 150.946/320, SD.

25. Mudge to the President, 16 February 1934, 150.946/323, SD.

26. Members and Friends of the Central M.E. Church of Stockton to the President, 3 March 1934, 150.946/325, SD.

27. Busch to Hull, 11 April 1934, 150.946/343, SD.

28. Mutō to Hirota, 10 March 1934, BHZIS; *China Press Weekly,* 16 June 1934.

29. Hutchason (Women's Club of San Bernardino) to Hull, 21 February 1934, 150.946/329; Resident of Los Angeles to Hull, 22 March 1934, 150.946/335, SD.

30. Hosokawa, *JACL in Quest of Justice,* 83.

31. McClatchy to Hornbeck, 26 February 1934, 150.946/321 1/2, SD.

32. *FRUS,* 1934, 3:636–37.

33. *Washington Evening Star,* 13 February 1934.

34. FCN, 1930, 63; 1931, 63; 1932, 62; 1933, 52; 1934, 2:51.

35. *New York Times,* 11 April 1934; *New York Herald-Tribune,* 11 April 1934; *New Orleans Tribune,* 12 April 1934; *Houston Post,* 12 April 1934; *New Orleans Item,* 12 April 1934.

36. *New Orleans States,* 29 May 1934.

37. *Grizzly Bear,* May 1934.

38. *San Francisco Daily News,* 23 March 1934.

39. *San Francisco Chronicle*, 29 March 1934; McClatchy to Hornbeck, 31 March 1934, and Hornbeck to McClatchy, 10 April 1934, 150.946/336, SD.

40. Hume to Hull, 29 April 1934, and Simmons to Hume, 10 May 1934, 150.946/347, SD.

41. CJIC, Release #390, 27 March 1934, Scharrenberg Papers.

42. CJIC, Release #387, 6 March 1934, Scharrenberg Papers.

43. CJIC, Release #391, 3 April 1934, Scharrenberg Papers.

44. CJIC, Release #392, 5 April 1934, Scharrenberg Papers.

45. Nakamura to Hirota, 8 May 1934, BHZIS.

46. Uchiyama to Hirota, 8 May 1934, BHZIS.

47. Grew to Hull, 22 March 1934, 711.94/919, SD; *New York Times*, 22 March 1934; *Hochi*, 24 March 1934, quoted in Grew to Hull, 711.94/925, SD; *Time Magazine*, 2 April 1934.

48. *Time Magazine*, 7 May 1934.

49. *Sacramento Bee*, 11 May 1934; *San Francisco Examiner*, 12 May 1934.

50. *Grizzly Bear*, June 1934.

51. Tomii to Hirota, 19 June 1934, BHZIS; CJIC, Release #398 and #400, 22 May 1934, Press Releases and Documents of the CJIC; *Labor Clarion*, 25 May 1934.

52. *Grizzly Bear*, June 1934.

53. CJIC, Release #394, 23 April 1934, CJIC Collection; McClatchy made a similar criticism in Release #401, dated 28 May, in ibid.

54. CJIC, Release #404, 1 June 1934, Press Releases and Documents of the CJIC.

55. Nixon, *Roosevelt*, 2:54–63.

56. Nakauchi to Hirota, 8 September 1934, BHZIS.

57. Uchiyama to Hirota, 21 September 1934, BHZIS.

58. Holden to Hume, 5 September 1934, BHZIS.

59. Jikichirō Kawahara, "Beikoku ni okeru hainichi undō no kaiko 1" [Review of the History of the Anti-Japanese Movement in the United States, part 1], *Gaikō Jihō*, 1 March 1934, 120–21.

60. Jikichirō Kawahara, "Beikoku ni okeru hainichi undō no kaiko 2" [Review of the History of the Anti-Japanese Movement in the United States, part 2], *Gaikō Jihō*, 1 April 1934, 236–47.

61. Kiichi Kanzaki, "Nichibei kankei no kōten" [Improvement of U.S.-Japanese Relations], *Gaikō Jihō*, 1 April 1934, 201–14.

62. Ujirō Ōyama, "Beikoku hainichi iminhō dai jūichi nen" [The Eleventh Anniversary of the Anti-Japanese Immigration Law of the United States], *Gaikō Jihō*, 15 July 1934, 71–84.

63. Kido nikki kenkyūkai, *Kido Kōichi kankei monjo*, 155.

64. Grew to Hull, 31 May 1935, 711.94/1035, SD.

65. Amau, *Amau Eiji nikki/shiryōshū*, 2:668–71.

66. Ibid., 2:769–70.

67. Nixon, *Roosevelt*, 2:250–54.

68. Ibid., 2:263.

69. NCCWP, *A Message to the Churches and World Peace* (pamphlet), 11.

70. Sawada to Hirota, 19 November 1934, KHZB.

71. Castle Journals, 27 November 1934. Although it is typed as 26 December in the diary stored at the Houghton Library, Harvard University, the date must be 27 November for this part because it is located between 26 November and 28 November and because of the content of the writing.

72. Conversation between Reifsnider and Hornbeck, 27 November 1934, 150.946/371, SD.

73. Gulick to Roosevelt, 8 January 1935, box 20, Gulick Family Papers.

74. Gulick, *Toward Understanding Japan*, 235–37, 245.

75. Uchiyama to Hirota, 12 December 1934, BHZIS; Martin, *Who Shall Enter Our Gates?* (pamphlet), 13.

76. Tamura to Hirota, 8 January 1935, KHZB.

77. *New York Times*, 6 January 1935.

78. Ibid., 10 February 1935.

79. *Houston Post*, 16 February 1935; Chief of the American Bureau to Army and Navy(?), 2 April 1935, BHZIS; North to Hull, 20 March 1935, 150.946/385, SD; "Oriental Exclusion," 150.946/386, SD.

80. President of the Women's Missionary Council to Hull, 15 March 1935, 150.946/384, SD; "Resolution on Exclusion Act," 11 April 1935, 150.946/392, SD; Little Rock Conference of the Women's Missionary Society to Hull, 6 April 1935, 150.946/393, SD; Slaton to Hull, 25 April 1935, 150.946/404, SD.

81. George Blakeslee, "America and Japan in the Pacific," Blakeslee Papers.

82. Shakai mondai kenkyūkai, *Teikoku gikai shi*, series 1, 23:195–98.

83. "Nichi Bei kankei chōsei no kyūmu" [A Pressing Need for Adjustment of U.S.-Japanese Relations], *Gaikō Jihō*, 15 March 1935, 1–4.

84. Ujirō Ōyama, "Hainichi iminhō dai jūni nen" [The Twelfth Anniversary of the Japanese Exclusion Law], *Gaikō Jihō*, 1 July 1935, 45–56.

85. Shakai mondai kenkyūkai, *Teikoku gikai shi*, series 1, 23:199–203.

86. Prayers of Ajia Renmei Kyōkai, 1 July 1935, KHZB.

87. CJIC, Release #407, 5 February 1935, Press Releases and Documents of the CJIC.

88. CJIC, Release #408, 6 February 1935, CJIC Collection.

89. CJIC, Release #414, 11 December 1934, Press Releases and Documents of the CJIC.

90. Shiozaki to Arita, 30 November 1936, KHZB; CJIC, Release #460, 15 August 1936, Press Releases and Documents of the CJIC; *San Francisco Chronicle*, 30 October 1936.

91. *Tokyo Asahi Shimbun*, 7 January 1937; *Yomiuri*, 7 January 1937.

92. Arita to Saitō, 9 January 1937, BHZIS.

93. Saitō to Arita, 13 January 1937, BHZIS; Saitō to Arita, 16 January 1937, KHZB.

94. Shiozaki to Arita, 13 January 1937, BHZIS.

Chapter 9

1. Japan, Teikoku Gikai Shūgiin [The House of Representatives of the Imperial Diet], *Teikoku gikai shūgiin yosan iinkaigiroku* [Proceedings of the Budget Committee], 70th sess., 23 March 1937.

2. *Tokyo Asahi Shimbun*, 24 March 1937.

3. *Los Angeles Times*, 24 March 1937.

4. *Honolulu Advertiser*, 10 March 1937.

5. *Oregonian*, 29 April 1937.

6. Ibid., 30 April 1937; Tsurumi to Satō, 30 April 1937, BHZIS.

7. *New York Herald-Tribune*, 19 April 1937.

8. *Grizzly Bear*, June 1938.

9. *Sacramento Bee*, 1 June 1937.

10. *San Francisco Examiner*, 27 May 1937.

11. Ibid., 18 June 1937.

12. *Labor Clarion*, 30 April and 18 June 1937.

13. CJIC, Release #500, 18 June 1937, carton 1, Scharrenberg Papers.

14. CJIC to Roosevelt, 30 August 1937, Hiram Johnson Papers.

15. Shiozaki to Satō, 10 May 1937, KHZB; *Transactions of the Commonwealth Club* 32, no. 4 (4 May 1938): 196–99, 216–21.

16. "General Questions concerning Commerce and Special Questions of Japan with Great Britain, the United States, and Germany," 10 April 1937, KHZB.

17. Wu, *Japan: The World's Enemy* (pamphlet).

18. China Information Committee, *Destruction of Schools by Japanese Invaders* (pamphlet).

19. Federation of Chinese Cultural Associations, *The Indiscriminate Aerial Bombing of Non-Combatants in China by Japanese* (pamphlet).

20. Willoughby, *The Significance to the World of the Conflict in the Far East* (pamphlet).

21. Japanese Chamber of Commerce of Los Angeles, *Japan's Position in the Shanghai and North China Hostilities* (pamphlet).

22. Foreign Affairs Association of Japan, *What Happened at Tungchow?* (pamphlet).

23. Japanese Chamber of Commerce of New York, *The Sino-Japanese Crisis, 1937* (pamphlet).

24. Lamont to Wakasugi, 17 September 1937, box 187, Lamont Collection.

25. Lamont to Kadono, 24 September 1924, box 187, Lamont Collection.

26. Hayashi, *"For the Sake of Our Japanese Brethren,"* 137.

27. Ibid., 133–38; Takahashi, *Nisei/Sansei*, 58–60; Ichioka, "Dai Nisei Mondai," 764–73.

28. "A Memorial Service for Wallace McKinney Alexander, 1869–1939," no. 99, Takagi Collection.

29. "Address at the Memorial Service for Mr. Wallace Alexander, Tokyo Union Church, 13 December 1939," Grew Diary.

30. Salisbury to Marcy, 9 June 1938, NCAJR Papers.

31. CJIC, Release #523, 18 October 1938, Hiram Johnson Papers.

32. *San Francisco Daily News*, 17 May 1938; Shiozaki to Hirota, 17 May 1938, KHZB; Fisk to Johnson, 25 October 1938, Hiram Johnson Papers.

33. Beard and Beard, *America in Midpassage*, 1:204, 439–40; *Labor Clarion*, 30 June 1939.

34. American Federation of Labor, *Report of Proceedings of the Fifty-Ninth Annual Convention*, 1939, 134–35.

35. *Grizzly Bear*, May 1938.

36. Axling, *Far Eastern Crisis*.

37. Cohen, *America's Response to China*, 146–49; American Committee for Non-Participation in Japanese Aggression, *America's Share in Japan's War Guilt* (pamphlet). For more information about this organization, see Friedman, *The Road from Isolation*.

38. *New York Times*, 14 February 1938.

39. Shiozaki to Ugaki, 22 July 1938, KHZB.

40. Gauss to Hull, 3 May 1939, 711.94/1267, SD.

41. "Nichibei no kinjō" [The Recent Conditions of Japan-U.S. Relations], *Gaikō Jihō*, 15 April 1939, 1–4; Ujirō Ōyama, "Hainichi iminhō dai jūrokushūnen wo tomurau" [Paying Condolences to the Sixteenth Anniversary of the Japanese Exclusion Immigration Law], *Gaikō Jihō*, 1 July 1939, 80–89.

42. Shigeo Suehiro, "Nihonjin fubyōdō taigū to gen seikyoku" [The

Discriminatory Treatment of the Japanese and the Present Situation], *Gaikō Jihō*, 15 December 1940, 1–15.

43. *Foreign Relations of the United States: Japan: 1931–1941*, 2:171 (hereafter cited as *FRUS: Japan*).

44. Conversation between Ōhashi and Dooman, 26 February 1941, 711.94/1996, SD.

45. "The Outline of the Anti-Japanese Movement of the United States of America," KHZB.

46. Ibid.

47. Ibid.

48. *FRUS: Japan*, 2:394–95.

49. Ibid., 409.

50. Japan, Gaimushō [Ministry of Foreign Affairs], *Nihon gaikō bunsho: Nichibei kōshō, 1941 nen, jō ge* [Documents on Japanese Foreign Policy: Japan-U.S. Talks in 1941], 1:28 (hereafter cited as *NGBNK*).

51. *FRUS: Japan*, 2:398–402; Utley, *Going to War with Japan*, 142; for John Doe Associates, see Butow, *John Doe Associates*.

52. *NGBNK*, 1:37.

53. *FRUS: Japan*, 2:406–10.

54. Prepared on 16 April 1941 by Mr. Hamilton and Mr. Ballantine as a tentative basis for a possible counterdraft to the Japanese draft of 9 April 1941, 711.94/2066–6/9, SD.

55. *NGBNK*, 1:20; Butow, *John Doe Associates*, 164–65.

56. *NGBNK*, 1:28.

57. *NGBNK*, 1:60, 66; *FRUS: Japan*, 2:422.

58. *FRUS: Japan*, 2:446–51.

59. *FRUS: Japan*, 2:453.

60. *FRUS: Japan*, 2:486–92; *NGBNK*, 1:114–25.

61. *NGBNK*, 1:146–54.

62. *NGBNK*, 1:151–54.

63. *FRUS: Japan*, 2:764.

64. National Foreign Trade Convention. *Official Report*, 1941, viii.

65. Ford to Hull, 18 August 1941, and Chief of Visa Division to Ford, 4 September 1941, 150.946/488, SD.

66. George H. Blakeslee, "Is There a Peaceful Solution of American-Japanese Issues?" 11 November 1941, Blakeslee Papers.

67. Hart to Welles, 4 December 1941, and Welles to Hart, 19 December 1941, 150.946/491, SD.

Conclusion

1. Ugaki, *Nikki*, 1:674, 769.

2. Kitaoka, *Kiyosawa Kiyoshi*, 50.

3. Taylor, *Advocate of Understanding.*

4. For example, Taylor, *Advocate of Understanding*; Burkman, "Nitobe Inazo"; and Kitaoka, "Prophet Without Honor."

Epilogue

1. See Dower, *War Without Mercy.*

2. Macnaughton to Hull, 8 June 1943, 150.946/495, SD.

3. Peter T. Conmy, *The History of California's Japanese Problem and the Part Played by the Native Sons of the Golden West in its Solution* (brochure), 1 July 1942, fF870.J3C6, Bancroft Library.

4. *Grizzly Bear*, March, 1942.

5. Dower, *War Without Mercy*, 167.

6. House Committee on Immigration and Naturalization, *Samples of Japanese-Controlled Radio Comments on America's Exclusion Act*, 78th Cong., 1st sess., 1943, Confidential Committee Print.

7. *Japan Times and Advertiser*, 20 February 1942.

8. Riggs, *Pressures on Congress*, 162.

9. Ibid., 48–49.

10. Ibid., 92–95.

11. Ibid., 96–102.

12. Yu, *To Save China*, 132.

13. Riggs, *Pressures on Congress*, 114–15.

14. Yu, *To Save China*, 133–35.

15. Riggs, *Pressures on Congress*, 57.

16. Charles N. Spinks, "Repeal Chinese Exclusion!" *Asia and the Americas*, February 1942, 92–93.

17. Richard J. Walsh, "Repeal Exclusion Laws Now," *Asia and the Americas*, June 1943, 322–23.

18. Riggs, *Pressures on Congress*, 57–63.

19. *Congressional Record*, 78th Cong., 1st sess., 1943, 89, pt. 8:9991.

20. House Committee on Immigration and Naturalization, *Repeal of the Chinese Exclusion Acts: Hearings on H.R. 1882 and H.R. 2309*, 78th Cong., 1st sess., 6 October 1943, 175–87.

21. House Committee, *Repeal of the Chinese Exclusion Acts*, 175–87.

22. *Grizzly Bear*, July 1943.

23. *Congressional Record*, 78th Cong., 1st sess., 1943, 89, pt. 8:10019, 10539, 10882.

24. *Nippon Times*, 5 and 7 December 1943.

25. Ibid., 17 December 1943.

26. Ibid., 25 December 1943.

27. Ibid., 23 December 1943, 8 January and 1 February 1944.

28. *Congressional Record*, 79th Cong., 2d sess., 1946, 92, pt. 6:6918, 7957.

29. Divine, *American Immigration Policy*, 153–54.

30. Hosokawa, *JACL in Quest of Justice*, 286.

31. *Rafu Shimpō*, 4, 8, and 22 February 1947.

32. *Imin kika kongōhō seiritsu kinengō* [Special Issue to Commemorate the Passage of the Omnibus Immigration Bill] (San Francisco: Nichibei Jiji-sha, 1952).

33. *Hawaii Times*, 8 March 1947.

34. The first goal was about $15,000 for each city.

35. House subcommittee on Immigration and Naturalization of the Judiciary Committee, *Providing for Equality under Naturalization and Immigration Laws: Hearings on H.R. 5004*, 80th Cong., 2d sess., 1948, 85; Takeshita, *Yamato Damashi*, 174–75.

36. Koshiro, *Trans-Pacific Racisms*, 127–34.

37. *Congressional Record*, 80th Cong., 2d sess., 94, pt. 1:331; House Subcommittee, *Providing for Equality under Naturalization and Immigration Laws*, 35, 56-57.

38. Takeshita, *Yamato Damashi*, 214–28; Masaoka, *Moses*, 220–22.

39. Senate subcommittee of the Committee on the Judiciary, *Naturalization of Asian and Pacific Peoples: Hearing on H.R. 199*, 81st Cong., 1st sess., 19 and 20 July 1949, 49–55; Takeshita, *Yamato Damashi*, 239–46.

40. Masaoka, *Moses*, 224; *Rafu Shimpō*, 28 April 1950.

41. *Congressional Record*, 82d Cong., 2d sess., 98, pt. 6:8082–85.

42. Ibid., pt. 6:8254.

43. Ibid., pt. 6:8217–18.

44. Ibid., pt. 6:8225–26, 8267–68.

45. *Osaka Mainichi Shimbun*, 27 June 1952.

46. *Osaka Asahi Shimbun*, 28 June 1952.

Bibliography

Principal Manuscript Collections and Archives

ARCHIVES DU MINISTÈRE DES AFFAIRES ÉTRANGÈRES. PARIS, FRANCE.

Asie-Océanie, Japon: Gouvernement et Politique intérieure
Asie-Océanie, Japon: Politique étrangère
Correspondance politique et commerciale: États-Unis

BŌEICHŌ (SELF-DEFENSE AGENCY).
BŌEIKENKYŪSHO (NATIONAL INSTITUTE FOR DEFENSE STUDIES).
SENSHIBU (DEPARTMENT OF WAR HISTORY). TOKYO, JAPAN.

Dai nikki [General Files]
Mitsu dai nikki [Confidential General Files]
Fujita Kikuichi nisshi [Diary of Kikuichi Fujita]

CLARK UNIVERSITY. WORCESTER, MASSACHUSETTS.
GODDARD LIBRARY.

George Hubbard Blakeslee Papers

COLUMBIA UNIVERSITY. NEW YORK, N.Y. BUTLER LIBRARY.

Carnegie Council on Ethics and International Affairs Papers (formerly the Church

Peace Union Papers, and then Council on Religion and International Affairs
Papers)

COLUMBIA UNIVERSITY. NEW YORK, N.Y.
COLUMBIA UNIVERSITY ORAL HISTORY COLLECTION.

Eugene H. Dooman Interview

DUKE UNIVERSITY. DURHAM, N.C.
WILLIAM R. PERKINS LIBRARY.

John Caldwell Calhoun Newton Papers

GAIMUSHO (MINISTRY OF FOREIGN AFFAIRS).
GAIKO SHIRŌKAN (DIPLOMATIC RECORD OFFICE).
TOKYO, JAPAN.

1924 nen iminhō ni taisuru ippan yoron: Shūsei undō [Public Opinion Relating to
the 1924 Immigration Law: The Modification Movement]

Beikoku hainichi iminhō ni taisuru honpō ni okeru undō jōkyō chōsa [Survey of
Movements in Japan against the United States Exclusion Immigration Law]

Beikoku ni okeru hainichi mondai ikken: 1924 nen iminhō seiritsu ni taisuru
naigaino hantai undō [Documents Relating to Anti-Japanese Movements in
the United States: Protests against the 1924 Immigration Law at Home and
Abroad] (abbreviated as BHNG in Notes)

Beikoku ni okeru hainichi mondai zakken: Beikoku iminhō ni taisuru haibei jōhō
[Miscellaneous Documents Relating to Anti-Japanese Problems in the United
States: Anti-American Information Relating to the United States Immigration
Law] (abbreviated as BIHJ in Notes)

Beikoku ni okeru hainichi mondai zakken: Iminhō shūsei kankei [Miscellaneous
Documents Relating to Anti-Japanese Problems in the United States: Docu-
ments Relating to the Amendment of the Immigration Law] (abbreviated as
BHZIS in Notes)

Iminhō seiritsu ni taisuru naigai hantai undō jyōkyō chōsa [Survey of Protests
against the Immigration Law at Home and Abroad]

Kakkoku ni okeru hainichi kankei zakken: Beikoku no bu [Miscellaneous
Documents Relating to Anti-Japanese Movements in Foreign Countries:
United States] (abbreviated as KHZB in Notes)

Zai naigai kyōkai kankei zakken: Zainai no bu [Miscellaneous Documents
Relating to Associations at Home and Abroad: Associations at Home]

HARVARD BUSINESS SCHOOL. BOSTON, MASS.
BAKER LIBRARY.

Thomas W. Lamont Collection

HARVARD UNIVERSITY. CAMBRIDGE, MASS.
HOUGHTON LIBRARY.

American Board of Commissioners for Foreign Missions Papers
William R. Castle Journals
Joseph C. Grew, Diary, Grew Papers
Sidney L. Gulick Family Papers

HERBERT HOOVER PRESIDENTIAL LIBRARY.
WEST BRANCH, IOWA.

Herbert Hoover Papers

HOOVER INSTITUTION ON WAR, REVOLUTION AND
PEACE ARCHIVES. STANFORD, CALIF.

Stanley K. Hornbeck Papers

KNOX COLLEGE LIBRARY. GALESBURG, ILL.
SPECIAL COLLECTIONS AND ARCHIVES.

Edgar A. Bancroft Papers

LIBRARY OF CONGRESS. WASHINGTON, D.C.

William Borah Papers
Roy W. Howard Papers
Nelson T. Johnson Papers
Roland S. Morris Papers

NATIONAL ARCHIVES. WASHINGTON, D.C.

U.S. Department of State Files, Record Group 59

PRESBYTERIAN DEPARTMENT OF HISTORY. PHILADELPHIA, PA.

Papers of the National Council of the Churches of Christ in the United States of
America (formerly called the Federal Council of the Churches of Christ in
America)

PUBLIC RECORD OFFICE. LONDON, UNITED KINGDOM.

Colonial Office 532
Foreign Office 115, 371
War Office 106

SWARTHMORE COLLEGE. SWARTHMORE, PA.
SWARTHMORE COLLEGE PEACE COLLECTION.

Jane Addams Papers
National Committee on American-Japanese Relations Papers
National Committee on the Churches and World Peace Papers
Records of the Women's International League for Peace and Freedom
World Alliance for International Friendship through Churches Papers

UNIVERSITY OF CALIFORNIA, BERKELEY. BERKELEY, CALIF.
BANCROFT LIBRARY.

California Joint Immigration Committee Collection, 1924–1936
David P. Barrows Papers
Hiram Johnson Papers
James D. Phelan Papers
Press Releases and Documents of the CJIC
Chester H. Rowell Papers
Paul Scharrenberg Papers

UNIVERSITY OF CALIFORNIA, LOS ANGELES. LOS ANGELES, CALIF.
UNIVERSITY RESEARCH LIBRARY, SPECIAL COLLECTIONS.

Japanese American Research Project Collection

UNIVERSITY OF TOKYO. TOKYO, JAPAN.
CENTER FOR AMERICAN STUDIES.

Takagi Collection

Newspapers and Periodicals

Albuquerque Tribune
American Lumberman
Annals of the American Academy of Political and Social Science

Asia (later published as *Asia and the Americas*)
Atlanta Constitution
Atlantic Monthly
Bungei shunjū (Tokyo)
California Legionnaire
Chicago Daily Tribune
Chicago Defender
China Press Weekly (Shanghai)
China Weekly Review (Shanghai)
Christian Century
Christian Science Monitor
Chūgai Shōgyō Shimpō (Tokyo)
Chung Sai Yat Po (San Francisco)
Chūō kōron (Tokyo)
Coast Seamen's Journal
Collier's
The Commonweal
Commonwealth
(San Francisco) Daily Commercial News
Daily (Olympia, Wash.) Olympian
Denver Post
Far Eastern Survey
Federal Council Bulletin
Foreign Affairs
Fresno Bee
Fresno Republican
Gaikō Jihō (Tokyo)
Grizzly Bear
Hawai Hōchi
Hawaii Times
Helena (Montana) Daily Independent
Honolulu Advertiser
Honolulu Star-Bulletin
Houston Post
International Goodwill
Interpreter Release

JACL Reporter
Japan Times and Advertiser (Tokyo)
Japan Times and Mail (Tokyo)
Kaikōsha kiji (Tokyo)
Kaizō (Tokyo)
Kashū Mainichi [*Japan-California Daily News*] (Los Angeles)
Kokumin Shimbun (Tokyo)
Labor Clarion
Literary Digest
Los Angeles Examiner
Los Angeles Times
Manshū Nichinichi Shimbun (Dairen)
Maui Shimbun
Melbourne Herald
Missionary Review of the World
Nation's Business
Negro World
New Orleans Item
New Orleans States
New Orleans Tribune
New York Herald Tribune
New York Times
New York World
(Japan Society of New York) News Bulletin
Newsweek
Nichi Bei [*Japanese American News*] (San Francisco)
Nihon oyobi nihonjin [*Japan and the Japanese*]
Nippu Jiji (Honolulu)
Nippon Times (Tokyo)
Oakland Tribune
(Portland) Oregonian
Organized Labor
Osaka Asahi Shimbun
Osaka Mainichi Shimbun
Outlook
Pacific Citizen

297

Providence (Rhode Island) Journal
Philadelphia Evening Bulletin
Quota
Rafu Shimpō [*Los Angeles Daily News*]
Sacramento Bee
San Francisco Bulletin
San Francisco Call
San Francisco Call-Bulletin
San Francisco Chronicle
San Francisco Daily News
San Francisco Examiner
(Los Angeles) Saturday Night
Scribner's Magazine
Seattle Daily Times
Seattle Post-Intelligencer
Seattle Star
Seisho no kenkyū [*Bible Study*] (Tokyo)
Seiyū (monthly publication of the Japanese Seiyū Party)
Selma Enterprise
Selma Irrigator
Shinsekai [*New World Daily*] (later published as *Shinsekai Asahi New World Sun*] (San Francisco)
Southern California Business
Time Magazine
Tokyo Asahi Shimbun (later published as *Asahi Shimbun*)
Tokyo Mainichi Shimbun
Tokyo Nichinichi Shimbun
(Seattle) Town Crier
Tōyōkeizai Shinpō [*The Oriental Economist*]
Transactions of the Commonwealth Club (part 2 of *The Commonwealth*)
Trans-Pacific
Washington Daily News
Washington Evening Star
Washington Post
West Coast Lumberman
(New York) World Telegram

World Tomorrow

Yomiuri Shimbun (Tokyo)

Governmental Documents and Publications

Japan. Gaimushō [Ministry of Foreign Affairs]. *Nihon gaikō bunsho* [Documents on Japanese Foreign Policy]. Annual volumes, 1924–1926, and volumes for 1927–1931.

Japan. Gaimushō. *Nihon gaikō bunsho: Taibei imin mondai keika gaiyō* [Documents on Japanese Foreign Policy: Summary of the Course of Negotiations between Japan and the United States concerning the Problems of Japanese Immigration in the United States].

Japan. Gaimushō. *Nihon gaikō bunsho: Manshū jihen* [Documents on Japanese Foreign Policy: The Manchurian Incident].

Japan. Gaimushō. *Nihon gaikō bunsho: Nichibei kōshō, 1941 nen, jō ge* [Documents on Japanese Foreign Policy: Japan–U.S. Talks, 1941, vols. 1 and 2].

Japan. Gaimushō. *Nihon gaikō bunsho: Shōwa-ki* [Documents on Japanese Foreign Policy: Showa Era].

Japan. Sūmitsuin [The Privy Council]. *Sūmitsuin kaigi gijiroku* [Proceedings in the Privy Council], vol. 35: *1924*. Tokyo: Tokyo daigaku shuppankai, 1986.

Japan. Teikoku Gikai Kizokuin [House of Peers of the Imperial Diet]. *Kizokuin tsūjōkai giji sokkiroku* [Proceedings in the Imperial Diet of Japan, House of Peers]. 1890/91–1947.

Japan. Teikoku Gikai Shūgiin [House of Representatives of the Imperial Diet]. *Shūgiin tsūjōkai giji sokkiroku* [Proceedings in the Imperial Diet of Japan, House of Representatives]. 1890/91–1947.

Japan. Teikoku Gikai Shūgiin [The House of Representatives of the Imperial Diet]. *Teikoku gikai shūgiin yosan iinkaigiroku* [Proceedings of Budget Committee in the Imperial Diet of Japan, House of Representatives]. 1937.

U.K. *Parliamentary Debates*, Commons. 5th ser., vol. 174 (1924).

U.S. Congress. *Congressional Record.* 1924–1952. Washington, D.C.

U.S. Congress. House. Committee on Immigration and Naturalization. *Repeal of the Chinese Exclusion Acts: Hearings on H.R. 1882 and H.R. 2309.* 78th Cong., 1st sess., 6 October 1943.

———. *Repeal of the Chinese Exclusion Acts: Hearings on H.R. 1882 and H.R. 2309.* 78th Cong., 1st sess., 1943.

———. *To Grant a Quota to Eastern Hemisphere Indians and To Make Them Racially Eligible for Naturalization: Hearings on H.R. 173, H.R. 1584, H.R. 1624, H.R. 1746, H.R. 2256, H.R. 2609.* 79th Cong., 1st sess., 1945.

U.S. Congress. House. Subcommittee on Immigration and Naturalization of the Committee on the Judiciary. *Providing for Equality under Naturalization and Immigration Laws: Hearings on H.R. 5004.* 80th Cong., 2d sess., 1948.

———. *Naturalization of Asian and Pacific Peoples: Hearing on H.R. 199.* 81st Cong., 1st sess., 19 and 20 July 1949.

U.S. Congress. Senate. Subcommittee of the Committee on the Judiciary. *Naturalization of Asian and Pacific Peoples: Hearings on H.R. 199*, 81st Cong., 1st sess., 19 and 20 July 1949.

U.S. Department of Commerce. *Foreign Commerce and Navigation of the United States.* 1909–1941. Washington: Government Printing Office, 1909–1944.

U.S. Department of State. *Foreign Relations of the United States.* Annual volumes, 1924–1941. Washington: Government Printing Office, 1939–1959.

U.S. Department of State. *Foreign Relations of the United States: Japan: 1931–1941.* 2 vols. Washington: Government Printing Office, 1943.

Pamphlets and Leaflets

Alexander, Wallace M. *The United States's View of Trade Relations with Japan.* N.p.: California Council on Oriental Relations, 1932.

American Committee for Non-Participation in Japanese Aggression. *Americans' Share in Japan's War Guilt.* New York: American Committee for Non-Participation in Japanese Aggression, 1938.

American Friends Service Committee. *Message to the American People on Japan.* Philadelphia: AFSC, 1927.

Axling, William. *Japan Wonders Why?* New York: Commission on International Justice and Goodwill, 1924.

———. *Toward An Understanding of the Far Eastern Crisis.* Tokyo: Misaki Kaikan, 1938.

Be Patient, Neighbor Japan [in Takagi Collection].

California Joint Immigration Committee. *America and Japan.* San Francisco: CJIC, 1925.

———. *An Appeal to the Japanese Vote.* San Francisco: CJIC, 1924 [in Hiram Johnson Papers].

———. *California's Answer to Japan.* San Francisco: CJIC, 1924.

———. *Congress and Japan.* San Francisco: CJIC, 1924.

———. *Japanese Immigration Drops.* San Francisco: CJIC, 1925 [in Hiram Johnson Papers].

———. *Japan, Geneva, and Congress.* San Francisco: CJIC, 1924 [in Hiram Johnson Papers].

——. *Japan's Cure for Dual Citizenship.* San Francisco: CJIC, 1924 [in Hiram Johnson Papers].

——. *McClatchy to the Editor of Collier's.* CJIC, 1925.

——. *Quota for Japan: Conflicting Views of Hawaii and California.* San Francisco: CJIC, 1931.

——. *Tourist Brides from Japan.* San Francisco: CJIC, 1924 [in Hiram Johnson Papers].

China Information Committee. *Destruction of Schools by Japanese Invaders.* Shanghai: China Information Committee, 1937.

Federation of Chinese Cultural Associations. *The Indiscriminate Aerial Bombing of Non-Combatants in China by Japanese.* Shanghai: Federation of Chinese Cultural Associations, 1937.

Foreign Affairs Association of Japan. *What Happened at Tungchow?* Tokyo: Foreign Affairs Association of Japan, 1937.

Gulick, Sidney L. *New Factors in American Japanese Relations and a Constructive Proposal.* New York: NCAJR, 1924.

——. *The Proposal: Reestablishment of Right Relations between America and Japan.* New York: CIJG, 1924.

Honganji. *Hainichi mondai to kokumin no kakugo* [The Japanese Exclusion Question and National Determination]. Kyoto: Honganji, 1924.

Hume, Samuel J. *The Square Deal in the Pacific.* Berkeley: CCOR, 1932.

Japanese Chamber of Commerce of Los Angeles. *Japan's Position in the Shanghai and North China Hostilities.* Los Angeles: Japanese Chamber of Commerce of Los Angeles, 1937.

Japanese Chamber of Commerce of New York. *The Sino-Japanese Crisis, 1937.* New York: Japanese Chamber of Commerce of New York, 1937.

Martin, Charles E. *Who Shall Enter Our Gates?* Los Angeles: The Los Angeles University of International Relations, 1934.

McClatchy, V. S. *Guarding the Immigration Gates.* San Francisco: CJIC, 1925.

National Committee on American-Japanese Relations. *America and Japan.* New York: NCAJR, 1924.

——. *National Committee on American-Japanese Relations.* New York: NCAJR, 1924, 1925 [in NCCWP Papers].

——. *Toward an Understanding of Japan.* New York: NCAJR, 1927.

National Committee on the Churches and World Peace. *The Churches and World Peace.* New York: NCCWP, 1930.

——. *A Message to the Churches and World Peace.* New York, 1934.

Northern Baptist Convention. *Race Prejudice: Part of the Annual Address of Corwin S. Shank. May 28–June 3, 1924.* N.p., 1924.

Scharrenberg, Paul. *An Answer to Dr. Henry S. Pritchett Who Insists that a Few California Politicians Are Solely Responsible for Excluding the Japanese.* San Francisco: CJIC, 1928.

Willoughby, W. W. *The Significance to the World of the Conflict in the Far East.* New York: Chinese Cultural Society, 1937.

World Alliance for International Friendship through Churches, *Welcome and Christian Fellowship by Migrating People.* WAIFTC, n.d. [in WAIFTC Papers].

Wu, H. C., ed. *Japan: The World's Enemy.* Shanghai: Cheng Zung Publishing Society, 1937.

Books, Articles, and Proceedings

Abrams, Bruce A. "A Muted Cry: White Opposition to the Japanese Exclusion Movement, 1911–1924." Ph.D. diss., City University of New York, 1987.

Amau, Eiji. *Amau Eiji nikki/shiryōshū* [The Diary of Eiji Amau and Related Materials]. 5 vols. Tokyo: Eiji Amau nikki/shiryōshū kankōkai, 1982–1992.

American Federation of Labor. *Report of the Executive Council.* Annual reports, 1931–1933. Washington, D.C.: AFL, 1931–1933.

American Federation of Labor. *Report of Proceedings of the Annual Convention of the American Federation of Labor.* Annual volumes, 1924–1939. Washington, D.C.: AFL, 1924–1939.

American Legion. *Summary of Proceedings, National Conventions of the American Legion.* Annual volumes, 1924–1952. Washington, D.C.: Government Printing Office, 1924–1952.

American Legion, Department of California. *Summary of Proceedings of the Annual Convention of the American Legion, Department of California.* Annual volumes, 1924–1941. N.p.: American Legion of California, 1924–1941.

Ariyama, Teruo. "1924 nen iminhō to *Rafu Sinpō*" [The Immigration Law of 1924 and *Rafu Shimpō*]. In *Seigi ha ware ni ari* [Right and Justice Is on Our Side], edited by Norio Tamura. Tokyo: Shakai hyōronsha, 1995.

Aruga, Tadashi, and Akira Iriye, eds. *Senkanki no Nihon gaikō* [Japanese Foreign Policy during the Interwar Period]. Tokyo: Tokyo daigaku shuppankai, 1984.

Asada, Sadao. "Japan and the United States, 1915–1925." Ph.D. diss., Yale University, 1963.

———. *Ryō taisenkan no Nichibei kankei* [Japanese American Relations between the Wars]. Tokyo: Tokyo daigaku shuppankai, 1993.

Barnhart, Michael A. *Japan Prepares for Total War: The Search for Economic Security, 1919–1941.* Ithaca, N.Y.: Cornell University Press, 1987.

Beard, Charles, and Mary Beard. *America in Midpassage.* Vol. 1. New York: Macmillan, 1939.

Blakeslee, George. "The Japanese Monroe Doctrine." *Foreign Affairs* 11 (July 1933): 671–81.

Bōeichō Bōeikenshūsho Senshishitsu [Department of War History, National Institute of Defense Studies, Defense Agency]. *Daihon'ei Kaigunbu Rengōkantai* [Imperial Headquarters, Navy: Combined Fleet], vol. 1. Tokyo: Asagumo Shimbunsha, 1975.

Borg, Dorothy, and Shumpei Okamoto, eds. *Pearl Harbor as History.* New York: Columbia University Press, 1973.

Burkman, Thomas W. "Nitobe Inazo: From World Order to Regional Order." In *Culture and Identity: Japanese Intellectuals during the Interwar Years,* edited by J. Thomas Rimer. Princeton: Princeton University Press, 1990.

Butow, R. J. C. *The John Doe Associates: Backdoor Diplomacy for Peace, 1941.* Stanford, Calif.: Stanford University Press, 1974.

California State Federation of Labor. *Proceedings of the Annual Convention.* Annual volumes, 1924–1950. N.p.: California State Federation of Labor, 1924–1950.

Cavert, Samuel McCrea, ed. *Twenty Years of Church Federation: Report of the Federal Council of the Churches of Christ in America, 1924–1928.* New York: FCCCA, 1929.

———. *United in Service: Report of the Federal Council of the Churches of Christ in America, 1920–1924.* New York: FCCCA, 1925.

Chamber of Commerce of the United States. *Annual Meeting.* Annual volumes, 1924–1932. Washington, D.C.: Chamber of Commerce of the United States, 1924–1932.

Chambers, Clarke A. *California Farm Organizations: A Historical Study of the Grange, the Farm Bureau, and the Associated Farmers, 1929–1941.* Berkeley: University of California Press, 1952.

Chan, Sucheng. *Asian Americans: An Interpretive History.* New York: Twayne, 1991.

Chang, Gordon H. *Morning Glory, Evening Shadow: Yamato Ichihashi and His Internment Writings, 1942–1945.* Stanford, Calif.: Stanford University Press, 1997.

Chapman, Charles E. *The Native Son Fellowships.* San Francisco, n.d.

Chinese Historical Society of America. *The Repeal and Its Legacy: Proceedings of the Conference on the 50th Anniversary of the Repeal of the Exclusion Acts.* San Francisco: Chinese Historical Society of America, 1994.

Chuman, Frank F. *The Bamboo People: The Law and Japanese-Americans.* Del Mar, Calif.: Publishers Inc., 1976.

Cohen, Warren I. *America's Response to China: An Interpretative History of Sino-American Relations.* 2d ed. New York: Knopf, 1971.

———. *The Chinese Connection: Roger S. Greene, Thomas W. Lamont, George E. Sokolsky, and American–East Asian Relations.* New York: Columbia University Press, 1978.

———, ed. *New Frontiers in American–East Asian Relations: Essays Presented to Dorothy Borg.* New York: Columbia University Press, 1983.

———. *Pacific Passage: The Study of American–East Asian Relations on the Eve of the Twenty-First Century.* New York: Columbia University Press, 1996.

Claudel, Paul. *Correspondence Diplomatique: Tokyo, 1921–1927.* Paris: Gallimard, 1995.

Condliffe, J. B. ed. *Problems of the Pacific: Proceedings of the Second Conference of the Institute of Pacific Relations, Honolulu, Hawaii, July 15 to 29, 1927.* Chicago: University of Chicago Press, 1928.

Conmy, Peter Thomas. *The Origin and Purposes of the Native Sons and Native Daughters of the Golden West.* San Francisco: Dolores Press, 1956.

Daniels, Roger. *Asian America: Chinese and Japanese in the United States since 1850.* Seattle: University of Washington Press, 1988.

———. *The Politics of Prejudice: The Anti-Japanese Movement in California and the Struggle for Japanese Exclusion.* Berkeley: University of California Press, 1962.

Dean, Arthur L. *Alexander & Baldwin, Ltd. and the Predecessor Partnerships.* Honolulu: Alexander & Baldwin, Ltd., 1950.

DeBeneditti, Charles. *Origins of the Modern American Peace Movement, 1915–1929.* Millwood, N.Y.: KTO Press, 1978.

DeConde, Alexander. *Ethnicity, Race, and American Foreign Policy: A History.* Boston: Northeastern University Press, 1992.

Dingman, Roger. *Power in the Pacific.* Chicago: University of Chicago Press, 1976.

Divine, Robert A. *American Immigration Policy, 1924–1952.* New Haven, Conn.: Yale University Press, 1957.

Doenecke, Justus D., comp. *The Diplomacy of Frustration: The Manchurian Crisis of 1931–1933 as Revealed in the Papers of Stanley K. Hornbeck.* Stanford, Calif.: Hoover Institution Press, 1981.

———. *When the Wicked Rise: American Opinion-Makers and the Manchurian Crisis of 1931–1933.* Lewisburg, Pa.: Bucknell University Press, 1984.

Dower, John W. *War Without Mercy: Race and Power in the Pacific War.* New York: Pantheon, 1986.

Edwards, Lee. *Missionary for Freedom: The Life and Times of Walter Judd*. New York: Paragon, 1990.

Federal Council of the Churches of Christ in America. *Annual Report*. Annual volumes, 1924–1950. New York: FCCCA, 1924–1950.

Fletcher, William Miles, III. *The Japanese Business Community and National Trade Policy, 1920–1942*. Chapel Hill: University of North Carolina Press, 1989.

Flowers, Montaville. *The Japanese Conquest of American Opinion*. New York: George H. Doran Co., 1917.

Friday, Chris. *Organizing Asian American Labor: The Pacific Coast Canned-Salmon Industry, 1870–1942*. Philadelphia: Temple University Press, 1994.

Friedman, Donald J. *The Road from Isolation: The Campaign of the American Committee for Non-Participation in Japanese Aggression, 1938–1941*. Cambridge, Mass.: Harvard University Press, 1968.

Gaimushō gaikō shiryōkan nihon gaikōshi jiten hensan iinkai, eds. [Committee for the Compilation of a Dictionary of Japanese Diplomatic History]. *Nihon gaikōshi jiten* [A Dictionary of Japanese Diplomatic History]. Tokyo: Yamakawa shoten, 1992).

Grodzins, Morton. *Americans Betrayed: Politics and the Japanese Evacuation*. Chicago: University of Chicago Press, 1949.

Gulick, Sidney L. "American-Japanese Relations: The Logic of the Exclusionists." *Annals of the American Academy of Political Science* 122 (Nov. 1925): 181–87.

———. *Toward Understanding Japan: Constructive Proposals for Removing the Menace of War*. New York: Macmillan, 1935.

Hara, Kakuten. *Gendai Ajia kenkyū seiritsu shiron: Mantetsu chōsabu, Tōakenkyūsho, IPR no kenkyū* [A Historical Study of the Formation of Modern Asian Studies: A Study of the Research Department of the South Manchurian Railway Company, the Oriental Institute, and the Institute of Pacific Relations]. Tokyo: Keisō shobō, 1984.

Hata, Donald Teruo, Dominguez Hills, and Nadine Ishitani Hata. *Japanese Americans and World War II: Exclusion, Internment, and Redress*. Wheeling, Ill.: Harlan Davidson, 1974.

Hata, Ikuhiko. *Taiheiyō kokusai kankeishi: Nichibei oyobi Nichiro kiki no keifu, 1900–1935* [Pacific International Relations: History of the Japanese-American and the Russo-Japanese Crises, 1900–1935]. Tokyo: Fukumura shuppan, 1972.

Hayashi, Brian Masaru. *"For the Sake of Our Japanese Brethren": Assimilation, Nationalism, and Protestantism among the Japanese of Los Angeles, 1895–1942*. Stanford, Calif.: Stanford University Press, 1995.

Heinrichs, Waldo H., Jr. *American Ambassador: Joseph C. Grew and the Development of the United States Diplomatic Tradition*. Boston: Little, Brown, 1966.

———. *Threshold of War: Franklin D. Roosevelt and American Entry into World War II*. New York: Oxford University Press, 1988.

Hellwig, David J. "Afro-American Reactions to the Japanese and the Anti-Japanese Movement, 1906–1924." *Phylon* 38, no. 1 (1977): 93–104.

Herzberg, James R. *A Broken Bond: American Economic Policies towards Japan, 1931–1941*. New York: Garland, 1988.

Higham, John. *Strangers in the Land: Patterns of American Nativism, 1860–1925*. 1955; reprint, New York: Atheneum, 1977.

Hirobe, Izumi. "American Attitudes Toward the Japanese Immigration Question, 1924–1931." *Journal of American–East Asian Relations* 2 (fall 1993): 275–301.

———. "Nijusseiki shotō san furanshisuko ni okeru han nikkeijin undō [Anti-Japanese Movements in San Francisco in the Early Twentieth Century]." Master's thesis, University of Tokyo, 1991.

Hogan, Michael J., and Thomas G. Paterson. *Explaining the History of American Foreign Relations*. Cambridge: Cambridge University Press, 1991.

Hooper, Paul F., ed. *Rediscovering the IPR: Proceedings of the First International Research Conference on the Institute of Pacific Relations*. Honolulu: Center for Arts & Humanities, University of Hawaii, 1994.

Hornbeck, Stanley K. *The Diplomacy of Frustration: The Manchurian Crisis of 1931–1933 as Revealed in the Papers of Stanley K. Hornbeck*. Compiled by Justus D. Doenecke. Stanford, Calif.: Hoover Institution Press, 1981.

Hosokawa, Bill. *JACL in Quest of Justice: The History of the Japanese American Citizens League*. New York: William Morrow and Company, 1982.

———. *Nisei: The Quiet Americans*. New York: Morrow, 1969.

Hunter, Jane. *The Gospel of Gentility: American Women Missionaries in Turn-of-the-Century China*. New Haven, Conn.: Yale University Press, 1984.

Hutchinson, E. P. *Legislative History of American Immigration Policy, 1789–1965*. Philadelphia: University of Pennsylvania Press, 1981.

Ichihashi, Yamato. *Japanese in the United States: A Critical Study of the Problems of the Japanese Immigrants and their Children*. Stanford, Calif.: Stanford University Press, 1932.

Ichioka, Yuji. "'Attorney for the Defense': Yamato Ichihashi and Japanese Immigration." *Pacific Historical Review* 55 (May 1986): 192–225.

———. "'Dai Nisei mondai': 1902 nen–1941 nen [The Nisei Question: 1902–1941]. In *Hokubei Nihonjin Kirisutokyō undō shi* [A History of the Japanese Christian Movement in North America], edited by *Dōshisha daigaku jinbun kagaku kenkyūsho*. Tokyo: PMC shuppan, 1991.

———. "The Early Japanese Immigrant Quest for Citizenship: The Background of the 1922 Ozawa Case." *Amerasia Journal* 4, no. 2 (1977): 1–22.

———. "An Instance of Private Japanese Diplomacy: Suzuki Bunji, Organized American Labor, and Japanese Immigrant Workers, 1915–1916." *Amerasia Journal* 10 (spring/summer 1983): 1–22.

———. *The Issei: The World of the First Generation Japanese Immigrants, 1885–1924.* New York: Free Press, 1988.

———. "Japanese Associations and the Japanese Government: A Special Relationship, 1909–1926." *Pacific Historical Review* 46, no. 3 (1977): 409–37.

———. "Japanese Immigrant Nationalism: The Issei and the Sino-Japanese War, 1937–1941." *California History* 69, no. 3 (1990): 260–75.

———. "Kengakugan: The Origin of Nisei Study Tours of Japan." *California History* 73 (spring 1994): 30–43.

———. "A Study in Dualism: James Yoshinori Sakamoto and the *Japanese American Courier*, 1928–1942." *Amerasia* 13, no. 2 (1986–1987): 49–81.

———, et al., comps. *A Buried Past: An Annotated Bibliography of the Japanese American Research Project Collection.* Berkeley: University of California Press, 1974.

Inoue, Junnosuke. *Taiheiyō mondai* [Pacific Issues]. Tokyo: Taiheiyō mondai chōsa kai, 1927.

Institute of Pacific Relations. *Institute of Pacific Relations.* Honolulu: IPR, 1925.

Iriye, Akira. *Across the Pacific: An Inner History of American–East Asian Relations.* Rev. ed. Chicago: Imprint Publications, 1992.

———. *Cultural Internationalism and World Order.* Baltimore: Johns Hopkins University Press, 1997.

———. "Japan as a Competitor, 1895–1917." In *Mutual Images: Essays in American-Japanese Relations*, edited by Akira Iriye. Cambridge, Mass.: Harvard University Press, 1975.

———. *Nijisseiki no sensō to heiwa* [War and Peace in the Twentieth Century]. Tokyo: University of Tokyo Press, 1986.

———. *The Origins of the Second World War in Asia and the Pacific.* London: Longman, 1987.

———. *Pacific Estrangement: Japanese and American Expansion, 1897–1911.* Cambridge, Mass.: Harvard University Press, 1972.

———. "Tenkanki no nichibei kankei, 1896–1914" [Japan-U.S. Relations at a Turning Point, 1896–1914]. In *Nichibei kankei tsūshi* [A History of Japan-US Relations], edited by Chihiro Hosoya. Tokyo: Tokyo daigaku shuppankai, 1995).

———, ed. *Mutual Images: Essays in American Japanese Relations.* Cambridge, Mass.: Harvard University Press, 1975.

Ishimaru, Tōta. *Nichibei Sensō: Nihon ha makenai* [Japan–U.S. War: Japan Won't Be Beaten]. Tokyo: Konishi Shoten, 1934.

Ishiwara, Kanji. *Ishiwara Kanji senshū.* 2 vols. Tokyo: Tamairabo, 1985.

Issacs, Harold R. *Scratches on Our Minds: American Views of China and India.* 1958. Reprint, Armonk, N.Y.: M. E. Sharpe, Inc., 1980.

Issel, William, and Robert W. Cherny. *San Francisco, 1865–1932: Politics, Power, and Urban Development.* Berkeley: University of California Press, 1986.

Itō, Takashi, and Yoshihiro Hirose, eds. *Makino Nobuatsu nikki* [The Diary of Nobuatsu Makino]. Tokyo: Chūōkōronsha, 1990.

Kajima heiwa kenkyūsho, ed. *Nihon gaikō shi* [A Diplomatic History of Japan]. Vol. 24, *Daitōa sensō, Senji gaikō* [Great East Asia War and Wartime Diplomacy]. Tokyo: Kajima kenkyūsho shuppan, 1971.

Katagiri, Yasuo. "Taiheiyō mondai chōsakai (IPR) to imin mondai: Daiikkai hawai kaigi o chūshintoshite" [The Institute of Pacific Relations and the Immigration Question: A Perspective on the First Conference in Hawaii]. Parts 1 and 2. *Hōgaku kenkyū* 58, no. 6 (June 1985): 37–56; no. 7 (July 1985): 26–44.

————. "Taiheiyō mondai chōsakai (IPR) to imin mondai: Dainikai hawai kaigi o chūshintoshite" [The Institute of Pacific Relations and the Immigration Question: A Perspective on the Second Conference in Hawaii]. *Hōgaku kenkyū* 65, no. 2 (February 1992): 155–84.

Kawakami, K. K. *Manchukuo: Child of Conflict.* New York: Macmillan Company, 1933.

Kearney, Reginald. *African American Views of the Japanese: Solidarity or Sedition?* Albany: State University of New York, 1998.

Kidonikki kenkyūkai, ed. *Kido Kōichi kannkei monjo* [Papers Relating to Kōichi Kido]. Tokyo: Tokyo daigaku shuppankai, 1966.

Kimura, Masato. *Shibusawa Eiichi: Minkan keizai gaikō no sōshisha* [Shibusawa Eiichi: The Founder of Private Economic Diplomacy]. Tokyo: Chūōkōronsha, 1991.

Kinoshita, Hanji. *Nihon kokkashugi undōshi* [A History of the Nationalism Movement in Japan]. Vol. 1. Tokyo: Fukumurashoten, 1971.

Kitaoka, Shin'ichi. *Kiyosawa Kiyoshi* [Kiyoshi Kayosawa]. Tokyo: Chūōkōronsha, 1987.

————. "Prophet Without Honor: Kiyosawa Kiyoshi's View of Japanese-American Relations." In *The Ambivalence of Nationalism,* edited by James White et al. Lanham, Md.: University Press of America, 1990.

Ko Sakatani Sishaku kinen jigyōkai, ed. *Sakatani Yoshirō den* [The Life of Yoshirō Sakatani]. Tokyo: Ko Sakatani sishaku kinen jigyōkai, 1951.

Kokuryū kurabu, ed. [Kokuryū Club]. *Kokushi Uchida Ryōhei den* [The Life of Ryōhei Uchida, A Patriot]. Tokyo: Hara shobō, 1967.

Koria kenkyūsho, ed. and trans. *Kesareta genron, seiji hen: Nihon tōchika no Tōanippō/Chōsen nippō ōshū kijishū* [Erased Speech, Politics: Seized Articles of *Tonga ilbo* and *Choson ilbo* under Japanese Rule]. Tokyo: Miraisha, 1990.

Koshiro, Yukiko. *Trans-Pacific Racisms and the U.S. Occupation of Japan.* New York: Columbia University Press, 1999.

Kurosawa, Fumitaka. "Nihon rikugun no taibei ninshiki" [Japanese Military Perceptions of the United States]. *Kokusai seiji* 91 (May 1989): 19–38.

Leonard, Kevin Allen. "Years of Hope, Days of Fear: The Impact of World War II on Race Relations in Los Angeles." Ph.D. diss., University of California, Davis, 1992.

Lopez, Espiridion Barrientos. "The History of the California State Federation of Labor." Master's thesis, University of California, Berkeley, 1932.

Macfarland, Charles S. *Christian Unity in the Making: The First Twenty-Five Years of the Federal Council of the Churches of Christ in America, 1905–1930.* New York: FCCCA, 1948.

Makela, Lee Arne. "Japanese Attitudes Towards the United States Immigration Act of 1924." Ph.D. diss., Stanford University, 1973.

Masaoka, Mike, with Bill Hosokawa. *They Call Me Moses Masaoka: An American Saga.* New York: Morrow, 1987.

May. Ernest. *American Imperialism.* New York: Atheneum, 1968.

May, Ernest R., and James C. Thomson, Jr., eds. *American–East Asian Relations: A Survey.* Cambridge, Mass.: Harvard University Press, 1972.

McWilliams, Carey. *Prejudice, Japanese-Americans: Symbol of Racial Intolerance.* Boston: Little, Brown, 1944.

Miller, Edward S. *War Plan Orange: The U.S. Strategy to Defeat Japan, 1897–1945.* Annapolis, Md.: Naval Institute Press, 1991.

Miller, Stuart Creighton. *The Unwelcome Immigrant: The American Image of the Chinese, 1785–1882.* Berkeley: University of California Press, 1969.

Minohara, Toshihiro. "Kariforunia ni okeru hainichi undō to 1924 nen iminhō no seiritsu katei: Iminhō o meguru nichibei kankei, 1906–1924" [The Anti-Japanese Movement in California and the Enactment of the Immigration Act: U.S.-Japan Relations from the Perspective of the Immigration Issue, 1906–1924]. Ph.D. diss., Kobe University, 1997.

———. "The Road to Exclusion: The 1920 California Alien Land Law and U.S.-Japan Relations." *Kobe University Law Review* 30 (1996): 51–55.

Miwa, Kimitada. "Tokutomi Sohō no rekishizō to nichibei sensō no genriteki kaishi: Taishō 13 nen 7 gatsu 1 nichi, hanichi iminhō no jisshi o megutte" [The Historical Image of Sohō Tokutomi and the Theoretical Beginning of the Japanese-American War: Concerning the Enforcement of the Anti-

Japanese Immigration Law on July 1, 1924]. In *Seiyō no Shōgeki to Nihon* [The Western Impact and Japan], edited by Tōru Haga et al. Tokyo: Tokyo daigaku shuppankai, 1973.

Modell, John. *The Economics and Politics of Racial Accommodation: The Japanese of Los Angeles, 1900–1942*. Urbana: University of Illinois Press, 1977.

Mullins, William H. *The Depression and the Urban West Coast, 1929–1933*. Bloomington: Indiana University Press, 1991.

Nagai, Shōzō, ed. *Nichibei Bunka Kōsho-shi* [A History of Japan-U.S. Cultural Intercourse]. 5 vols. Tokyo: Yōyō-sha, 1955.

National Foreign Trade Convention. *Official Reports*. Annual convention reports, 1924–32. New York: Secretary, NFTC Headquarters, 1924–1932.

Newmann, William L. *America Encounters Japan: From Perry to MacArthur*. Baltimore: Johns Hopkins Press, 1963.

Nixon, Edgar B., ed. *Franklin D. Roosevelt and Foreign Affairs*. 3 vols. Cambridge, Mass.: Harvard University Press, 1969.

Okamoto, Shirō, ed. *Jūdai naru kekka* [Grave Consequences]. Tokyo: Minyūsha, 1924.

Ōshiro, Jōji. *Nitobe Inazō: Kokusaishugi no kaitakusha* [Inazō Nitobe: A Pioneer of Internationalism]. Tokyo: Chūō daigaku shuppanbu, 1992.

Pajus, Jean. *The Real Japanese California*. Berkeley, Calif.: James J. Gillick Co., 1937.

Pencak, William. *For God and Country: The American Legion, 1919–1941*. Boston: Northwestern University Press, 1989.

Rappaport, Armin. *Henry L. Stimson and Japan, 1931–33*. Chicago: University of Chicago Press, 1963.

Reed, James. *The Missionary Mind and American East Asian Policy, 1911–1915*. Cambridge, Mass.: Harvard University Press, 1983.

Riggs, Fred W. *Pressures on Congress: A Study of the Repeal of Chinese Exclusion*. New York: King's Crown Press, 1950.

Roosevelt, Franklin D. *Franklin D. Roosevelt and Foreign Affairs*. Edited by Edgar Nixon. 3 vols. Cambridge, Mass.: Harvard University Press, 1969.

Rosenberg, Emily S. *Spreading the American Dream: American Economic and Cultural Expansion, 1890–1945*. New York: Hill and Wang, 1982.

Rotary International. *Proceedings: Twenty-Third Annual Convention of Rotary International, Seattle, Washington, U.S.A., June 20–24, 1932*. Chicago: Rotary International, 1932.

Rydell, Robert W. *All the World's A Fair: Visions of Empire at American International Expositions, 1876–1916*. Chicago: University of Chicago Press, 1984.

Saitō, Hirosi. *Japan's Policies and Purposes: Selections from Recent Addresses and Writings*. Boston: Marshall Jones Co., 1935.

Satō, Ryūtarō. "Kumakō no Gensetsu" [The Comments of Kumakō], *Bungei shunjū* 2 (June 1924): 41–43.

Scharrenberg, Paul. "Japanese Exclusion by Law." *American Federationist* 32 (June 1925): 419–24.

Shakai mondai kenkyūkai, ed. *Teikoku gikai shi* [The Journal of the Imperial Diet]. Series 1: 54 vols., 1928–1947. Tokyo: Tōyō bunka sha, 1975–1979.

Shankman, Arnold. "'Asiatic Ogre' or 'Desirable Citizen'? The Image of Japanese Americans in the Afro-American Press, 1867–1933." *Pacific Historical Review* 46 (November 1977): 567–87.

Shepard, Bernard A. "C. K. McClatchy and the *Sacramento Bee*, 1883–1936." Ph.D. diss., Syracuse University, 1960.

Shibusawa, Eiichi. "Peace on the Pacific—Japan and the United States." *Pacific Affairs* 3 (March 1930): 273–77.

Shibusawa seien kinen zaidan ryūmonsha, comp. *Shibusawa Eiichi denki shiryō* [Biographical Materials on Eiichi Shibusawa]. 58 vols. Tokyo: Shibusawa Eiichi denki shiryō kankōkai, 1955–1971.

Shidehara, Kijūrō. *Gaikō gojūnen* [Fifty Years of Diplomacy]. Tokyo: Yomiuri shimbunsha, 1951.

Shimazu, Naoko. *Japan, Race and Equality: The Racial Equality Proposal of 1919*. London: Routledge, 1998.

Shiozaki, Hiroaki. "Gaimushō kakushinha no genjōdaha ninshiki to seisaku" [The 'Progressive' (kakushin) School in Japan's Ministry of Foreign Affairs: Its Ideology and Policy against the Status Quo]. *Nenppo Kindai Nihon Kenkyū* [Journal of Modern Japanese Studies], vol. 7 (1985): 151–85.

Skrepetos, Venetta. "A Study of the California State Grange as a Pressure Group in California Politics." Master's thesis, University of California, Berkeley, 1958.

Smith, Fred W., comp. *History, Department of California, 1919–1928*. Paso Robles: American Legion, California, 1929(?).

Stanford University Survey of Race Relations, *Tentative Findings of the Survey of Race Relations: A Canadian-American Study of the Oriental on the Pacific Coast*. Stanford, Calif.: Stanford University, 1925.

Stemen, John Roger. "The Diplomacy of the Immigration Issue: A Study in Japanese-American Relations, 1894–1941." Ph.D. diss., Indiana University, 1960.

Stimson, Henry L. *The Far Eastern Crisis: Recollections and Observations*. New York: Howard Fertig, 1974.

Strong, Edward K., Jr. *The Second-Generation Japanese Problem*. Stanford, Calif.: Stanford University Press, 1934.

Taft, Henry W. *Japan and America: A Journey and a Political Survey*. New York: Macmillan, 1932.

Takahashi, Jere. *Nisei/Sansei: Shifting Japanese American Identities and Politics*. Philadelphia: Temple University Press, 1992.

Takeshita, Tōmasu K. *Yamato Damashii to seijōki* [Yamato-Damashii under the Stars and Stripes]. Tokyo: Sannō shobō, 1967.

Takezawa, Yasuko I. *Breaking the Silence: Redress and Japanese American Ethnicity*. Ithaca, N.Y.: Cornell University Press, 1995.

Tamura, Norio, and Teruo Ariyama. "1924—Immigration Act and Japanese American Newspapers." *Journal of Humanities and Natural Sciences* 75 (March 1987): 135–68.

Tatsu, Sakutarō. *Beikoku gaikōjō no shoshugi* [Some Principles of American Diplomacy]. Tokyo: Nihon hyōronsha, 1942.

Taylor, Sandra C. *Advocate of Understanding: Sidney Gulick and the Search for Peace with Japan*. Kent, Ohio: Kent State University Press, 1984.

tenBroek, Jacobus, Edward N. Barnhart, and Floyd W. Matson. *Prejudice, War, and the Constitution*. Berkeley: University of California Press, 1954.

Terasaki, Hidenari, and Mariko Terasaki Miller. *Shōwatennō dokuhakuroku/ Terasaki Hidenari goyōkakari nikki* [A Monologue of Shiōwa Emperor/The Diary of Hidenari Terasaki, Aide to the Emperor]. Tokyo: Bungei shunjū, 1991.

Thorne, Christopher. *Allies of a Kind: The United States, Britain, and the War Against Japan, 1941–1945*. New York: Oxford University Press, 1978.

Tsunoda, Jun, ed. *Ishiwara Kanji shiryō*. Vol. 2, *Kokubō ronsaku* [Papers Relating to Kanji Ishiwara. Vol. 2, Treaties on National Defense]. Tokyo: Hara shobō, 1967.

Tsurumi, Yūsuke. *Present Day Japan*. New York: Columbia University Press, 1926.

Tupper, Eleanor, and George E. McReynolds. *Japan in American Public Opinion*. New York: Macmillan, 1937.

Uchida Ryōhei kankei bunsho kenkyūkai, ed. *Uchida Ryōhei kankei bunsho* [Papers Relating to Ryōhei Uchida]. 10 vols. Tokyo: Fuyōshobō, 1994.

Uehara Yūsaku kankei bunsho kenkyūkai, ed. *Uehara Yūsaku kankei bunsho* [Papers Relating to Yūsaku Uehara]. Tokyo: Tokyo daigaku shuppankai, 1976.

Uesugi, Shinkichi. *Nichibei shōtotsu no hisshi to kokumin no kakugo* [The Necessity of Japan–U.S. Clash and National Determination]. Tokyo: Dainihon yūben kai, 1924.

Ugaki, Kazushige. *Ugaki Kazushige nikki* [The Diary of Kazushige Ugaki]. 3 vols. Tokyo: Misuzu shobō, 1968.

Utley, Jonathan G. *Going to War with Japan, 1937–1941.* Knoxville: University of Tennessee Press, 1985.

Waldron, Gladys Hennig. "Antiforeign Movements in California, 1919–1929." Ph.D. diss., University of California, Berkeley, 1956.

Wilson, Joan Hoff. *American Business and Foreign Policy, 1920–1933.* Lexington: University Press of Kentucky, 1971.

Yoneda, Karl. *Ganbatte: Sixty-Year Struggle of a Kibei Worker.* Los Angeles: UCLA Asian American Studies Center, 1983.

Yoshimura, Michio. "Ningyō shisetsu kara ningen shisetsu e -Shōwa shoki kokusai kōryū shi no issetsu-" [From Goodwill Doll Exchange to Feminine Goodwill Delegates: One Aspect of International Exchange in the Early Shōwa Period]. *Gaikōshiryōkanpō* [Journal of the Diplomatic Record Office] 7 (March 1994): 40–53.

Yu, Renqiu. *To Save China, To Save Ourselves.* Philadelphia: Temple University Press, 1992.

Yui, Daizaburo. "From Exclusion to Integration: Asian Americans' Experiences in World War II." *Hitotsubashi Journal of Social Studies* 24 (December 1992): 55–67.

Index

115, 123–24; effect on Pacific Coast business, 131; Japanese reactions to, 9–10, 13–14, 17–18, 21–51, 80–82, 87–91, 102–3, 105, 107, 115, 125–26, 158, 167, 170, 176–77, 223–25; and private sector, 12–14. *See also* Immigration Act of 1924; Quotas, immigration

Executive Order 9066, 233

Exports to Japan, 184–85, 190, 197

Far East War Crimes Trial in Tokyo, 238
Farming, 3, 15–16, 72, 110
Farrell, James A., 222
Farrington, Wallace R., 144, 147, 151
Faunce, W. H. P., 57
Federal Council Bulletin, 123, 127
Federal Council of the Churches of Christ in America (FCCCA), 12; CJIC attacks on, 72–73, 104–5; and "Doll Project," 103–4; education campaign of, 96–101, 109–10, 118, 143, 201; inactivity of, 116; on Japanese military action in China, 214; on modification of exclusion clause, 60, 68, 77, 86–89, 91, 123–24; on passage of Immigration Act of 1924, 32; on quotas, 94–104, 127; and repeal of Chinese exclusion law, 235. *See also* Clergymen, American; Gulick, Sidney Lewis; Missionaries

Filene, Edward A., 58
Filipino immigrants. *See* Philippines, immigrants from
Finley, John H., 60
Fisk, James K., 71, 110, 145, 146, 155, 215
Fitzpatrick, F. Stuart, 145, 188
Flag incident at American Embassy, 43–44
Fleisher, B. W., 181, 193
Flournoy, Richard W., Jr., 168
Forbes, W. Cameron, 142, 149–50, 151, 153
Foreign Affairs Association of Japan, 213–14
Foreign Trade Club of Southern California, 185
Fouke, Robert H., 189
Franklin, James H., 128
Fraternal Order of Eagles, 137
Free, Arthur M., 125
Fresno Bee, 111, 137, 181
Fujita, Kikuichi, 1

Gaikō Jihō: on A. Johnson's immigration restriction proposal, 141; on anniversary of Immigration Act of 1924, 167; on anti-Japanese incident in Arizona, 207; on exclusion clause, 13, 25–26, 102, 115, 218, 224; on Howard's pro-quota campaign, 176; Kawahara's pro-Japanese articles in, 201–2; on U.S. Chamber of Commerce's pro-quota resolution, 146

Galveston, Tex., 190
Garfield, Harry A., 102
Garland, William M., 154
Garner, James W., 57
General Staff Office, 40–41
The Gentlemen's Agreement of 1907–1908, 4–5, 9, 53, 69, 78, 81, 189
Gibbony, Sam, 178
Gleason, George, 73, 84
Goldstone, M. A., 165
Gompers, Samuel, 27
Gospel of Gentility (Hunter), 11
Grady, Henry F., 170–71
Grays Harbor Washintonian, 138, 183
Great Forward Society. *See* Taikōsha
Green, William, 145, 187
Greene, Jerome D., 127, 128, 138
Grew, Joseph Clark, 61, 167, 170, 215
Griggs, E. G., 58
Grizzly Bear, 16; attack on *Literary Digest*'s pro-quota article, 183; on Burns's comments about exclusion, 112; on exclusion law, 78, 104–6, 163, 216; on FCCCA's pro-Japanese position, 100, 105; on Filipino immigration, 125, 132; on Mexican immigration, 110, 125; praise of McClatchy, 71; on "threat" of Asian immigration, 72

Guaranty Company of New York, 180
Guarding the Immigration Gates (McClatchy's), 94
Gulick, Sidney Lewis, 5, 12–13; on A. Johnson's immigration restriction plan, 138–39; appeal for veto of immigration bill, 60; criticism of, 105; and "Doll Project," 103–4; education campaign of, 96–101, 109–10, 118, 143, 201; honored by Saitō, 197; lack of public interest in anti-exclusion activities of, 101–2; pro-quota movement of, 68–70, 77–79, 82–89, 92–101, 117, 118, 123, 124, 127–28, 204–5, 228; visit to West Coast, 109. *See also* Federal